三家本礼

REIKO the ZOMBIE SHOP

②

REI MIKAMOTO

三家本礼

REIKO the ZOMBIE SHOP ②

CONTENTS

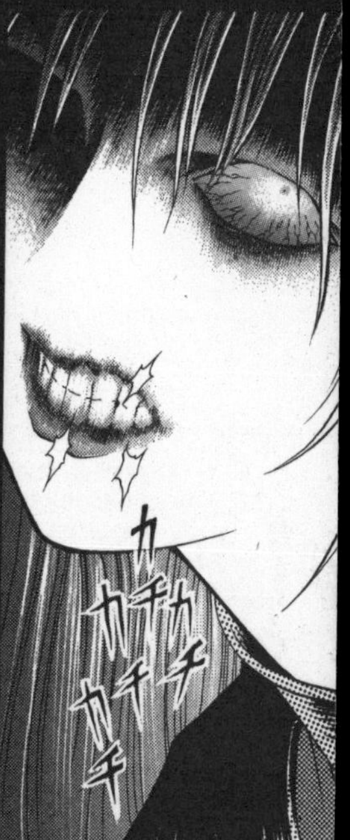

カチカチカチカチ

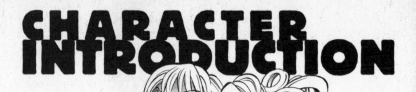

CHARACTER INTRODUCTION

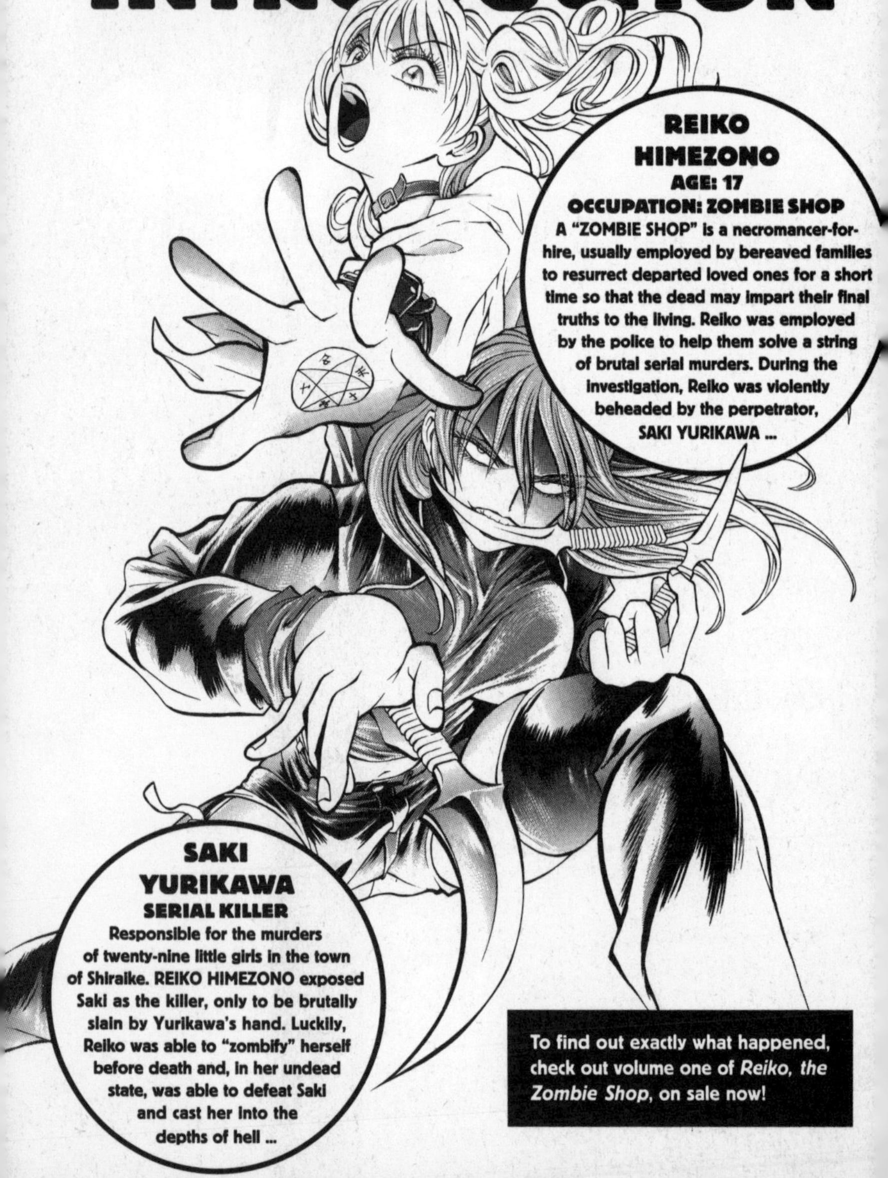
REIKO HIMEZONO
AGE: 17
OCCUPATION: ZOMBIE SHOP
A "ZOMBIE SHOP" is a necromancer-for-hire, usually employed by bereaved families to resurrect departed loved ones for a short time so that the dead may impart their final truths to the living. Reiko was employed by the police to help them solve a string of brutal serial murders. During the investigation, Reiko was violently beheaded by the perpetrator, SAKI YURIKAWA ...
SAKI YURIKAWA
SERIAL KILLER
Responsible for the murders of twenty-nine little girls in the town of Shiraike. REIKO HIMEZONO exposed Saki as the killer, only to be brutally slain by Yurikawa's hand. Luckily, Reiko was able to "zombify" herself before death and, in her undead state, was able to defeat Saki and cast her into the depths of hell ...
To find out exactly what happened, check out volume one of *Reiko, the Zombie Shop*, on sale now!

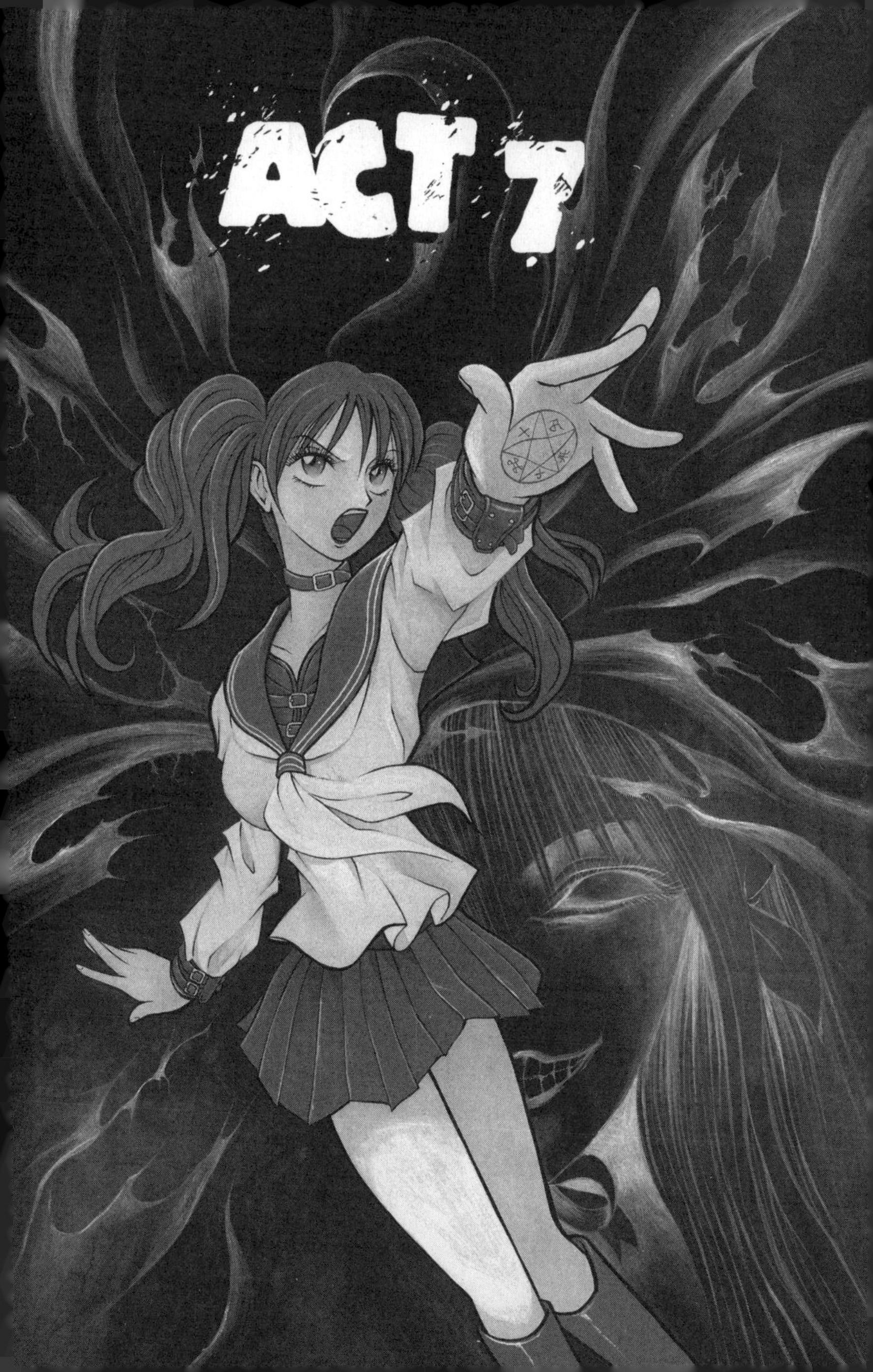
ACT 7

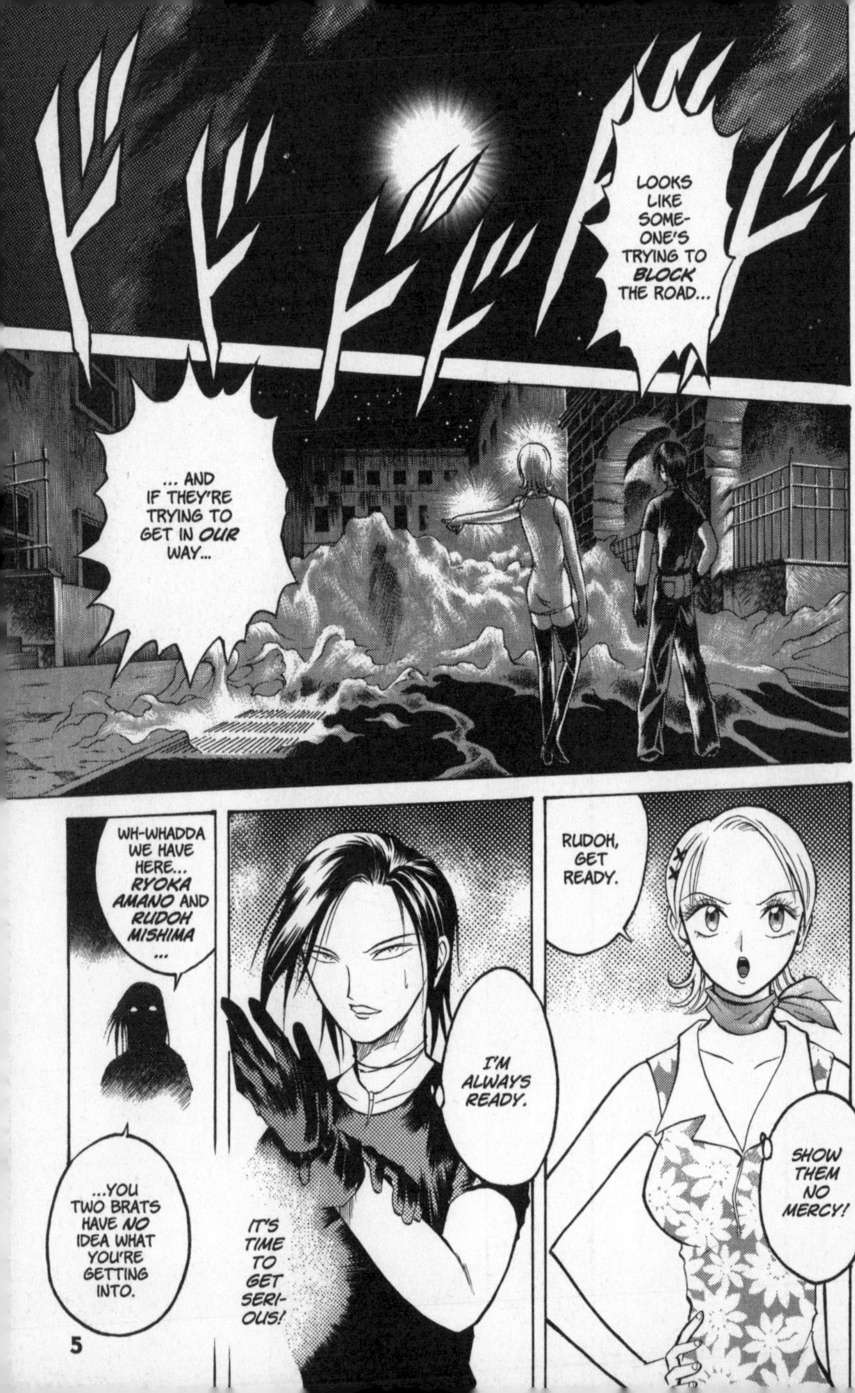
LOOKS LIKE SOME-ONE'S TRYING TO *BLOCK* THE ROAD...
... AND IF THEY'RE TRYING TO GET IN *OUR* WAY...
RUDOH, GET READY.
SHOW THEM NO MERCY!
I'M ALWAYS READY.
IT'S TIME TO GET SERI-OUS!
WH-WHADDA WE HAVE HERE... *RYOKA AMANO* AND *RUDOH MISHIMA* ...
...YOU TWO BRATS HAVE *NO* IDEA WHAT YOU'RE GETTING INTO.

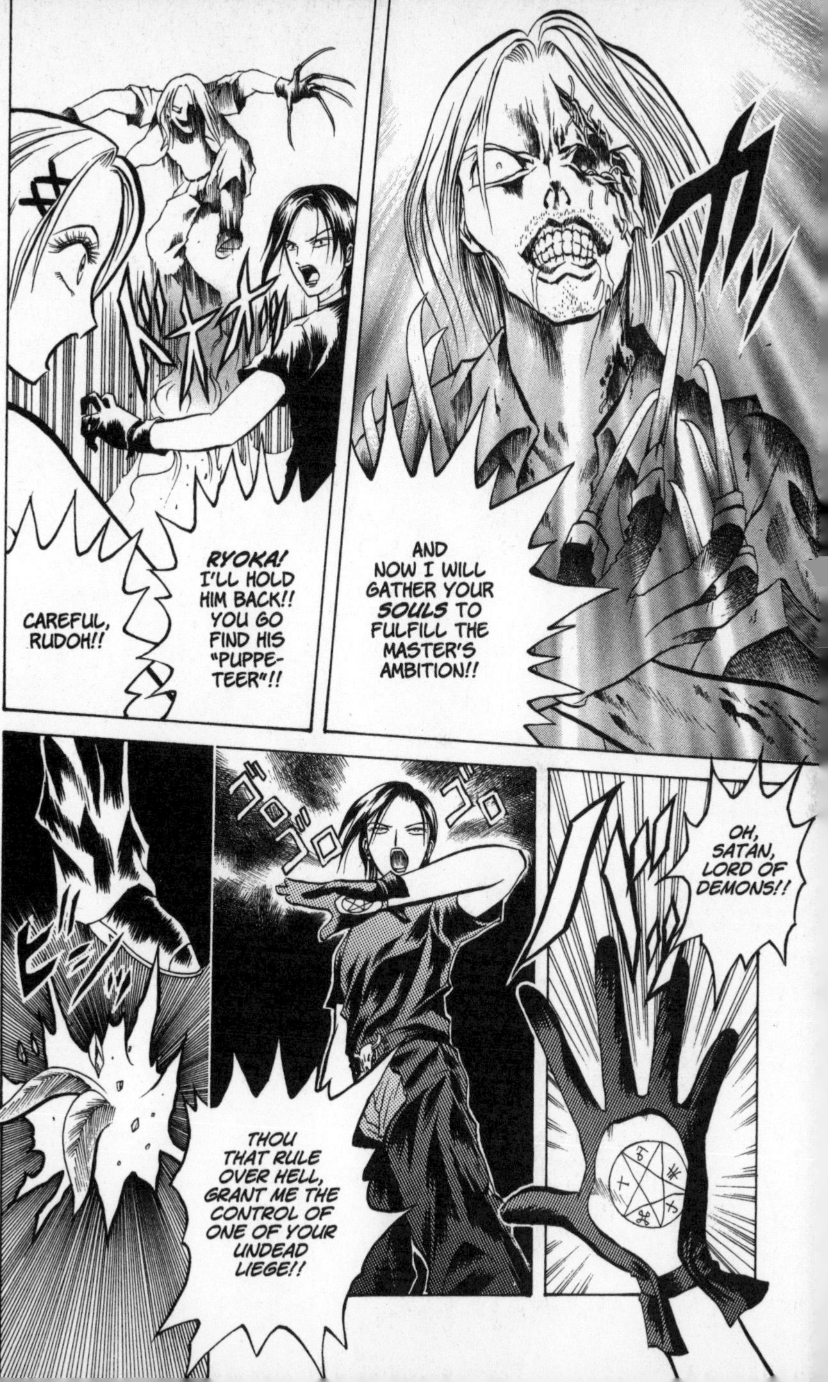
AND NOW I WILL GATHER YOUR SOULS TO FULFILL THE MASTER'S AMBITION!!
RYOKA! I'LL HOLD HIM BACK!! YOU GO FIND HIS "PUPPE-TEER"!!
CAREFUL, RUDOH!!
OH, SATAN, LORD OF DEMONS!!
THOU THAT RULE OVER HELL, GRANT ME THE CONTROL OF ONE OF YOUR UNDEAD LIEGE!!

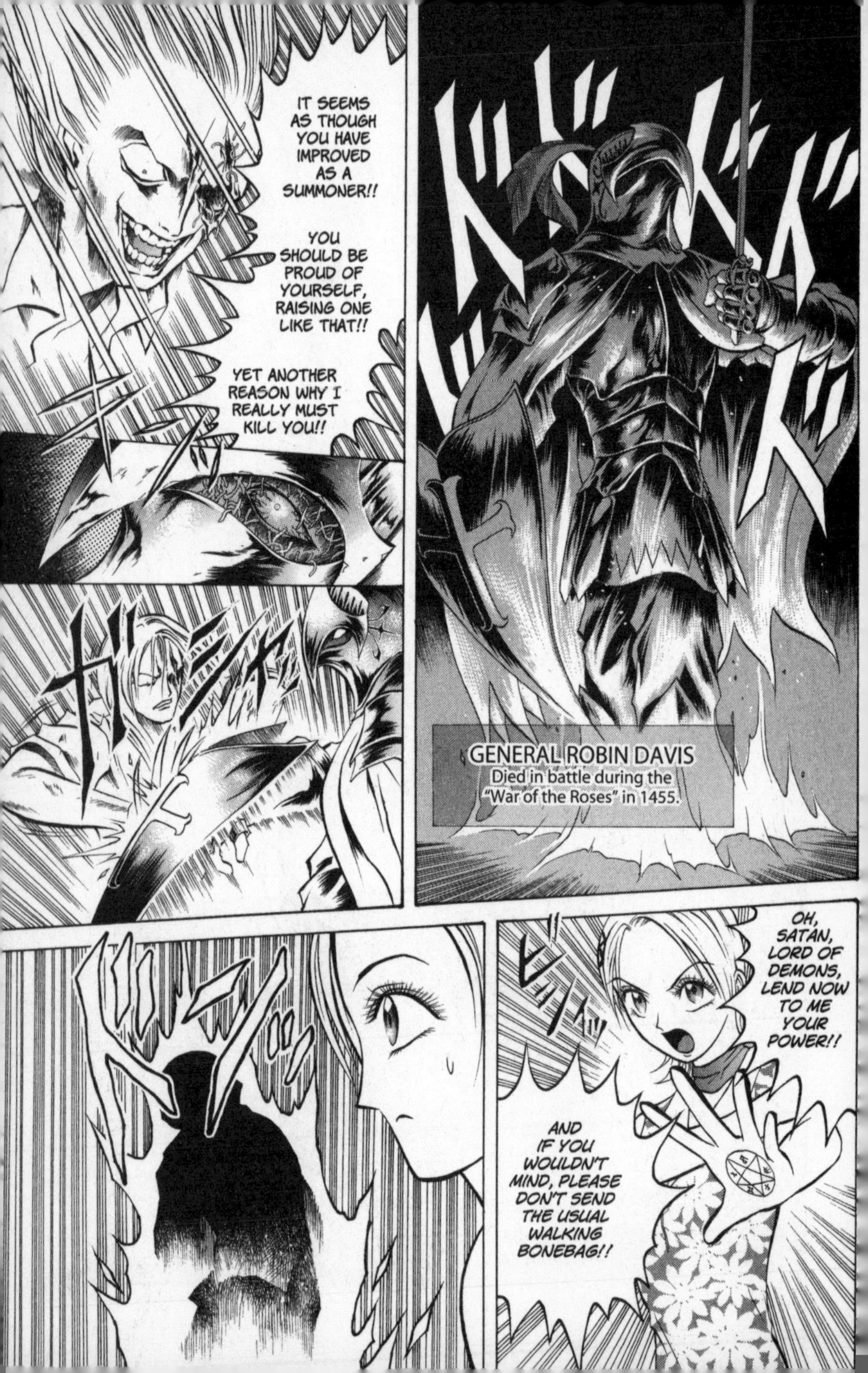
GENERAL ROBIN DAVIS
Died in battle during the "War of the Roses" in 1455.
IT SEEMS AS THOUGH YOU HAVE IMPROVED AS A SUMMONER!!
YOU SHOULD BE PROUD OF YOURSELF, RAISING ONE LIKE THAT!!
YET ANOTHER REASON WHY I REALLY MUST KILL YOU!!
OH, SATAN, LORD OF DEMONS, LEND NOW TO ME YOUR POWER!!
AND IF YOU WOULDN'T MIND, PLEASE DON'T SEND THE USUAL WALKING BONEBAG!!

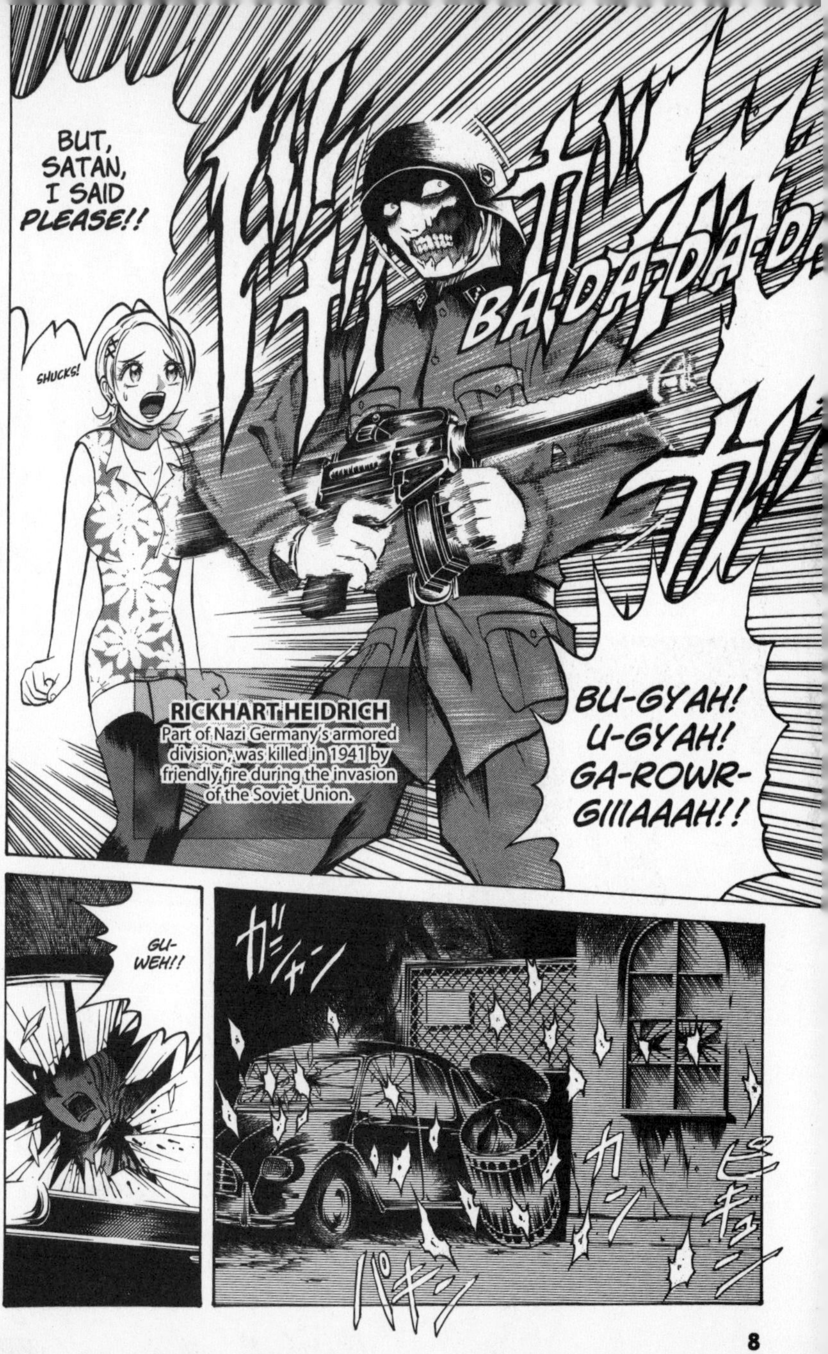
BA-DA-DA-DA-D...
BU-GYAH! U-GYAH! GA-ROWR-GIIIAAAH!!
BUT, SATAN, I SAID *PLEASE!!*
SHUCKS!
RICKHART HEIDRICH
Part of Nazi Germany's armored division, was killed in 1941 by friendly fire during the invasion of the Soviet Union.
ガシャン
ピキュン
カン
パキン
GU-WEH!!

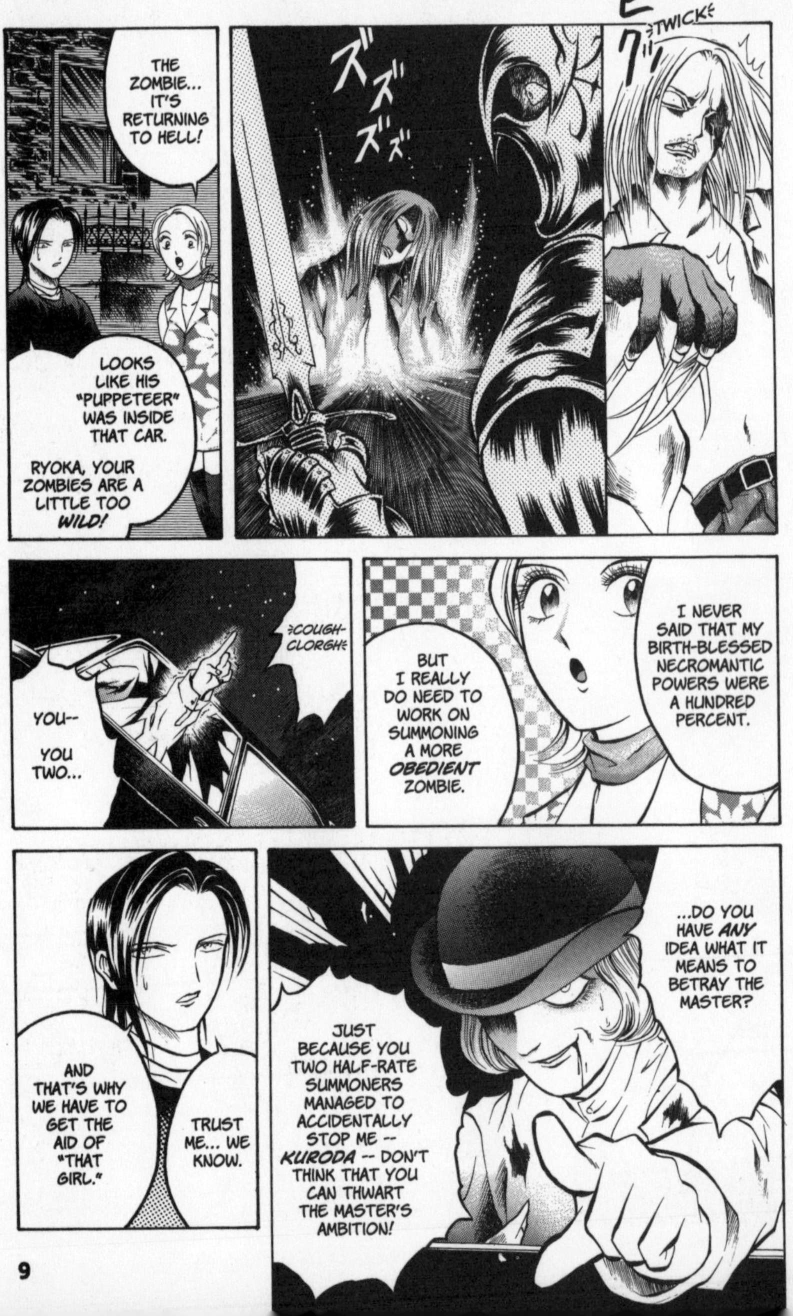

ビク
TWICK
ズズズズ
THE ZOMBIE... IT'S RETURNING TO HELL!
LOOKS LIKE HIS "PUPPETEER" WAS INSIDE THAT CAR.
RYOKA, YOUR ZOMBIES ARE A LITTLE TOO *WILD!*
I NEVER SAID THAT MY BIRTH-BLESSED NECROMANTIC POWERS WERE A HUNDRED PERCENT.
BUT I REALLY DO NEED TO WORK ON SUMMONING A MORE *OBEDIENT* ZOMBIE.
COUGH-CLORGH
YOU--
YOU TWO...
...DO YOU HAVE *ANY* IDEA WHAT IT MEANS TO BETRAY THE MASTER?
JUST BECAUSE YOU TWO HALF-RATE SUMMONERS MANAGED TO ACCIDENTALLY STOP ME -- *KURODA* -- DON'T THINK THAT YOU CAN THWART THE MASTER'S AMBITION!
TRUST ME... WE KNOW.
AND THAT'S WHY WE HAVE TO GET THE AID OF "THAT GIRL."

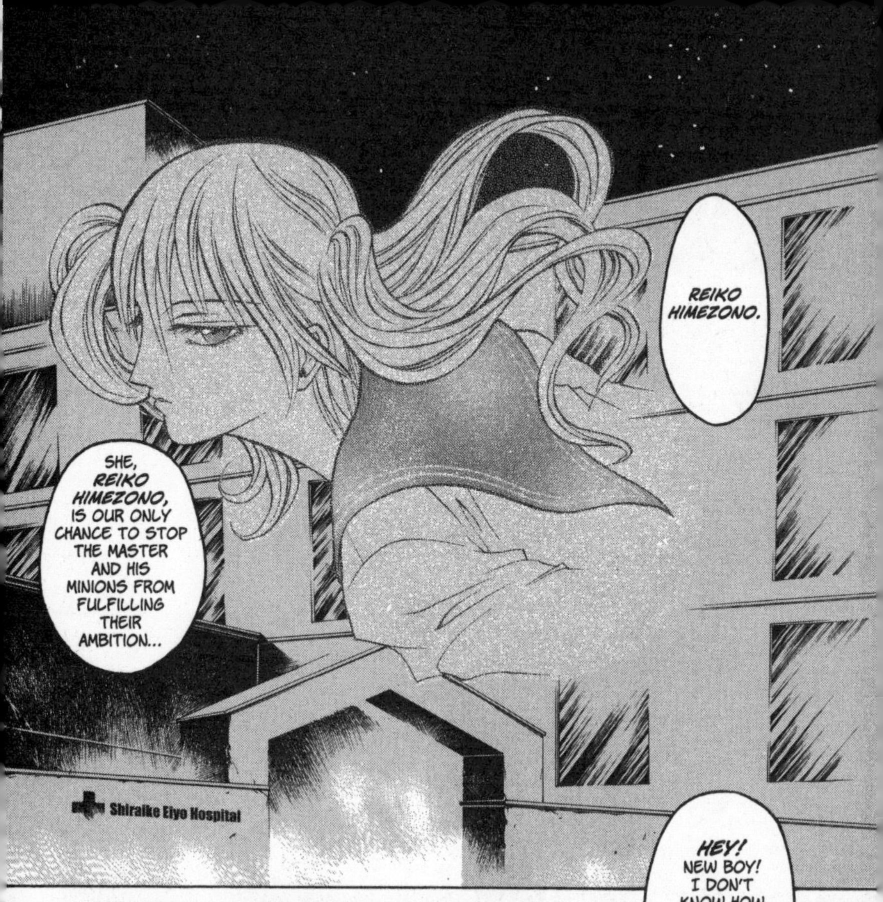
REIKO HIMEZONO.
SHE, REIKO HIMEZONO, IS OUR ONLY CHANCE TO STOP THE MASTER AND HIS MINIONS FROM FULFILLING THEIR AMBITION...
Shiraike Eiyo Hospital

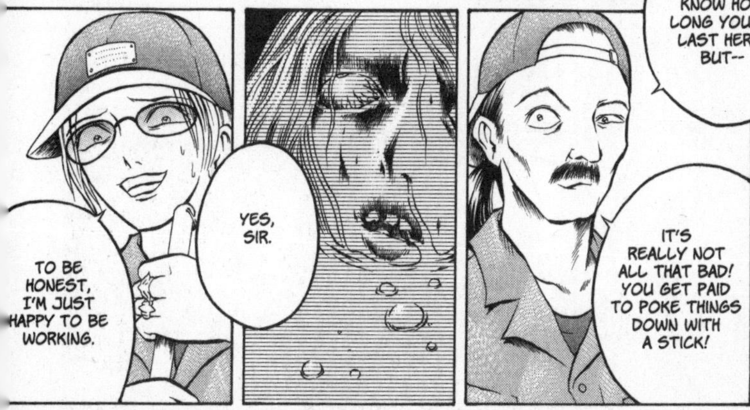
HEY! NEW BOY! I DON'T KNOW HOW LONG YOU'LL LAST HERE, BUT--
IT'S REALLY NOT ALL THAT BAD! YOU GET PAID TO POKE THINGS DOWN WITH A STICK!
YES, SIR.
TO BE HONEST, I'M JUST HAPPY TO BE WORKING.

TRANSLATOR'S NOTE: The interesting thing about this scene is that this was taken from a Japanese urban myth. There is a myth that there was a high-paying part time job at a certain hospital where one was paid merely to keep dead bodies under the surface of a formaldehyde pool by poking them with a stick. They had no next of kin and are merely lumped together until services could be procured. As this is merely an urban myth, the exact location of the hospital, as well as small details pertaining to the job, will vary from place to place.

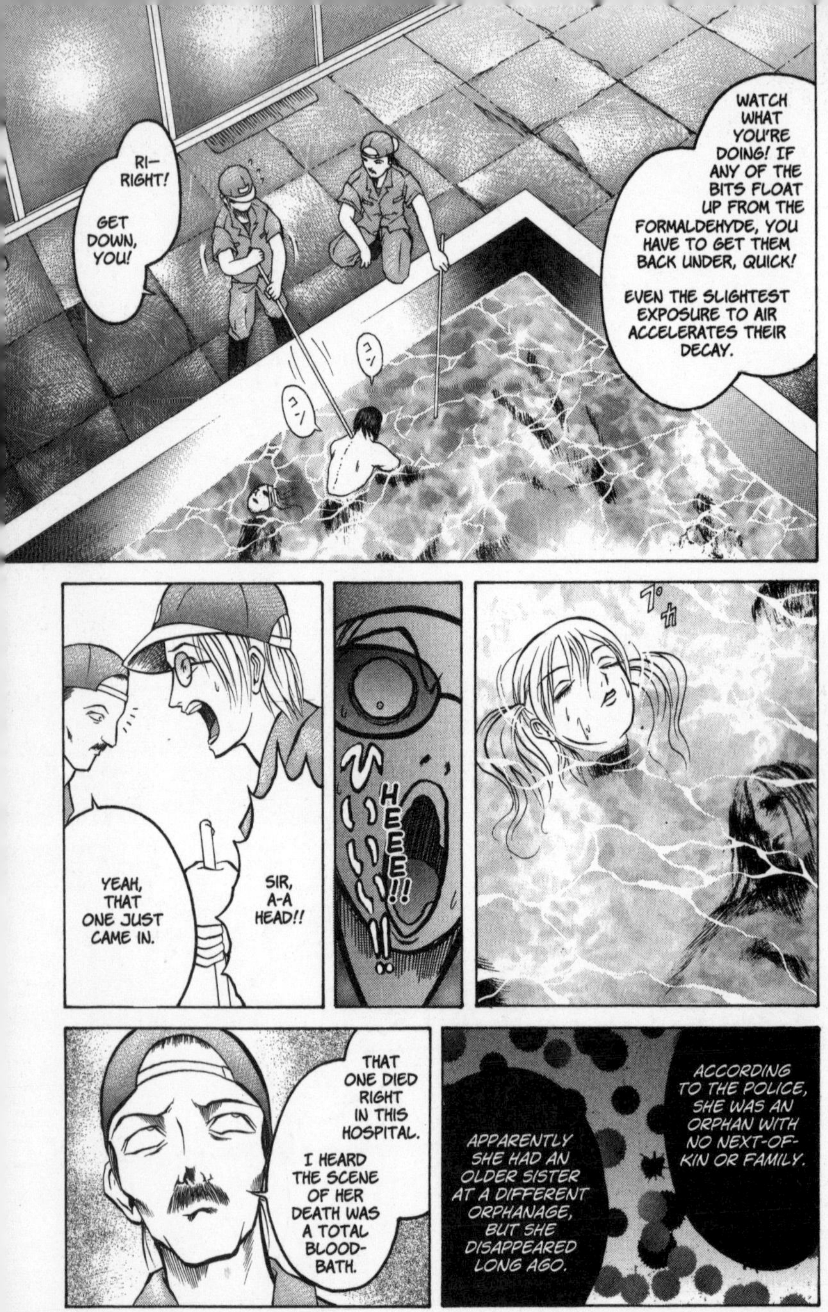
WATCH WHAT YOU'RE DOING! IF ANY OF THE BITS FLOAT UP FROM THE FORMALDEHYDE, YOU HAVE TO GET THEM BACK UNDER, QUICK!
EVEN THE SLIGHTEST EXPOSURE TO AIR ACCELERATES THEIR DECAY.
RI— RIGHT!
GET DOWN, YOU!
コン
コン
HEEEE!!
SIR, A-A HEAD!!
YEAH, THAT ONE JUST CAME IN.
ACCORDING TO THE POLICE, SHE WAS AN ORPHAN WITH NO NEXT-OF-KIN OR FAMILY.
APPARENTLY SHE HAD AN OLDER SISTER AT A DIFFERENT ORPHANAGE, BUT SHE DISAPPEARED LONG AGO.
THAT ONE DIED RIGHT IN THIS HOSPITAL.
I HEARD THE SCENE OF HER DEATH WAS A TOTAL BLOOD-BATH.

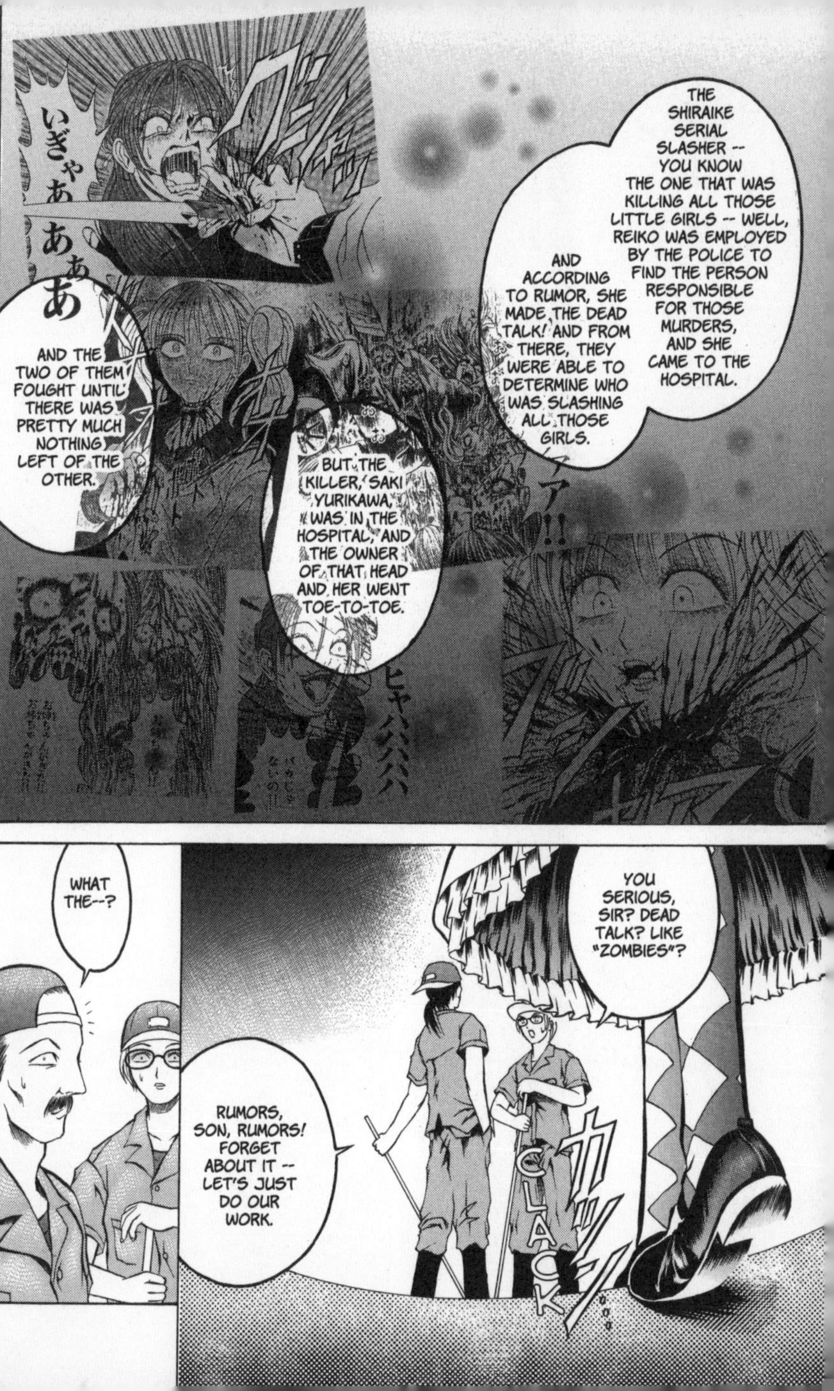
THE SHIRAIKE SERIAL SLASHER -- YOU KNOW THE ONE THAT WAS KILLING ALL THOSE LITTLE GIRLS -- WELL, REIKO WAS EMPLOYED BY THE POLICE TO FIND THE PERSON RESPONSIBLE FOR THOSE MURDERS, AND SHE CAME TO THE HOSPITAL.
AND ACCORDING TO RUMOR, SHE MADE THE DEAD TALK! AND FROM THERE, THEY WERE ABLE TO DETERMINE WHO WAS SLASHING ALL THOSE GIRLS.
いぎゃあああ
ア!!
BUT THE KILLER, SAKI YURIKAWA, WAS IN THE HOSPITAL, AND THE OWNER OF THAT HEAD AND HER WENT TOE-TO-TOE.
AND THE TWO OF THEM FOUGHT UNTIL THERE WAS PRETTY MUCH NOTHING LEFT OF THE OTHER.
ヒャハハハハ
YOU SERIOUS, SIR? DEAD TALK? LIKE "ZOMBIES"?
RUMORS, SON, RUMORS! FORGET ABOUT IT -- LET'S JUST DO OUR WORK.
CLACK
WHAT THE--?

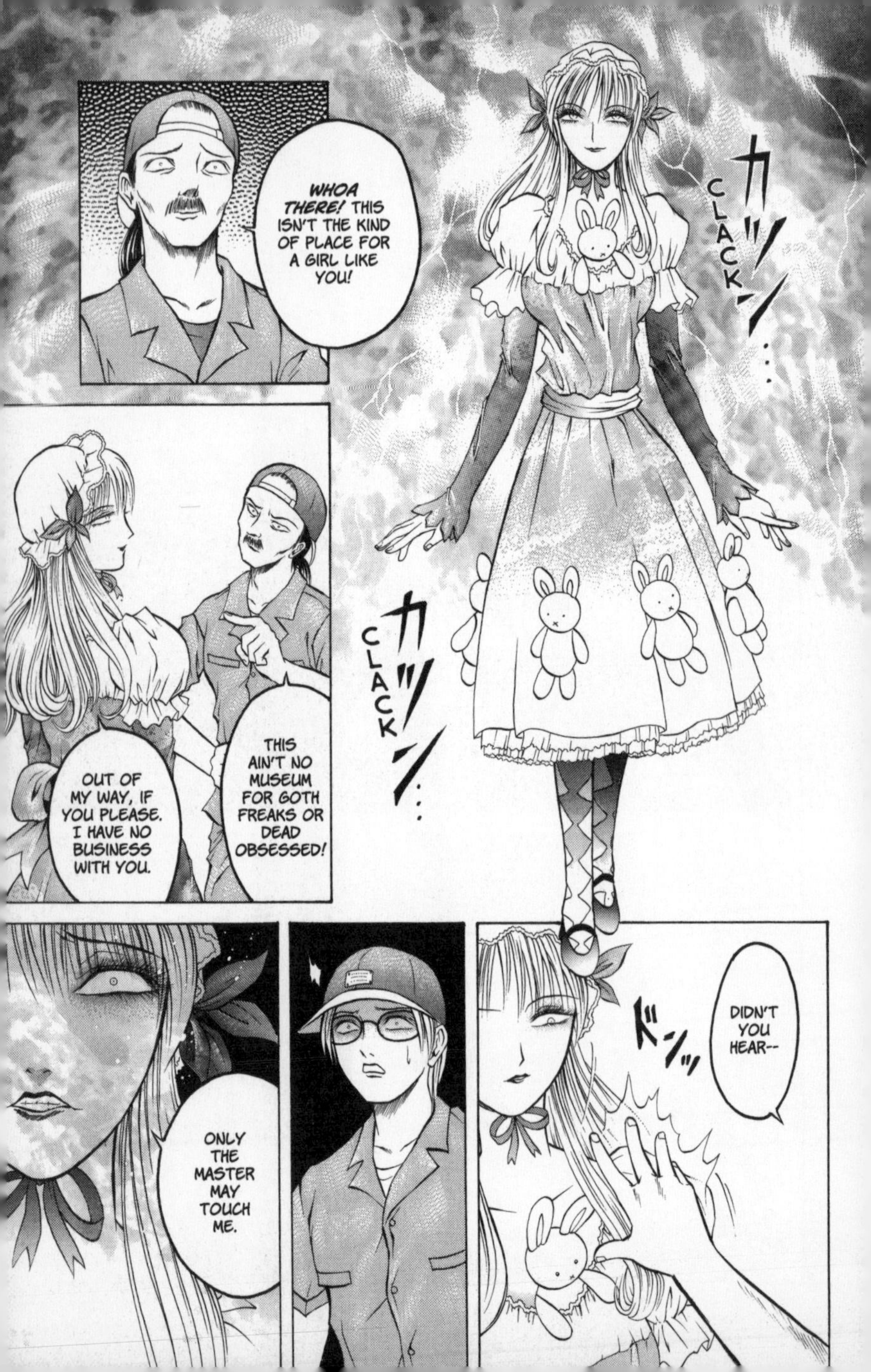
CLACK
CLACK
WHOA THERE! THIS ISN'T THE KIND OF PLACE FOR A GIRL LIKE YOU!
THIS AIN'T NO MUSEUM FOR GOTH FREAKS OR DEAD OBSESSED!
OUT OF MY WAY, IF YOU PLEASE. I HAVE NO BUSINESS WITH YOU.
DIDN'T YOU HEAR--
ONLY THE MASTER MAY TOUCH ME.

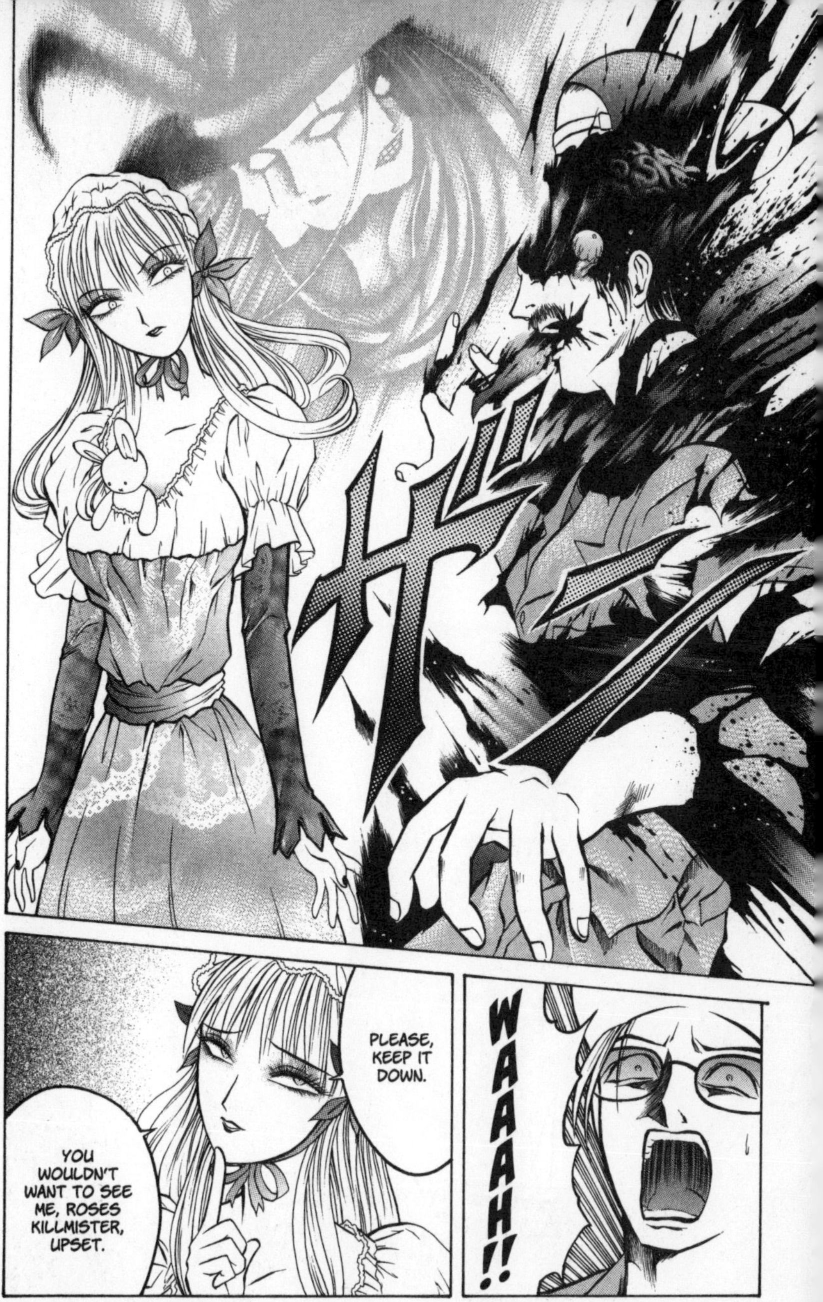
WAAAAAH!!
PLEASE, KEEP IT DOWN.
YOU WOULDN'T WANT TO SEE ME, ROSES KILLMISTER, UPSET.

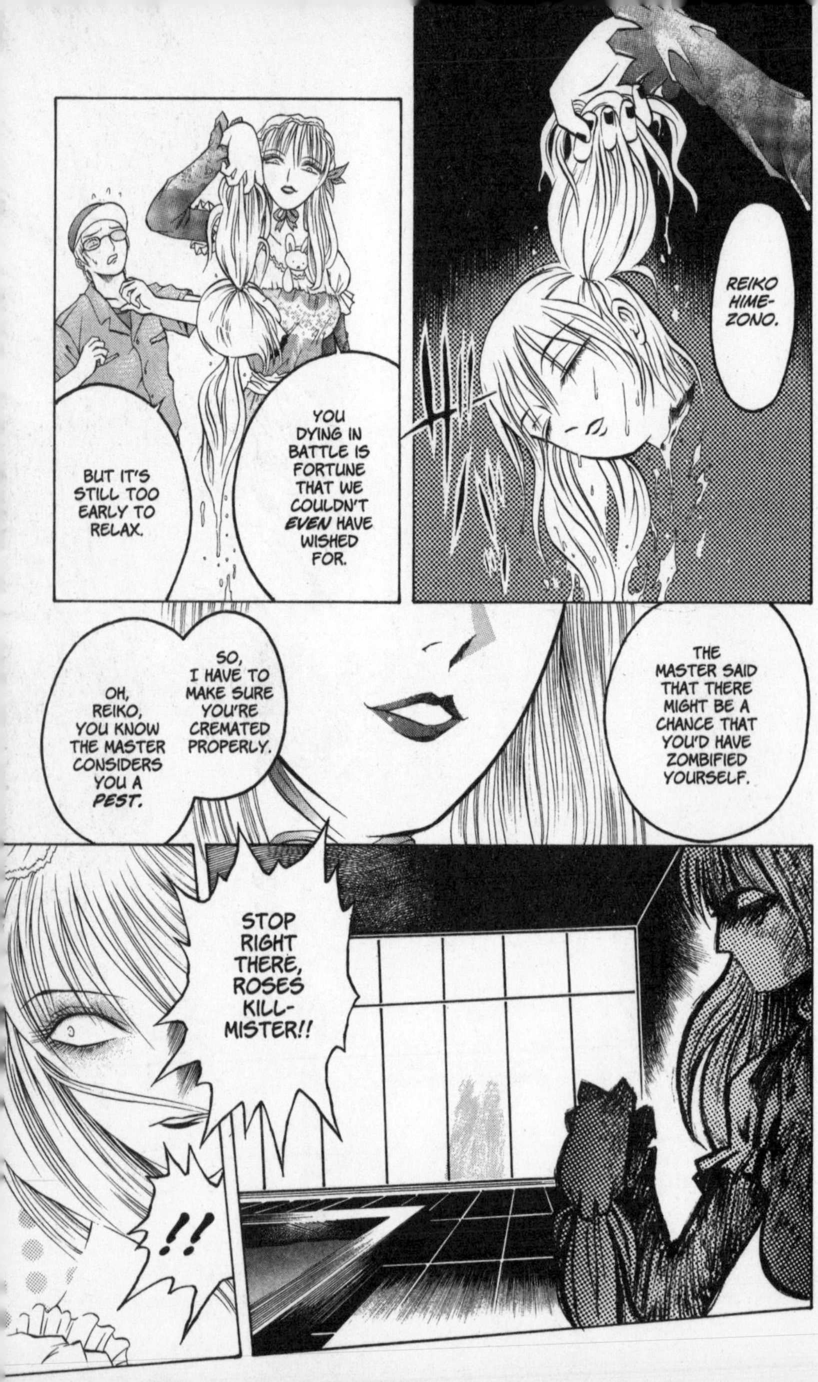

REIKO HIME-ZONO.
YOU DYING IN BATTLE IS FORTUNE THAT WE COULDN'T *EVEN* HAVE WISHED FOR.
BUT IT'S STILL TOO EARLY TO RELAX.
THE MASTER SAID THAT THERE MIGHT BE A CHANCE THAT YOU'D HAVE ZOMBIFIED YOURSELF.
SO, I HAVE TO MAKE SURE YOU'RE CREMATED PROPERLY.
OH, REIKO, YOU KNOW THE MASTER CONSIDERS YOU A *PEST*.
STOP RIGHT THERE, ROSES KILL-MISTER!!
!!

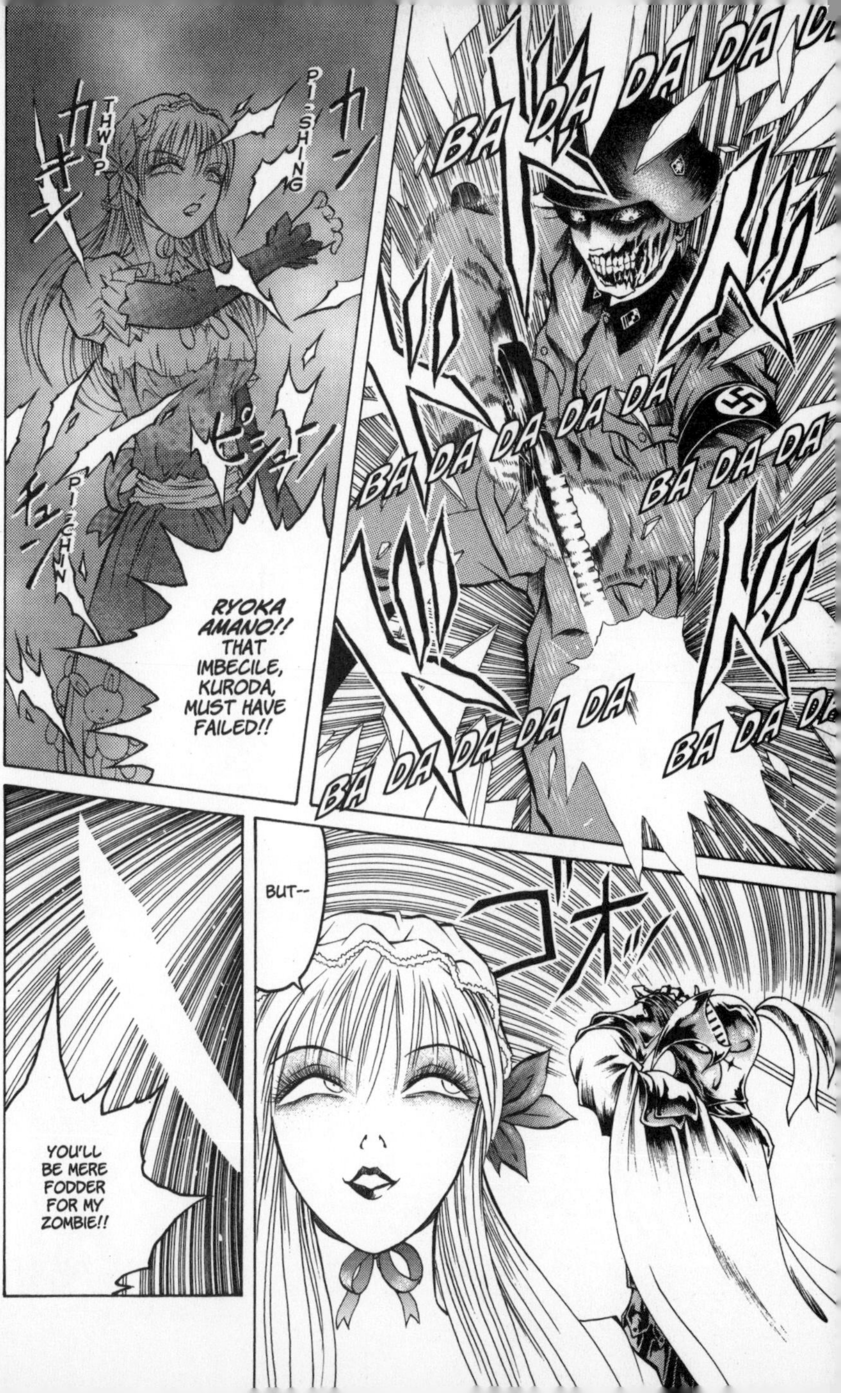
BA DA DA DA
BA DA DA DA DA
BA DA DA
BA DA DA DA DA
BA DA
PI-SHING
THWIP
PI-CHIN
RYOKA AMANO!! THAT IMBECILE, KURODA, MUST HAVE FAILED!!
BUT--
YOU'LL BE MERE FODDER FOR MY ZOMBIE!!

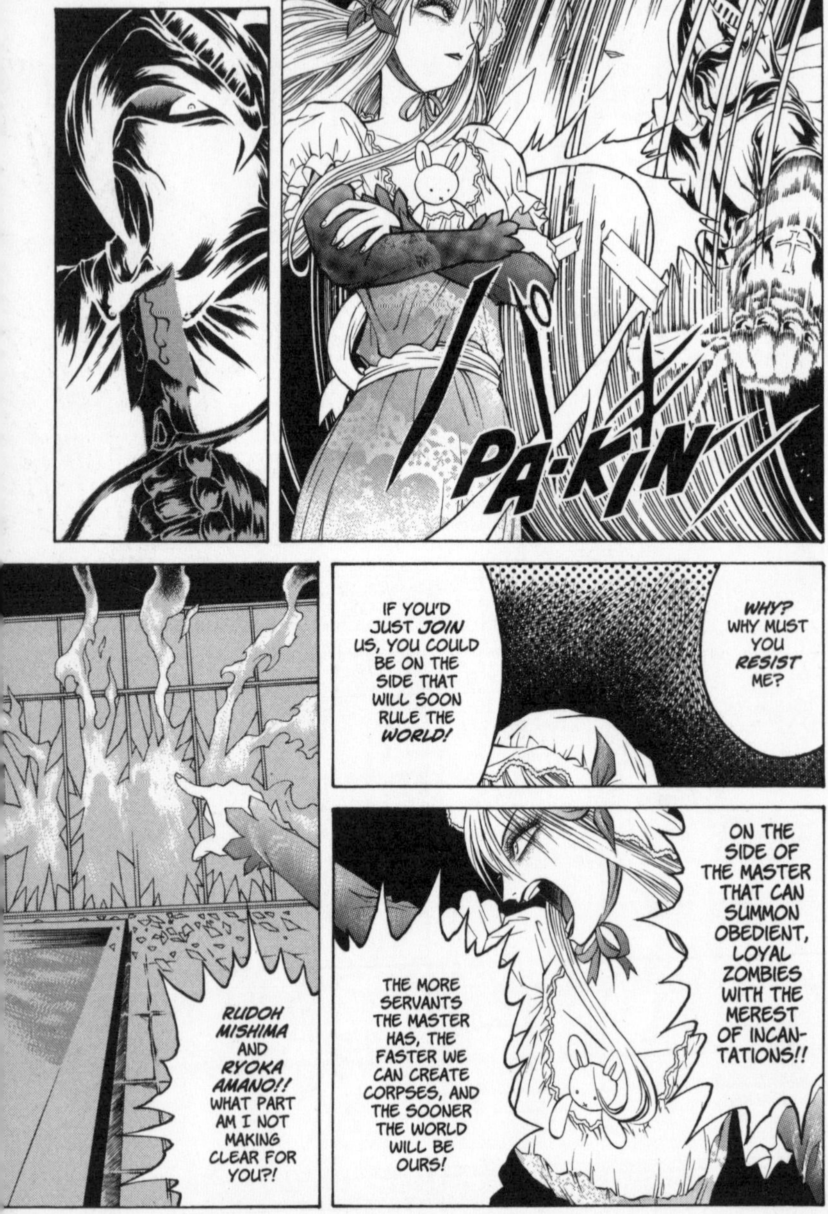
PA-KIN
WHY? WHY MUST YOU RESIST ME?
IF YOU'D JUST JOIN US, YOU COULD BE ON THE SIDE THAT WILL SOON RULE THE WORLD!
ON THE SIDE OF THE MASTER THAT CAN SUMMON OBEDIENT, LOYAL ZOMBIES WITH THE MEREST OF INCANTATIONS!!
THE MORE SERVANTS THE MASTER HAS, THE FASTER WE CAN CREATE CORPSES, AND THE SOONER THE WORLD WILL BE OURS!
RUDOH MISHIMA AND RYOKA AMANO!! WHAT PART AM I NOT MAKING CLEAR FOR YOU?!

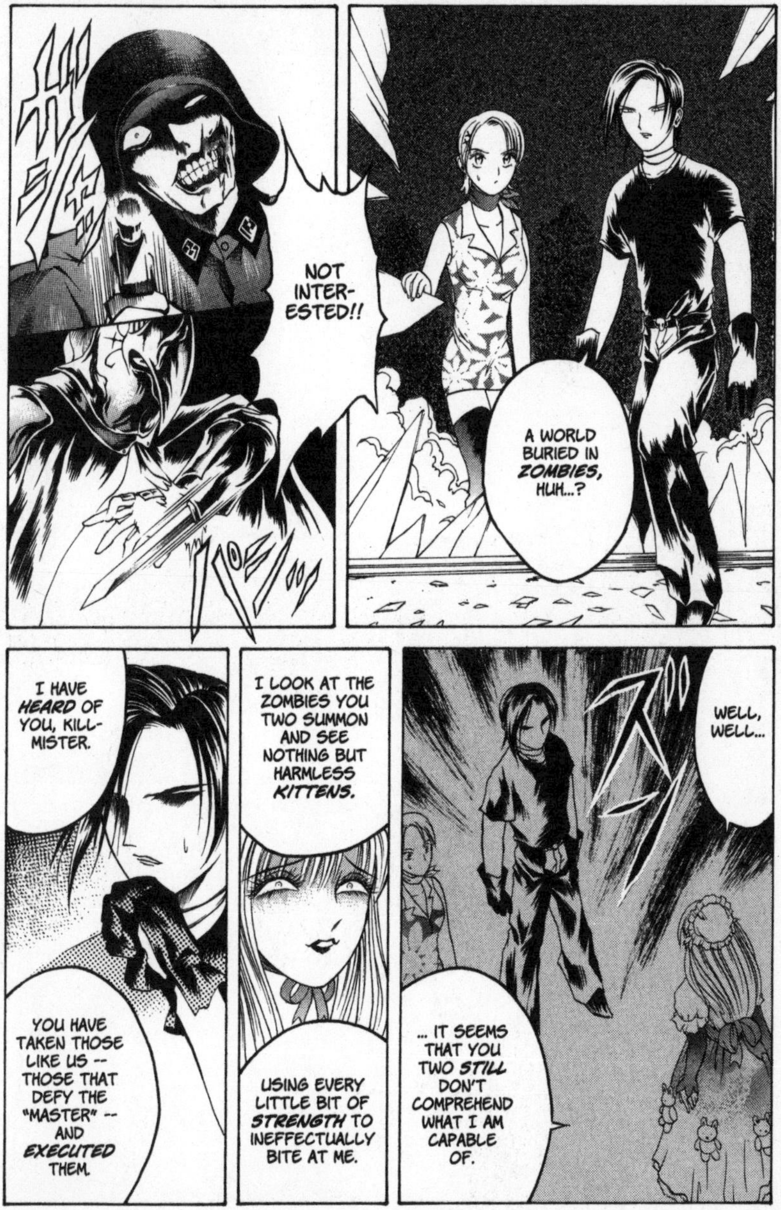
A WORLD BURIED IN ZOMBIES, HUH...?
NOT INTER-ESTED!!
WELL, WELL...
... IT SEEMS THAT YOU TWO STILL DON'T COMPREHEND WHAT I AM CAPABLE OF.
I LOOK AT THE ZOMBIES YOU TWO SUMMON AND SEE NOTHING BUT HARMLESS KITTENS.
USING EVERY LITTLE BIT OF STRENGTH TO INEFFECTUALLY BITE AT ME.
I HAVE HEARD OF YOU, KILL-MISTER.
YOU HAVE TAKEN THOSE LIKE US -- THOSE THAT DEFY THE "MASTER" -- AND EXECUTED THEM.

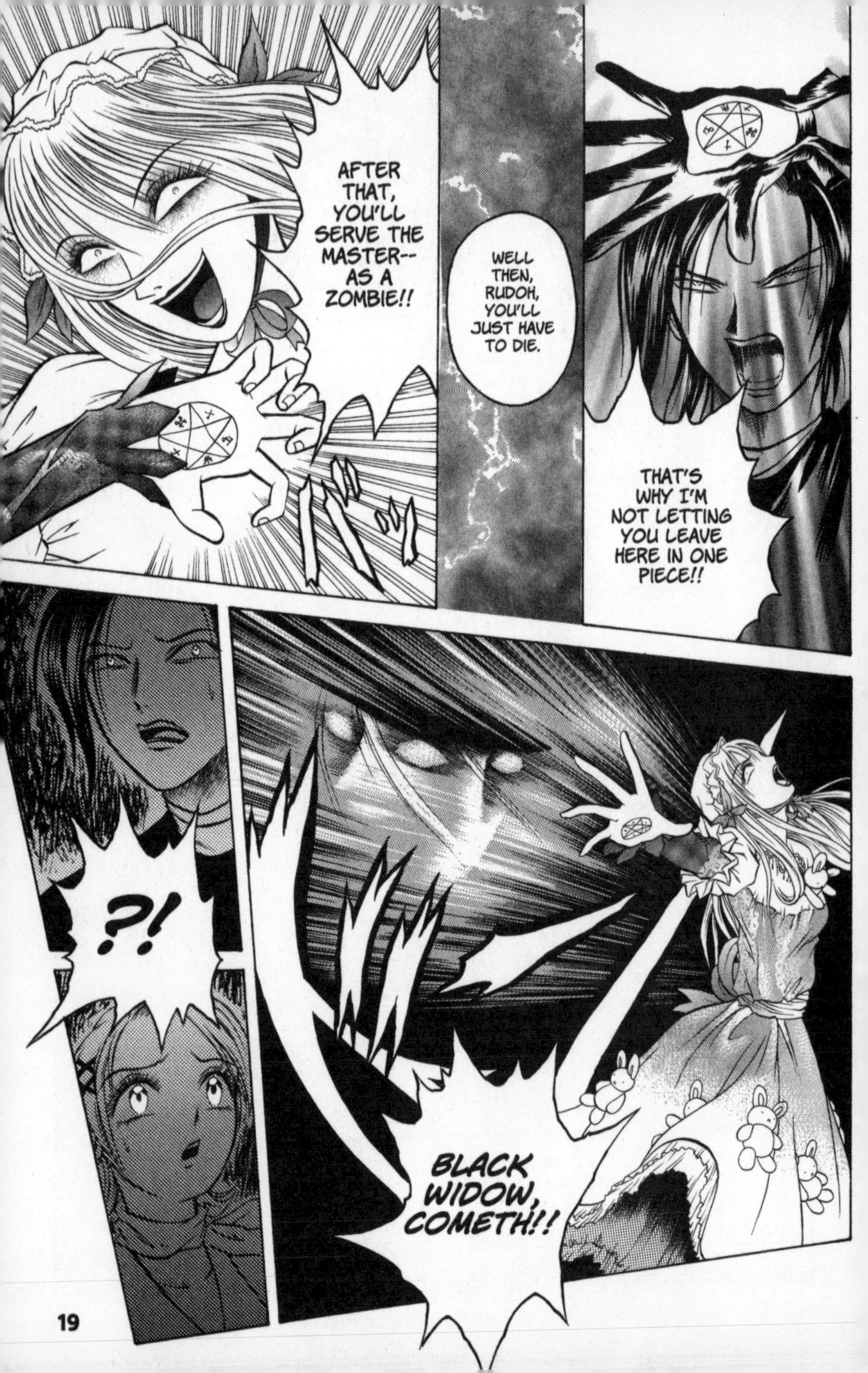
THAT'S WHY I'M NOT LETTING YOU LEAVE HERE IN ONE PIECE!!
WELL THEN, RUDOH, YOU'LL JUST HAVE TO DIE.
AFTER THAT, YOU'LL SERVE THE MASTER-- AS A ZOMBIE!!
BLACK WIDOW, COMETH!!
?!

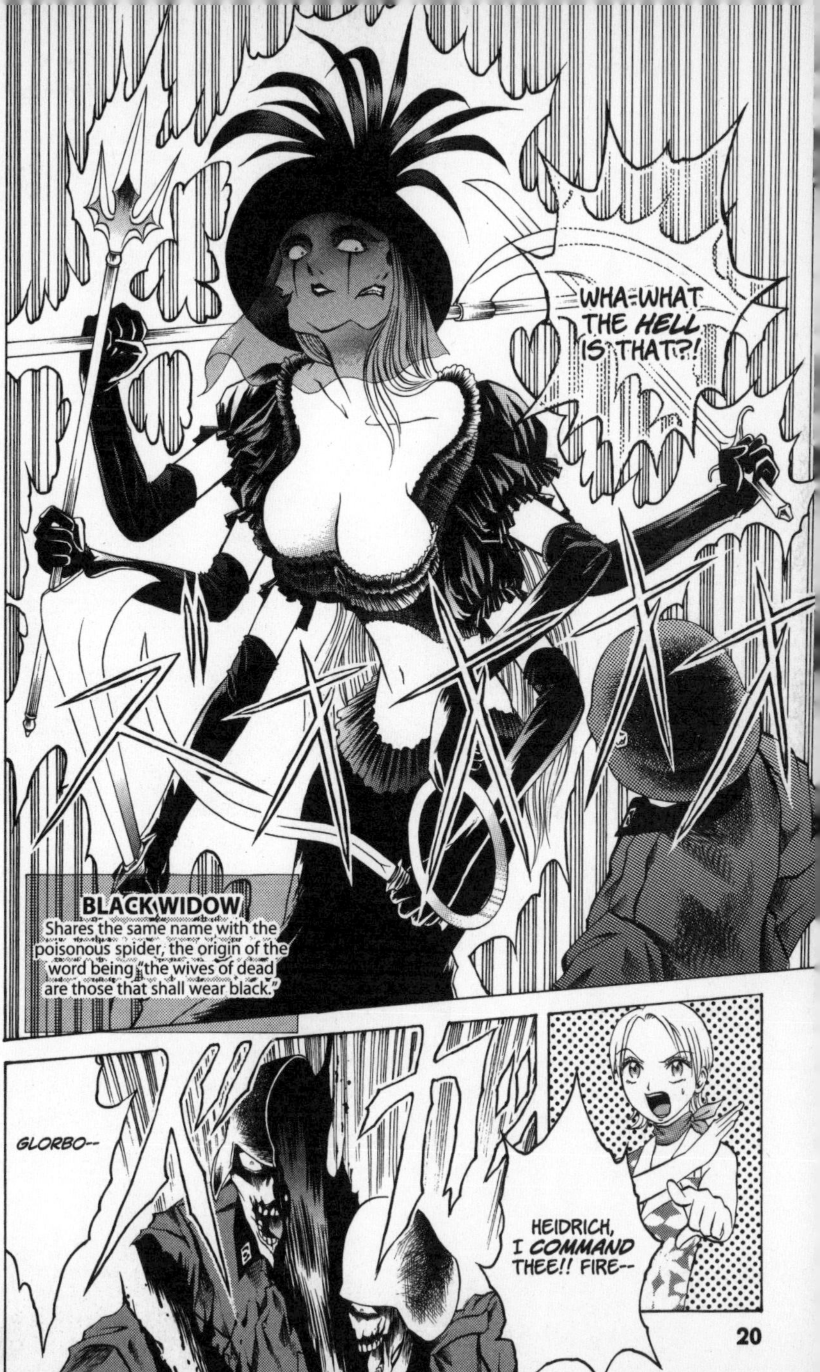
WHA-WHAT THE HELL IS THAT?!
BLACK WIDOW
Shares the same name with the poisonous spider, the origin of the word being "the wives of dead are those that shall wear black."
HEIDRICH, I COMMAND THEE!! FIRE--
GLORBO--

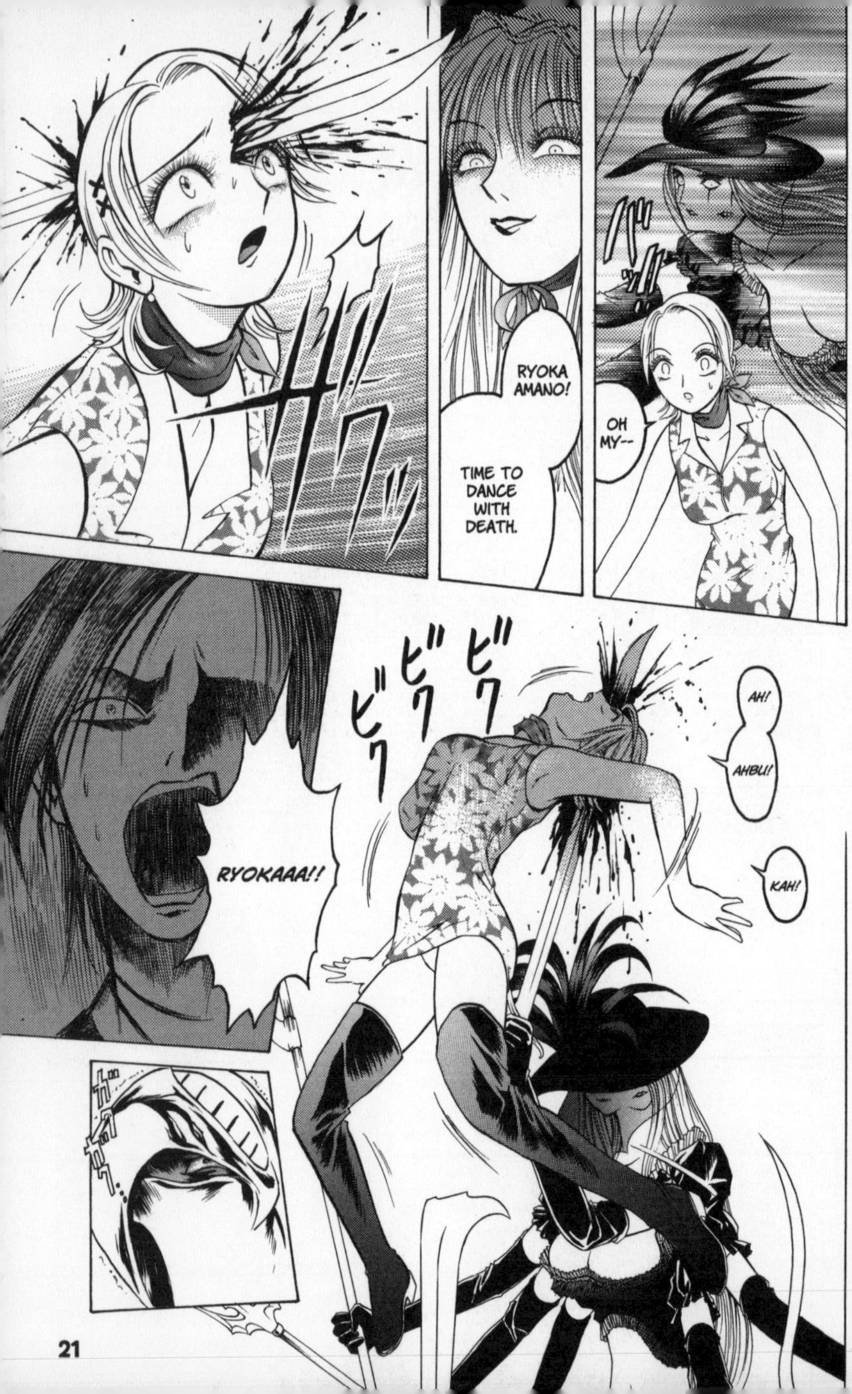
OH MY--
RYOKA AMANO!
TIME TO DANCE WITH DEATH.
AH!
AHBU!
KAH!
RYOKAAA!!

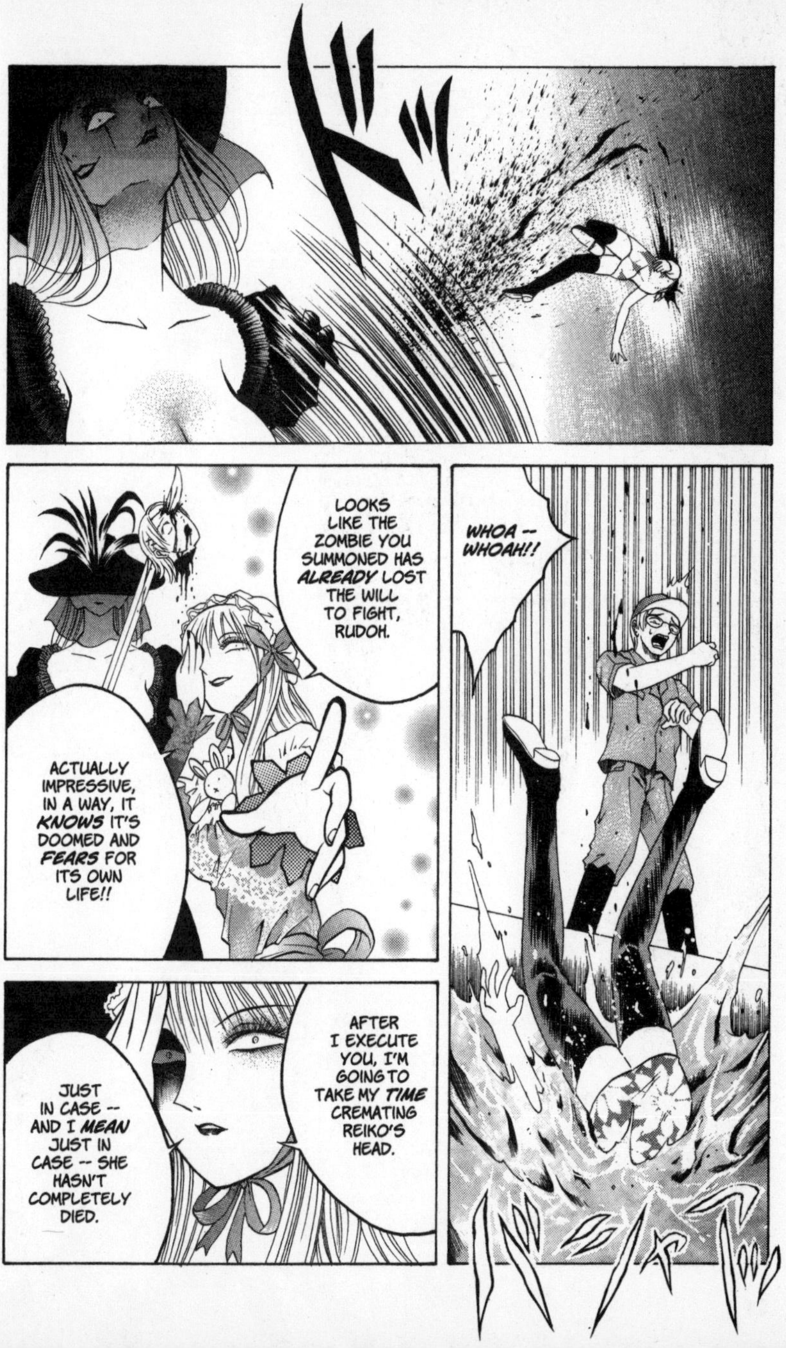
WHOA -- WHOAH!!
LOOKS LIKE THE ZOMBIE YOU SUMMONED HAS ALREADY LOST THE WILL TO FIGHT, RUDOH.
ACTUALLY IMPRESSIVE, IN A WAY, IT KNOWS IT'S DOOMED AND FEARS FOR ITS OWN LIFE!!
AFTER I EXECUTE YOU, I'M GOING TO TAKE MY TIME CREMATING REIKO'S HEAD.
JUST IN CASE -- AND I MEAN JUST IN CASE -- SHE HASN'T COMPLETELY DIED.

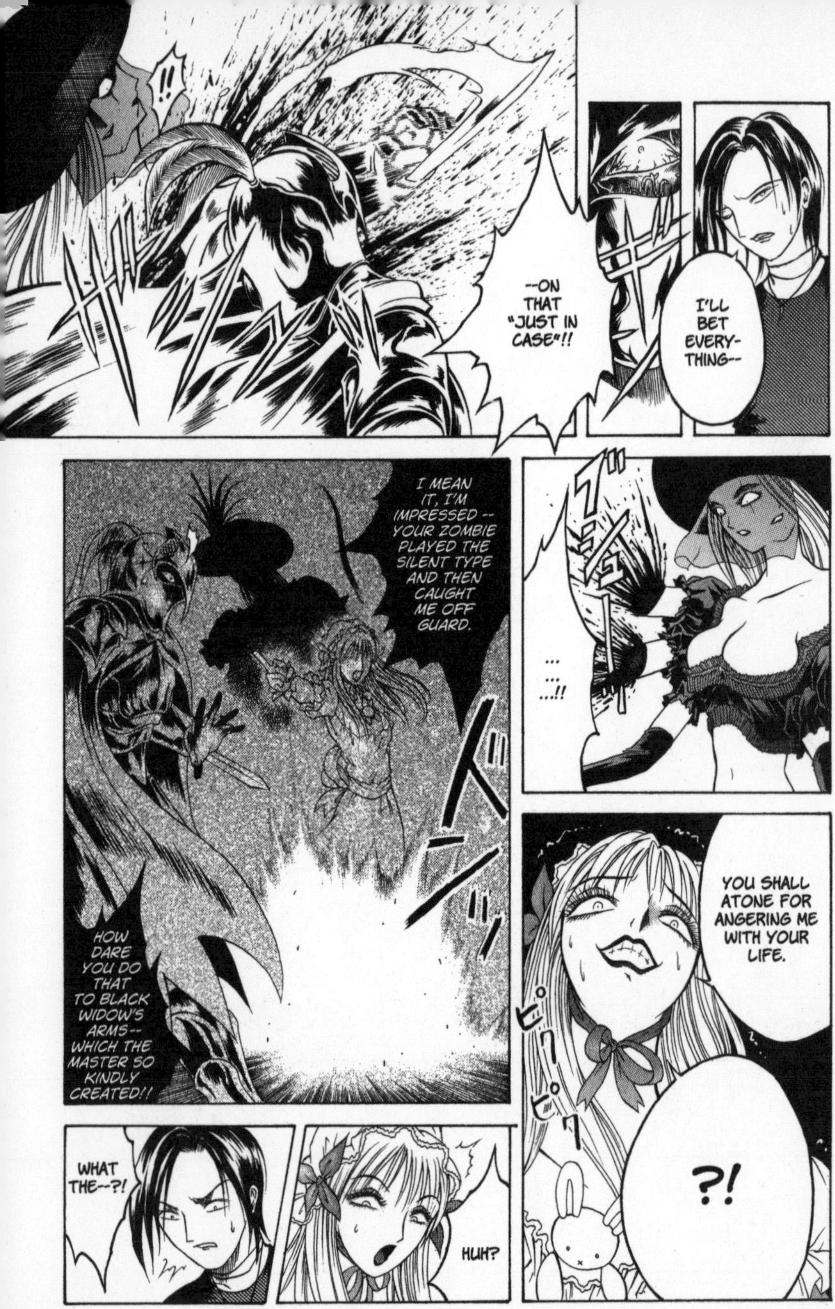
I'LL BET EVERY-THING--
--ON THAT "JUST IN CASE"!!
!!
...
...
...!!
I MEAN IT, I'M IMPRESSED -- YOUR ZOMBIE PLAYED THE SILENT TYPE AND THEN CAUGHT ME OFF GUARD.
HOW DARE YOU DO THAT TO BLACK WIDOW'S ARMS-- WHICH THE MASTER SO KINDLY CREATED!!
YOU SHALL ATONE FOR ANGERING ME WITH YOUR LIFE.
?!
HUH?
WHAT THE--?!

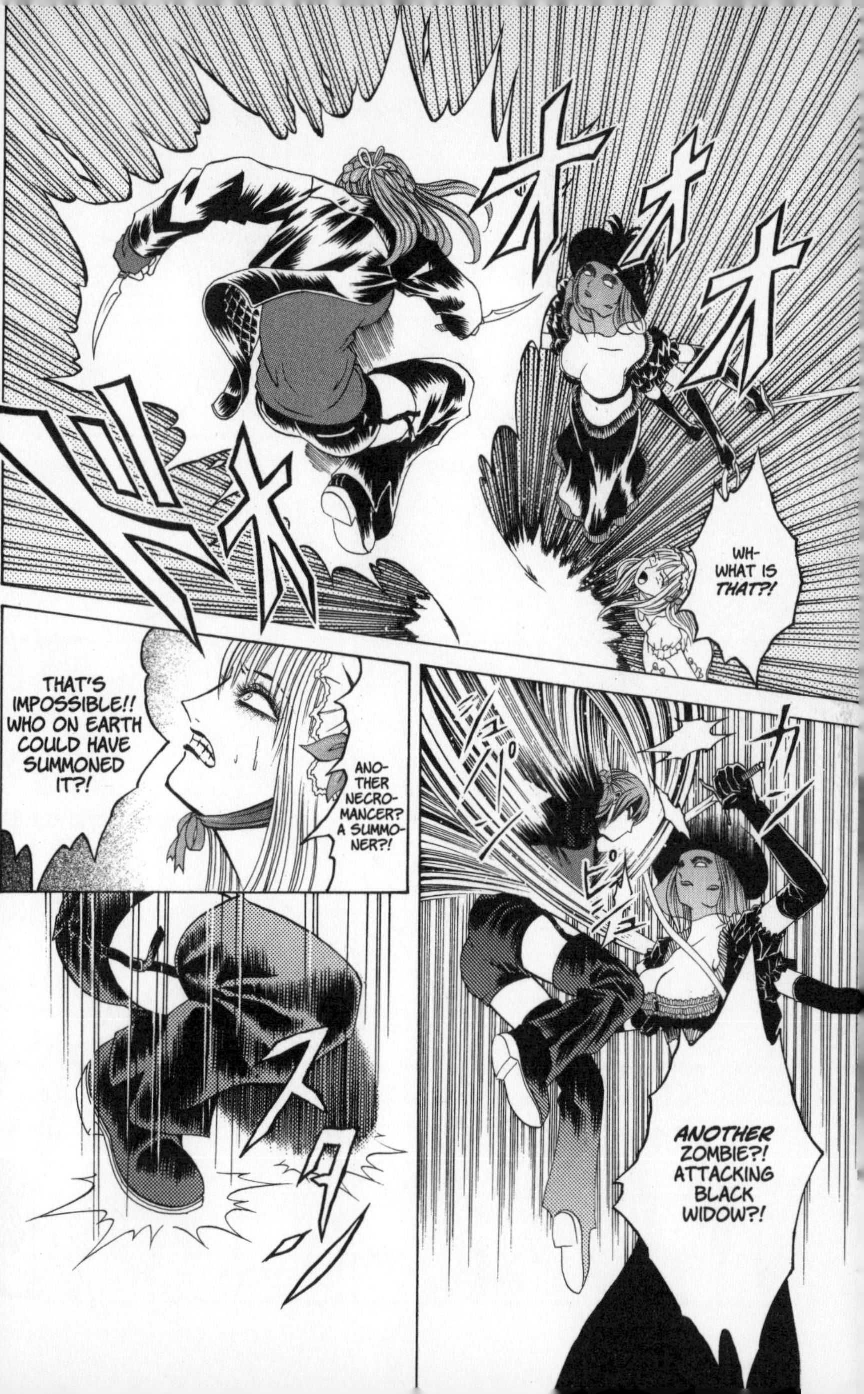
WH- WHAT IS *THAT?!*
ANOTHER ZOMBIE?! ATTACKING BLACK WIDOW?!
ANOTHER NECROMANCER? A SUMMONER?!
THAT'S IMPOSSIBLE!! WHO ON EARTH COULD HAVE SUMMONED IT?!

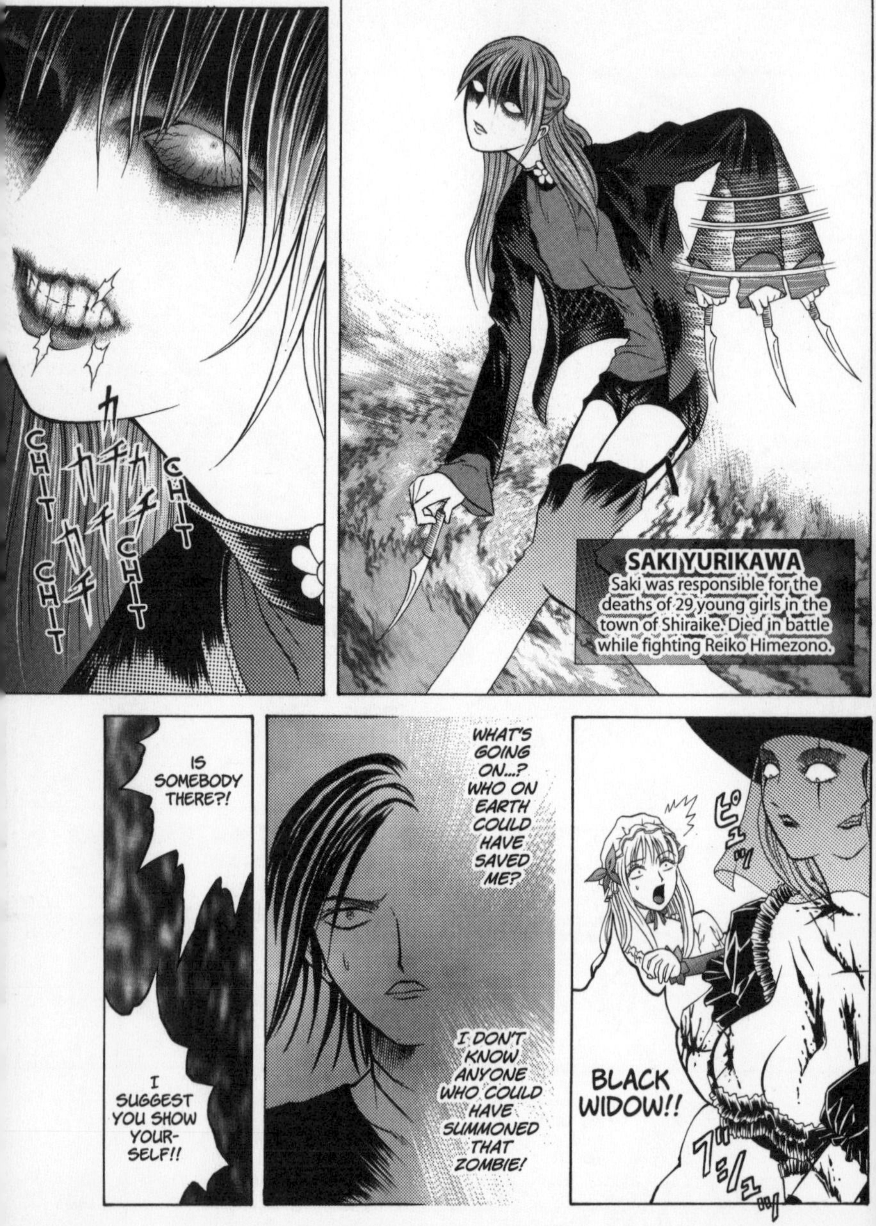
SAKI YURIKAWA
Saki was responsible for the deaths of 29 young girls in the town of Shiraike. Died in battle while fighting Reiko Himezono.
CHIT
CHIT
CHIT
CHIT
BLACK WIDOW!!
WHAT'S GOING ON...? WHO ON EARTH COULD HAVE SAVED ME?
I DON'T KNOW ANYONE WHO COULD HAVE SUMMONED THAT ZOMBIE!
IS SOMEBODY THERE?!
I SUGGEST YOU SHOW YOUR-SELF!!

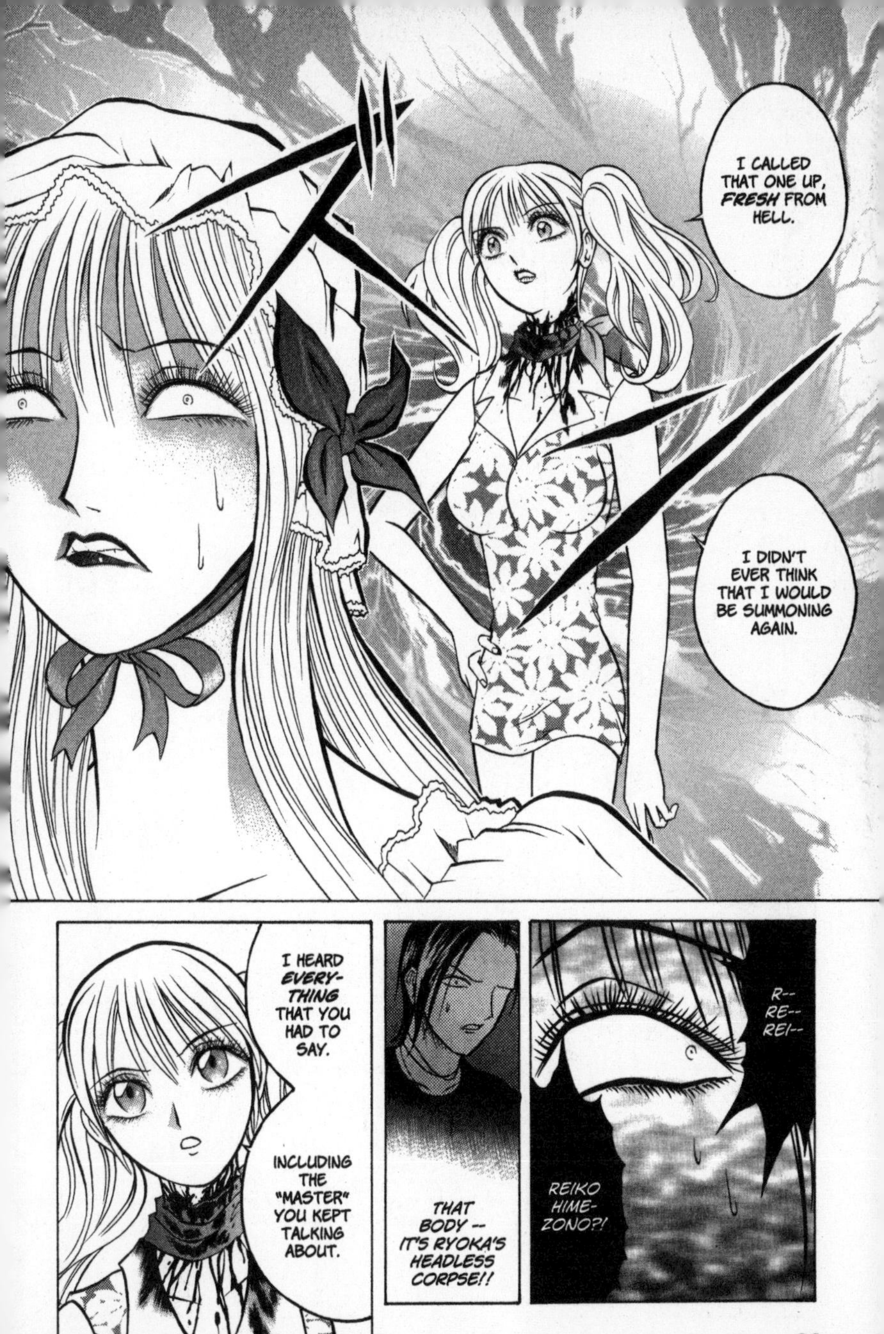
I CALLED THAT ONE UP, FRESH FROM HELL.
I DIDN'T EVER THINK THAT I WOULD BE SUMMONING AGAIN.
R-- RE-- REI--
REIKO HIME-ZONO?!
THAT BODY -- IT'S RYOKA'S HEADLESS CORPSE!!
I HEARD EVERY-THING THAT YOU HAD TO SAY.
INCLUDING THE "MASTER" YOU KEPT TALKING ABOUT.

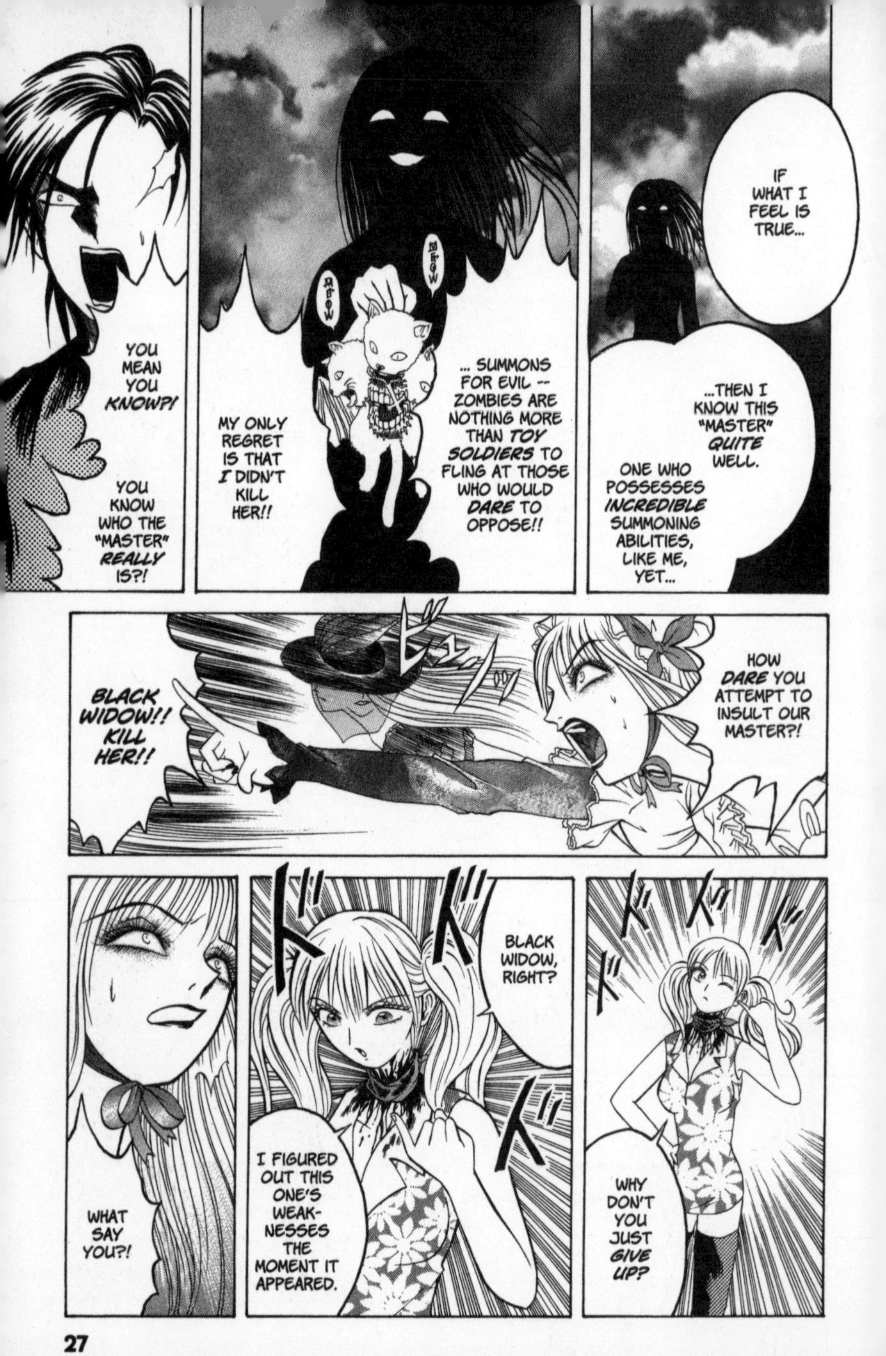
IF WHAT I FEEL IS TRUE...
...THEN I KNOW THIS "MASTER" QUITE WELL.
ONE WHO POSSESSES INCREDIBLE SUMMONING ABILITIES, LIKE ME, YET...
MEOW
MEOW
... SUMMONS FOR EVIL -- ZOMBIES ARE NOTHING MORE THAN TOY SOLDIERS TO FLING AT THOSE WHO WOULD DARE TO OPPOSE!!
MY ONLY REGRET IS THAT I DIDN'T KILL HER!!
YOU MEAN YOU KNOW?!
YOU KNOW WHO THE "MASTER" REALLY IS?!
HOW DARE YOU ATTEMPT TO INSULT OUR MASTER?!
BLACK WIDOW!! KILL HER!!
WHY DON'T YOU JUST GIVE UP?
BLACK WIDOW, RIGHT?
I FIGURED OUT THIS ONE'S WEAKNESSES THE MOMENT IT APPEARED.
WHAT SAY YOU?!

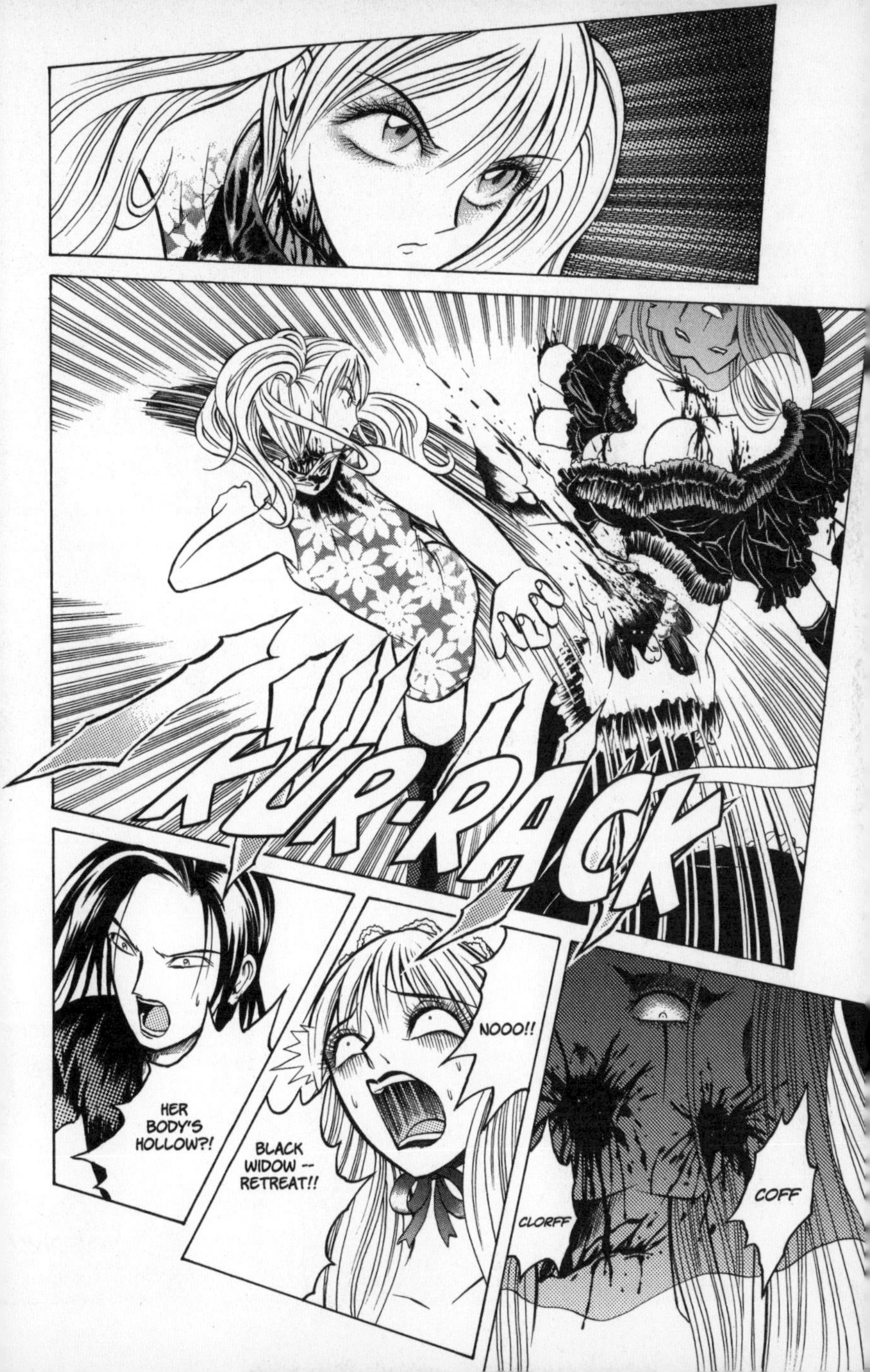
KUR-RACK
COFF
CLORFF
NOOO!!
BLACK WIDOW -- RETREAT!!
HER BODY'S HOLLOW?!

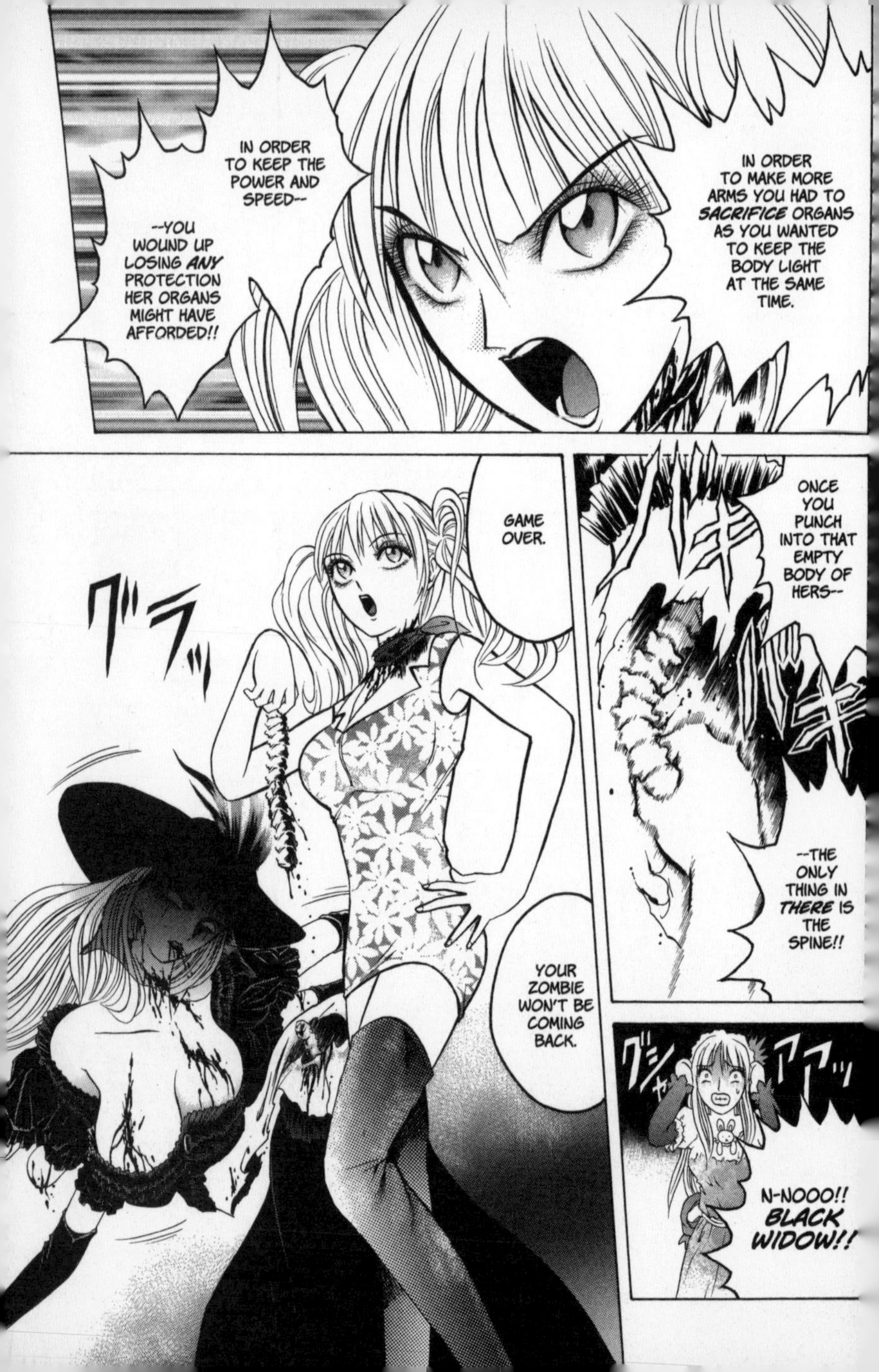
IN ORDER TO MAKE MORE ARMS YOU HAD TO *SACRIFICE* ORGANS AS YOU WANTED TO KEEP THE BODY LIGHT AT THE SAME TIME.
IN ORDER TO KEEP THE POWER AND SPEED--
--YOU WOUND UP LOSING *ANY* PROTECTION HER ORGANS MIGHT HAVE AFFORDED!!
ONCE YOU PUNCH INTO THAT EMPTY BODY OF HERS--
--THE ONLY THING IN *THERE* IS THE SPINE!!
グシャアアッ
N-NOOO!! *BLACK WIDOW!!*
GAME OVER.
グラッ
YOUR ZOMBIE WON'T BE COMING BACK.

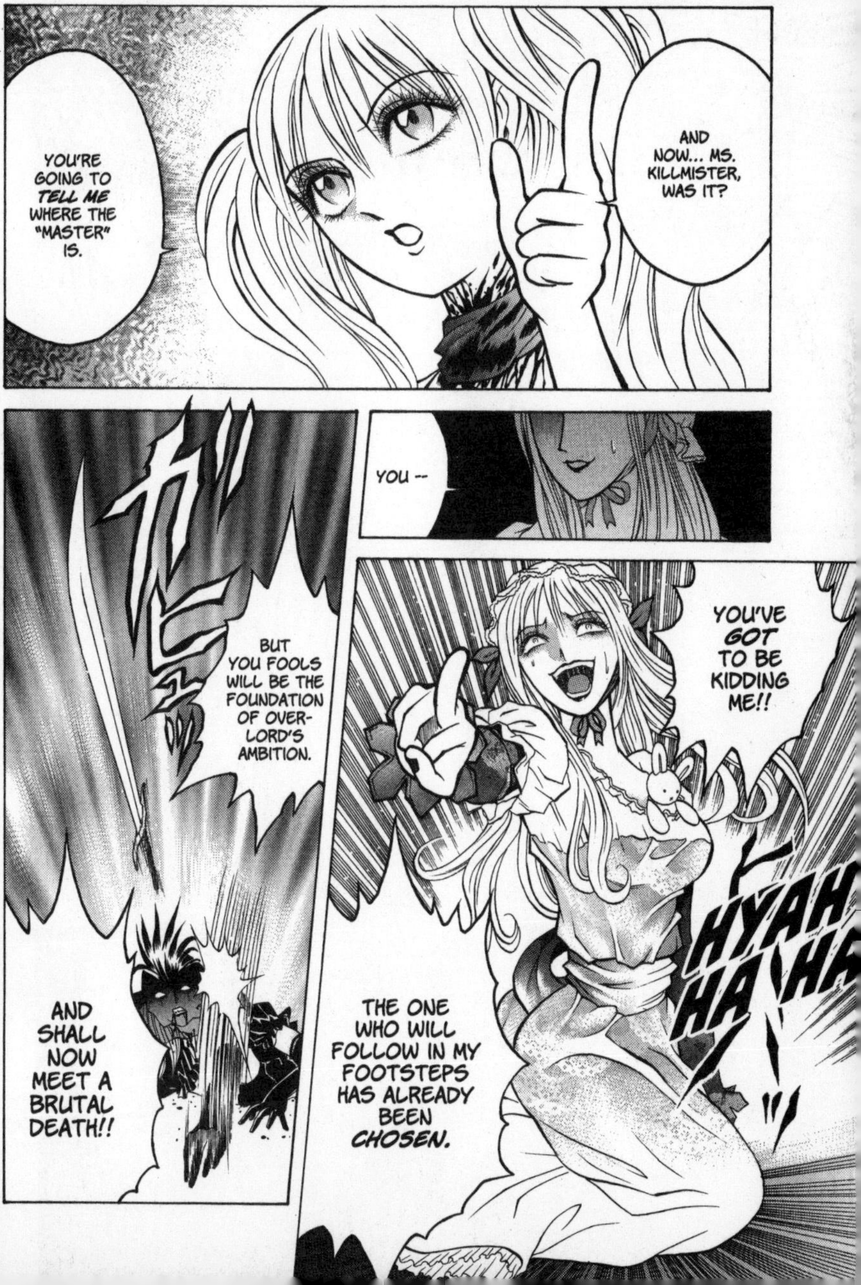
AND NOW... MS. KILLMISTER, WAS IT?
YOU'RE GOING TO *TELL ME* WHERE THE "MASTER" IS.
YOU --
YOU'VE *GOT* TO BE KIDDING ME!!
HYAH HA HA
!!
THE ONE WHO WILL FOLLOW IN MY FOOTSTEPS HAS ALREADY BEEN *CHOSEN.*
BUT YOU FOOLS WILL BE THE FOUNDATION OF OVER-LORD'S AMBITION.
AND SHALL NOW MEET A BRUTAL DEATH!!

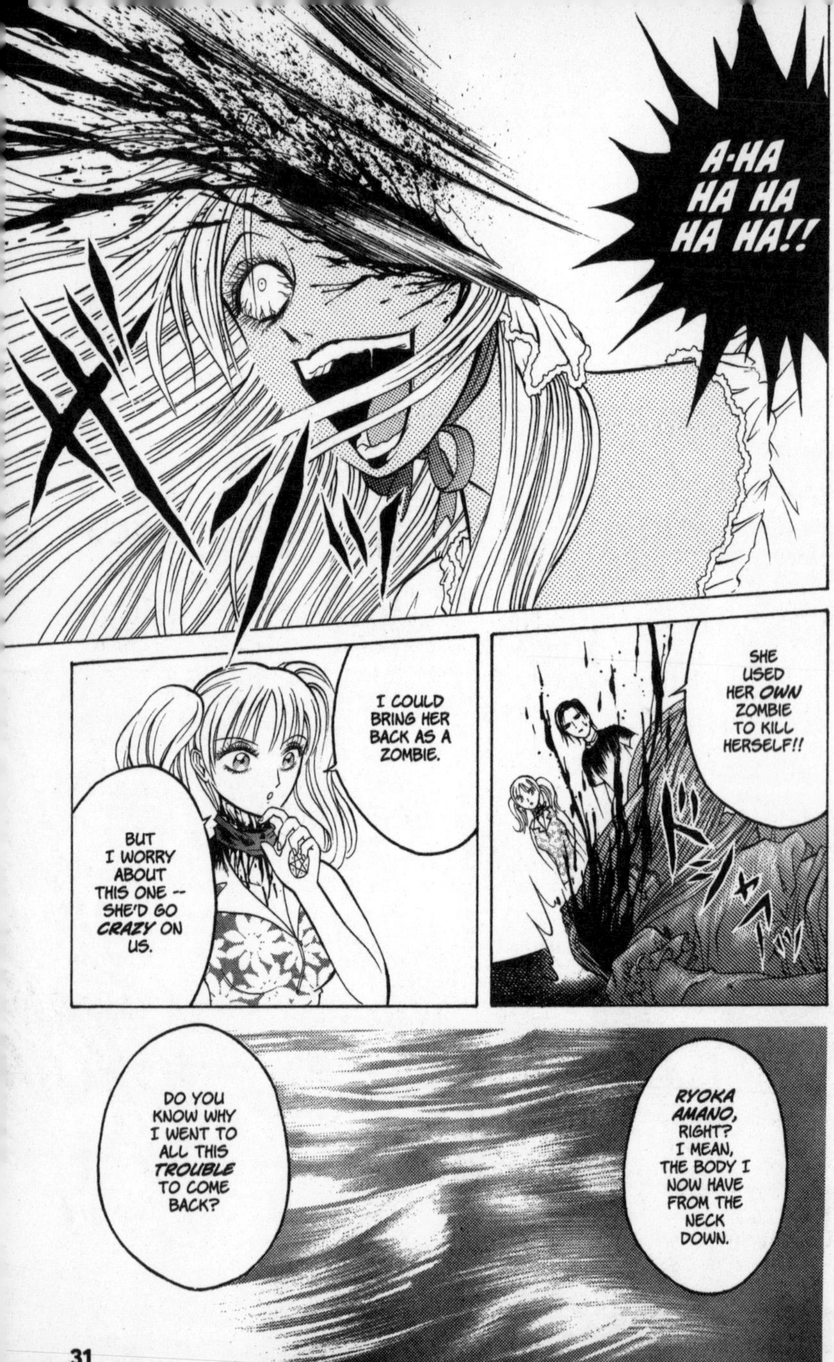
A-HA HA HA HA HA!!
SHE USED HER *OWN* ZOMBIE TO KILL HERSELF!!
I COULD BRING HER BACK AS A ZOMBIE.
BUT I WORRY ABOUT THIS ONE -- SHE'D GO *CRAZY* ON US.
RYOKA AMANO, RIGHT? I MEAN, THE BODY I NOW HAVE FROM THE NECK DOWN.
DO YOU KNOW WHY I WENT TO ALL THIS *TROUBLE* TO COME BACK?

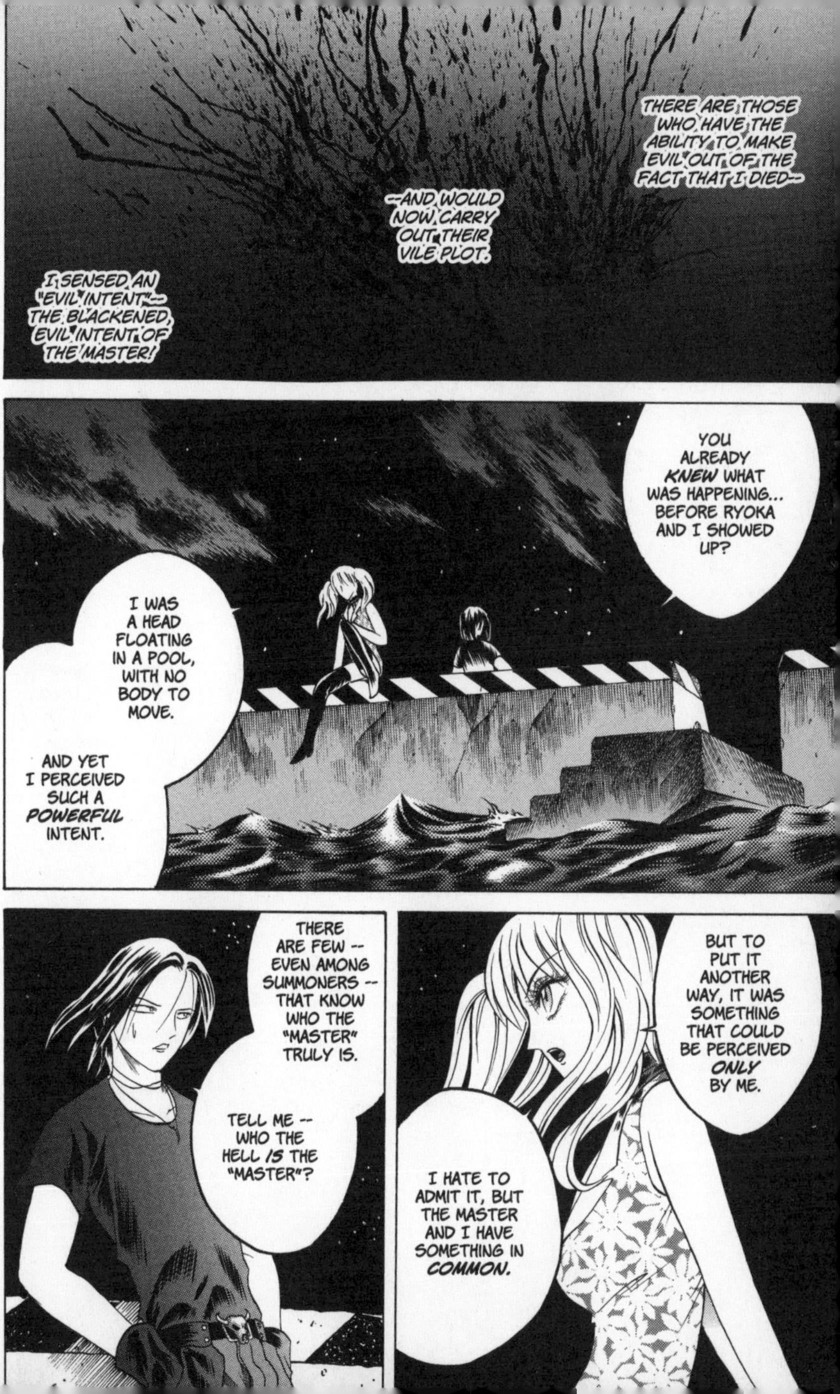
THERE ARE THOSE WHO HAVE THE ABILITY TO MAKE EVIL OUT OF THE FACT THAT I DIED--
--AND WOULD NOW CARRY OUT THEIR VILE PLOT.
I SENSED AN "EVIL INTENT"-- THE BLACKENED, EVIL INTENT OF THE MASTER!
YOU ALREADY KNEW WHAT WAS HAPPENING... BEFORE RYOKA AND I SHOWED UP?
I WAS A HEAD FLOATING IN A POOL, WITH NO BODY TO MOVE.
AND YET I PERCEIVED SUCH A POWERFUL INTENT.
BUT TO PUT IT ANOTHER WAY, IT WAS SOMETHING THAT COULD BE PERCEIVED ONLY BY ME.
I HATE TO ADMIT IT, BUT THE MASTER AND I HAVE SOMETHING IN COMMON.
THERE ARE FEW -- EVEN AMONG SUMMONERS -- THAT KNOW WHO THE "MASTER" TRULY IS.
TELL ME -- WHO THE HELL IS THE "MASTER"?

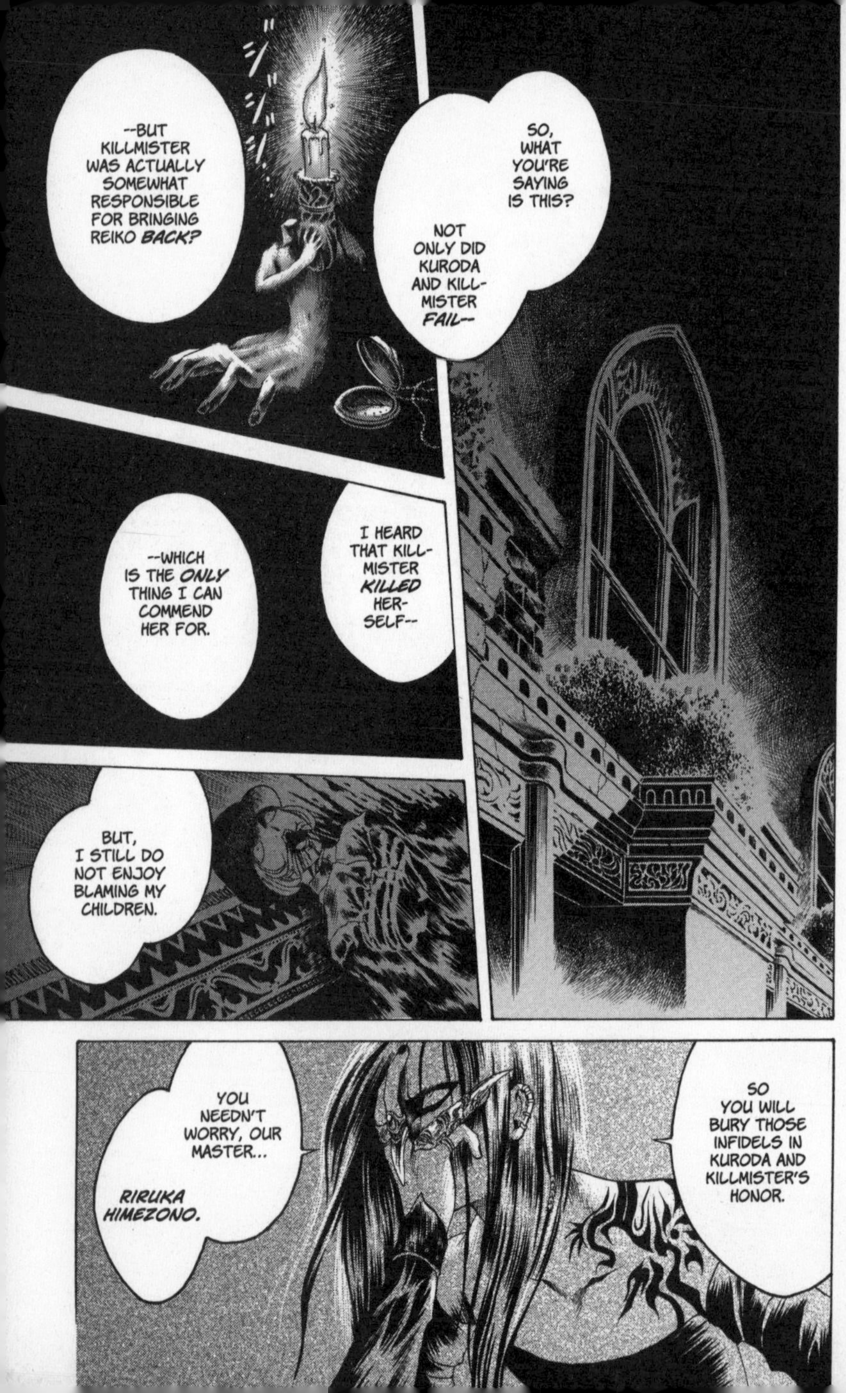
SO, WHAT YOU'RE SAYING IS THIS?
NOT ONLY DID KURODA AND KILL-MISTER FAIL--
--BUT KILLMISTER WAS ACTUALLY SOMEWHAT RESPONSIBLE FOR BRINGING REIKO BACK?
I HEARD THAT KILL-MISTER KILLED HER-SELF--
--WHICH IS THE ONLY THING I CAN COMMEND HER FOR.
BUT, I STILL DO NOT ENJOY BLAMING MY CHILDREN.
SO YOU WILL BURY THOSE INFIDELS IN KURODA AND KILLMISTER'S HONOR.
YOU NEEDN'T WORRY, OUR MASTER...
RIRUKA HIMEZONO.

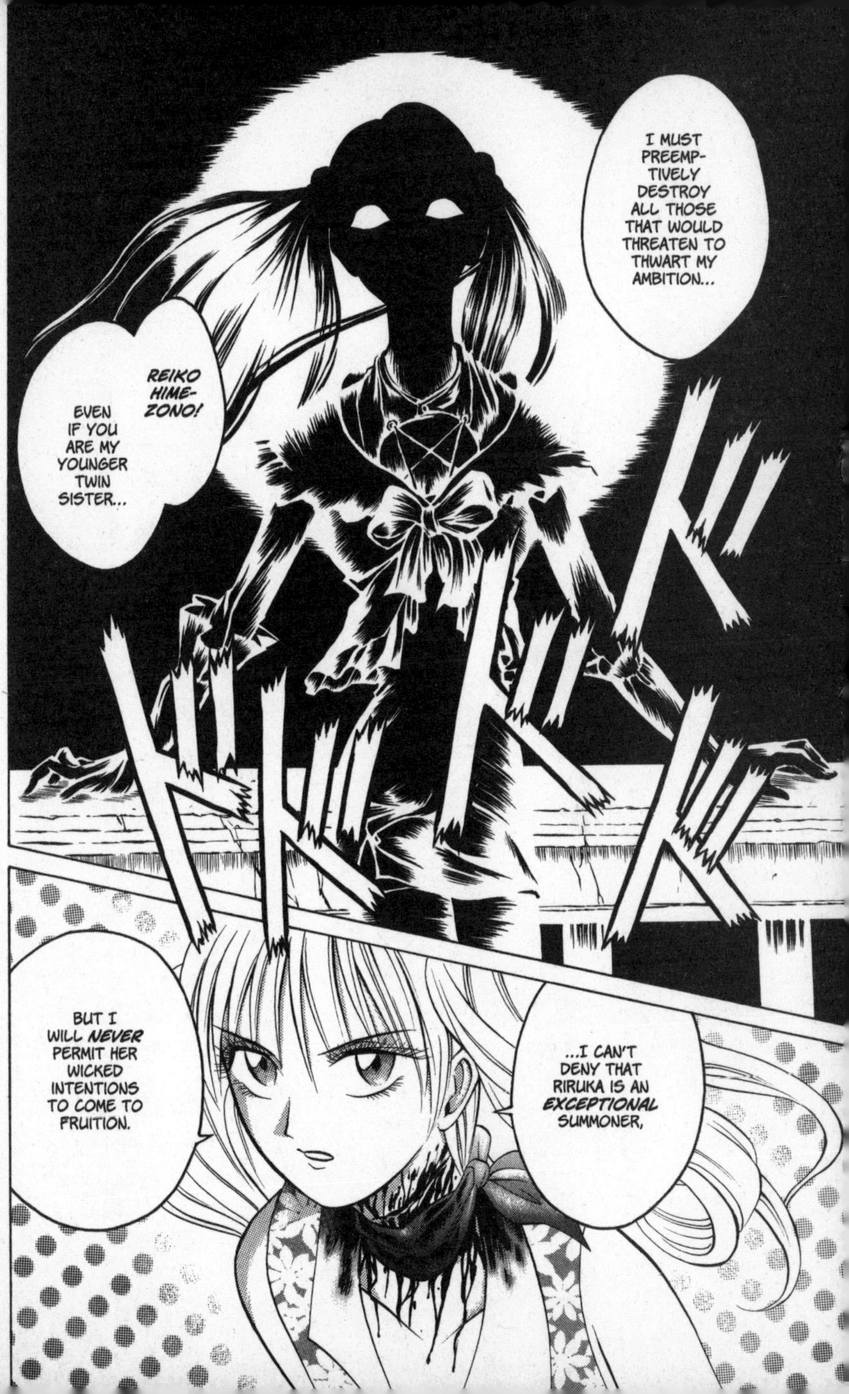
I MUST PREEMPTIVELY DESTROY ALL THOSE THAT WOULD THREATEN TO THWART MY AMBITION...
REIKO HIME-ZONO!
EVEN IF YOU ARE MY YOUNGER TWIN SISTER...
...I CAN'T DENY THAT RIRUKA IS AN *EXCEPTIONAL* SUMMONER,
BUT I WILL *NEVER* PERMIT HER WICKED INTENTIONS TO COME TO FRUITION.

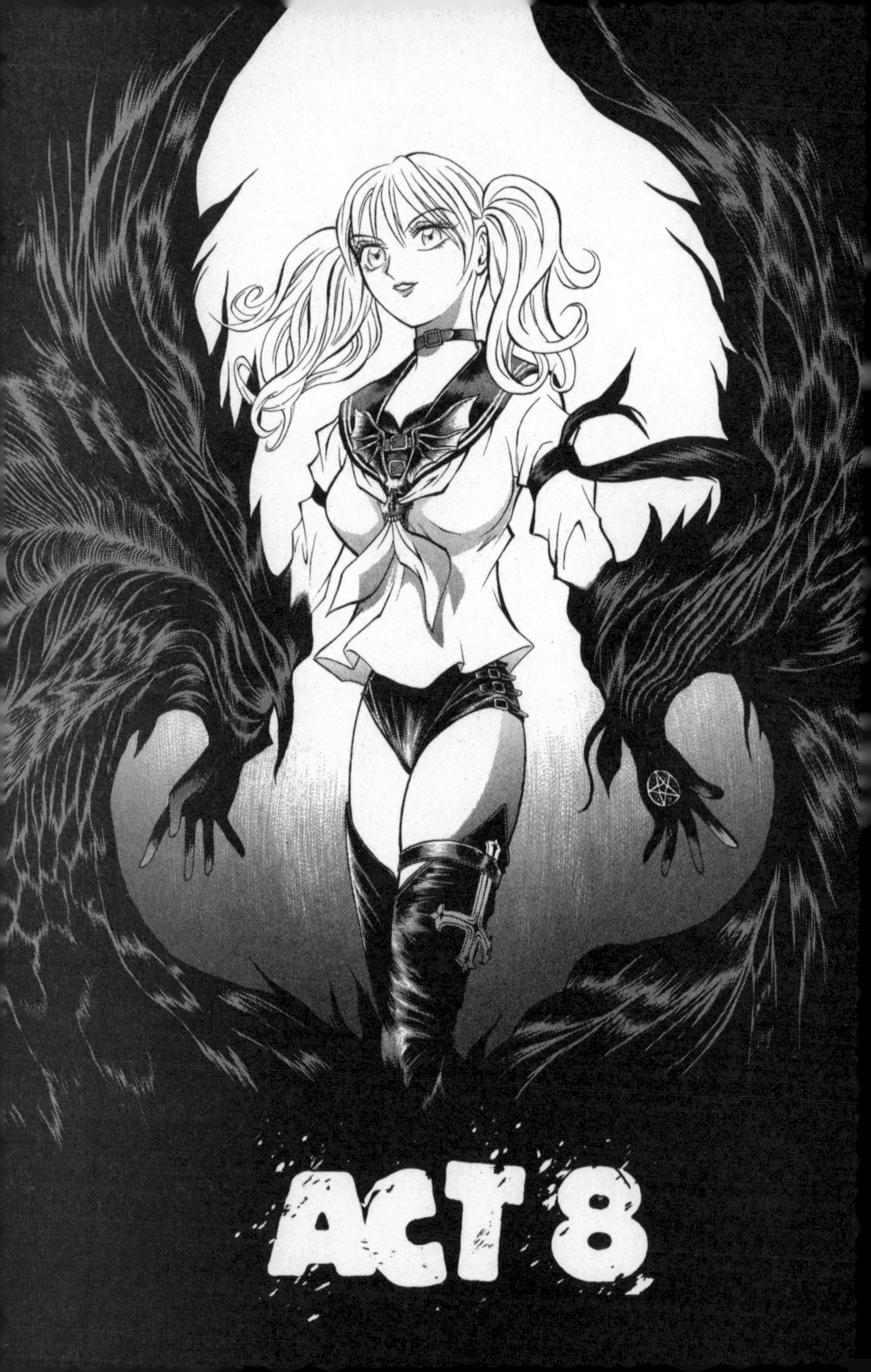
ACT 8

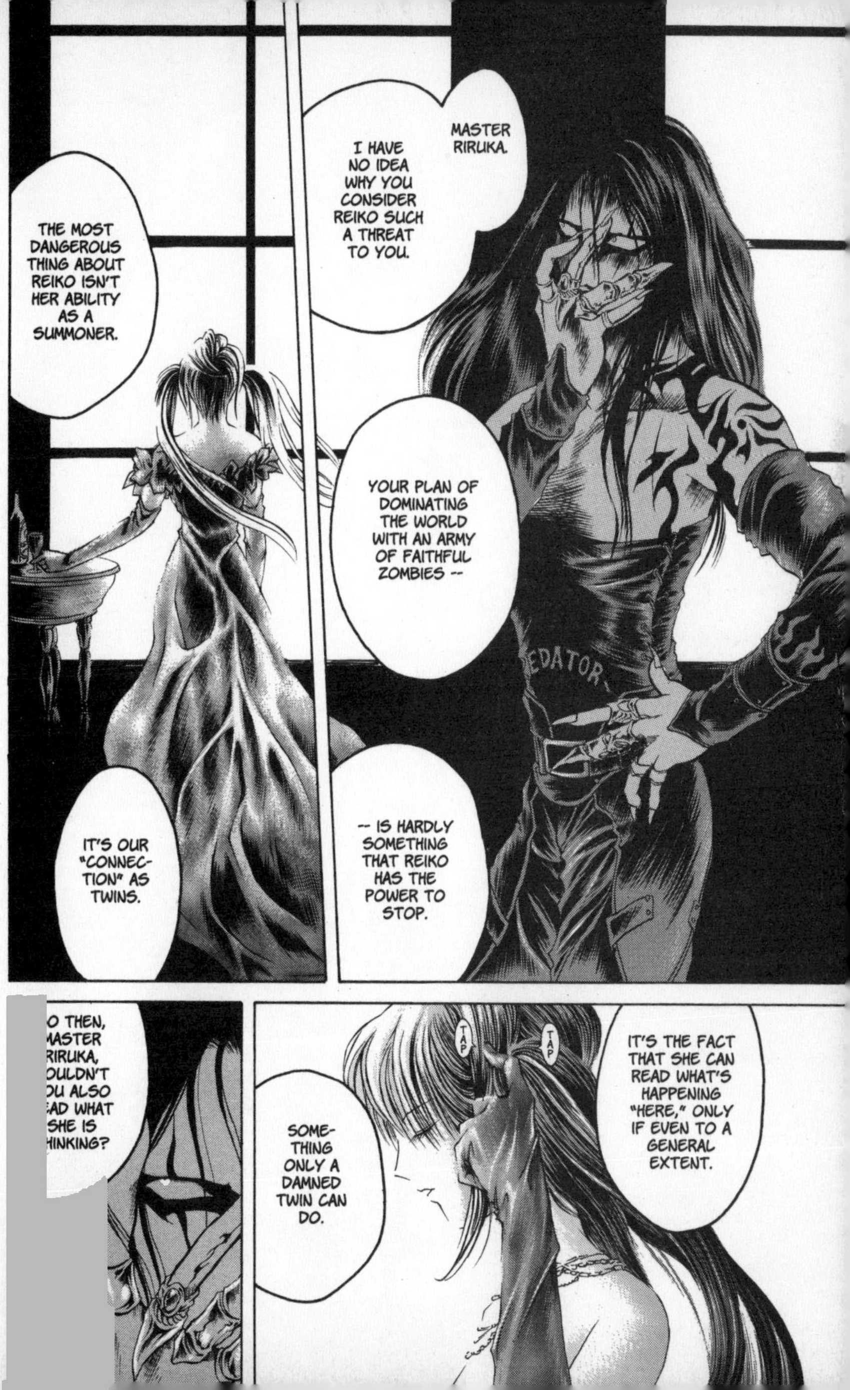
MASTER RIRUKA.
I HAVE NO IDEA WHY YOU CONSIDER REIKO SUCH A THREAT TO YOU.
YOUR PLAN OF DOMINATING THE WORLD WITH AN ARMY OF FAITHFUL ZOMBIES --
-- IS HARDLY SOMETHING THAT REIKO HAS THE POWER TO STOP.
THE MOST DANGEROUS THING ABOUT REIKO ISN'T HER ABILITY AS A SUMMONER.
IT'S OUR "CONNECTION" AS TWINS.
TAP
TAP
IT'S THE FACT THAT SHE CAN READ WHAT'S HAPPENING "HERE," ONLY IF EVEN TO A GENERAL EXTENT.
SOME-THING ONLY A DAMNED TWIN CAN DO.
O THEN, MASTER RIRUKA, OULDN'T OU ALSO EAD WHAT SHE IS HINKING?

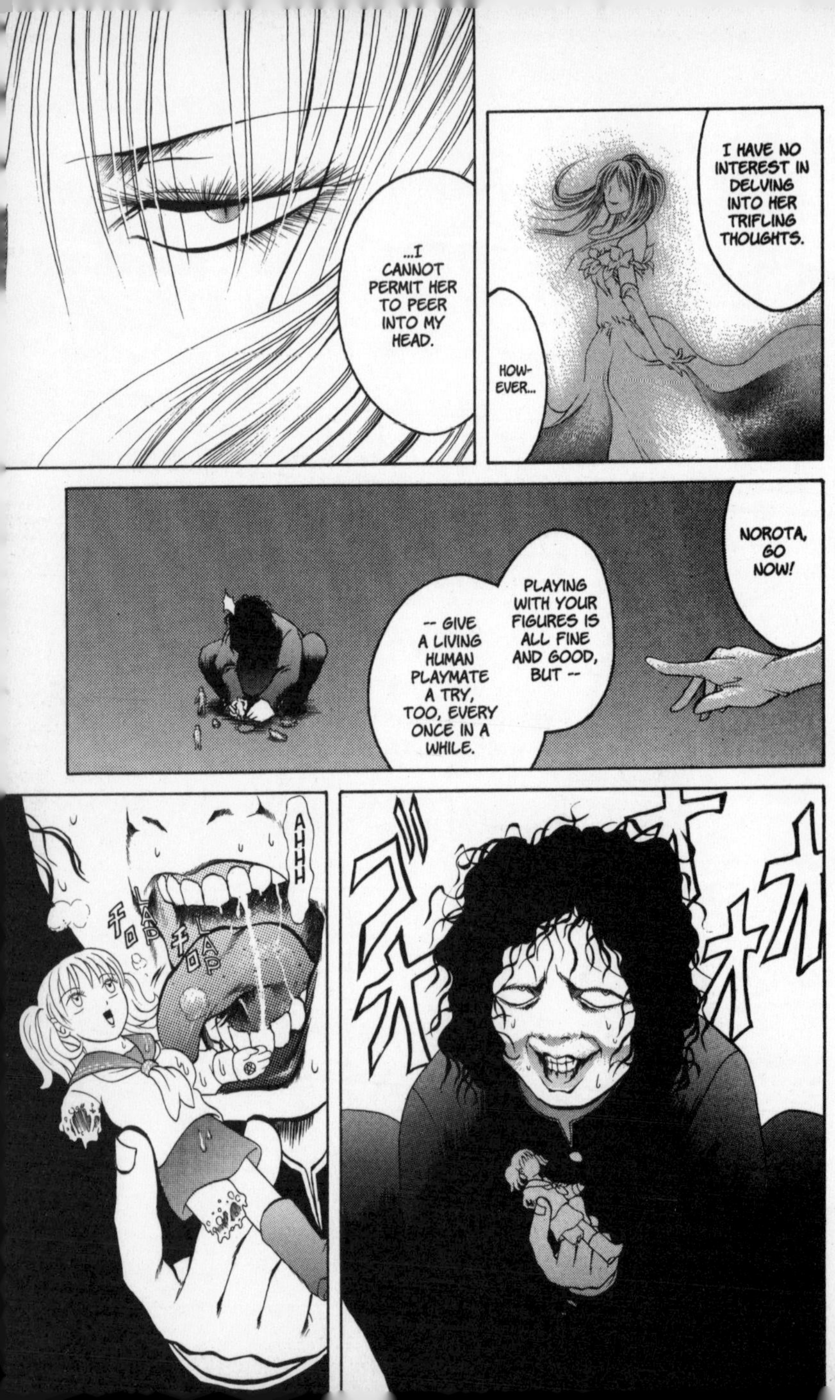
I HAVE NO INTEREST IN DELVING INTO HER TRIFLING THOUGHTS.
HOW-EVER...
...I CANNOT PERMIT HER TO PEER INTO MY HEAD.
NOROTA, GO NOW!
PLAYING WITH YOUR FIGURES IS ALL FINE AND GOOD, BUT --
-- GIVE A LIVING HUMAN PLAYMATE A TRY, TOO, EVERY ONCE IN A WHILE.
AHHH
LAP
LAP

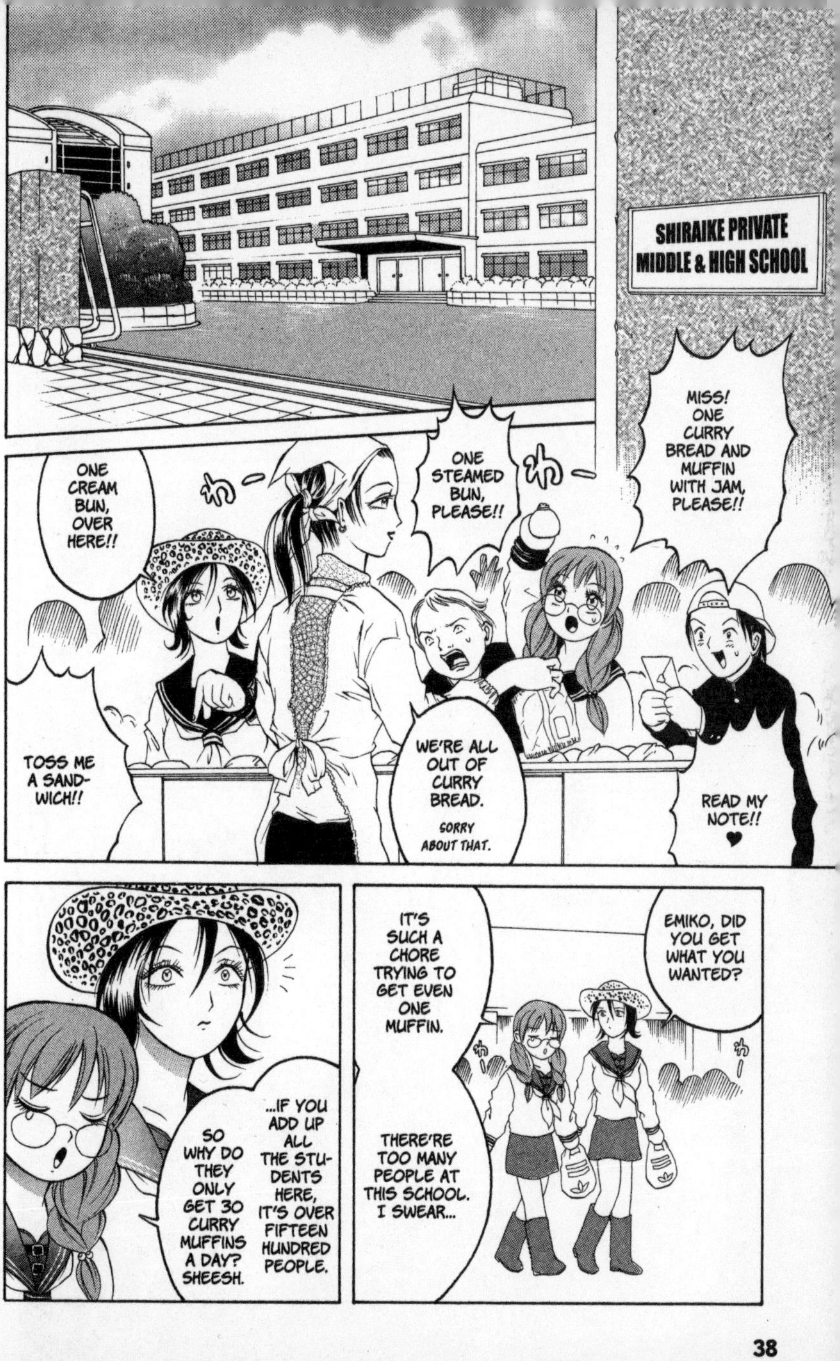
SHIRAIKE PRIVATE MIDDLE & HIGH SCHOOL
MISS! ONE CURRY BREAD AND MUFFIN WITH JAM, PLEASE!!
ONE STEAMED BUN, PLEASE!!
ONE CREAM BUN, OVER HERE!!
READ MY NOTE!! ♥
WE'RE ALL OUT OF CURRY BREAD.
SORRY ABOUT THAT.
TOSS ME A SAND-WICH!!
EMIKO, DID YOU GET WHAT YOU WANTED?
IT'S SUCH A CHORE TRYING TO GET EVEN ONE MUFFIN.
THERE'RE TOO MANY PEOPLE AT THIS SCHOOL. I SWEAR...
...IF YOU ADD UP ALL THE STU-DENTS HERE, IT'S OVER FIFTEEN HUNDRED PEOPLE.
SO WHY DO THEY ONLY GET 30 CURRY MUFFINS A DAY? SHEESH.

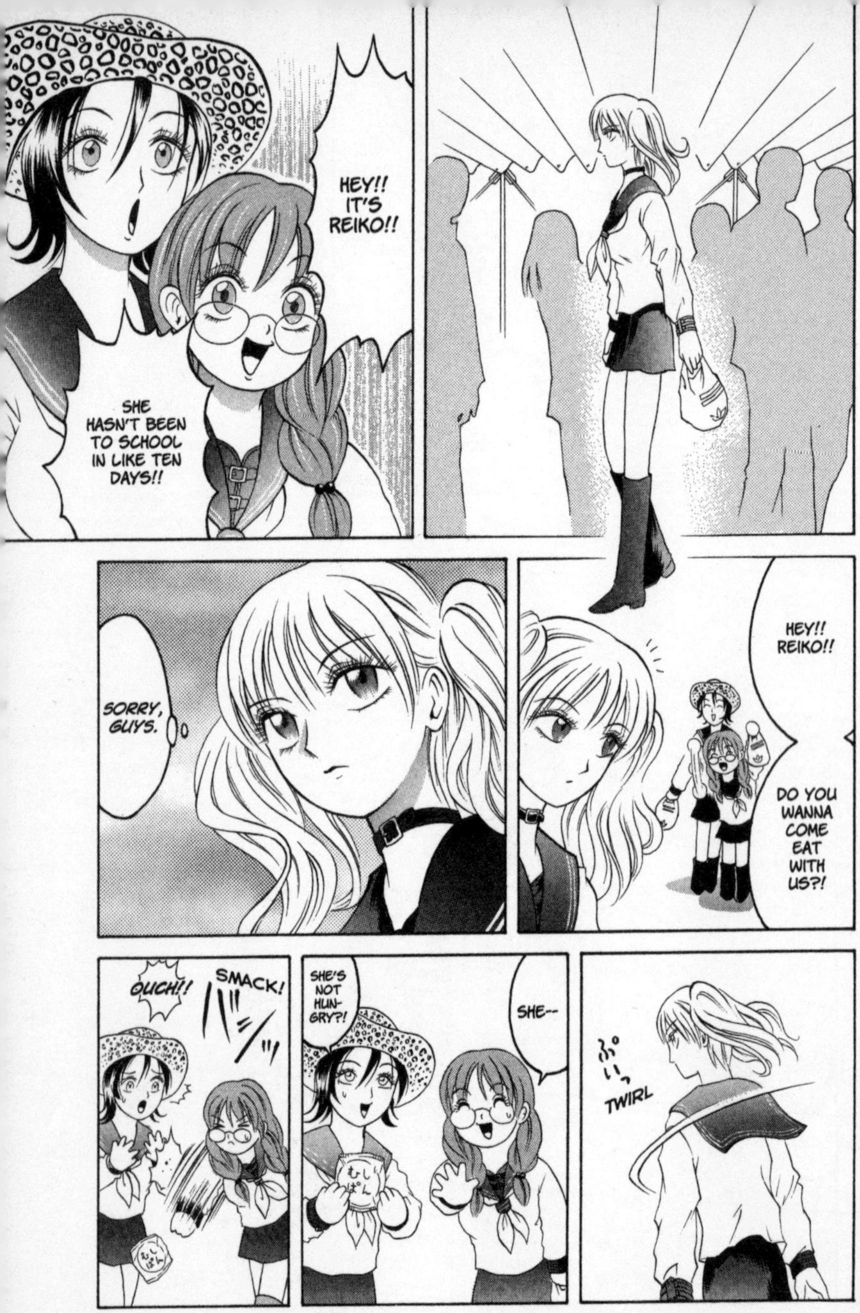
HEY!! IT'S REIKO!!
SHE HASN'T BEEN TO SCHOOL IN LIKE TEN DAYS!!
HEY!! REIKO!!
DO YOU WANNA COME EAT WITH US?!
SORRY, GUYS.
ぷいっ
TWIRL
SHE--
SHE'S NOT HUN-GRY?!
むしぱん
SMACK!
OUCH!!

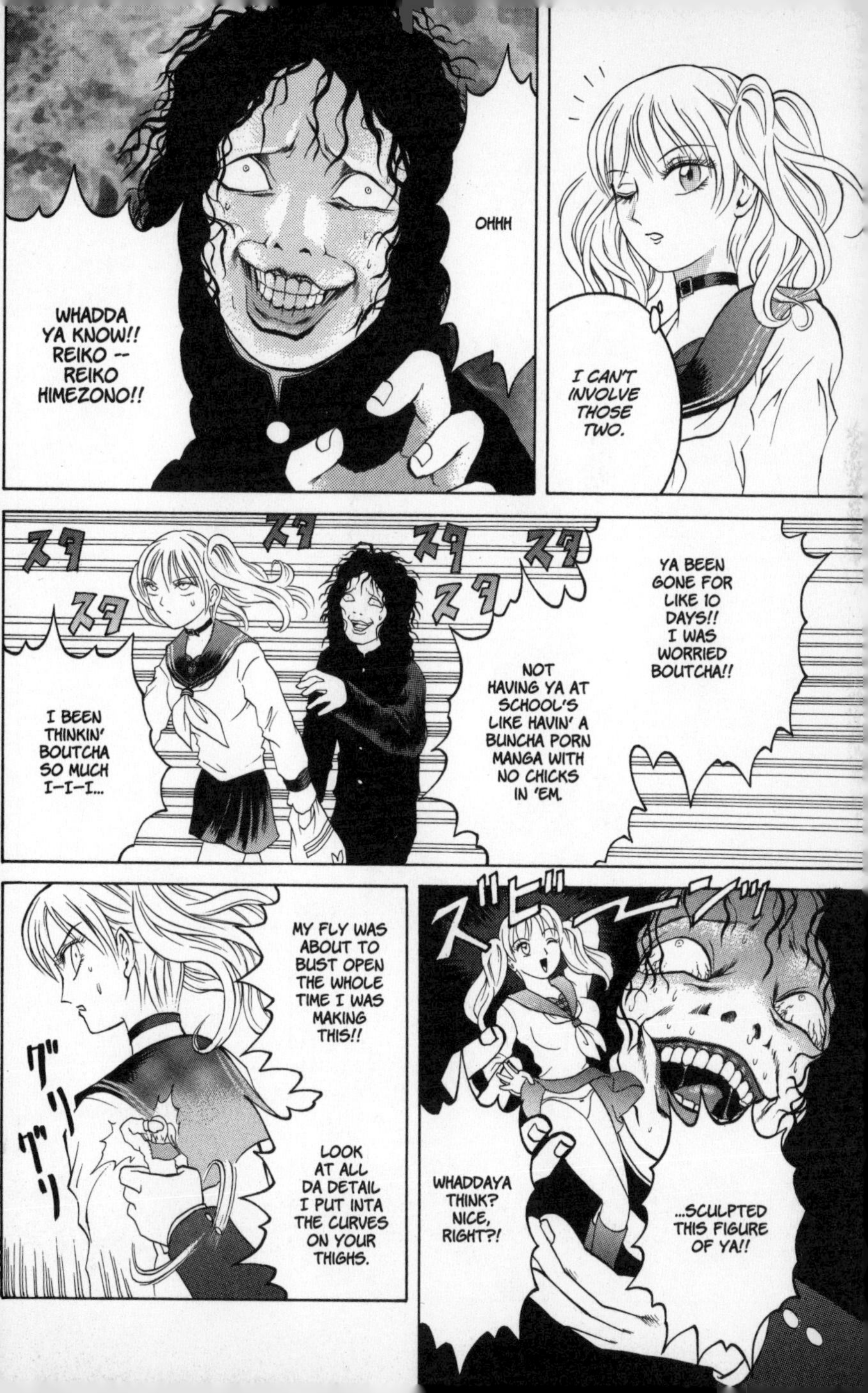
I CAN'T INVOLVE THOSE TWO.
OHHH
WHADDA YA KNOW!! REIKO -- REIKO HIMEZONO!!
スタ
スタ
スタ
スタ
スタ
スタ
YA BEEN GONE FOR LIKE 10 DAYS!! I WAS WORRIED BOUTCHA!!
NOT HAVING YA AT SCHOOL'S LIKE HAVIN' A BUNCHA PORN MANGA WITH NO CHICKS IN 'EM.
I BEEN THINKIN' BOUTCHA SO MUCH I-I-I...
...SCULPTED THIS FIGURE OF YA!!
WHADDAYA THINK? NICE, RIGHT?!
MY FLY WAS ABOUT TO BUST OPEN THE WHOLE TIME I WAS MAKING THIS!!
LOOK AT ALL DA DETAIL I PUT INTA THE CURVES ON YOUR THIGHS.
グリグリ

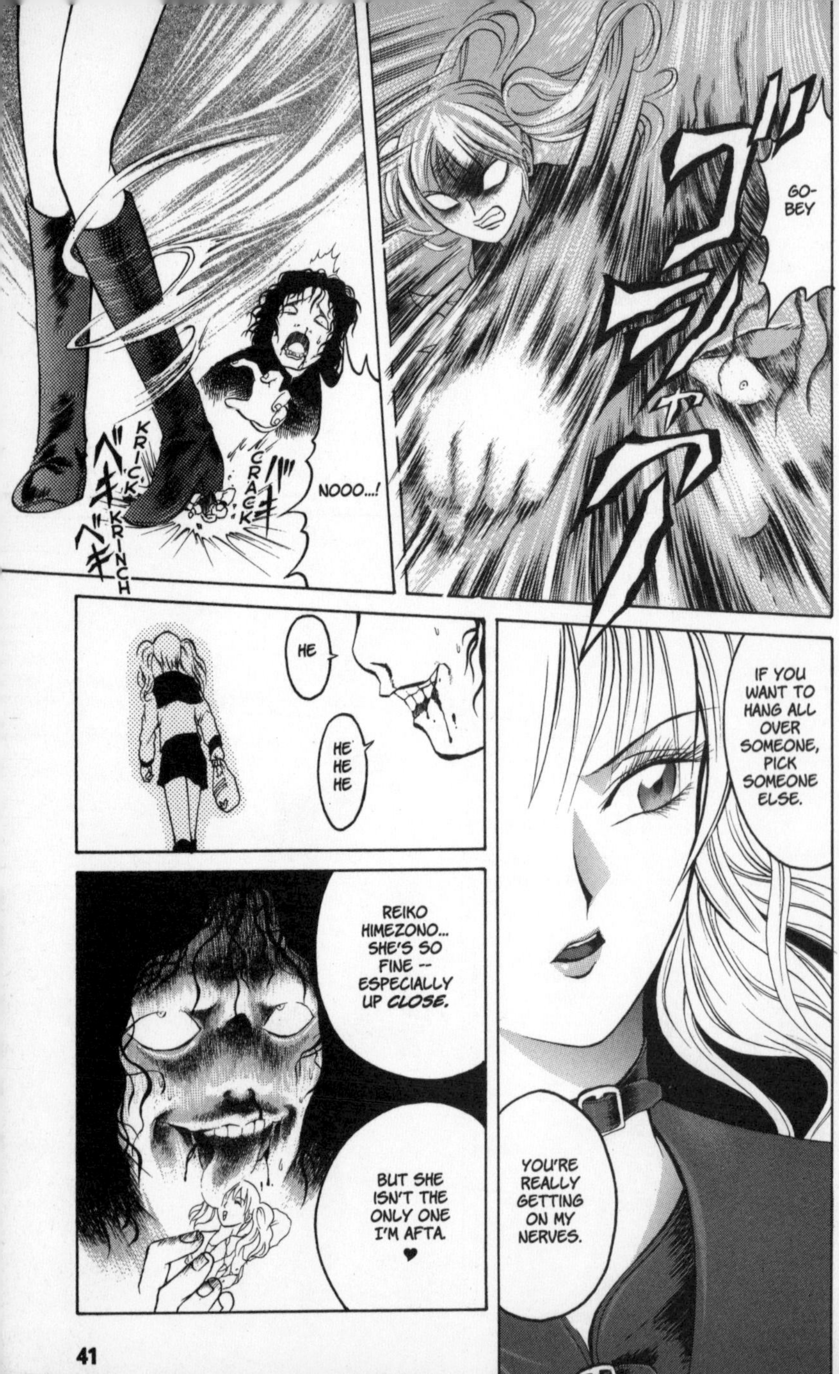
GO-
BEY
KRICK KRINCH
CRACK
NOOO...!
IF YOU WANT TO HANG ALL OVER SOMEONE, PICK SOMEONE ELSE.
YOU'RE REALLY GETTING ON MY NERVES.
HE
HE HE HE HE
REIKO HIMEZONO... SHE'S SO FINE -- ESPECIALLY UP *CLOSE.*
BUT SHE ISN'T THE ONLY ONE I'M AFTA. ♥

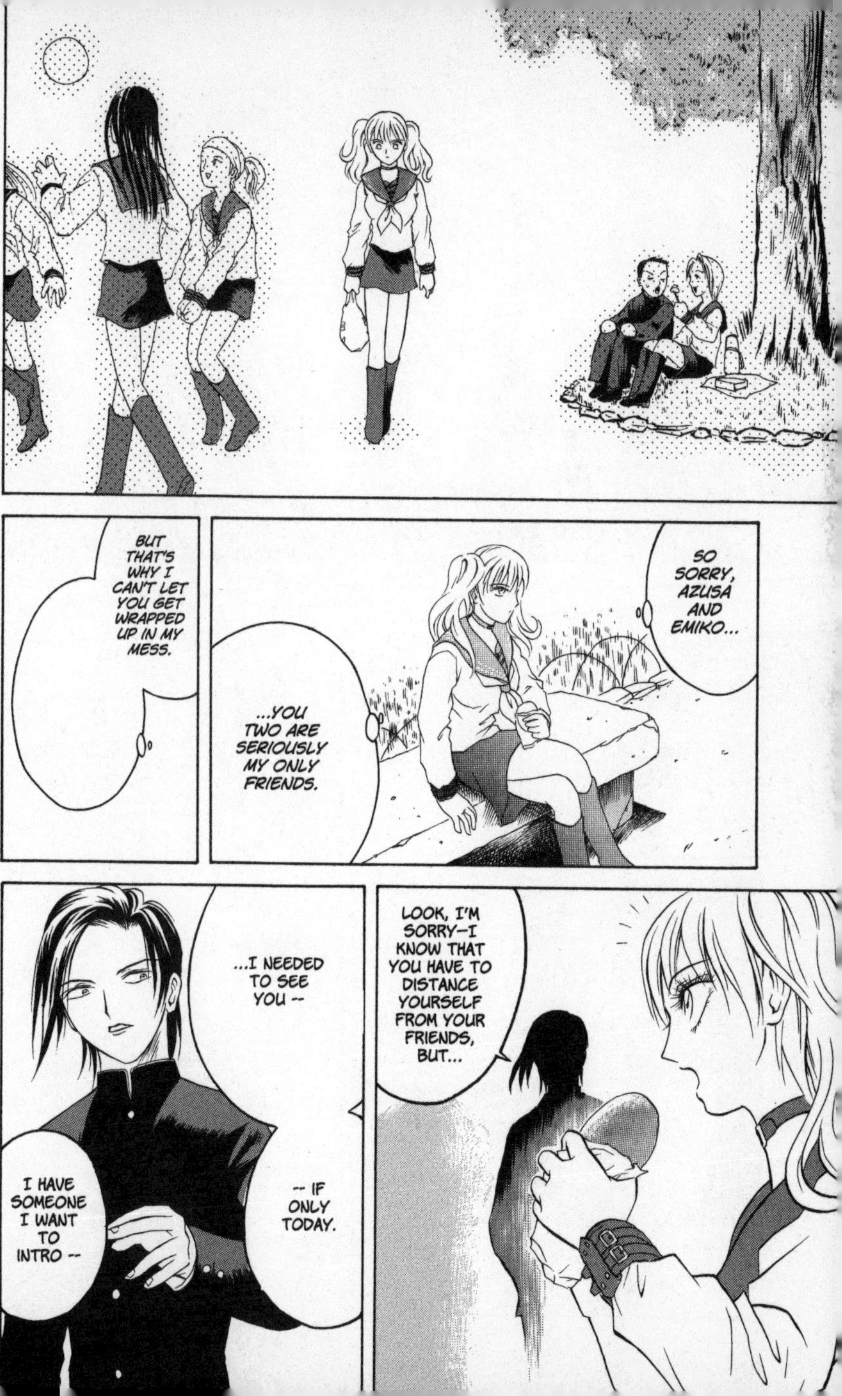
SO SORRY, AZUSA AND EMIKO...
...YOU TWO ARE SERIOUSLY MY ONLY FRIENDS.
BUT THAT'S WHY I CAN'T LET YOU GET WRAPPED UP IN MY MESS.
LOOK, I'M SORRY—I KNOW THAT YOU HAVE TO DISTANCE YOURSELF FROM YOUR FRIENDS, BUT...
...I NEEDED TO SEE YOU --
-- IF ONLY TODAY.
I HAVE SOMEONE I WANT TO INTRO --

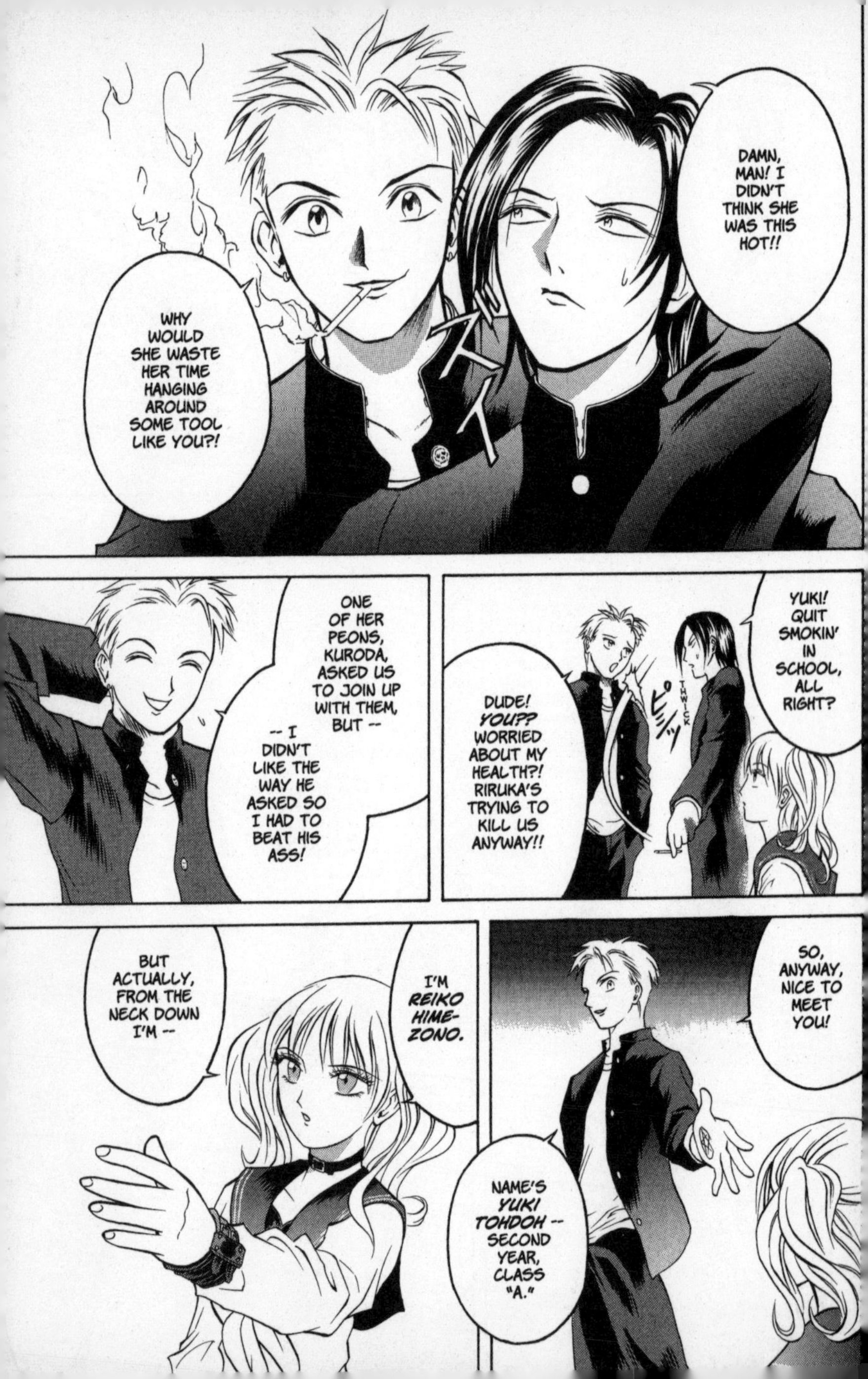
DAMN, MAN! I DIDN'T THINK SHE WAS THIS HOT!!
WHY WOULD SHE WASTE HER TIME HANGING AROUND SOME TOOL LIKE YOU?!
YUKI! QUIT SMOKIN' IN SCHOOL, ALL RIGHT?
THWICK
DUDE! *YOU??* WORRIED ABOUT MY HEALTH?! RIRUKA'S TRYING TO KILL US ANYWAY!!
ONE OF HER PEONS, KURODA, ASKED US TO JOIN UP WITH THEM, BUT --
-- I DIDN'T LIKE THE WAY HE ASKED SO I HAD TO BEAT HIS ASS!
SO, ANYWAY, NICE TO MEET YOU!
NAME'S *YUKI TOHDOH* -- SECOND YEAR, CLASS "A."
I'M *REIKO HIME-ZONO.*
BUT ACTUALLY, FROM THE NECK DOWN I'M --

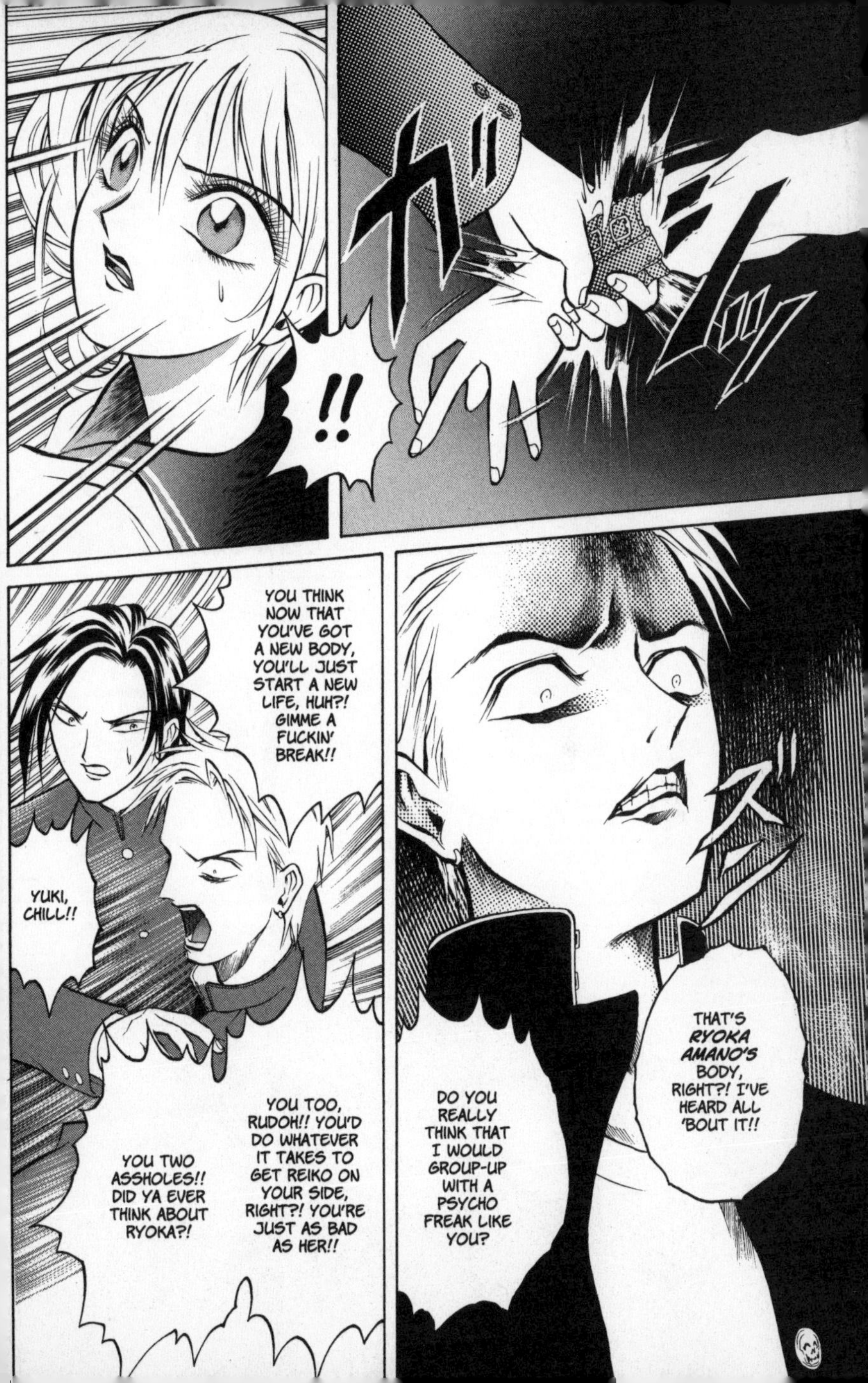
!!
THAT'S *RYOKA AMANO'S* BODY, RIGHT?! I'VE HEARD ALL 'BOUT IT!!
DO YOU REALLY THINK THAT I WOULD GROUP-UP WITH A PSYCHO FREAK LIKE YOU?
YOU THINK NOW THAT YOU'VE GOT A NEW BODY, YOU'LL JUST START A NEW LIFE, HUH?! GIMME A FUCKIN' BREAK!!
YUKI, CHILL!!
YOU TOO, RUDOH!! YOU'D DO WHATEVER IT TAKES TO GET REIKO ON YOUR SIDE, RIGHT?! YOU'RE JUST AS BAD AS HER!!
YOU TWO ASSHOLES!! DID YA EVER THINK ABOUT RYOKA?!

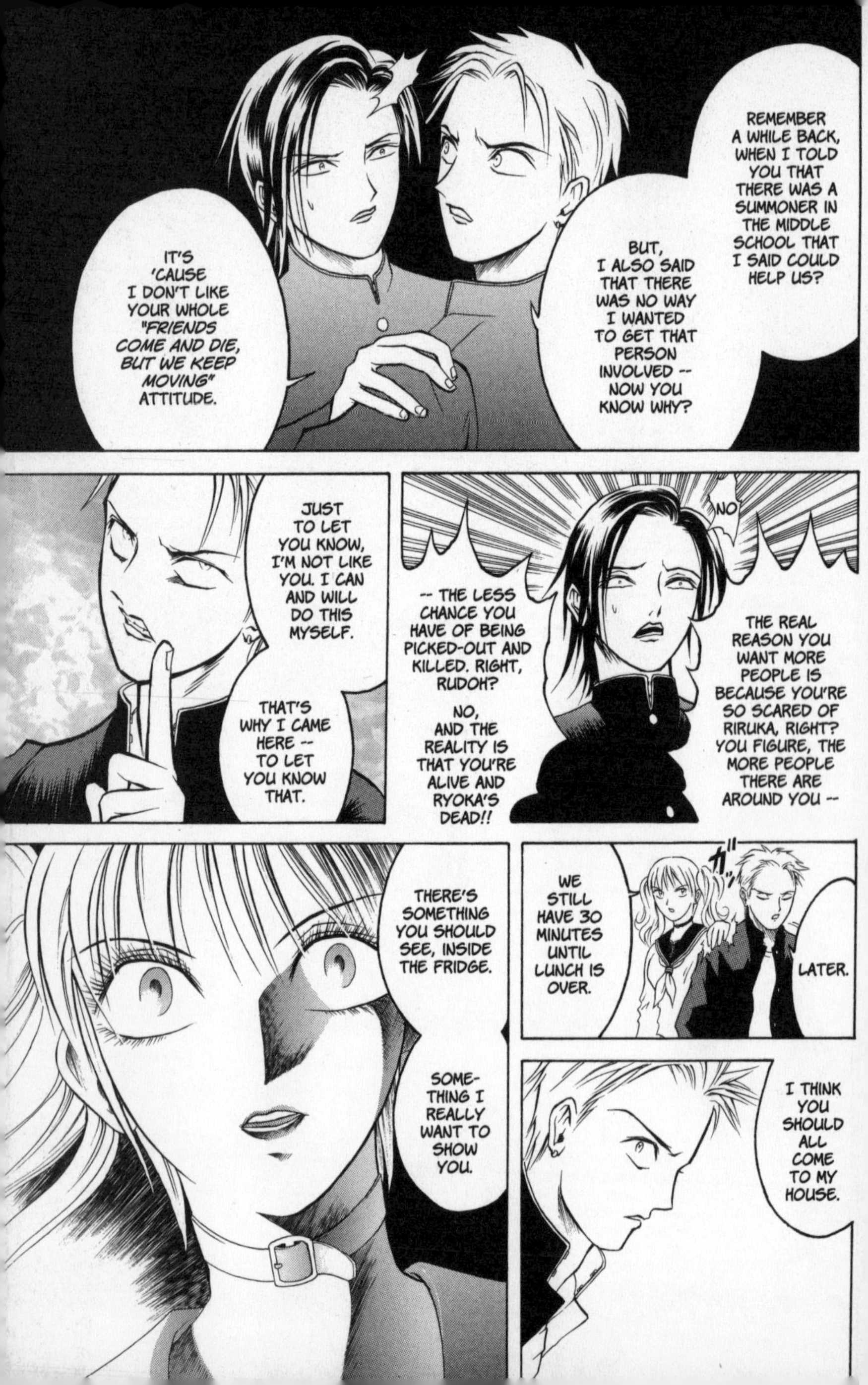
REMEMBER A WHILE BACK, WHEN I TOLD YOU THAT THERE WAS A SUMMONER IN THE MIDDLE SCHOOL THAT I SAID COULD HELP US?
BUT, I ALSO SAID THAT THERE WAS NO WAY I WANTED TO GET THAT PERSON INVOLVED -- NOW YOU KNOW WHY?
IT'S 'CAUSE I DON'T LIKE YOUR WHOLE "FRIENDS COME AND DIE, BUT WE KEEP MOVING" ATTITUDE.
NO
THE REAL REASON YOU WANT MORE PEOPLE IS BECAUSE YOU'RE SO SCARED OF RIRUKA, RIGHT? YOU FIGURE, THE MORE PEOPLE THERE ARE AROUND YOU --
-- THE LESS CHANCE YOU HAVE OF BEING PICKED-OUT AND KILLED. RIGHT, RUDOH?
NO, AND THE REALITY IS THAT YOU'RE ALIVE AND RYOKA'S DEAD!!
JUST TO LET YOU KNOW, I'M NOT LIKE YOU. I CAN AND WILL DO THIS MYSELF.
THAT'S WHY I CAME HERE -- TO LET YOU KNOW THAT.
LATER.
WE STILL HAVE 30 MINUTES UNTIL LUNCH IS OVER.
I THINK YOU SHOULD ALL COME TO MY HOUSE.
THERE'S SOMETHING YOU SHOULD SEE, INSIDE THE FRIDGE.
SOMETHING I REALLY WANT TO SHOW YOU.

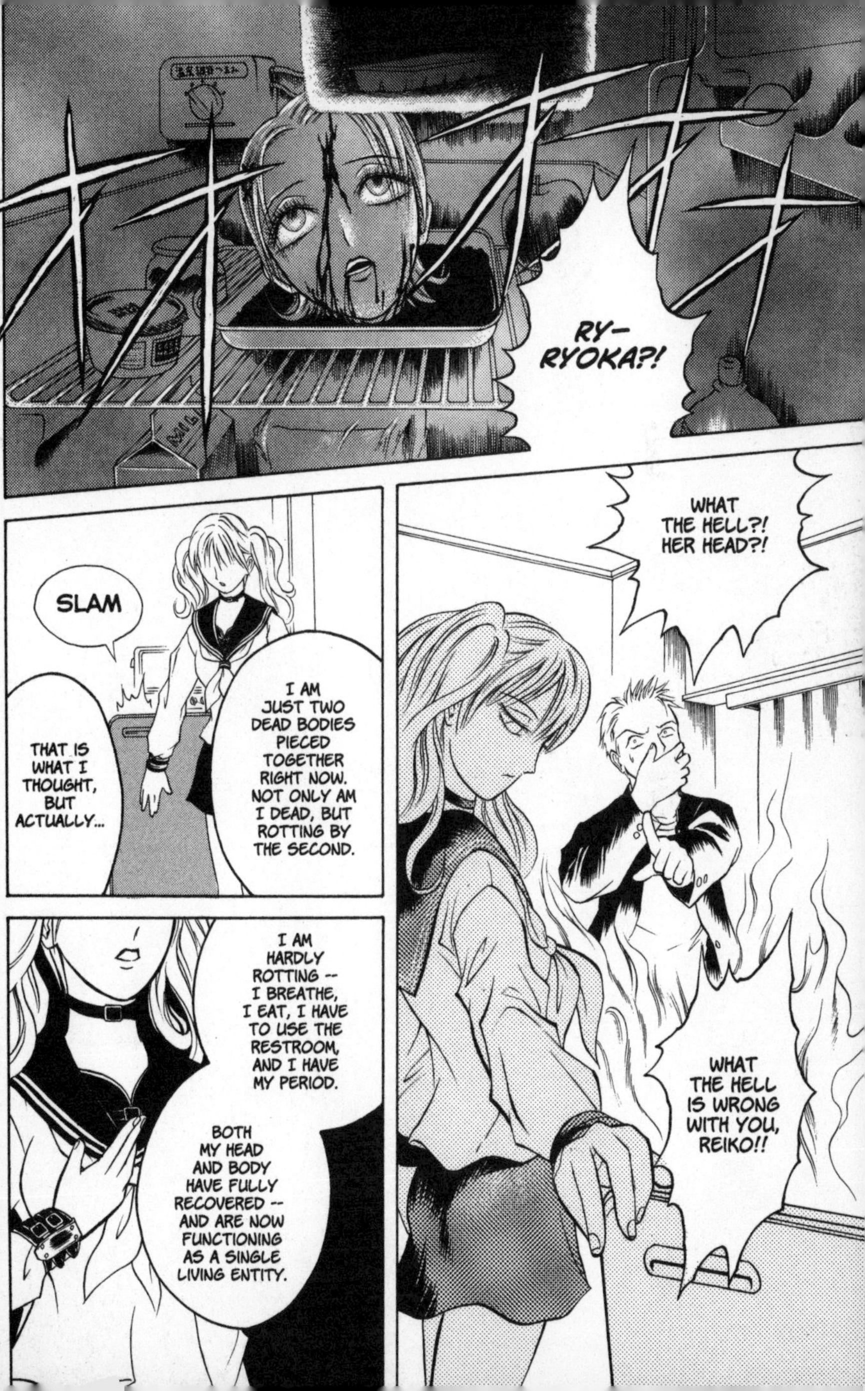
RY-
RYOKA?!
WHAT THE HELL?! HER HEAD?!
WHAT THE HELL IS WRONG WITH YOU, REIKO!!
SLAM
I AM JUST TWO DEAD BODIES PIECED TOGETHER RIGHT NOW. NOT ONLY AM I DEAD, BUT ROTTING BY THE SECOND.
THAT IS WHAT I THOUGHT, BUT ACTUALLY...
I AM HARDLY ROTTING -- I BREATHE, I EAT, I HAVE TO USE THE RESTROOM, AND I HAVE MY PERIOD.
BOTH MY HEAD AND BODY HAVE FULLY RECOVERED -- AND ARE NOW FUNCTIONING AS A SINGLE LIVING ENTITY.

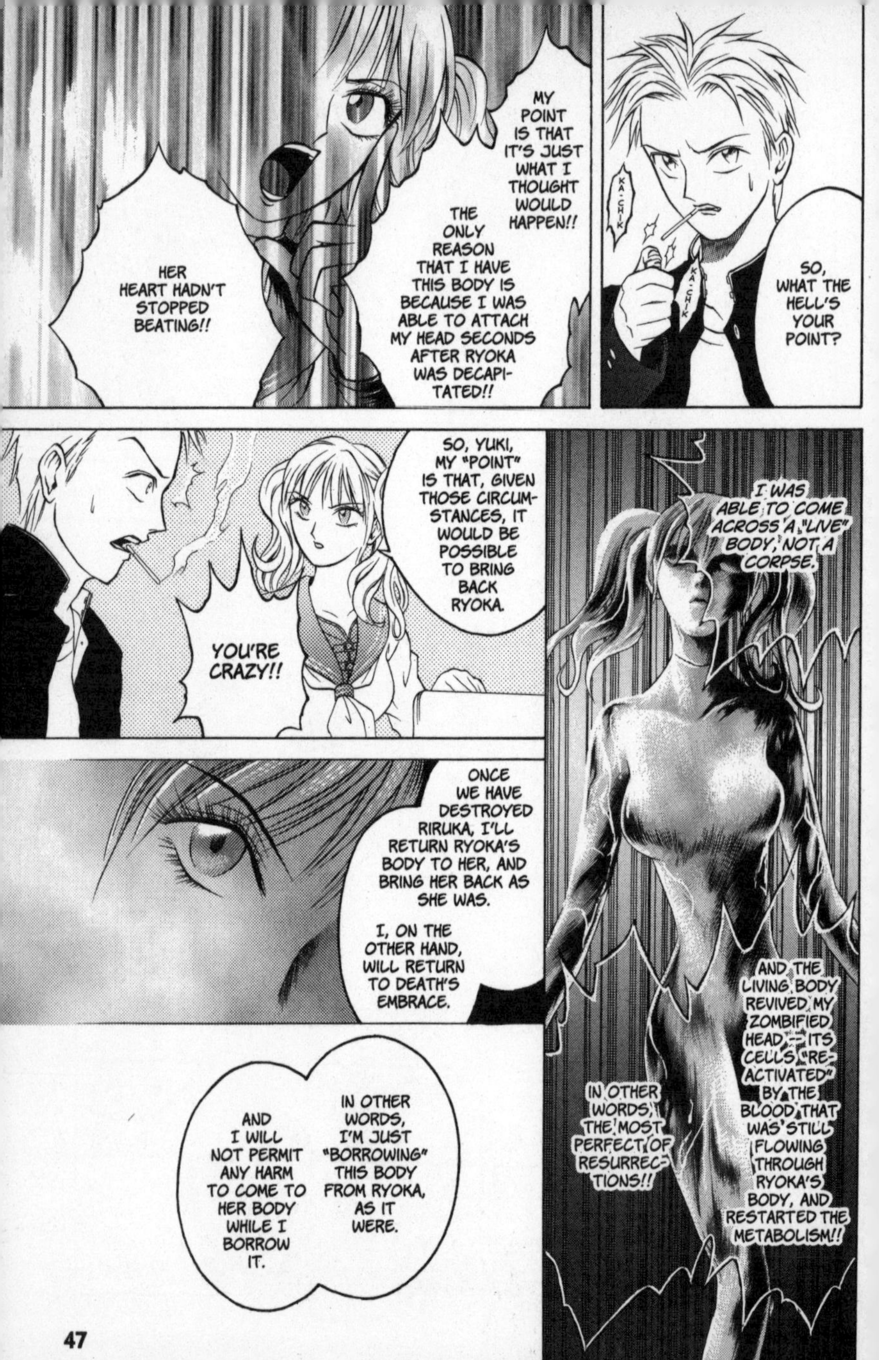
KA-CHIK
KA-CHIK
SO, WHAT THE HELL'S YOUR POINT?
MY POINT IS THAT IT'S JUST WHAT I THOUGHT WOULD HAPPEN!!
THE ONLY REASON THAT I HAVE THIS BODY IS BECAUSE I WAS ABLE TO ATTACH MY HEAD SECONDS AFTER RYOKA WAS DECAPITATED!!
HER HEART HADN'T STOPPED BEATING!!
I WAS ABLE TO COME ACROSS A "LIVE" BODY, NOT A CORPSE.
AND THE LIVING BODY REVIVED MY ZOMBIFIED HEAD -- ITS CELLS "RE-ACTIVATED" BY THE BLOOD THAT WAS STILL FLOWING THROUGH RYOKA'S BODY, AND RESTARTED THE METABOLISM!!
IN OTHER WORDS, THE MOST PERFECT OF RESURRECTIONS!!
SO, YUKI, MY "POINT" IS THAT, GIVEN THOSE CIRCUMSTANCES, IT WOULD BE POSSIBLE TO BRING BACK RYOKA.
YOU'RE CRAZY!!
ONCE WE HAVE DESTROYED RIRUKA, I'LL RETURN RYOKA'S BODY TO HER, AND BRING HER BACK AS SHE WAS.
I, ON THE OTHER HAND, WILL RETURN TO DEATH'S EMBRACE.
IN OTHER WORDS, I'M JUST "BORROWING" THIS BODY FROM RYOKA, AS IT WERE.
AND I WILL NOT PERMIT ANY HARM TO COME TO HER BODY WHILE I BORROW IT.

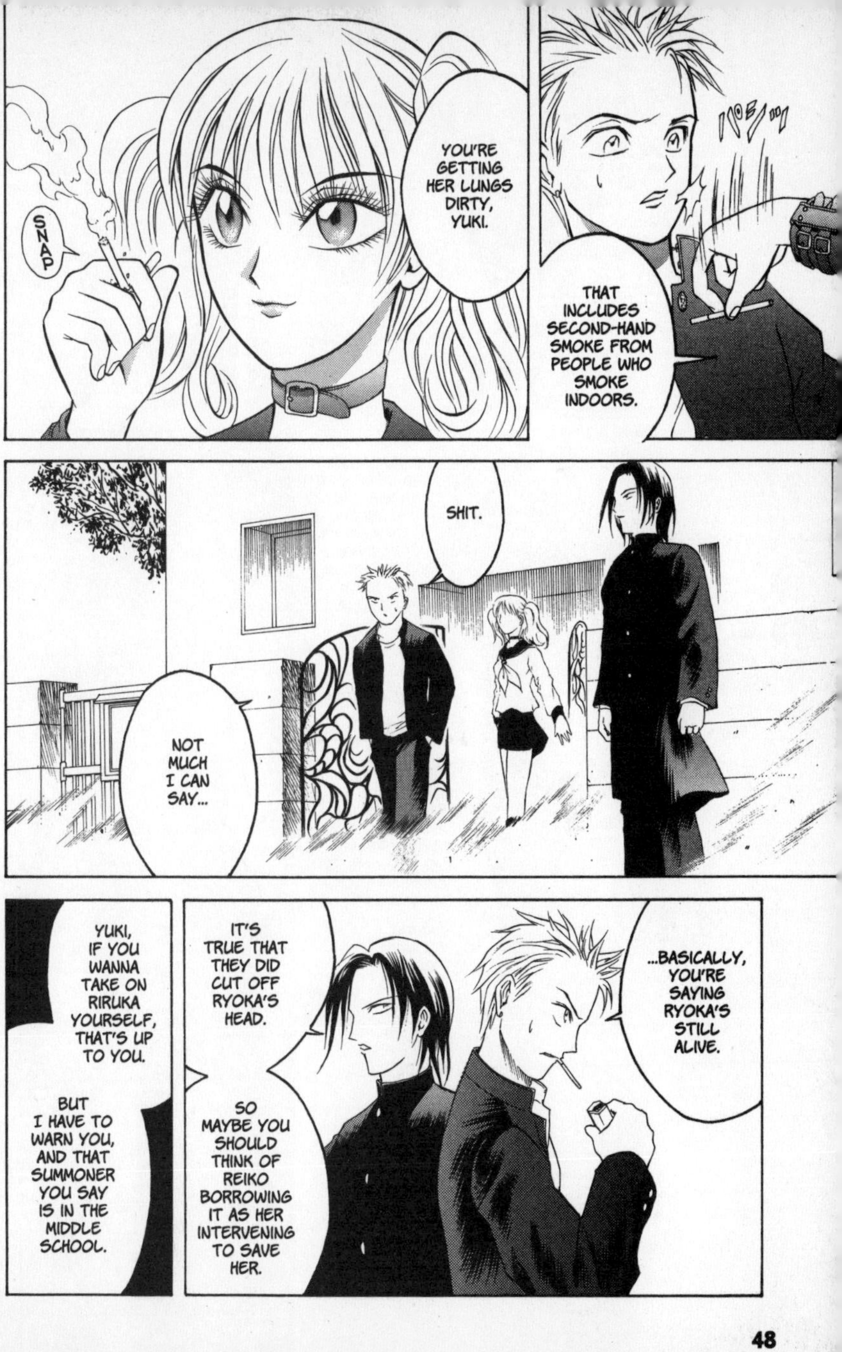
THAT INCLUDES SECOND-HAND SMOKE FROM PEOPLE WHO SMOKE INDOORS.
YOU'RE GETTING HER LUNGS DIRTY, YUKI.
SNAP
SHIT.
NOT MUCH I CAN SAY...
...BASICALLY, YOU'RE SAYING RYOKA'S STILL ALIVE.
IT'S TRUE THAT THEY DID CUT OFF RYOKA'S HEAD.
SO MAYBE YOU SHOULD THINK OF REIKO BORROWING IT AS HER INTERVENING TO SAVE HER.
YUKI, IF YOU WANNA TAKE ON RIRUKA YOURSELF, THAT'S UP TO YOU.
BUT I HAVE TO WARN YOU, AND THAT SUMMONER YOU SAY IS IN THE MIDDLE SCHOOL.

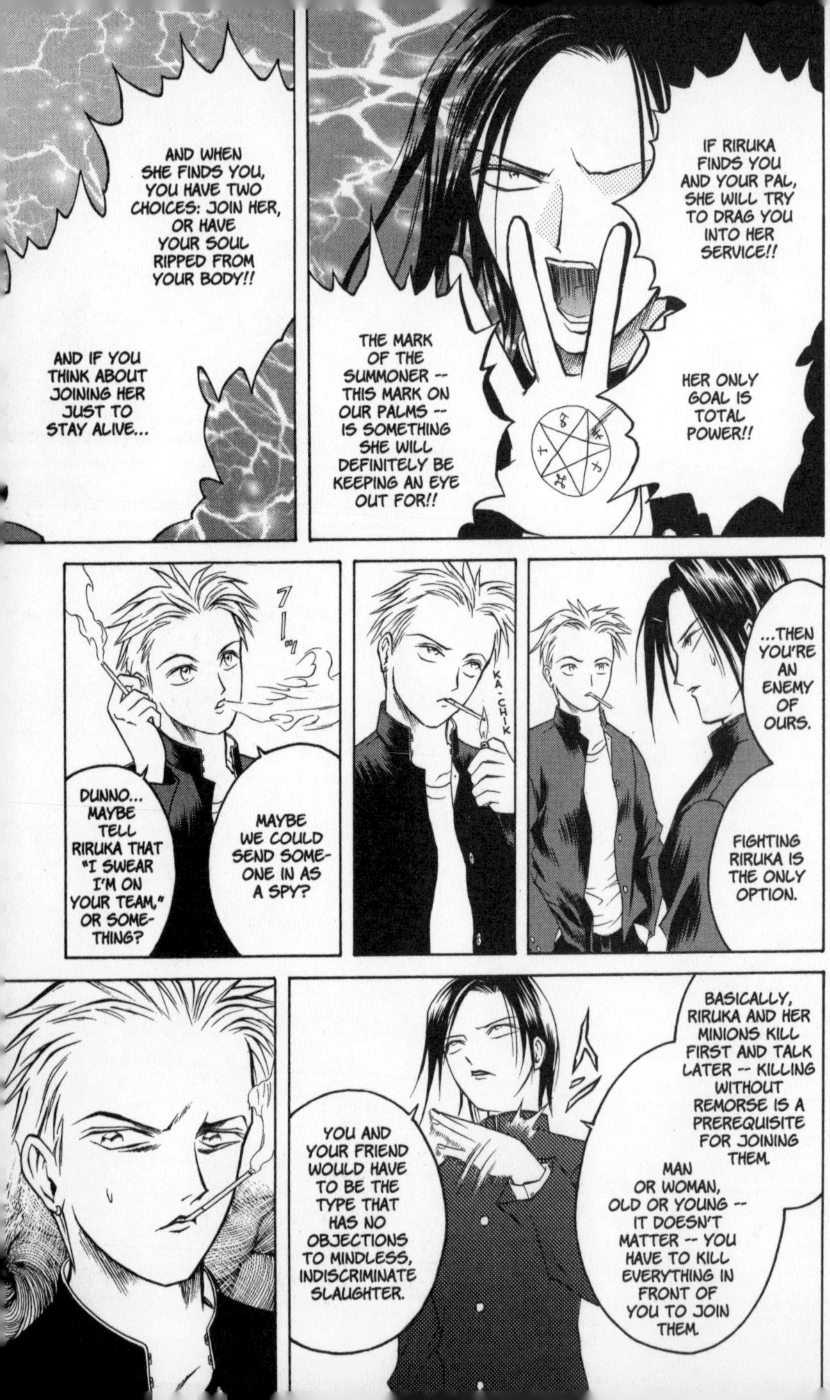
IF RIRUKA FINDS YOU AND YOUR PAL, SHE WILL TRY TO DRAG YOU INTO HER SERVICE!!
HER ONLY GOAL IS TOTAL POWER!!
THE MARK OF THE SUMMONER -- THIS MARK ON OUR PALMS -- IS SOMETHING SHE WILL DEFINITELY BE KEEPING AN EYE OUT FOR!!
AND WHEN SHE FINDS YOU, YOU HAVE TWO CHOICES: JOIN HER, OR HAVE YOUR SOUL RIPPED FROM YOUR BODY!!
AND IF YOU THINK ABOUT JOINING HER JUST TO STAY ALIVE...
...THEN YOU'RE AN ENEMY OF OURS.
FIGHTING RIRUKA IS THE ONLY OPTION.
KA-CHIK
MAYBE WE COULD SEND SOME-ONE IN AS A SPY?
DUNNO... MAYBE TELL RIRUKA THAT "I SWEAR I'M ON YOUR TEAM," OR SOME-THING?
BASICALLY, RIRUKA AND HER MINIONS KILL FIRST AND TALK LATER -- KILLING WITHOUT REMORSE IS A PREREQUISITE FOR JOINING THEM.
MAN OR WOMAN, OLD OR YOUNG -- IT DOESN'T MATTER -- YOU HAVE TO KILL EVERYTHING IN FRONT OF YOU TO JOIN THEM.
YOU AND YOUR FRIEND WOULD HAVE TO BE THE TYPE THAT HAS NO OBJECTIONS TO MINDLESS, INDISCRIMINATE SLAUGHTER.

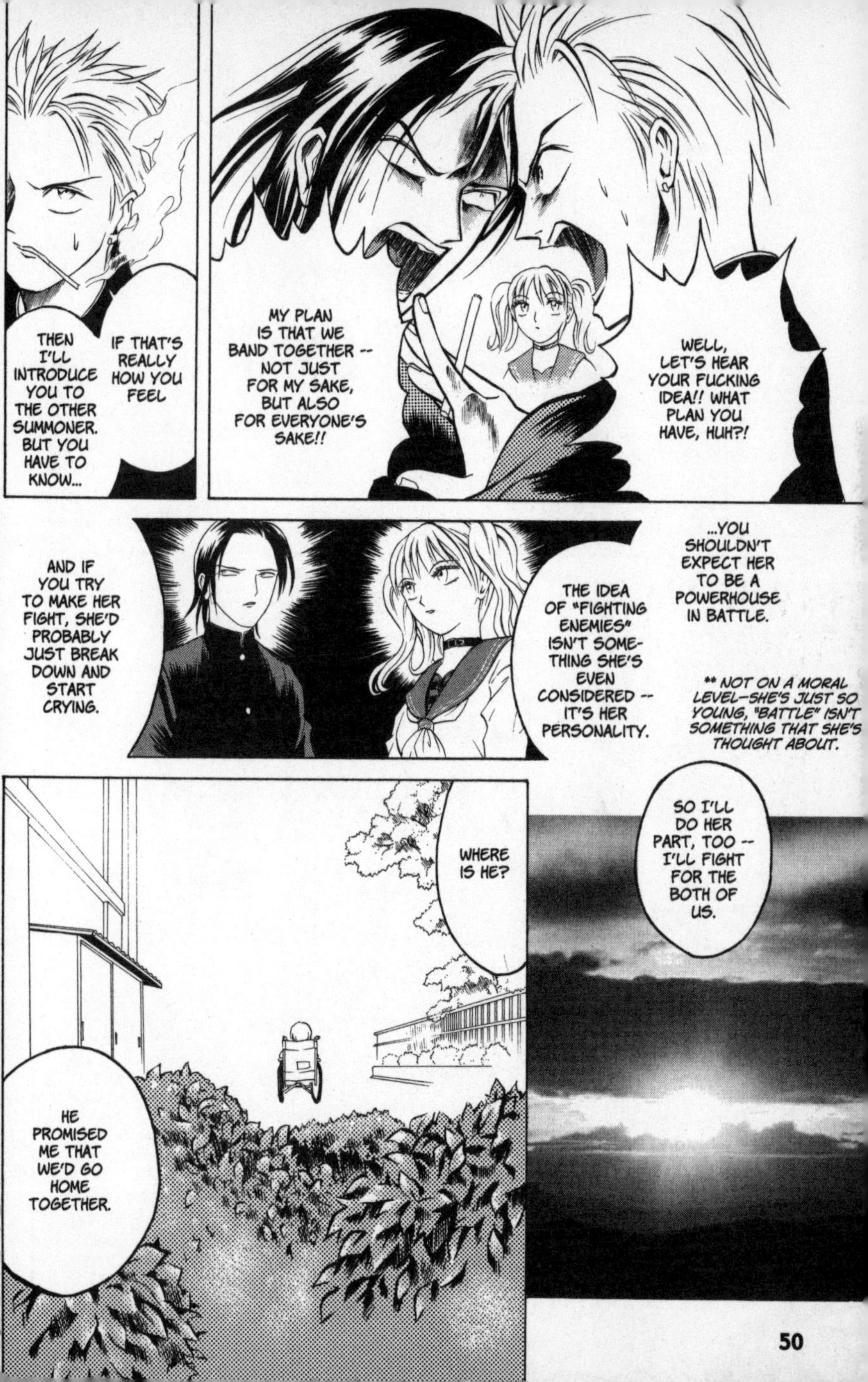
WELL, LET'S HEAR YOUR FUCKING IDEA!! WHAT PLAN YOU HAVE, HUH?!
MY PLAN IS THAT WE BAND TOGETHER -- NOT JUST FOR MY SAKE, BUT ALSO FOR EVERYONE'S SAKE!!
IF THAT'S REALLY HOW YOU FEEL
THEN I'LL INTRODUCE YOU TO THE OTHER SUMMONER. BUT YOU HAVE TO KNOW...
...YOU SHOULDN'T EXPECT HER TO BE A POWERHOUSE IN BATTLE.
** NOT ON A MORAL LEVEL–SHE'S JUST SO YOUNG, "BATTLE" ISN'T SOMETHING THAT SHE'S THOUGHT ABOUT.
THE IDEA OF "FIGHTING ENEMIES" ISN'T SOME-THING SHE'S EVEN CONSIDERED -- IT'S HER PERSONALITY.
AND IF YOU TRY TO MAKE HER FIGHT, SHE'D PROBABLY JUST BREAK DOWN AND START CRYING.
SO I'LL DO HER PART, TOO -- I'LL FIGHT FOR THE BOTH OF US.
WHERE IS HE?
HE PROMISED ME THAT WE'D GO HOME TOGETHER.

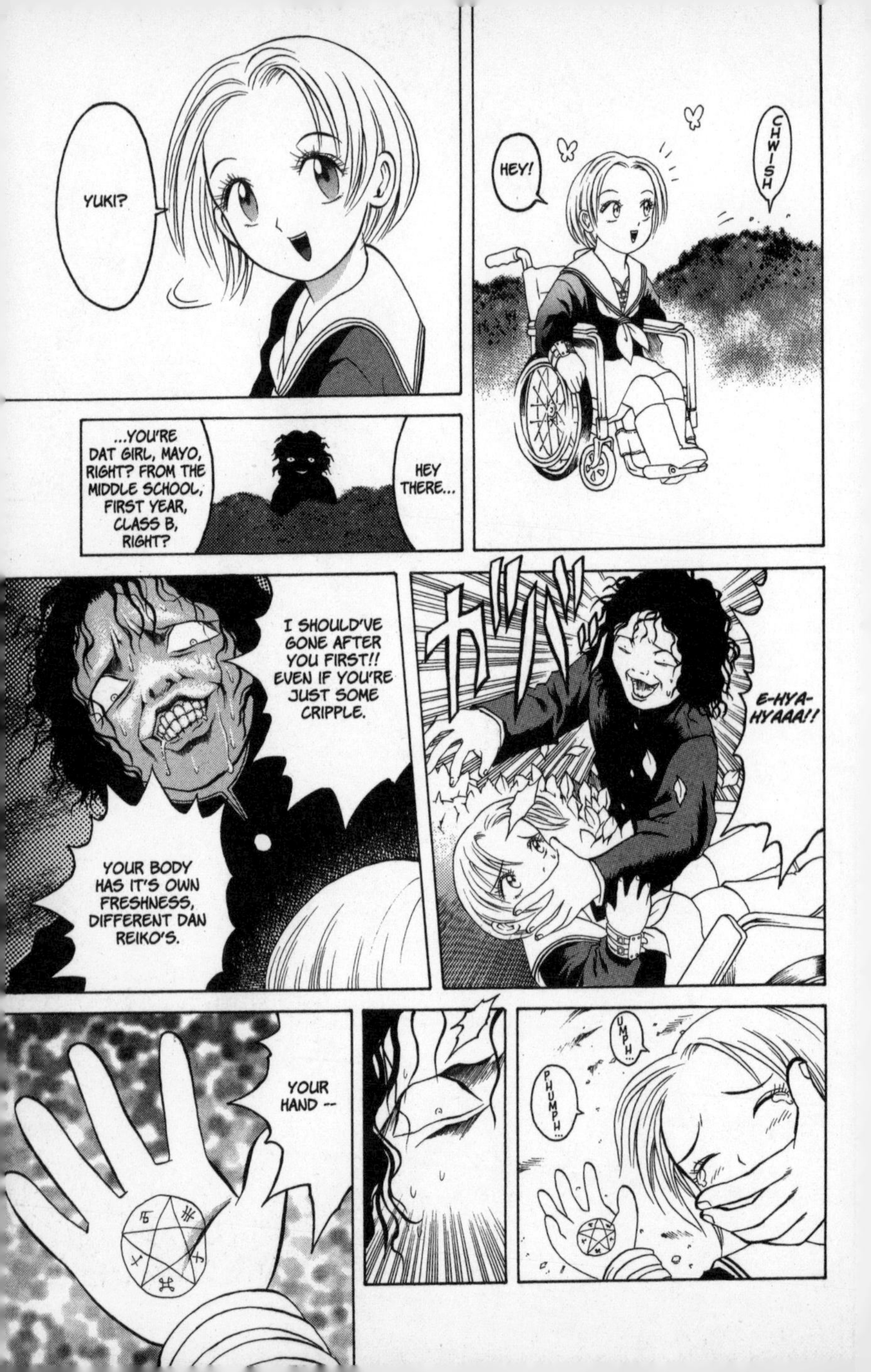
CHWISH
HEY!
YUKI?
HEY THERE...
...YOU'RE DAT GIRL, MAYO, RIGHT? FROM THE MIDDLE SCHOOL, FIRST YEAR, CLASS B, RIGHT?
E-HYA-HYAAA!!
I SHOULD'VE GONE AFTER YOU FIRST!! EVEN IF YOU'RE JUST SOME CRIPPLE.
YOUR BODY HAS IT'S OWN FRESHNESS, DIFFERENT DAN REIKO'S.
UMPH...
PHUMPH...
YOUR HAND --

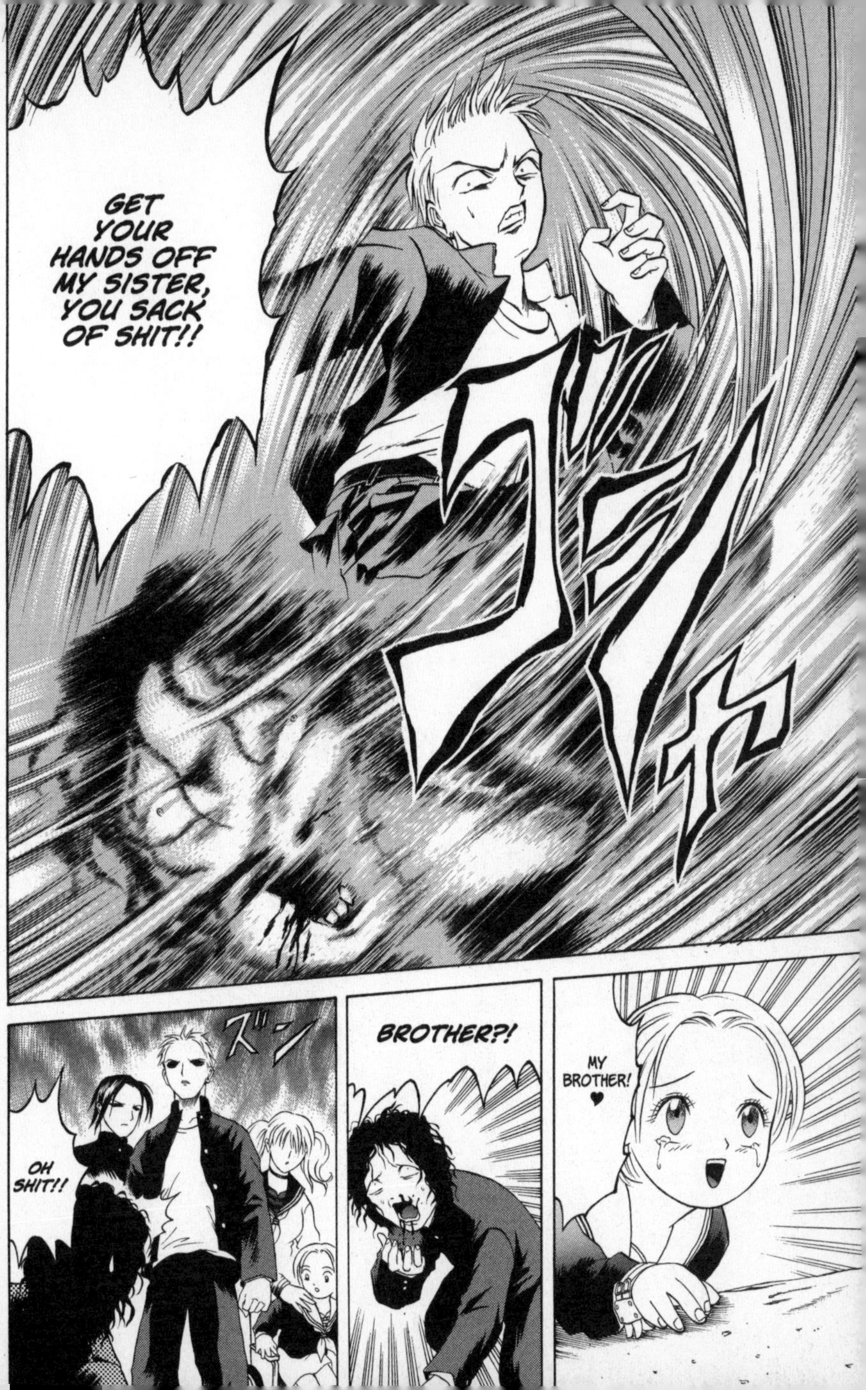
GET YOUR HANDS OFF MY SISTER, YOU SACK OF SHIT!!
MY BROTHER! ♥
BROTHER?!
ズン
OH SHIT!!

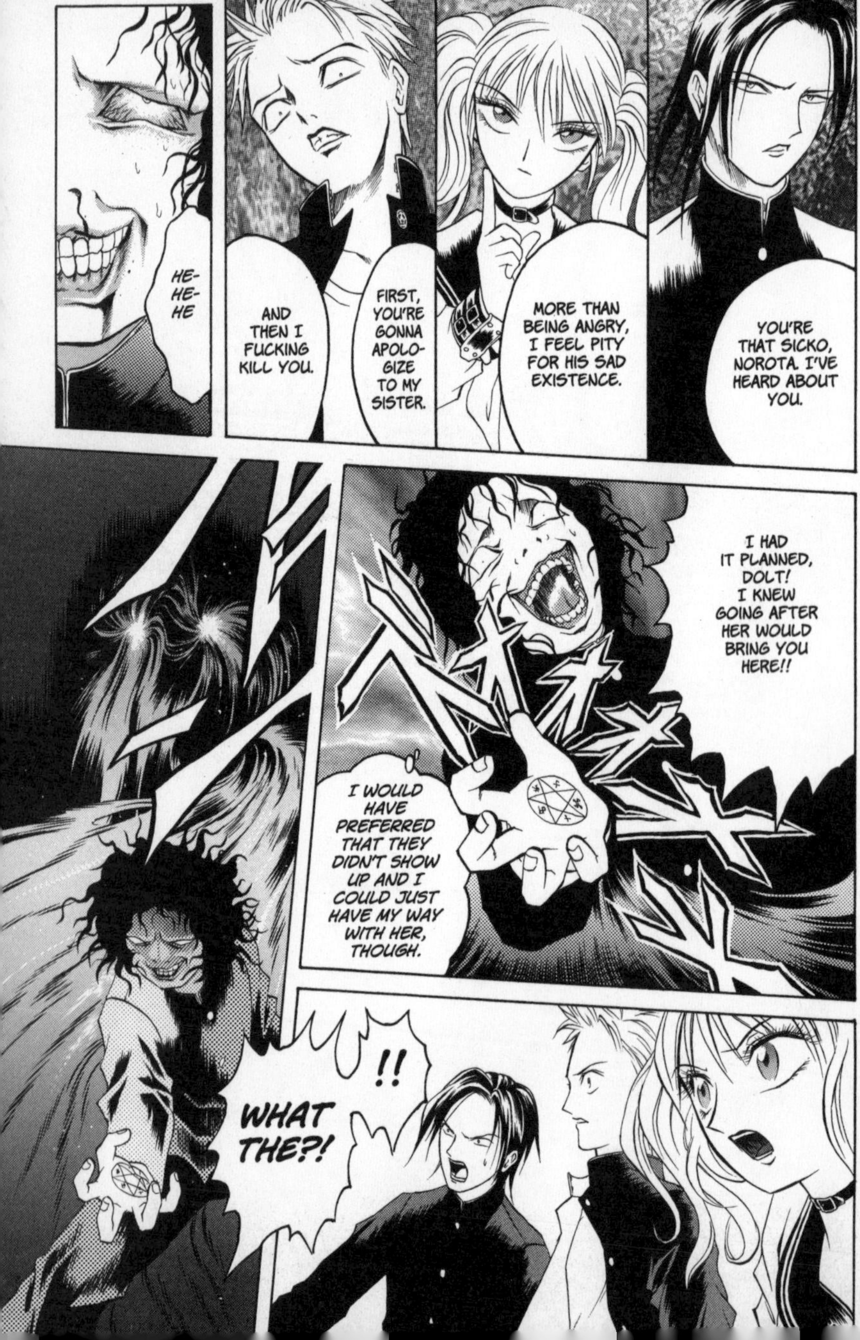
YOU'RE THAT SICKO, NOROTA. I'VE HEARD ABOUT YOU.
MORE THAN BEING ANGRY, I FEEL PITY FOR HIS SAD EXISTENCE.
FIRST, YOU'RE GONNA APOLO-GIZE TO MY SISTER.
AND THEN I FUCKING KILL YOU.
HE-HE-HE
I HAD IT PLANNED, DOLT! I KNEW GOING AFTER HER WOULD BRING YOU HERE!!
I WOULD HAVE PREFERRED THAT THEY DIDN'T SHOW UP AND I COULD JUST HAVE MY WAY WITH HER, THOUGH.
!!
WHAT THE?!

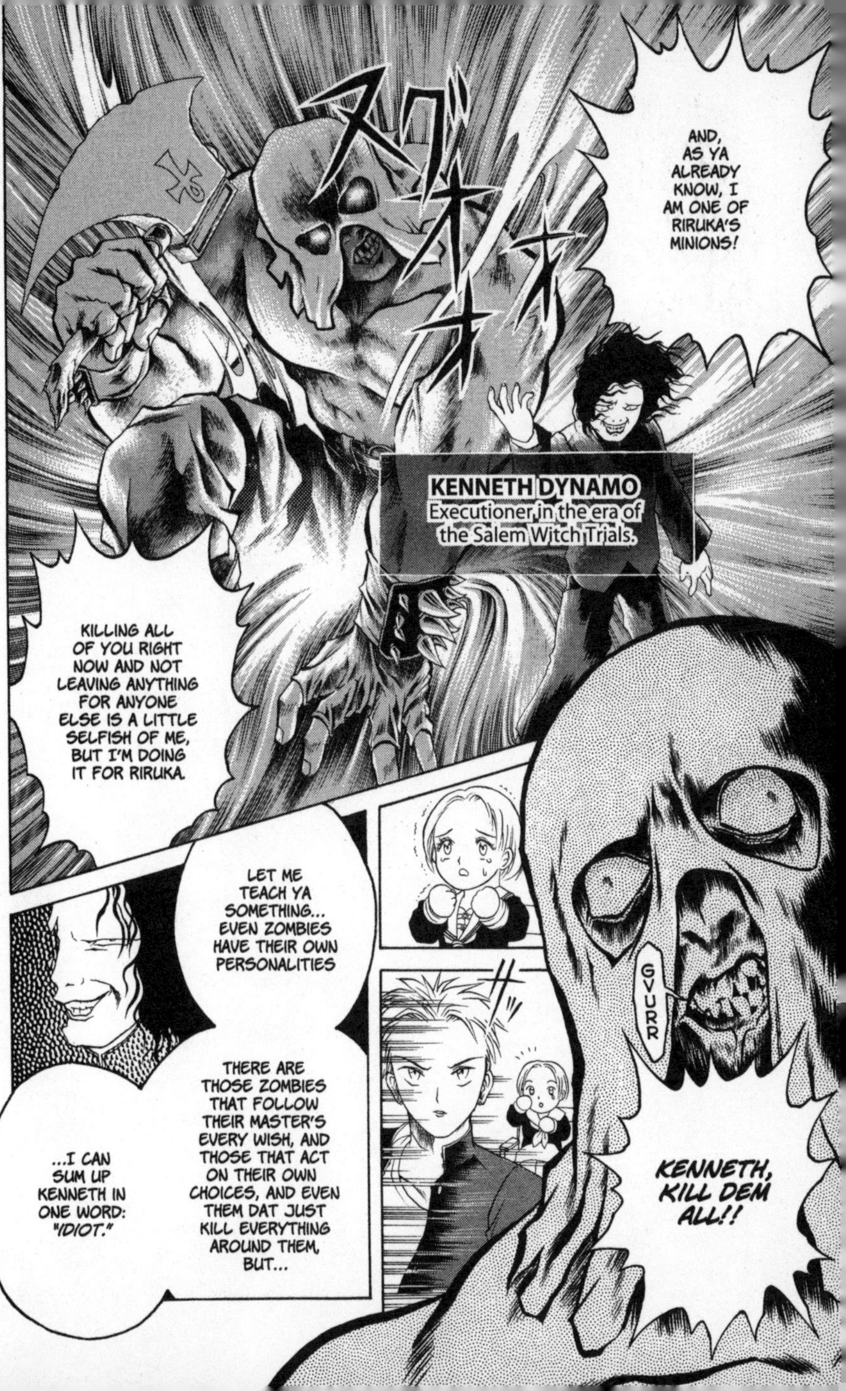
AND, AS YA ALREADY KNOW, I AM ONE OF RIRUKA'S MINIONS!
KENNETH DYNAMO
Executioner in the era of the Salem Witch Trials.
KILLING ALL OF YOU RIGHT NOW AND NOT LEAVING ANYTHING FOR ANYONE ELSE IS A LITTLE SELFISH OF ME, BUT I'M DOING IT FOR RIRUKA.
GVURR
KENNETH, KILL DEM ALL!!
LET ME TEACH YA SOMETHING... EVEN ZOMBIES HAVE THEIR OWN PERSONALITIES
THERE ARE THOSE ZOMBIES THAT FOLLOW THEIR MASTER'S EVERY WISH, AND THOSE THAT ACT ON THEIR OWN CHOICES, AND EVEN THEM DAT JUST KILL EVERYTHING AROUND THEM, BUT...
...I CAN SUM UP KENNETH IN ONE WORD: "IDIOT."

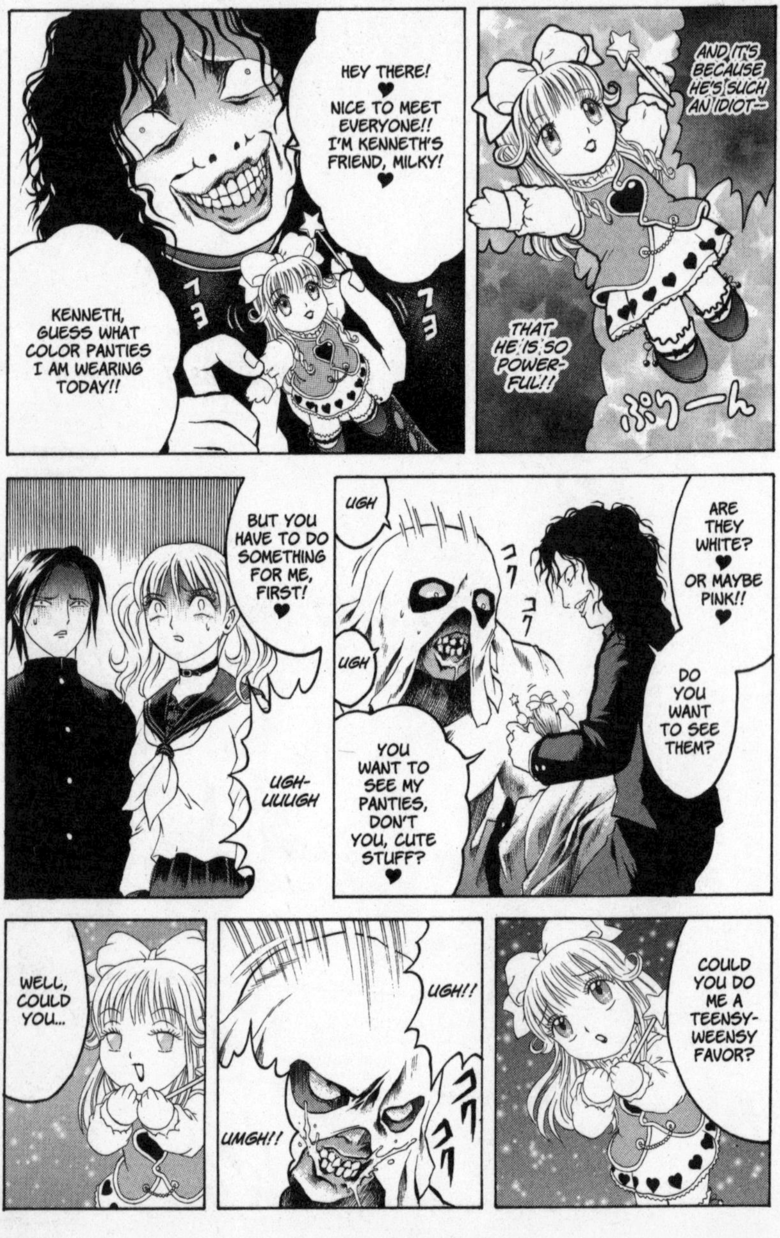
AND IT'S BECAUSE HE'S SUCH AN IDIOT—
THAT HE IS SO POWERFUL!!
ぷりーん
HEY THERE! ♥ NICE TO MEET EVERYONE!! I'M KENNETH'S FRIEND, MILKY! ♥
KENNETH, GUESS WHAT COLOR PANTIES I AM WEARING TODAY!!
ARE THEY WHITE? ♥ OR MAYBE PINK!! ♥
UGH
DO YOU WANT TO SEE THEM?
UGH
YOU WANT TO SEE MY PANTIES, DON'T YOU, CUTE STUFF? ♥
BUT YOU HAVE TO DO SOMETHING FOR ME, FIRST! ♥
UGH-UUUGH
COULD YOU DO ME A TEENSY-WEENSY FAVOR?
UGH!!
UMGH!!
WELL, COULD YOU...

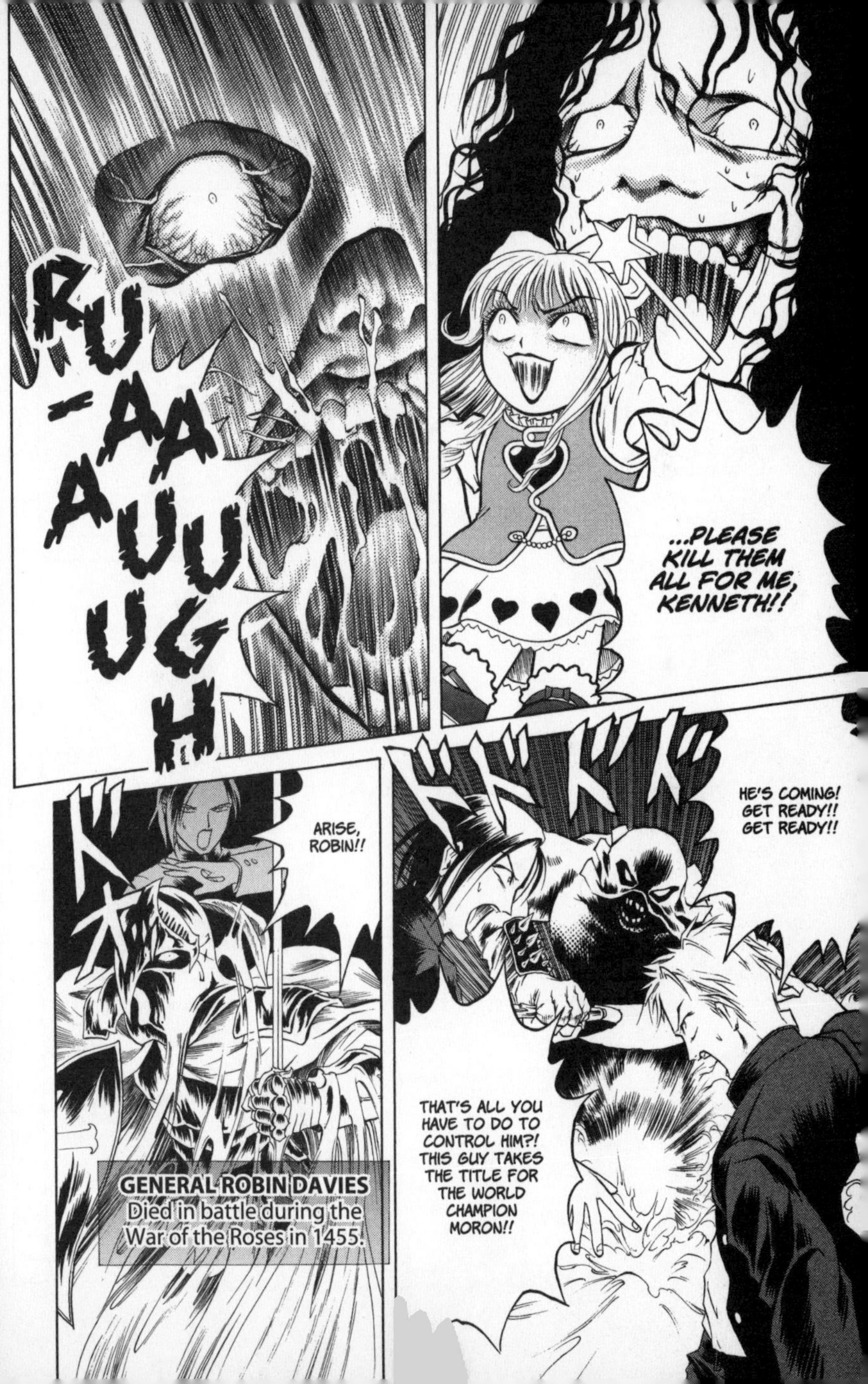
...PLEASE KILL THEM ALL FOR ME, KENNETH!!
RU-AAAUUUGH
ドドドド
HE'S COMING! GET READY!! GET READY!!
THAT'S ALL YOU HAVE TO DO TO CONTROL HIM?! THIS GUY TAKES THE TITLE FOR THE WORLD CHAMPION MORON!!
ARISE, ROBIN!!
GENERAL ROBIN DAVIES
Died in battle during the War of the Roses in 1455.

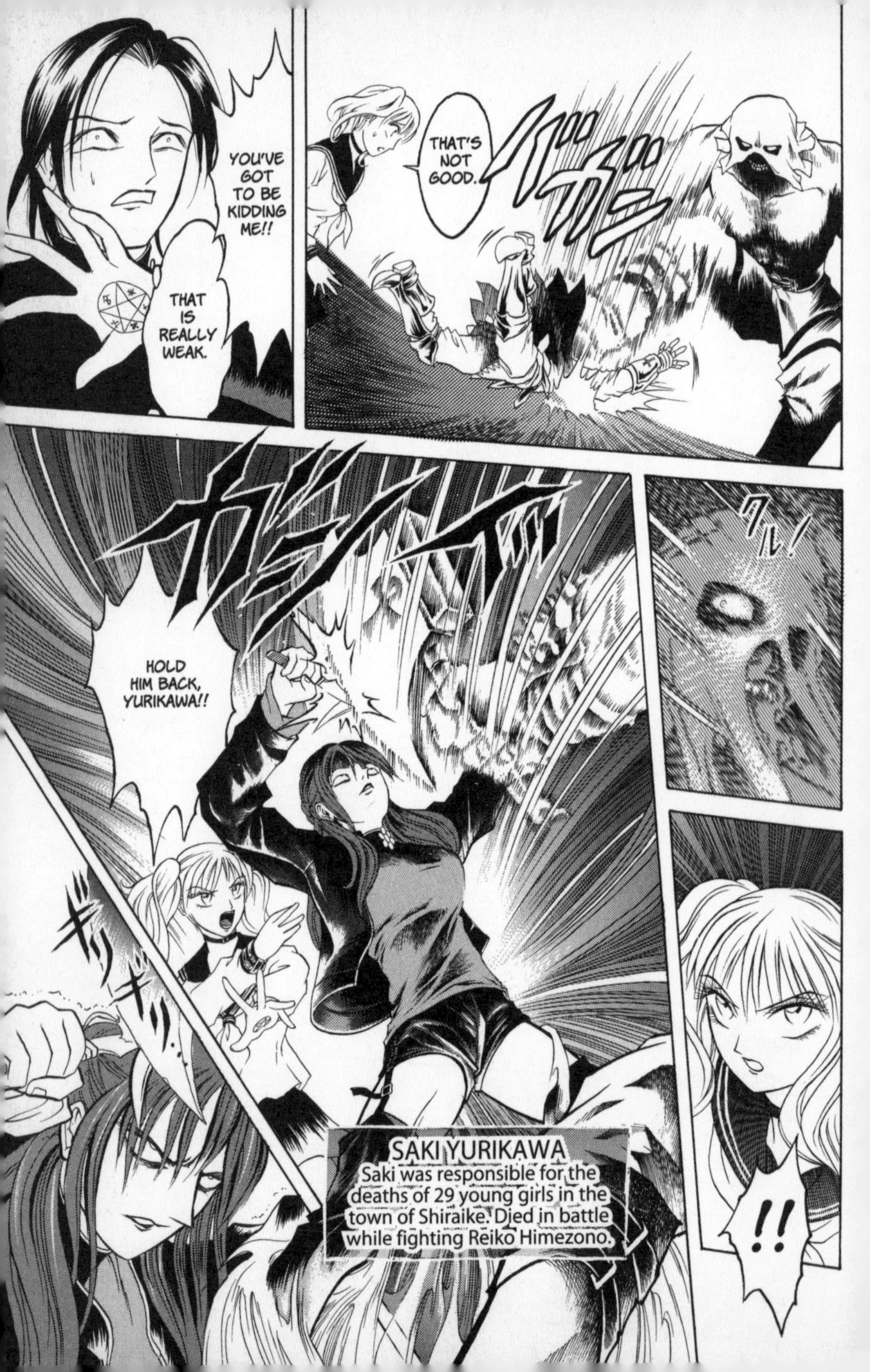
THAT'S NOT GOOD.
YOU'VE GOT TO BE KIDDING ME!!
THAT IS REALLY WEAK.
クル!
!!
HOLD HIM BACK, YURIKAWA!!
SAKI YURIKAWA
Saki was responsible for the deaths of 29 young girls in the town of Shiraike. Died in battle while fighting Reiko Himezono.

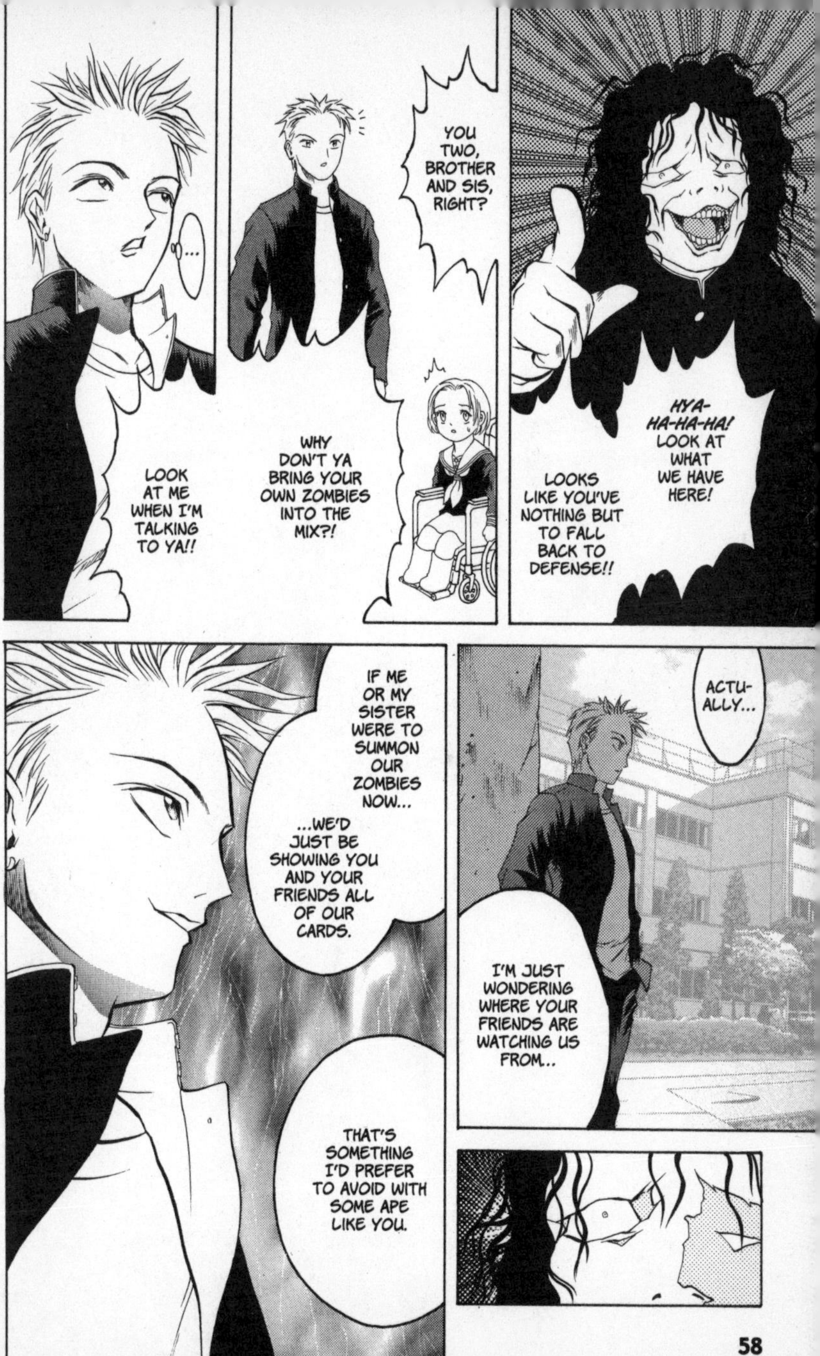
HYA-HA-HA-HA! LOOK AT WHAT WE HAVE HERE!
LOOKS LIKE YOU'VE NOTHING BUT TO FALL BACK TO DEFENSE!!
YOU TWO, BROTHER AND SIS, RIGHT?
WHY DON'T YA BRING YOUR OWN ZOMBIES INTO THE MIX?!
...
LOOK AT ME WHEN I'M TALKING TO YA!!
ACTU-ALLY...
I'M JUST WONDERING WHERE YOUR FRIENDS ARE WATCHING US FROM..
IF ME OR MY SISTER WERE TO SUMMON OUR ZOMBIES NOW...
...WE'D JUST BE SHOWING YOU AND YOUR FRIENDS ALL OF OUR CARDS.
THAT'S SOMETHING I'D PREFER TO AVOID WITH SOME APE LIKE YOU.

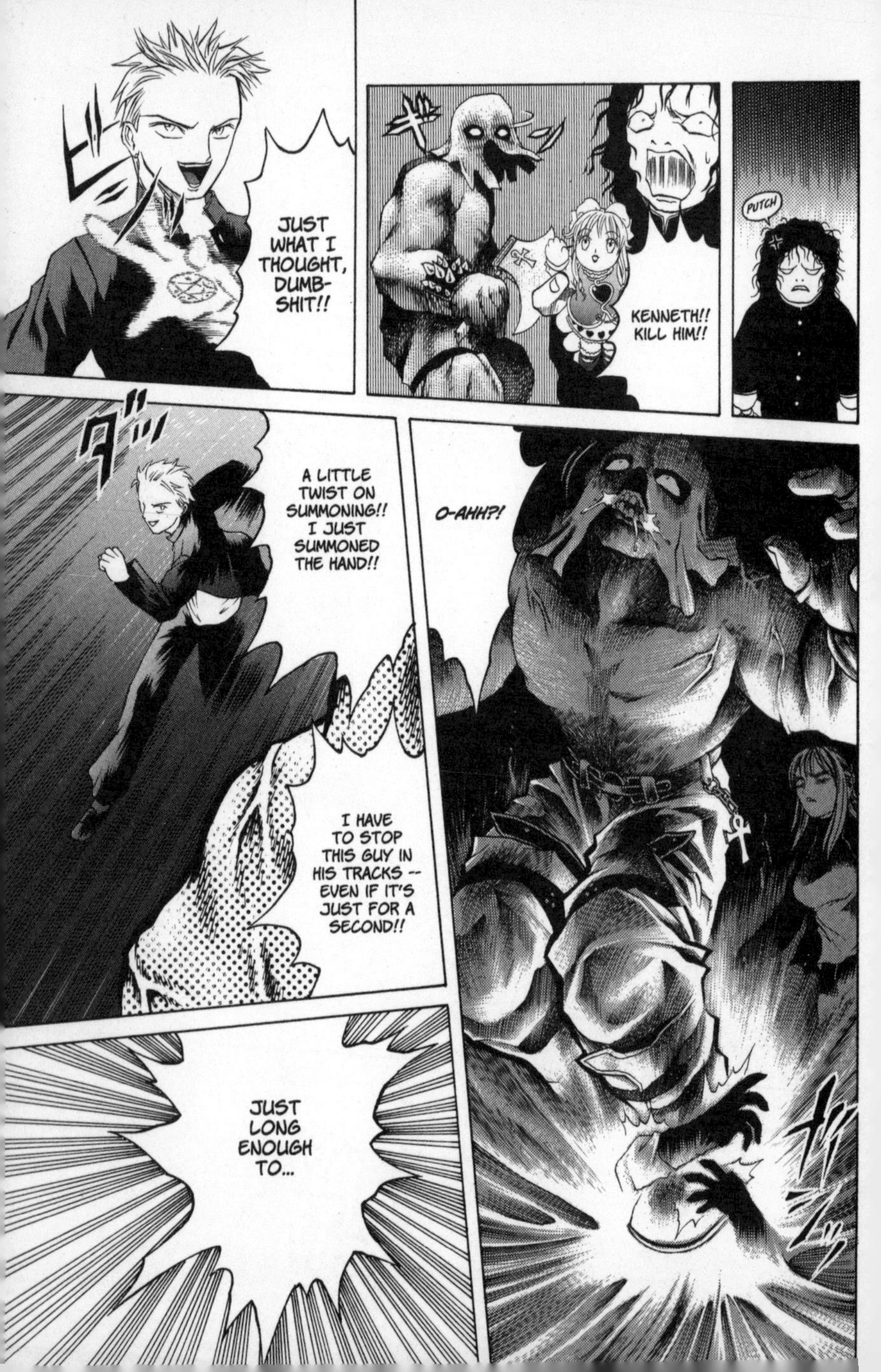
PUTCH
KENNETH!! KILL HIM!!
JUST WHAT I THOUGHT, DUMB-SHIT!!
O-AHH?!
A LITTLE TWIST ON SUMMONING!! I JUST SUMMONED THE HAND!!
I HAVE TO STOP THIS GUY IN HIS TRACKS -- EVEN IF IT'S JUST FOR A SECOND!!
JUST LONG ENOUGH TO...

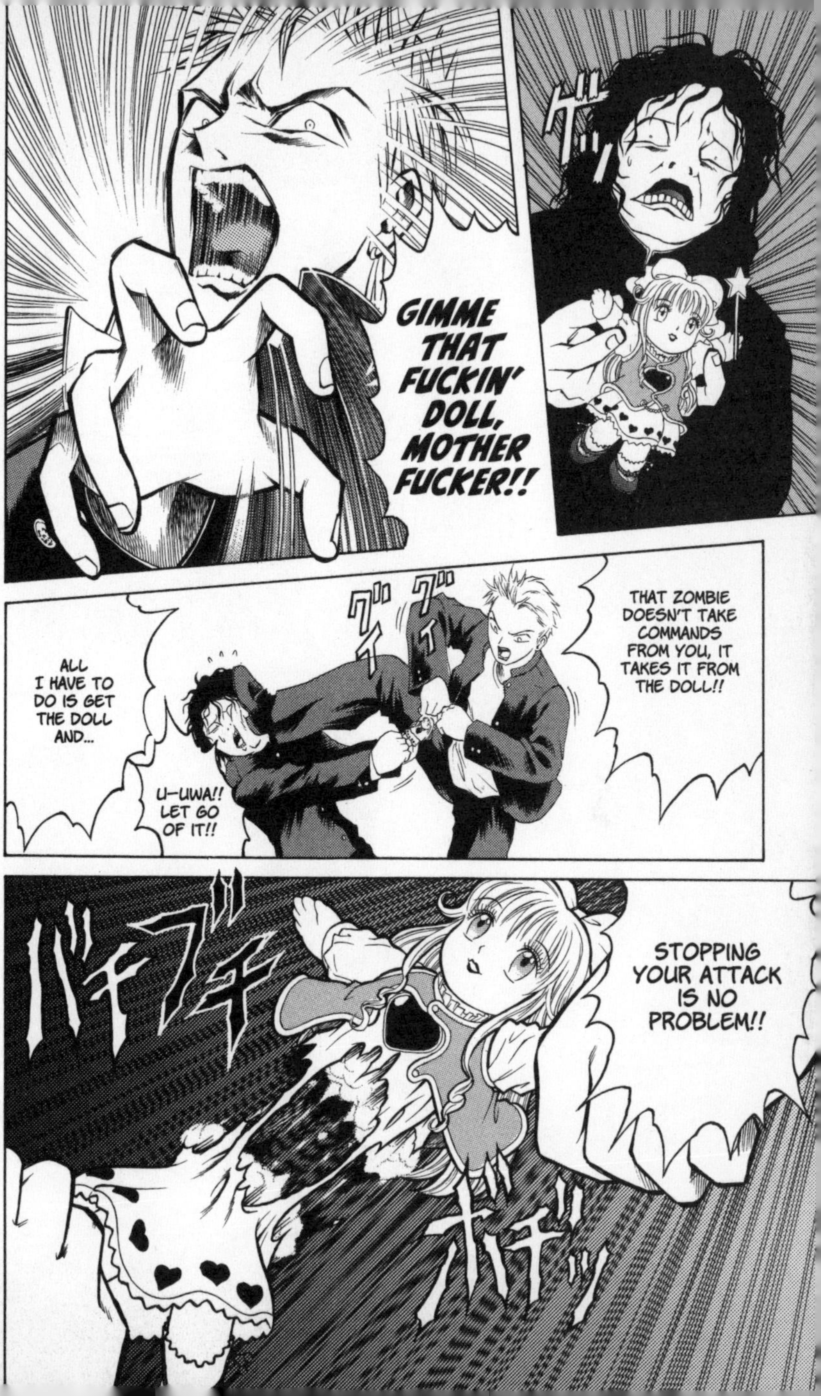
GIMME THAT FUCKIN' DOLL, MOTHER FUCKER!!
THAT ZOMBIE DOESN'T TAKE COMMANDS FROM YOU, IT TAKES IT FROM THE DOLL!!
ALL I HAVE TO DO IS GET THE DOLL AND...
U-UWA!! LET GO OF IT!!
STOPPING YOUR ATTACK IS NO PROBLEM!!

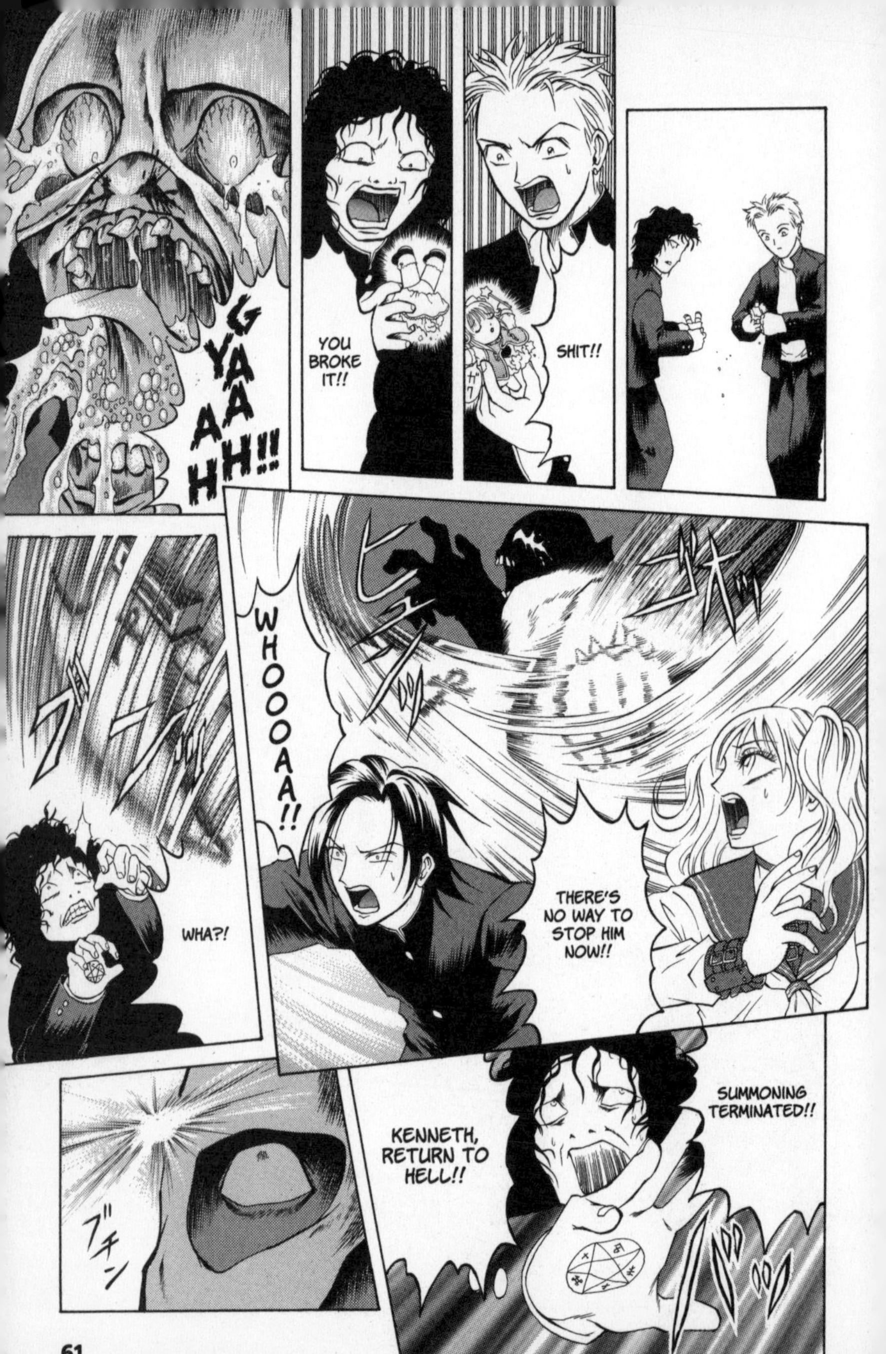
SHIT!!
YOU BROKE IT!!
GYAAAHH!!
WHOOOOAA!!
THERE'S NO WAY TO STOP HIM NOW!!
WHA?!
SUMMONING TERMINATED!!
KENNETH, RETURN TO HELL!!

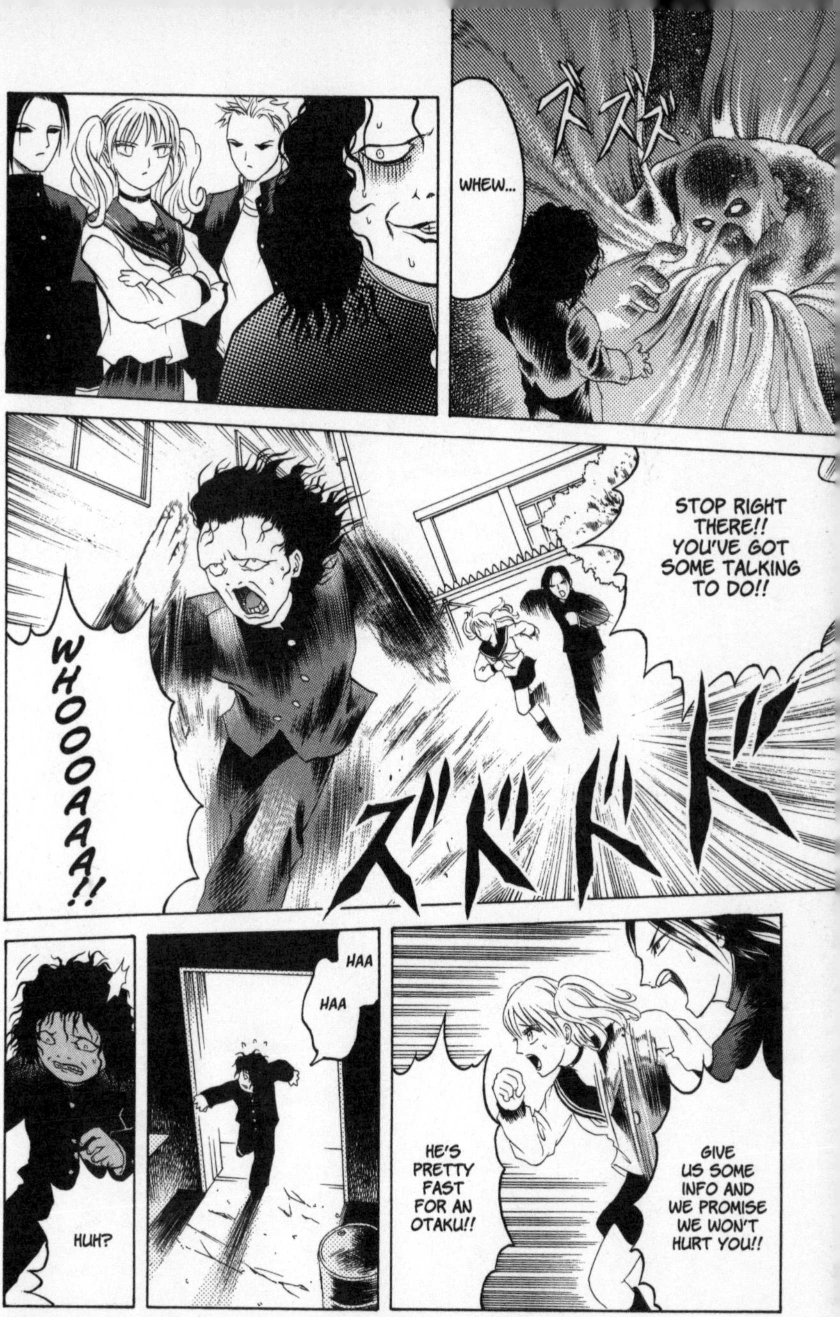
ズズズ
WHEW...
STOP RIGHT THERE!! YOU'VE GOT SOME TALKING TO DO!!
WHOOOOAAAA!!
ズドドド
GIVE US SOME INFO AND WE PROMISE WE WON'T HURT YOU!!
HE'S PRETTY FAST FOR AN OTAKU!!
HAA
HAA
HUH?

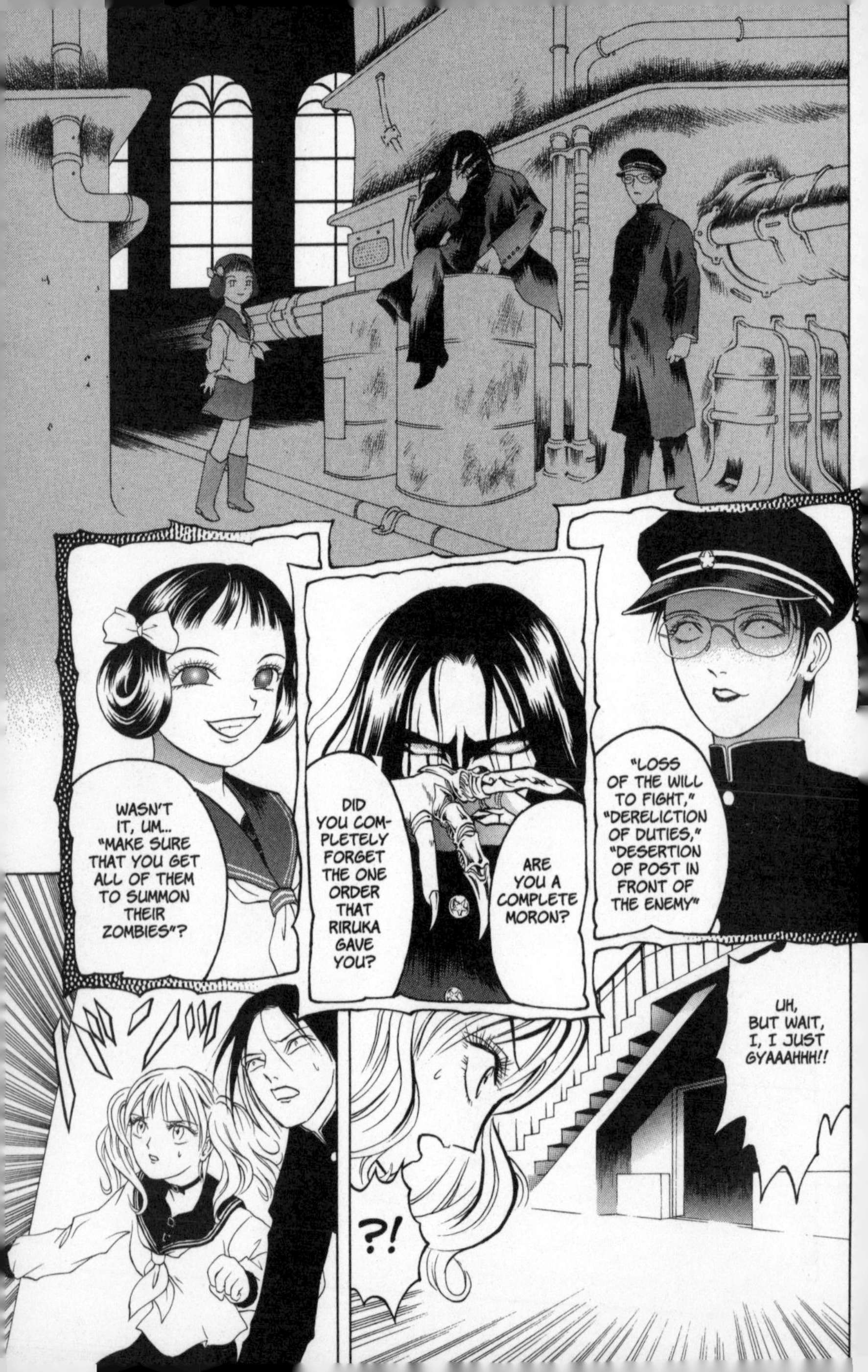
"LOSS OF THE WILL TO FIGHT," "DERELICTION OF DUTIES," "DESERTION OF POST IN FRONT OF THE ENEMY"
DID YOU COMPLETELY FORGET THE ONE ORDER THAT RIRUKA GAVE YOU?
ARE YOU A COMPLETE MORON?
WASN'T IT, UM... "MAKE SURE THAT YOU GET ALL OF THEM TO SUMMON THEIR ZOMBIES"?
UH, BUT WAIT, I, I JUST GYAAAHHH!!
?!

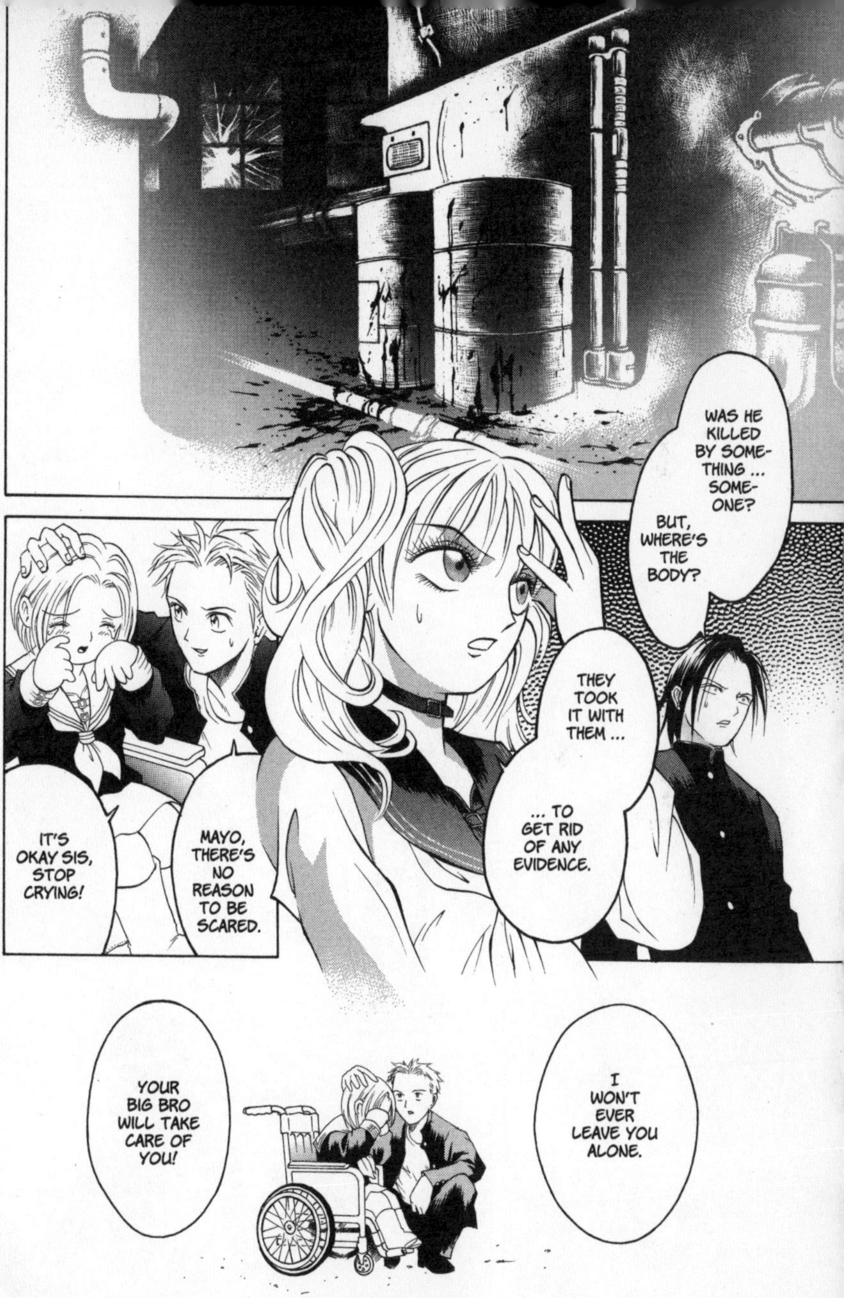
WAS HE KILLED BY SOME-THING ... SOME-ONE?
BUT, WHERE'S THE BODY?
THEY TOOK IT WITH THEM ...
... TO GET RID OF ANY EVIDENCE.
MAYO, THERE'S NO REASON TO BE SCARED.
IT'S OKAY SIS, STOP CRYING!
I WON'T EVER LEAVE YOU ALONE.
YOUR BIG BRO WILL TAKE CARE OF YOU!

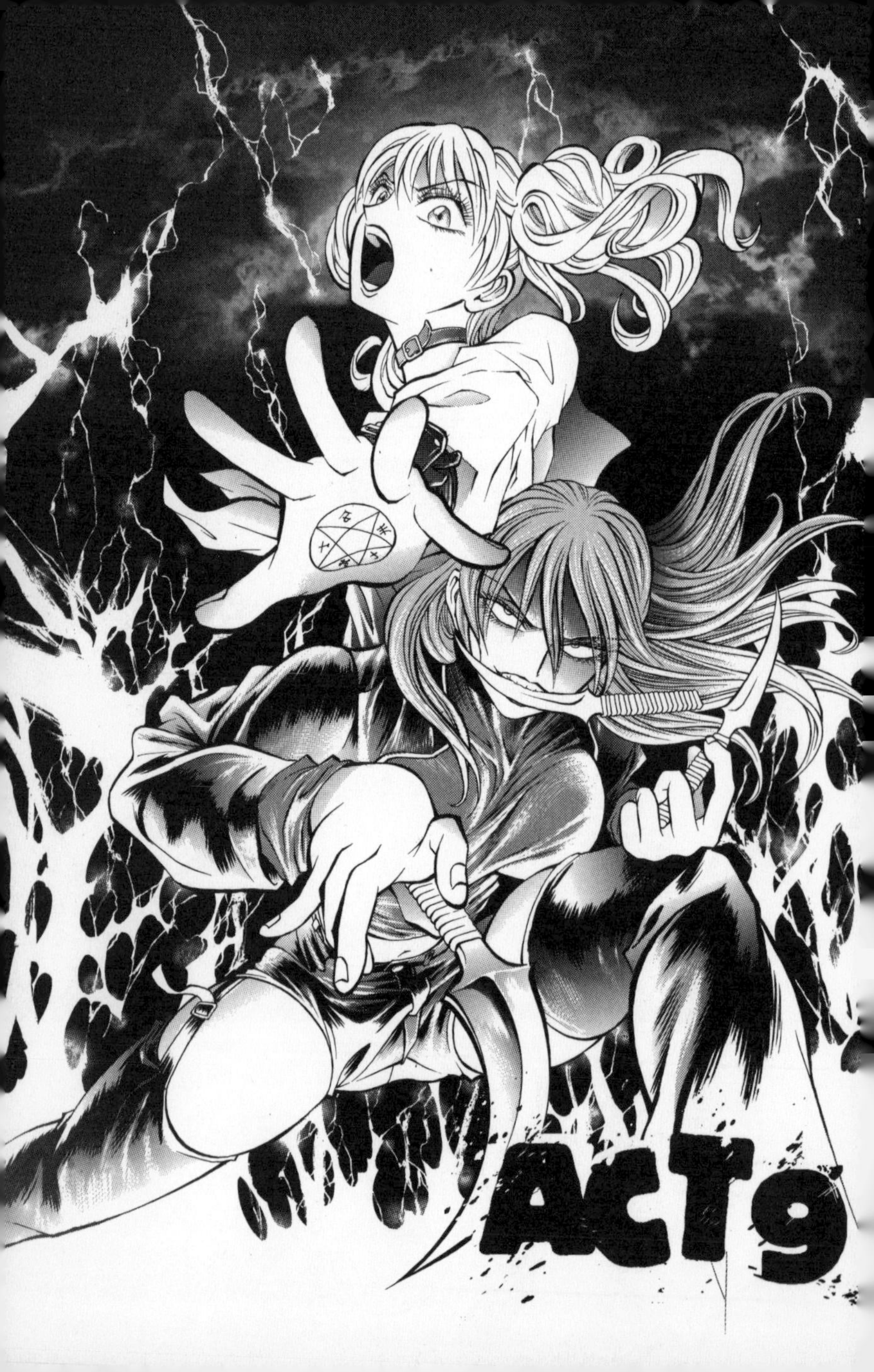
ACT 9

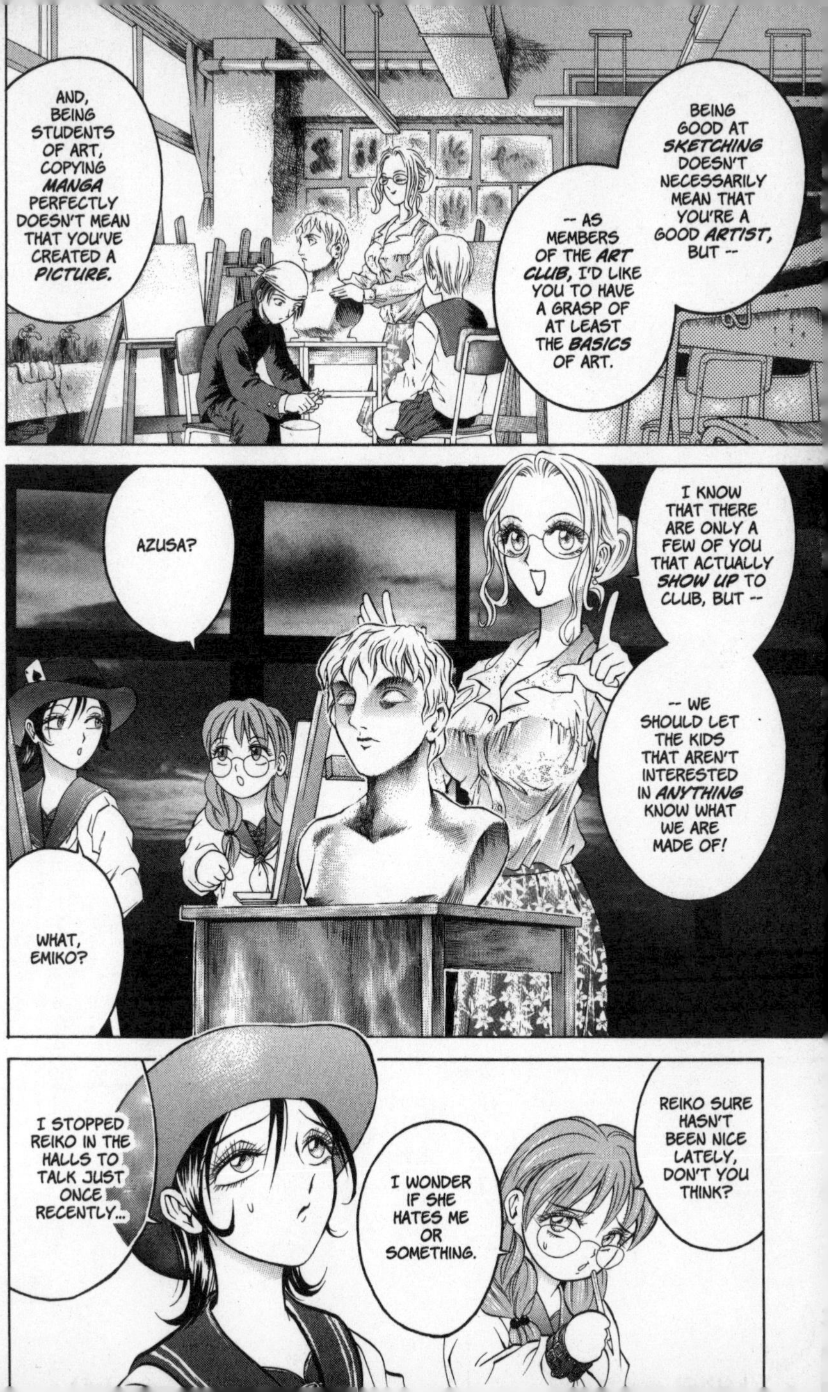
BEING GOOD AT *SKETCHING* DOESN'T NECESSARILY MEAN THAT YOU'RE A GOOD *ARTIST,* BUT --
-- AS MEMBERS OF THE *ART CLUB,* I'D LIKE YOU TO HAVE A GRASP OF AT LEAST THE *BASICS* OF ART.
AND, BEING STUDENTS OF ART, COPYING *MANGA* PERFECTLY DOESN'T MEAN THAT YOU'VE CREATED A *PICTURE.*
I KNOW THAT THERE ARE ONLY A FEW OF YOU THAT ACTUALLY *SHOW UP* TO CLUB, BUT --
-- WE SHOULD LET THE KIDS THAT AREN'T INTERESTED IN *ANYTHING* KNOW WHAT WE ARE MADE OF!
AZUSA?
WHAT, EMIKO?
REIKO SURE HASN'T BEEN NICE LATELY, DON'T YOU THINK?
I WONDER IF SHE HATES ME OR SOMETHING.
I STOPPED REIKO IN THE HALLS TO TALK JUST ONCE RECENTLY...

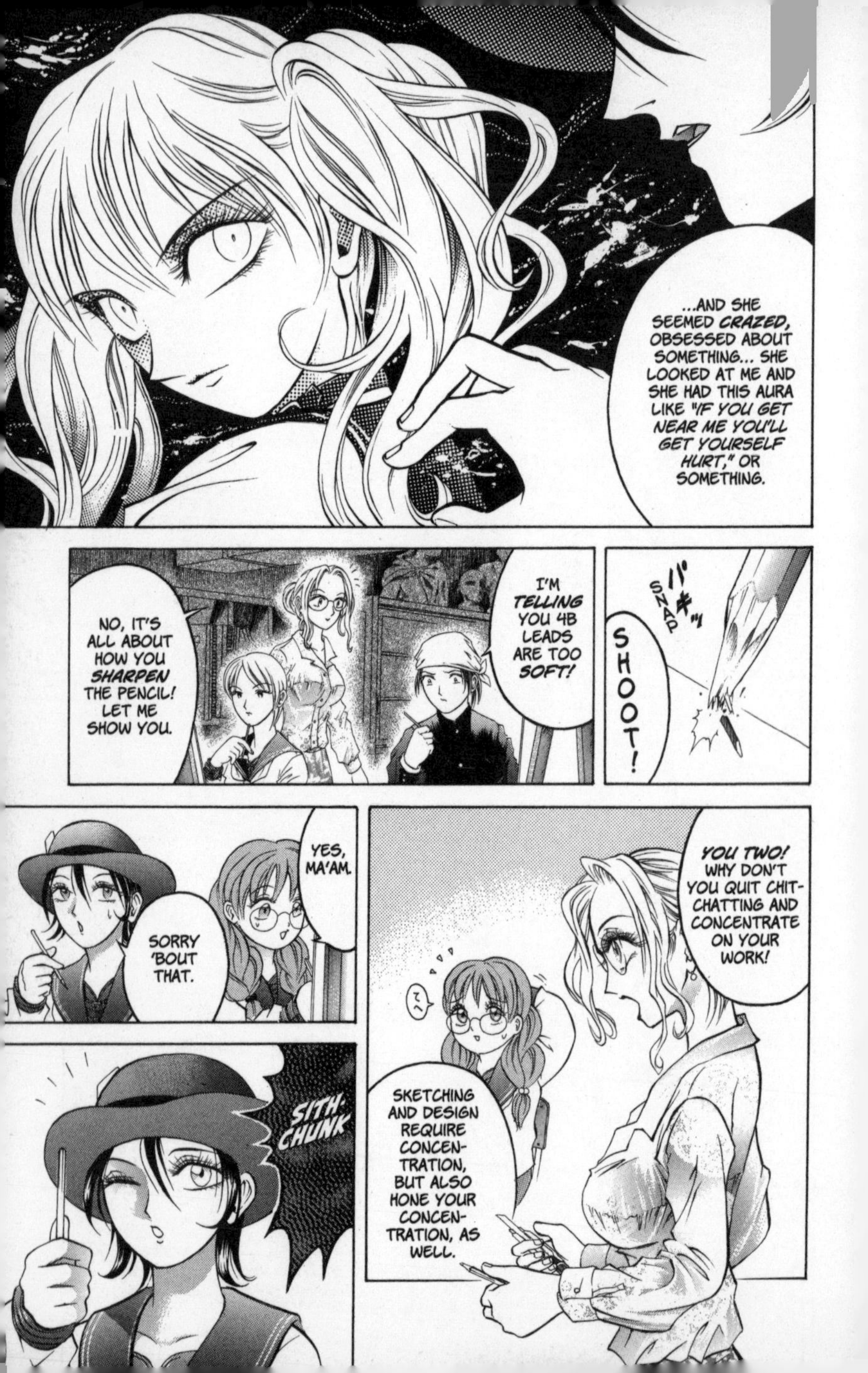
...AND SHE SEEMED CRAZED, OBSESSED ABOUT SOMETHING... SHE LOOKED AT ME AND SHE HAD THIS AURA LIKE "IF YOU GET NEAR ME YOU'LL GET YOURSELF HURT," OR SOMETHING.
SNAP
バキッ
SHOOT!
I'M TELLING YOU 4B LEADS ARE TOO SOFT!
NO, IT'S ALL ABOUT HOW YOU SHARPEN THE PENCIL! LET ME SHOW YOU.
YOU TWO! WHY DON'T YOU QUIT CHIT-CHATTING AND CONCENTRATE ON YOUR WORK!
SKETCHING AND DESIGN REQUIRE CONCEN-TRATION, BUT ALSO HONE YOUR CONCEN-TRATION, AS WELL.
YES, MA'AM.
SORRY 'BOUT THAT.
SITH-CHUNK

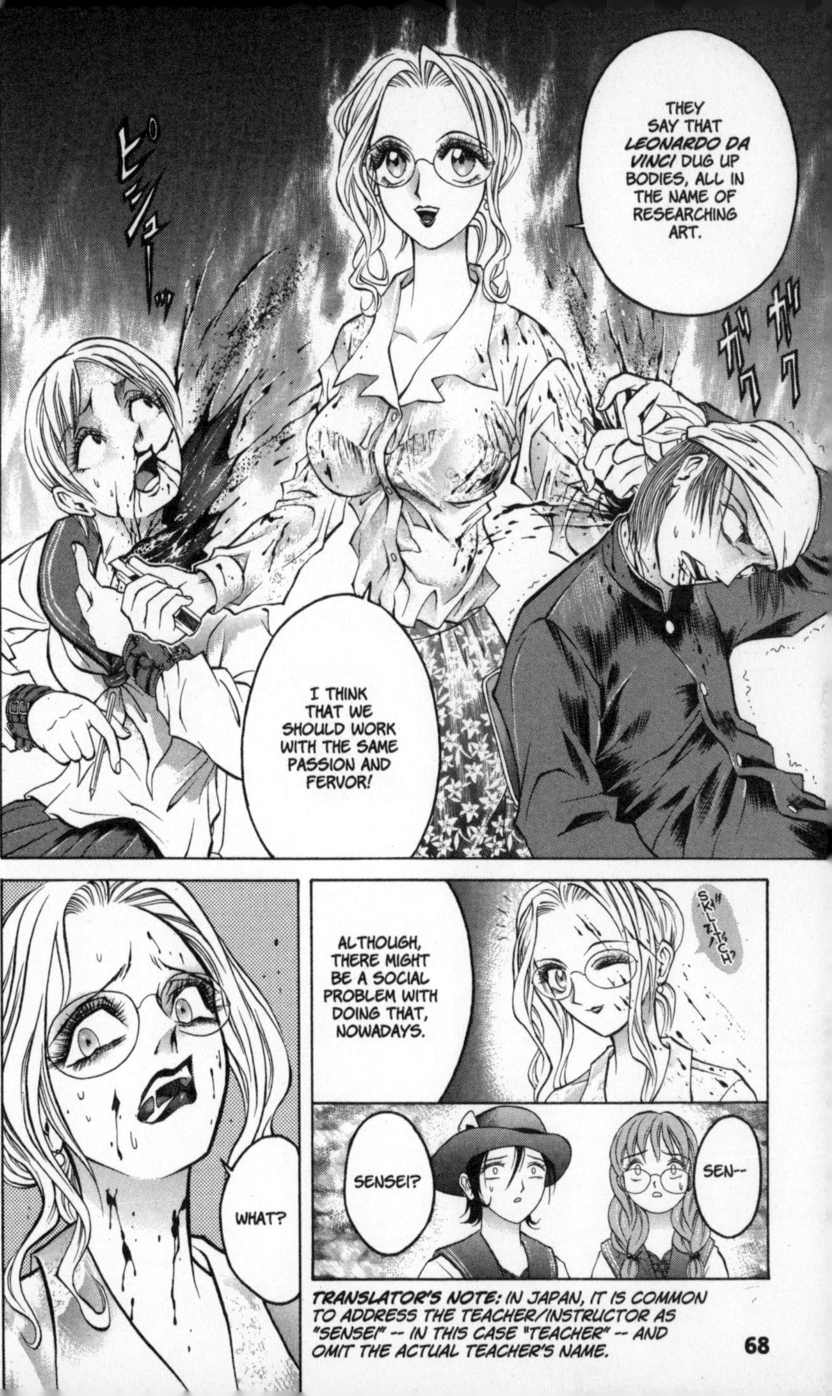
THEY SAY THAT *LEONARDO DA VINCI* DUG UP BODIES, ALL IN THE NAME OF RESEARCHING ART.
I THINK THAT WE SHOULD WORK WITH THE SAME PASSION AND FERVOR!
ALTHOUGH, THERE MIGHT BE A SOCIAL PROBLEM WITH DOING THAT, NOWADAYS.
SEN--
SENSEI?
WHAT?

TRANSLATOR'S NOTE: *IN JAPAN, IT IS COMMON TO ADDRESS THE TEACHER/INSTRUCTOR AS "SENSEI" -- IN THIS CASE "TEACHER" -- AND OMIT THE ACTUAL TEACHER'S NAME.*

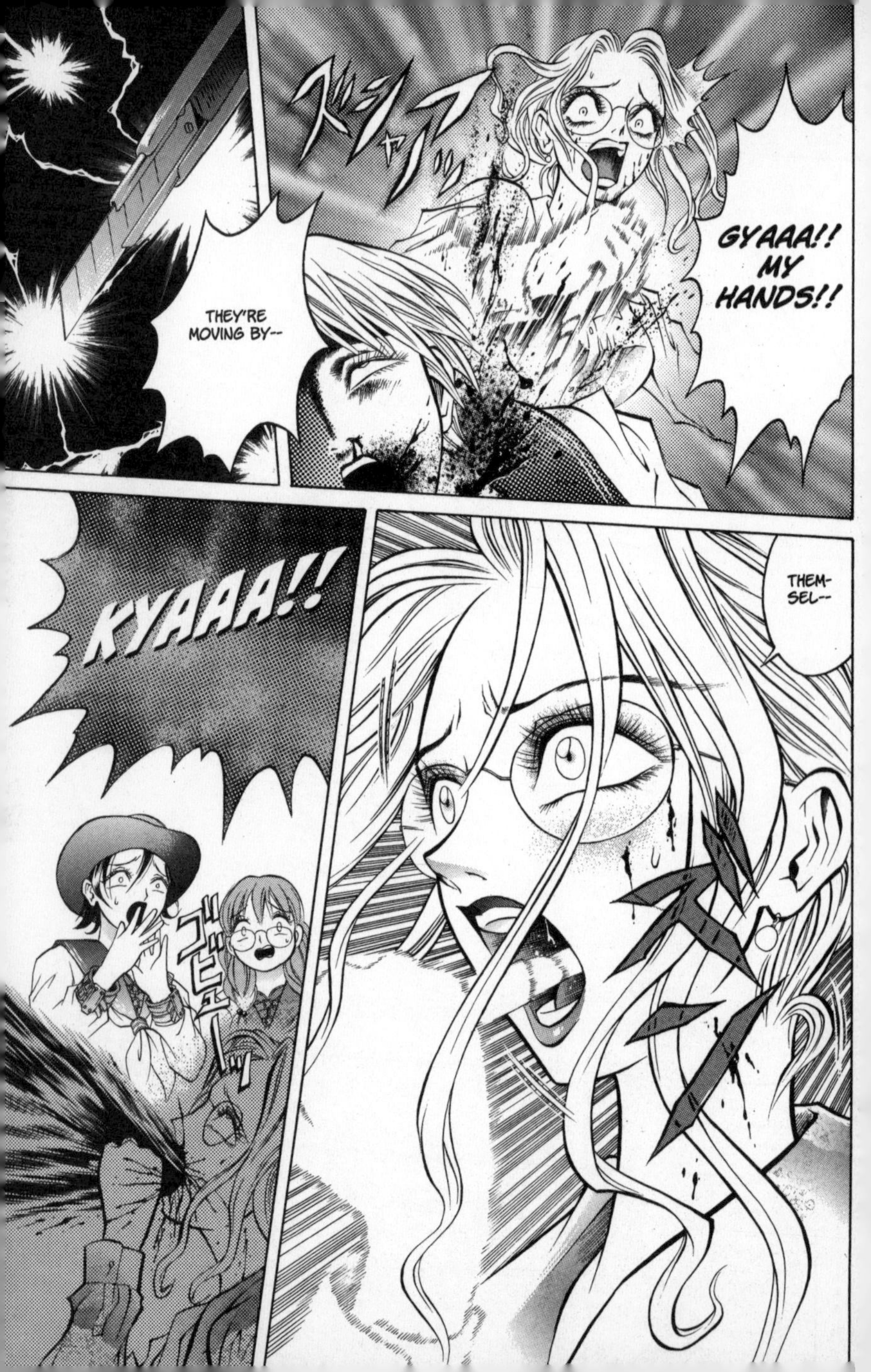
GYAAA!! MY HANDS!!
THEY'RE MOVING BY--
THEM-SEL--
KYAAA!!

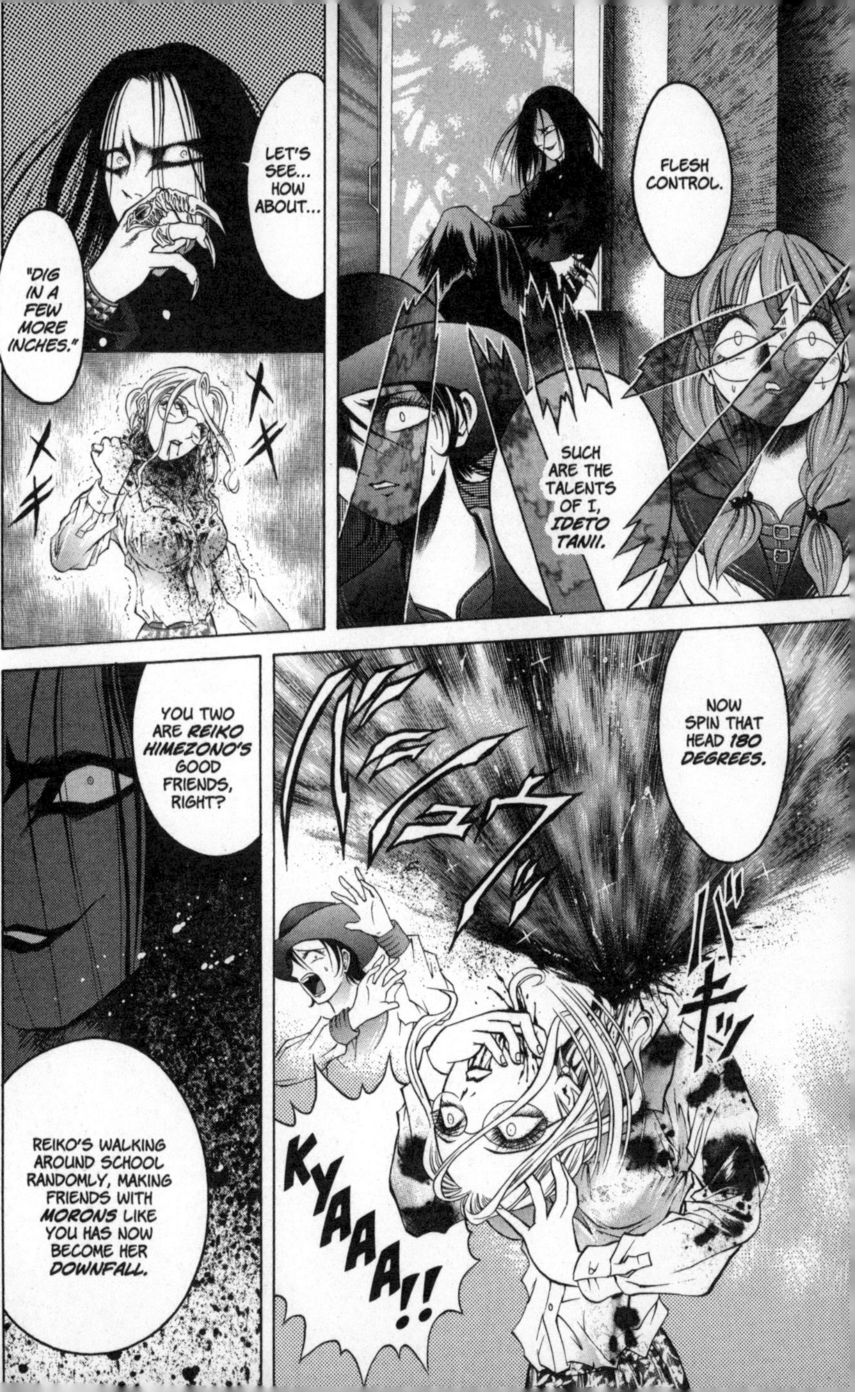
FLESH CONTROL.
SUCH ARE THE TALENTS OF I, *IDETO TANII.*
LET'S SEE... HOW ABOUT...
"DIG IN A FEW MORE INCHES."
NOW SPIN THAT HEAD *180 DEGREES.*
バシュウ
バキッ
KYAAAA!!
YOU TWO ARE *REIKO HIMEZONO'S* GOOD FRIENDS, RIGHT?
REIKO'S WALKING AROUND SCHOOL RANDOMLY, MAKING FRIENDS WITH *MORONS* LIKE YOU HAS NOW BECOME HER *DOWNFALL.*

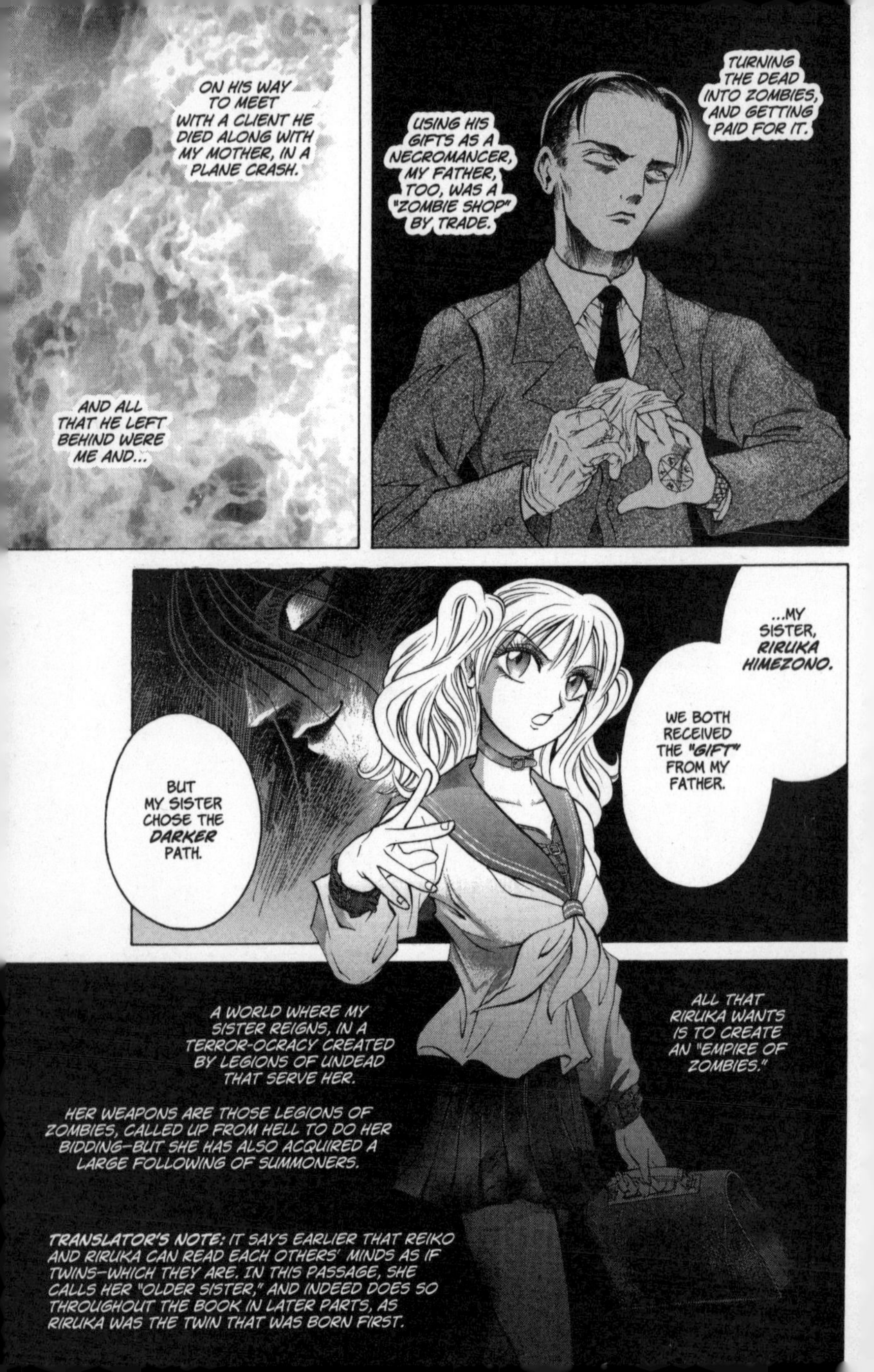
TURNING THE DEAD INTO ZOMBIES, AND GETTING PAID FOR IT.
USING HIS GIFTS AS A NECROMANCER, MY FATHER, TOO, WAS A "ZOMBIE SHOP" BY TRADE.
ON HIS WAY TO MEET WITH A CLIENT HE DIED ALONG WITH MY MOTHER, IN A PLANE CRASH.
AND ALL THAT HE LEFT BEHIND WERE ME AND...
...MY SISTER, **RIRUKA HIMEZONO.**
WE BOTH RECEIVED THE ***"GIFT"*** FROM MY FATHER.
BUT MY SISTER CHOSE THE ***DARKER*** PATH.
ALL THAT RIRUKA WANTS IS TO CREATE AN "EMPIRE OF ZOMBIES."
A WORLD WHERE MY SISTER REIGNS, IN A TERROR-OCRACY CREATED BY LEGIONS OF UNDEAD THAT SERVE HER.
HER WEAPONS ARE THOSE LEGIONS OF ZOMBIES, CALLED UP FROM HELL TO DO HER BIDDING—BUT SHE HAS ALSO ACQUIRED A LARGE FOLLOWING OF SUMMONERS.
TRANSLATOR'S NOTE: IT SAYS EARLIER THAT REIKO AND RIRUKA CAN READ EACH OTHERS' MINDS AS IF TWINS—WHICH THEY ARE. IN THIS PASSAGE, SHE CALLS HER "OLDER SISTER," AND INDEED DOES SO THROUGHOUT THE BOOK IN LATER PARTS, AS RIRUKA WAS THE TWIN THAT WAS BORN FIRST.

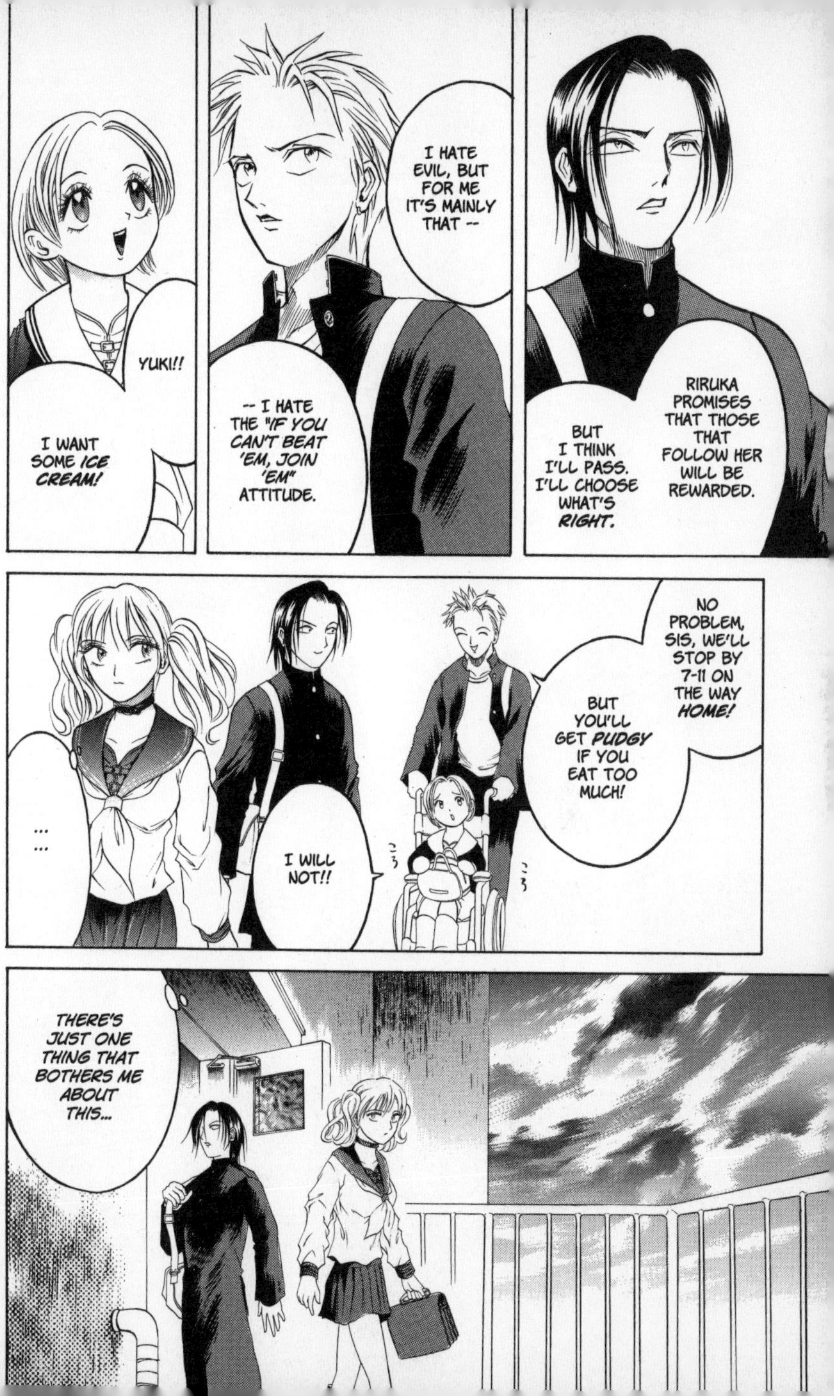
RIRUKA PROMISES THAT THOSE THAT FOLLOW HER WILL BE REWARDED.
BUT I THINK I'LL PASS. I'LL CHOOSE WHAT'S *RIGHT.*
I HATE EVIL, BUT FOR ME IT'S MAINLY THAT --
-- I HATE THE "*IF YOU CAN'T BEAT 'EM, JOIN 'EM*" ATTITUDE.
YUKI!!
I WANT SOME *ICE CREAM!*
NO PROBLEM, SIS, WE'LL STOP BY 7-11 ON THE WAY *HOME!*
BUT YOU'LL GET *PUDGY* IF YOU EAT TOO MUCH!
ころ
ころ
I WILL NOT!!
......
THERE'S JUST ONE THING THAT BOTHERS ME ABOUT THIS...

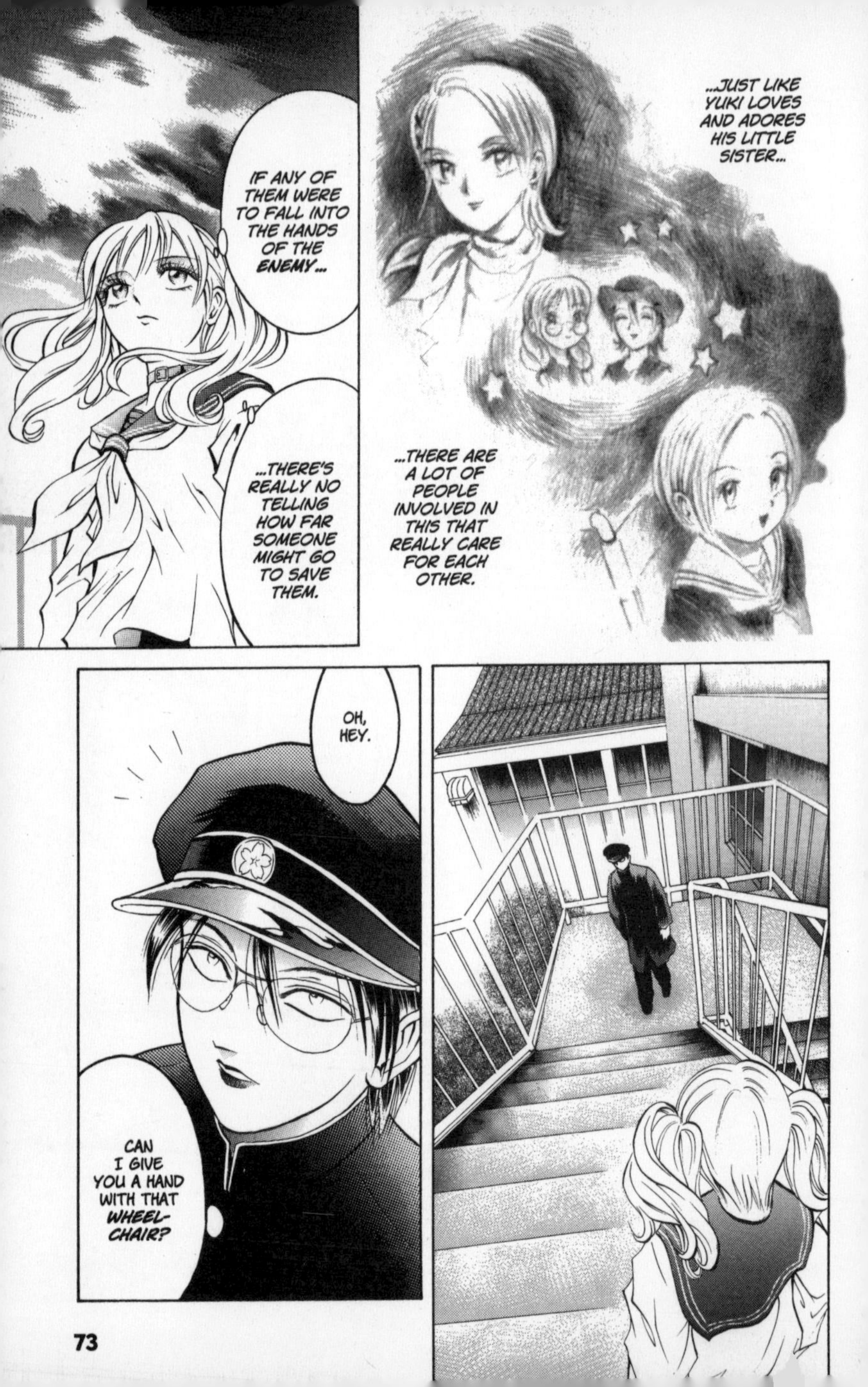
...JUST LIKE YUKI LOVES AND ADORES HIS LITTLE SISTER...
...THERE ARE A LOT OF PEOPLE INVOLVED IN THIS THAT REALLY CARE FOR EACH OTHER.
IF ANY OF THEM WERE TO FALL INTO THE HANDS OF THE ENEMY...
...THERE'S REALLY NO TELLING HOW FAR SOMEONE MIGHT GO TO SAVE THEM.
OH, HEY.
CAN I GIVE YOU A HAND WITH THAT WHEEL-CHAIR?

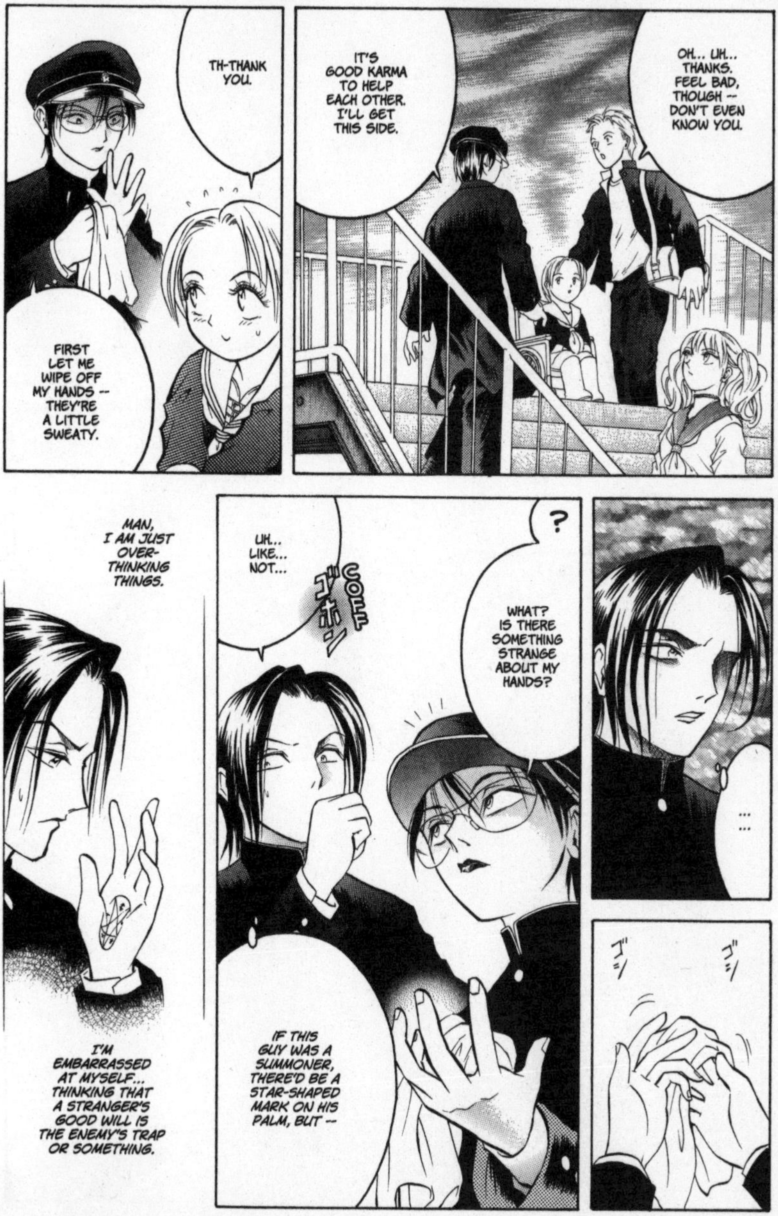

OH... UH... THANKS. FEEL BAD, THOUGH -- DON'T EVEN KNOW YOU.
IT'S GOOD KARMA TO HELP EACH OTHER. I'LL GET THIS SIDE.
TH-THANK YOU.
FIRST LET ME WIPE OFF MY HANDS -- THEY'RE A LITTLE SWEATY.
......
ゴシ
ゴシ
?
WHAT? IS THERE SOMETHING STRANGE ABOUT MY HANDS?
COFF
ゴホン
UH... LIKE... NOT...
IF THIS GUY WAS A SUMMONER, THERE'D BE A STAR-SHAPED MARK ON HIS PALM, BUT --
MAN, I AM JUST OVER-THINKING THINGS.
I'M EMBARRASSED AT MYSELF... THINKING THAT A STRANGER'S GOOD WILL IS THE ENEMY'S TRAP OR SOMETHING.

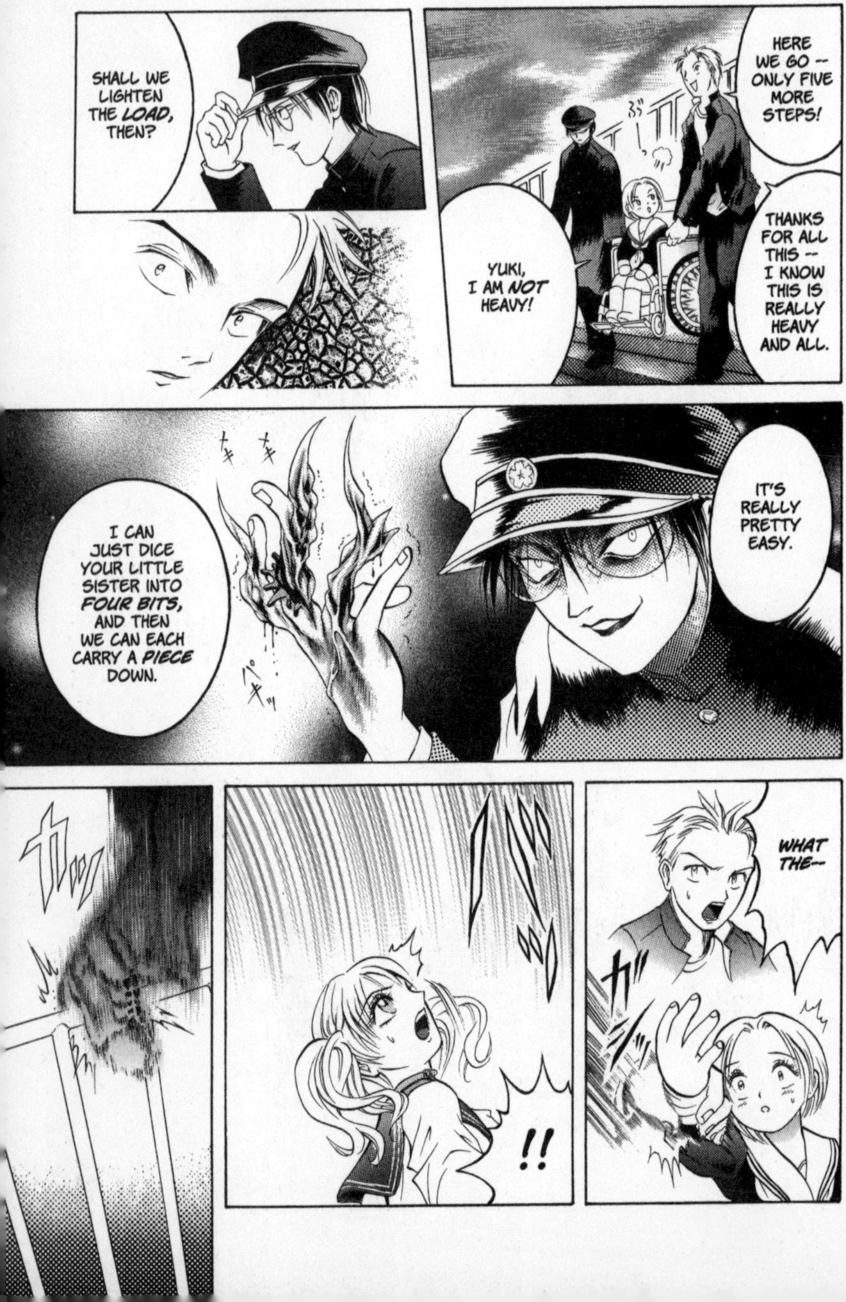
HERE WE GO -- ONLY FIVE MORE STEPS!
ぶ
THANKS FOR ALL THIS -- I KNOW THIS IS REALLY HEAVY AND ALL.
YUKI, I AM NOT HEAVY!
SHALL WE LIGHTEN THE LOAD, THEN?
IT'S REALLY PRETTY EASY.
メキ メキ
I CAN JUST DICE YOUR LITTLE SISTER INTO FOUR BITS, AND THEN WE CAN EACH CARRY A PIECE DOWN.
パキッ
WHAT THE--
!!

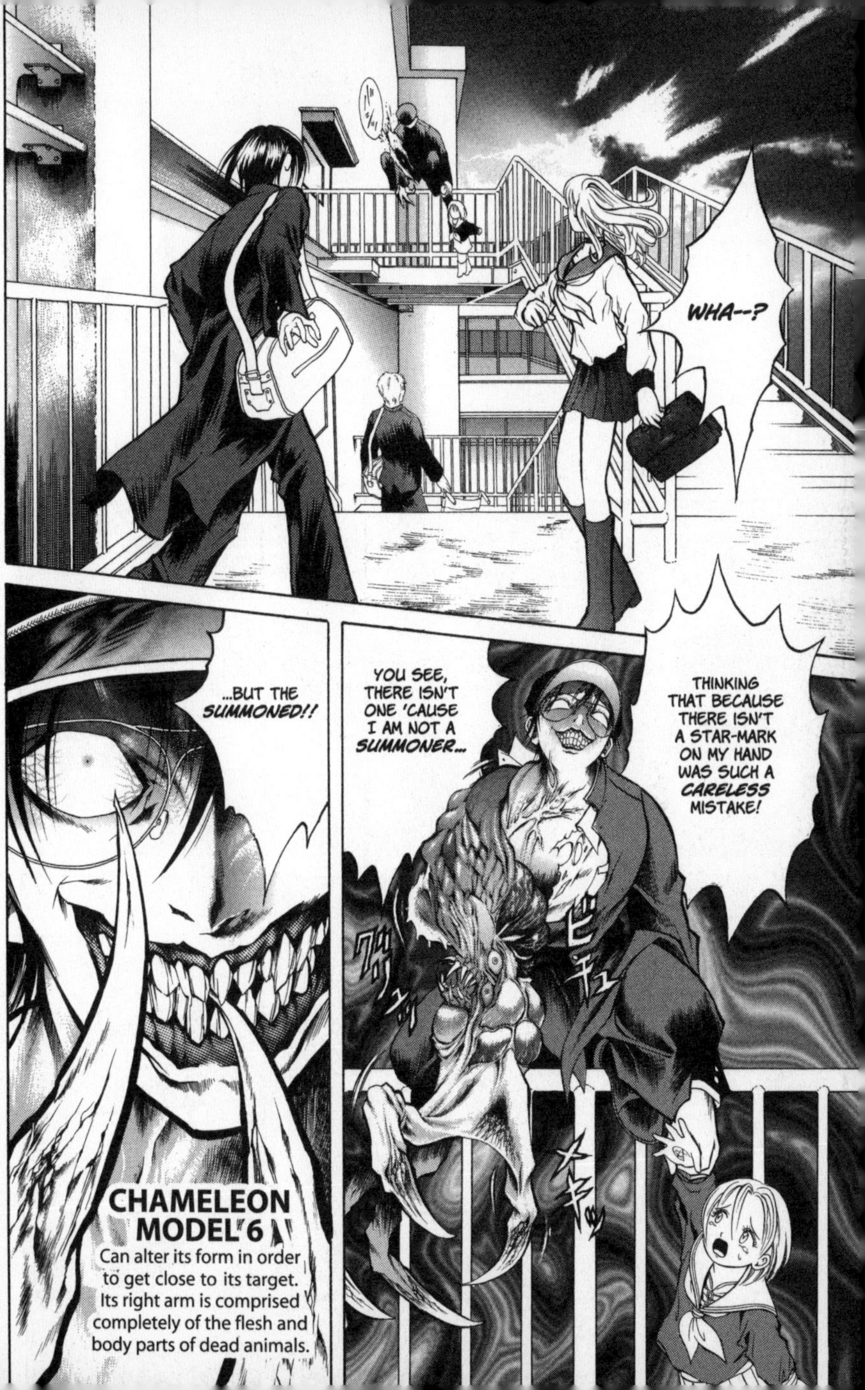
WHA--?
THINKING THAT BECAUSE THERE ISN'T A STAR-MARK ON MY HAND WAS SUCH A CARELESS MISTAKE!
YOU SEE, THERE ISN'T ONE 'CAUSE I AM NOT A SUMMONER...
...BUT THE SUMMONED!!
CHAMELEON MODEL 6
Can alter its form in order to get close to its target. Its right arm is comprised completely of the flesh and body parts of dead animals.

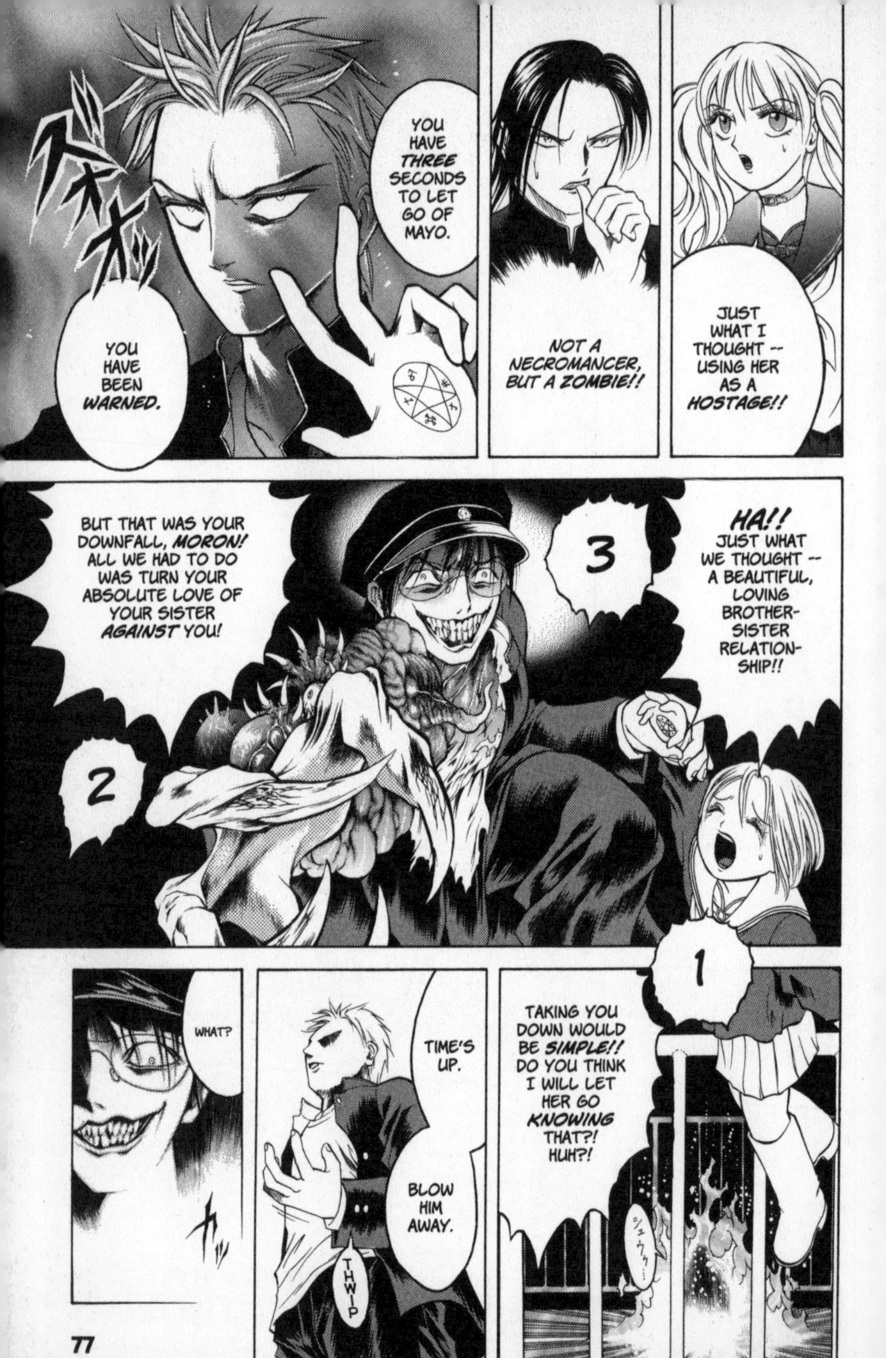

JUST WHAT I THOUGHT -- USING HER AS A HOSTAGE!!
NOT A NECROMANCER, BUT A ZOMBIE!!
YOU HAVE THREE SECONDS TO LET GO OF MAYO.
YOU HAVE BEEN WARNED.
HA!! JUST WHAT WE THOUGHT -- A BEAUTIFUL, LOVING BROTHER-SISTER RELATIONSHIP!!
3
BUT THAT WAS YOUR DOWNFALL, MORON! ALL WE HAD TO DO WAS TURN YOUR ABSOLUTE LOVE OF YOUR SISTER AGAINST YOU!
2
1
TAKING YOU DOWN WOULD BE SIMPLE!! DO YOU THINK I WILL LET HER GO KNOWING THAT?! HUH?!
TIME'S UP.
BLOW HIM AWAY.
THWIP
WHAT?

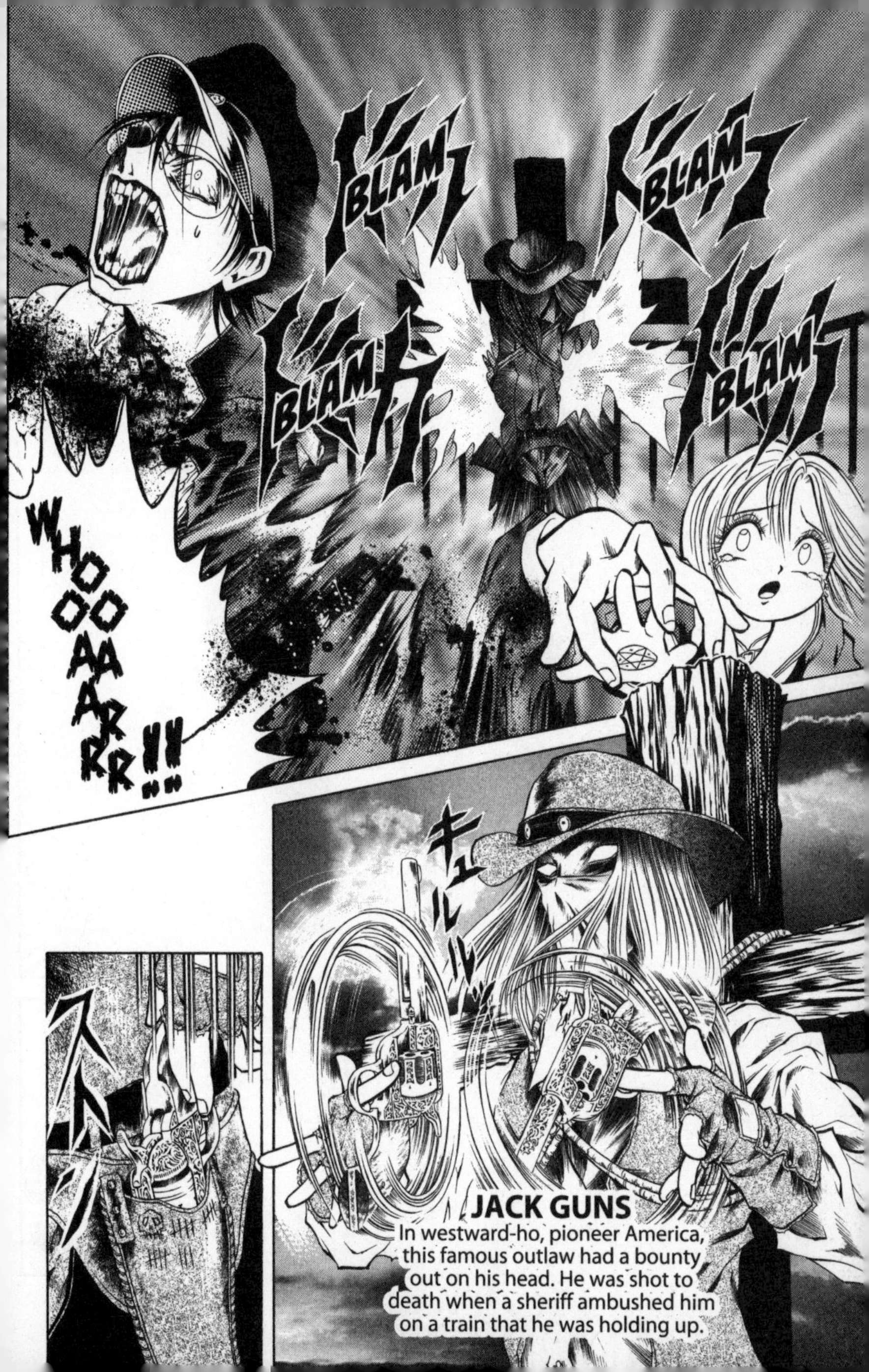
BLAM
BLAM
BLAM
BLAM
WHOOOAARRR!!
キュルルル
JACK GUNS
In westward-ho, pioneer America, this famous outlaw had a bounty out on his head. He was shot to death when a sheriff ambushed him on a train that he was holding up.

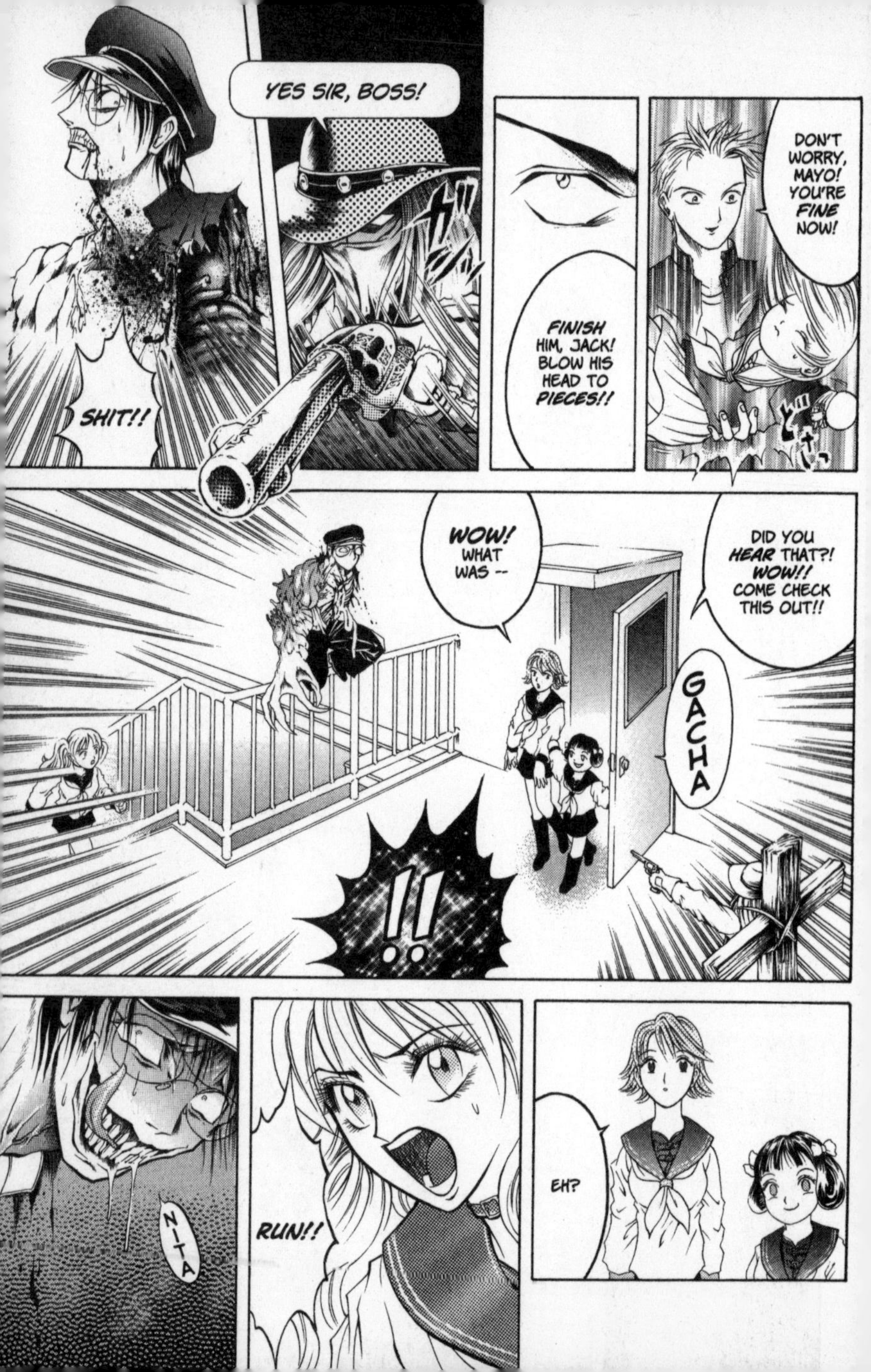
DON'T WORRY, MAYO! YOU'RE FINE NOW!
FINISH HIM, JACK! BLOW HIS HEAD TO PIECES!!
YES SIR, BOSS!
SHIT!!
DID YOU HEAR THAT?! WOW!! COME CHECK THIS OUT!!
GACHA
WOW! WHAT WAS --
!!
EH?
RUN!!
NITA

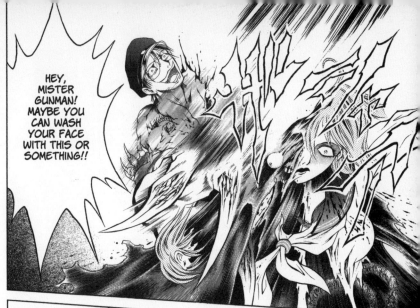

HEY, MISTER GUNMAN! MAYBE YOU CAN WASH YOUR FACE WITH THIS OR SOMETHING!!

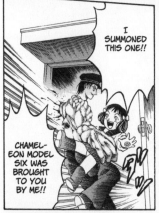

I SUMMONED THIS ONE!!

CHAMEL-EON MODEL SIX WAS BROUGHT TO YOU BY ME!!

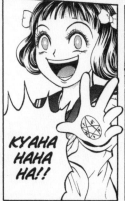

KYAHA HAHA HA!!

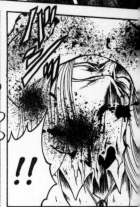

!!

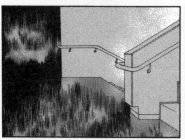

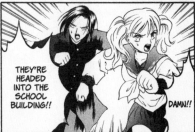

THEY'RE HEADED INTO THE SCHOOL BUILDING!!

DAMN!!

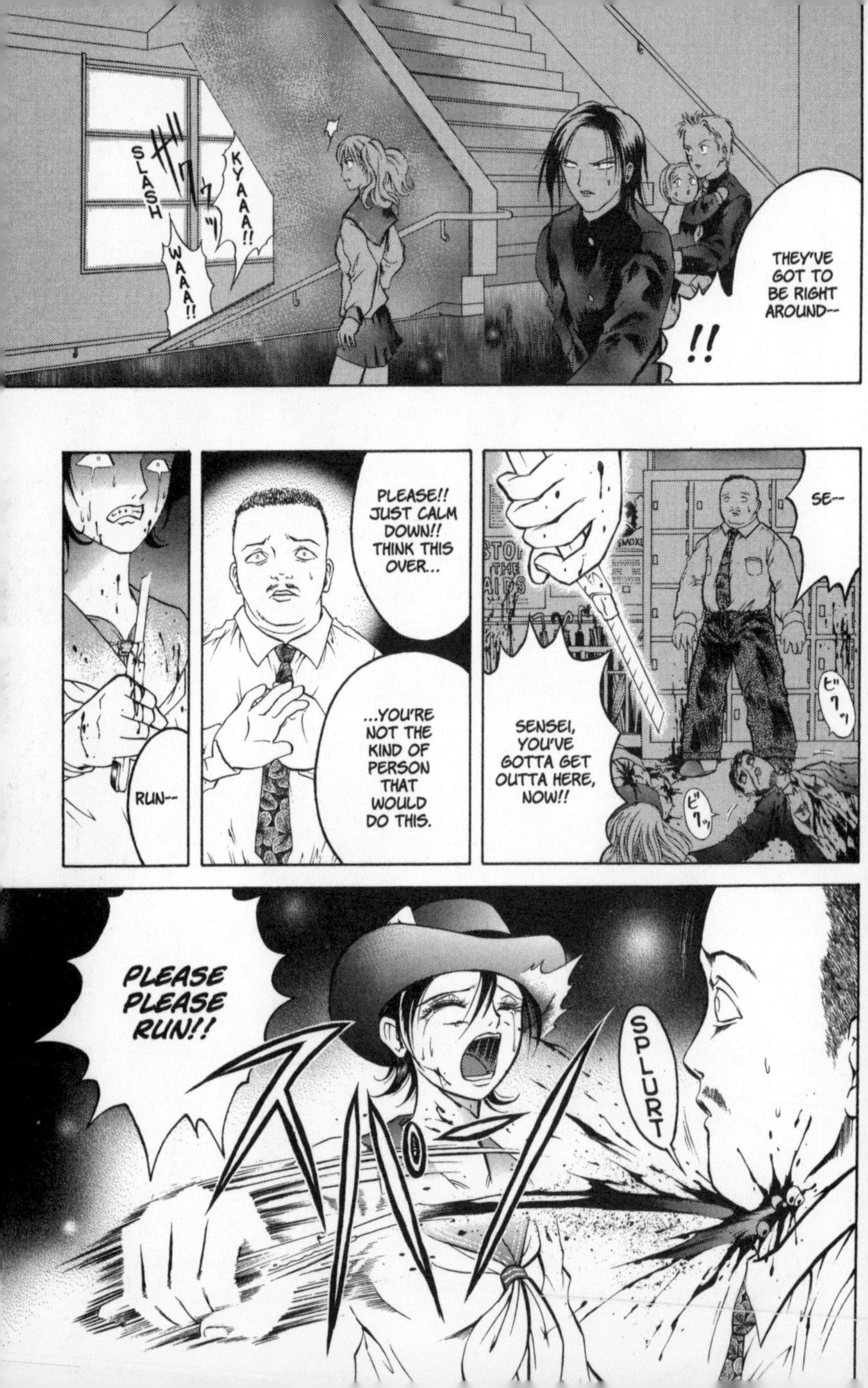
THEY'VE GOT TO BE RIGHT AROUND--
!!
KYAAAA!!
SLASH
WAAAA!!
SE--
SENSEI, YOU'VE GOTTA GET OUTTA HERE, NOW!!
PLEASE!! JUST CALM DOWN!! THINK THIS OVER...
...YOU'RE NOT THE KIND OF PERSON THAT WOULD DO THIS.
RUN--
SPLURT
PLEASE PLEASE RUN!!

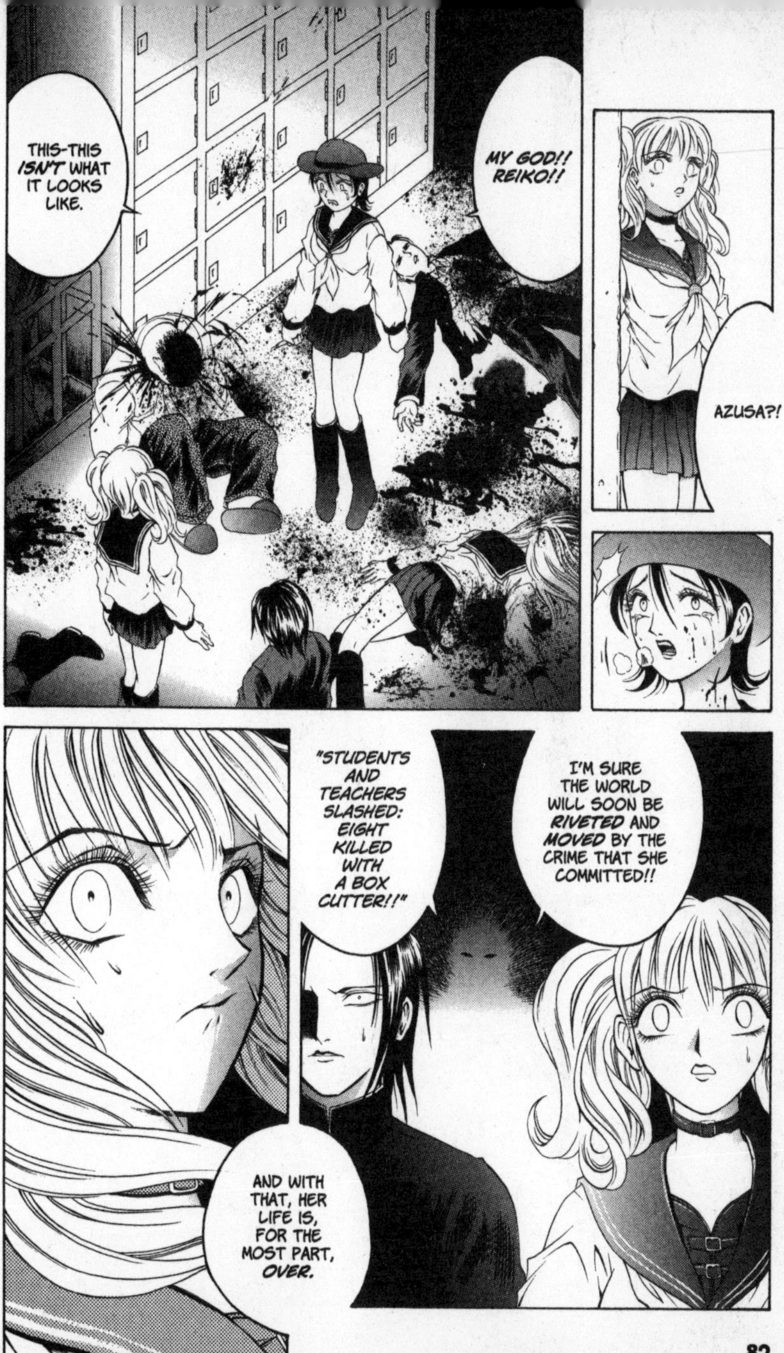
AZUSA?!
MY GOD!! REIKO!!
THIS-THIS *ISN'T* WHAT IT LOOKS LIKE.
I'M SURE THE WORLD WILL SOON BE *RIVETED* AND *MOVED* BY THE CRIME THAT SHE COMMITTED!!
"STUDENTS AND TEACHERS SLASHED: EIGHT KILLED WITH A BOX CUTTER!!"
AND WITH THAT, HER LIFE IS, FOR THE MOST PART, *OVER.*

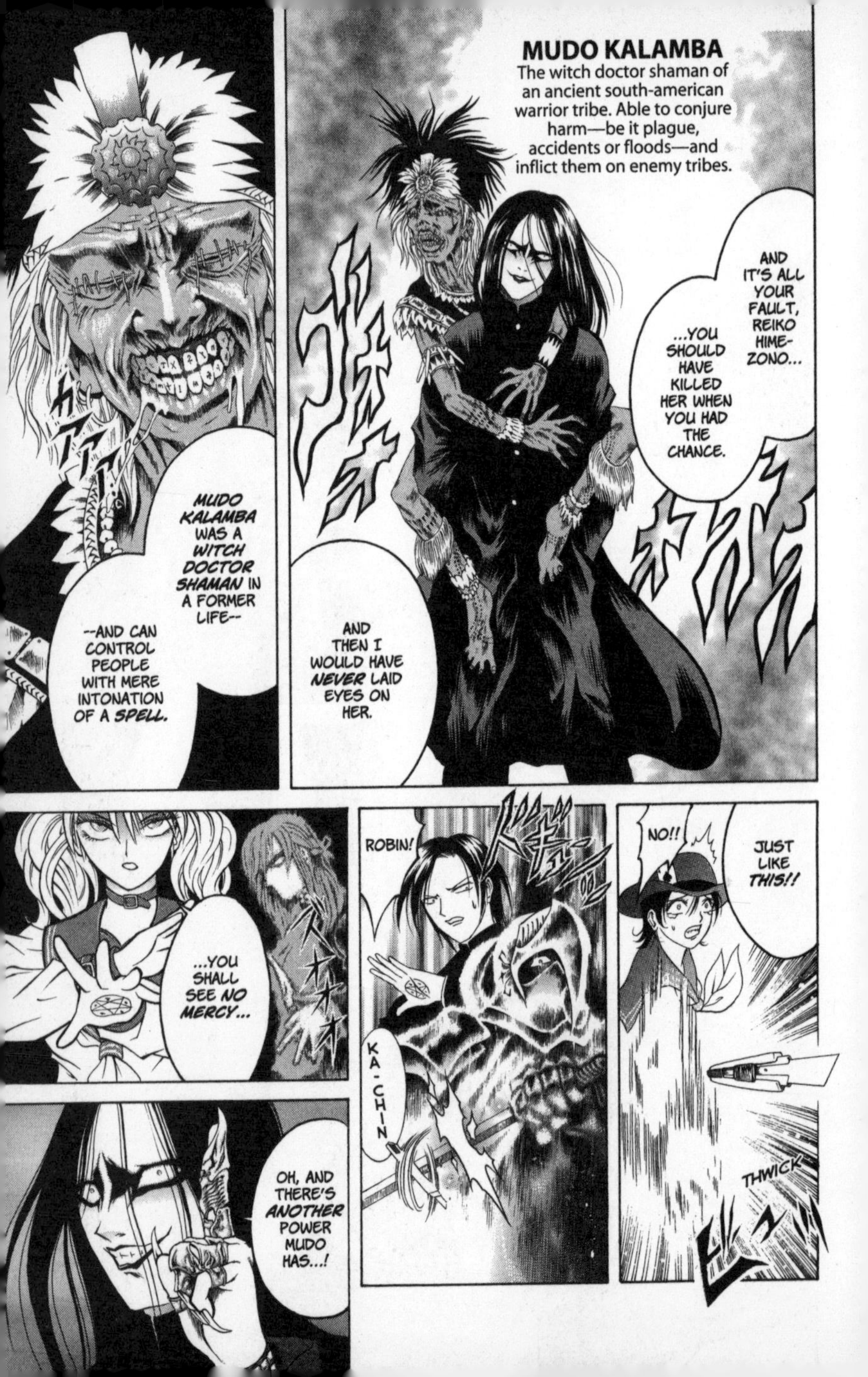
MUDO KALAMBA
The witch doctor shaman of an ancient south-american warrior tribe. Able to conjure harm—be it plague, accidents or floods—and inflict them on enemy tribes.
AND IT'S ALL YOUR FAULT, REIKO HIME-ZONO...
...YOU SHOULD HAVE KILLED HER WHEN YOU HAD THE CHANCE.
AND THEN I WOULD HAVE NEVER LAID EYES ON HER.
MUDO KALAMBA WAS A WITCH DOCTOR SHAMAN IN A FORMER LIFE--
--AND CAN CONTROL PEOPLE WITH MERE INTONATION OF A SPELL.
JUST LIKE THIS!!
NO!!
THWICK
ROBIN!
KA-CHIN
...YOU SHALL SEE NO MERCY...
OH, AND THERE'S ANOTHER POWER MUDO HAS...!

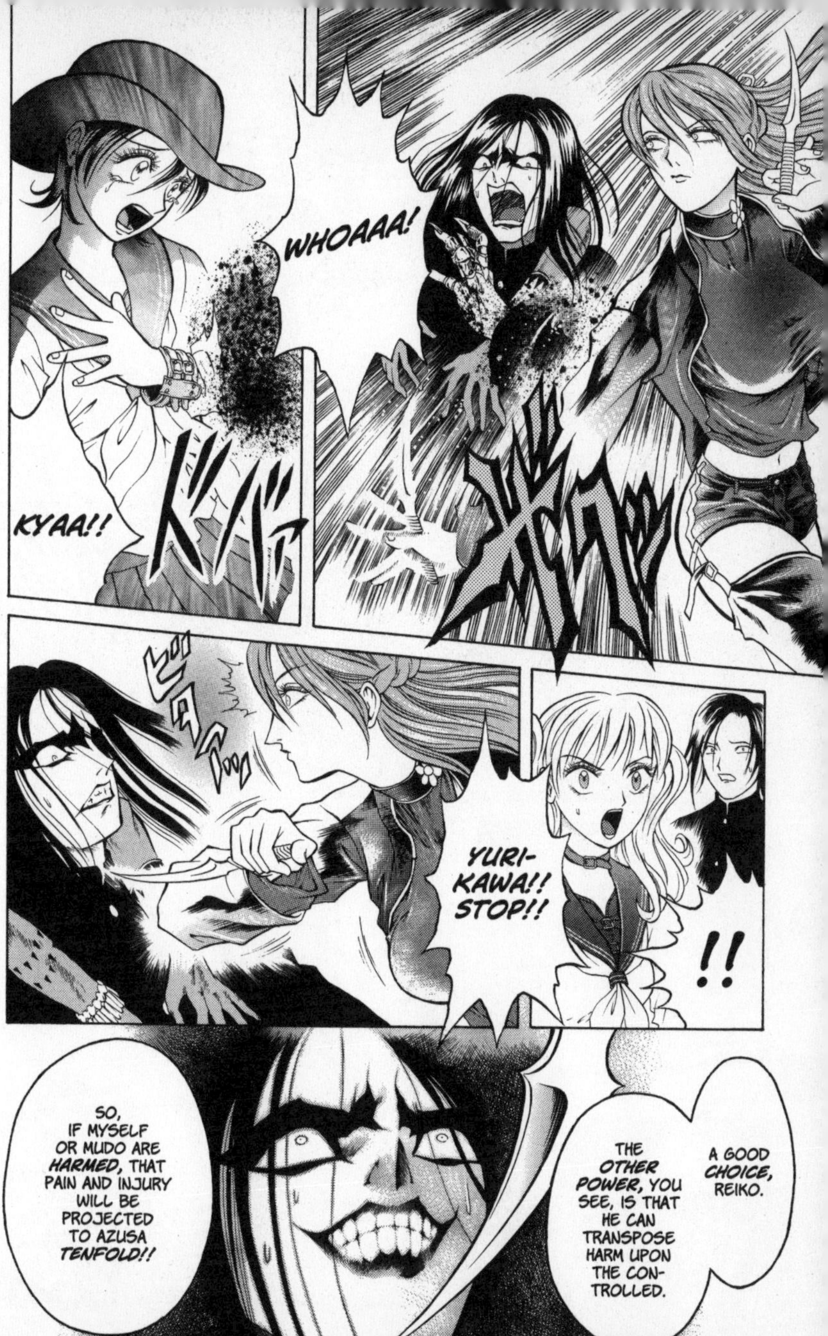
WHOAAA!
KYAA!!
YURI-KAWA!! STOP!!
!!
A GOOD CHOICE, REIKO.
THE OTHER POWER, YOU SEE, IS THAT HE CAN TRANSPOSE HARM UPON THE CON-TROLLED.
SO, IF MYSELF OR MUDO ARE HARMED, THAT PAIN AND INJURY WILL BE PROJECTED TO AZUSA TENFOLD!!

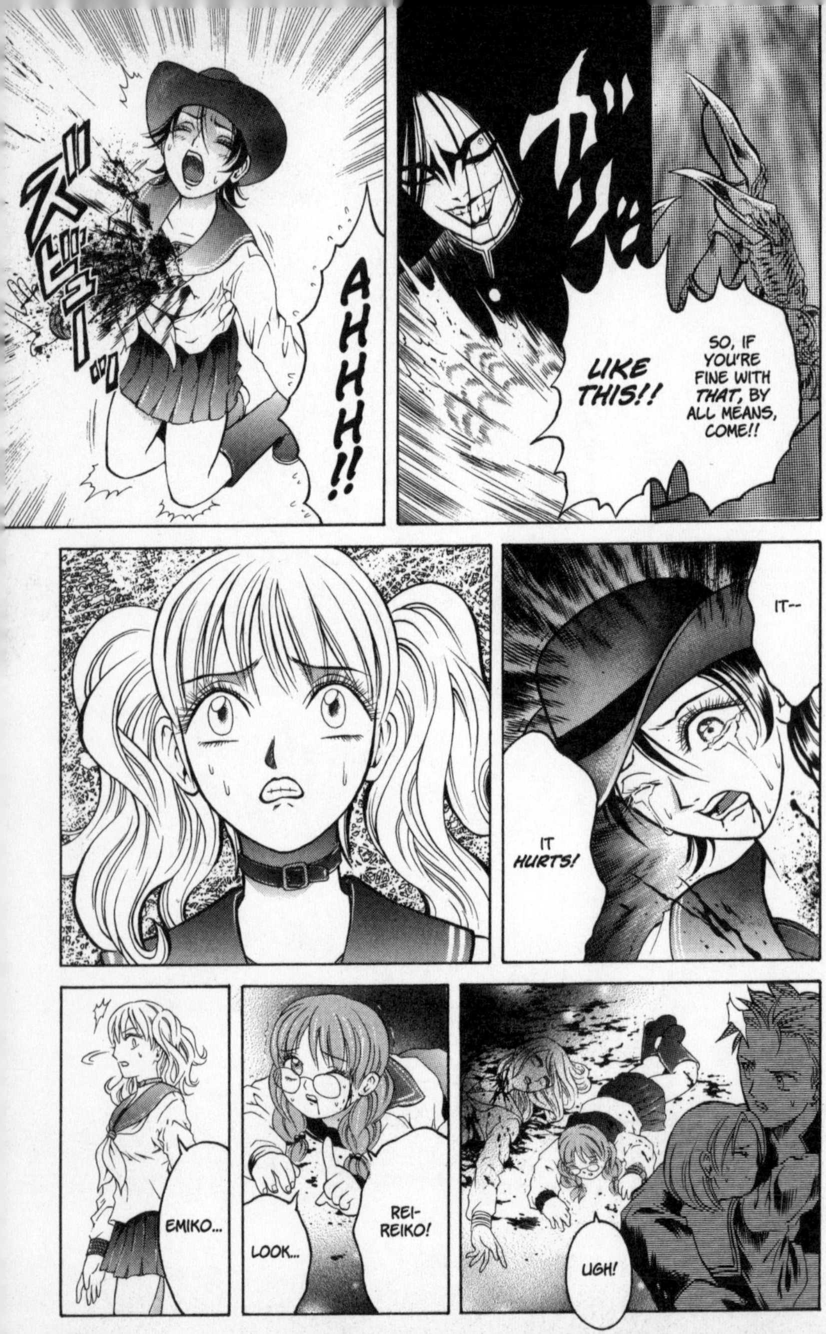
SO, IF YOU'RE FINE WITH *THAT*, BY ALL MEANS, COME!!
LIKE THIS!!
AHHHH!!
IT--
IT *HURTS!*
UGH!
REI-REIKO!
LOOK...
EMIKO...

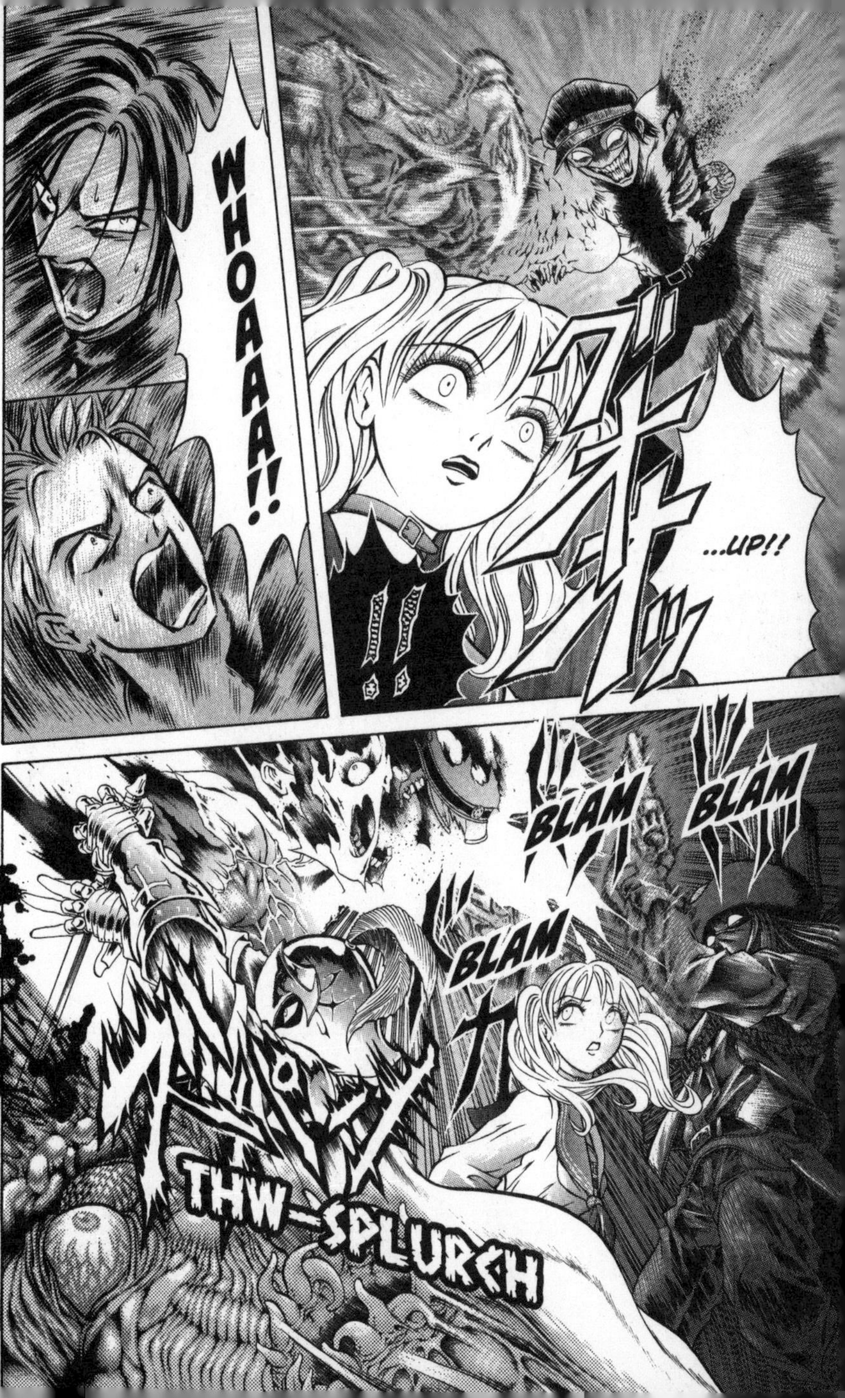
...UP!!
!!
WHOAAAA!!
BLAM
BLAM
BLAM
THW-SPLURCH

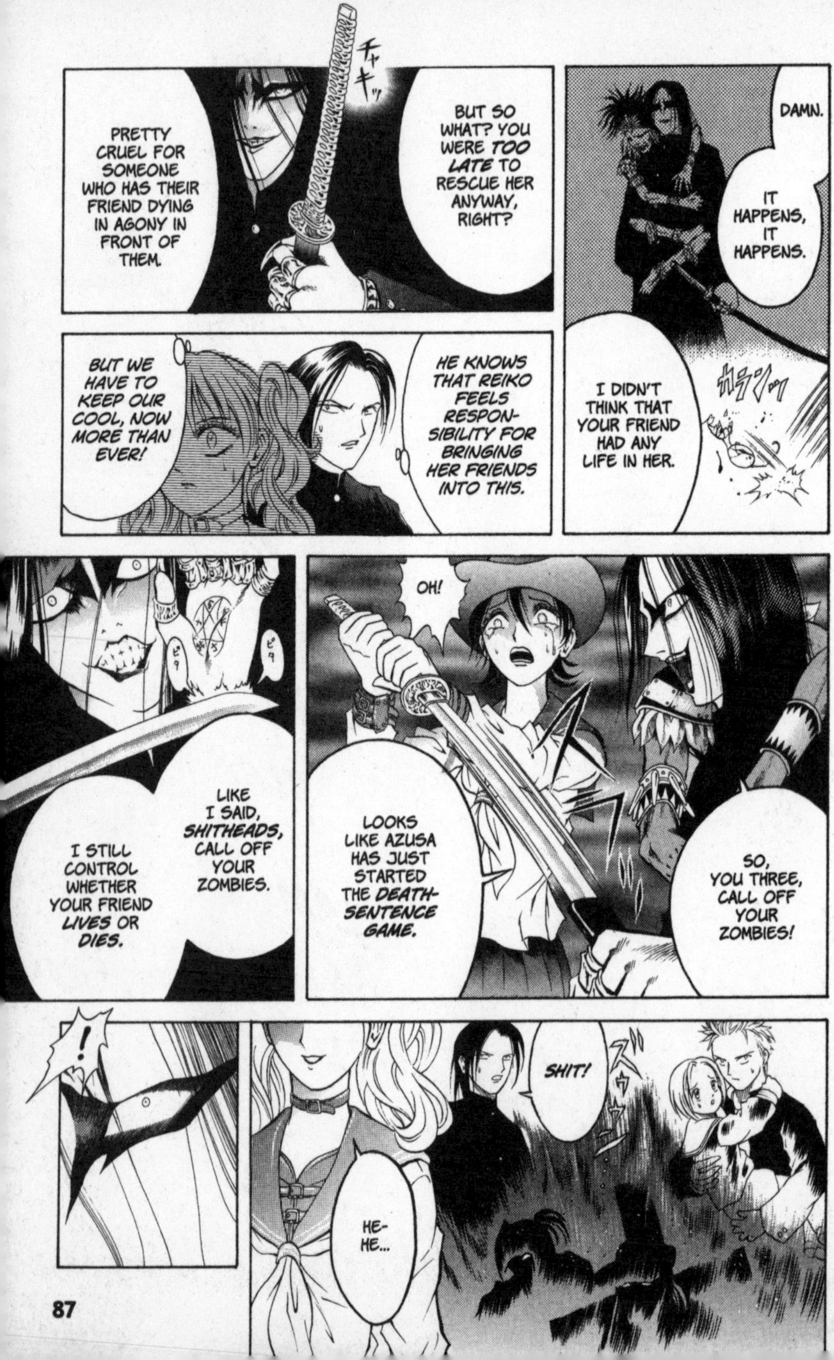
DAMN.
IT HAPPENS, IT HAPPENS.
I DIDN'T THINK THAT YOUR FRIEND HAD ANY LIFE IN HER.
チャキッ
BUT SO WHAT? YOU WERE *TOO LATE* TO RESCUE HER ANYWAY, RIGHT?
PRETTY CRUEL FOR SOMEONE WHO HAS THEIR FRIEND DYING IN AGONY IN FRONT OF THEM.
HE KNOWS THAT REIKO FEELS RESPON-SIBILITY FOR BRINGING HER FRIENDS INTO THIS.
BUT WE HAVE TO KEEP OUR COOL, NOW MORE THAN EVER!
OH!
SO, YOU THREE, CALL OFF YOUR ZOMBIES!
LOOKS LIKE AZUSA HAS JUST STARTED THE *DEATH-SENTENCE GAME.*
ピタ
ピタ
LIKE I SAID, *SHITHEADS,* CALL OFF YOUR ZOMBIES.
I STILL CONTROL WHETHER YOUR FRIEND *LIVES* OR *DIES.*
SHIT!
HE-HE...
!

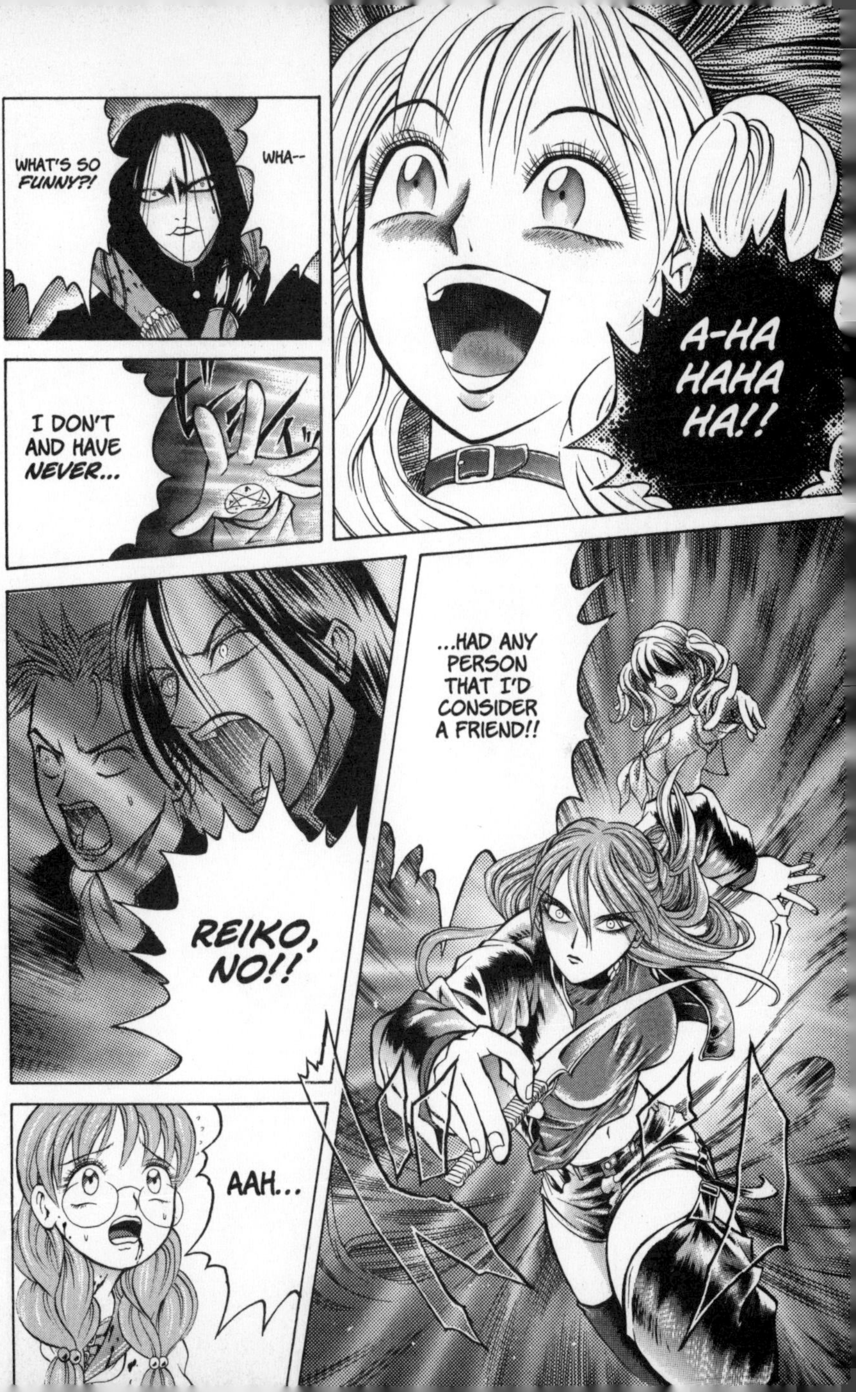
A-HA HAHA HA!!
WHA--
WHAT'S SO FUNNY?!
I DON'T AND HAVE NEVER...
...HAD ANY PERSON THAT I'D CONSIDER A FRIEND!!
REIKO, NO!!
AAH...

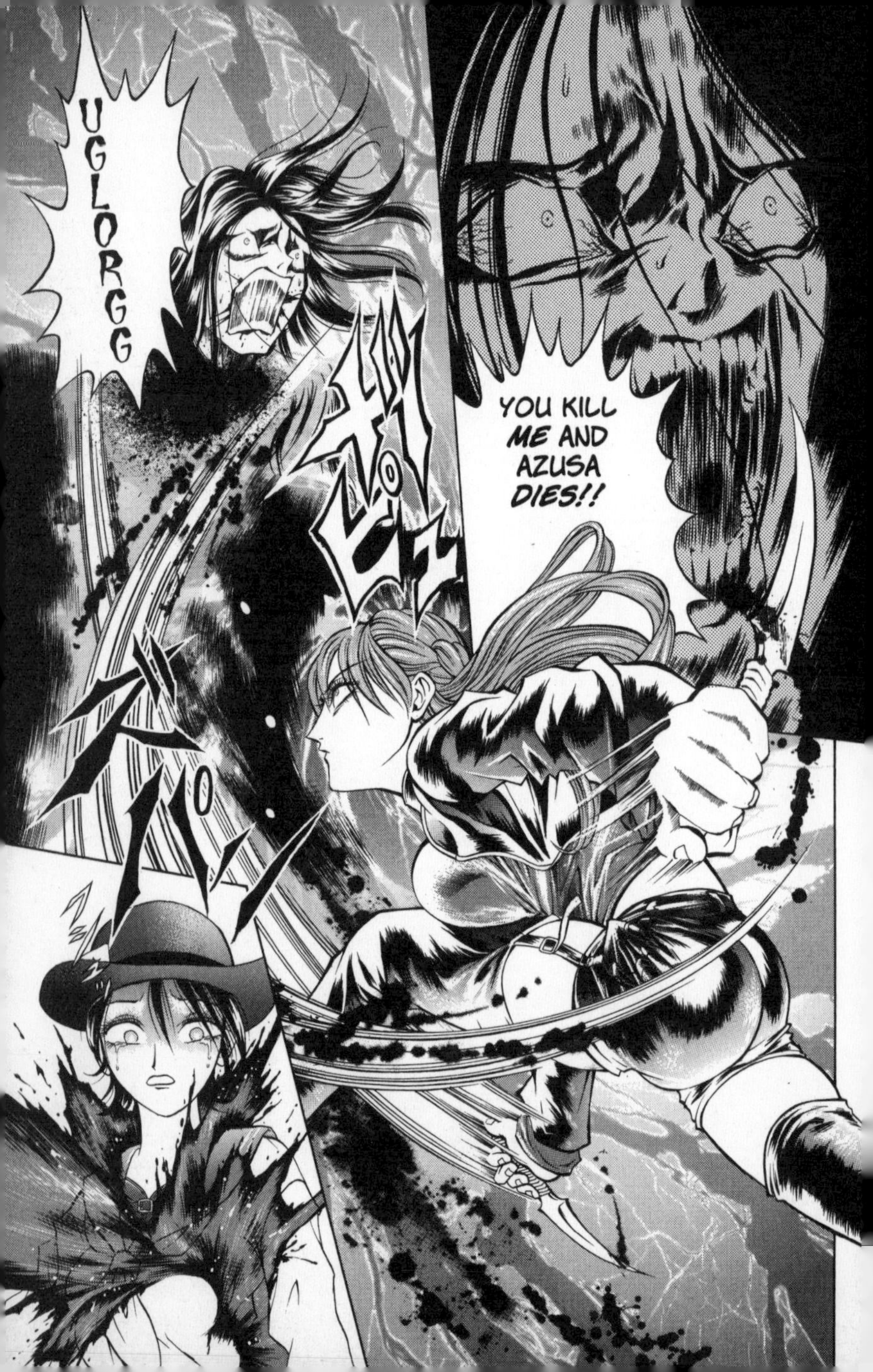
YOU KILL ME AND AZUSA DIES!!
UGLORGG

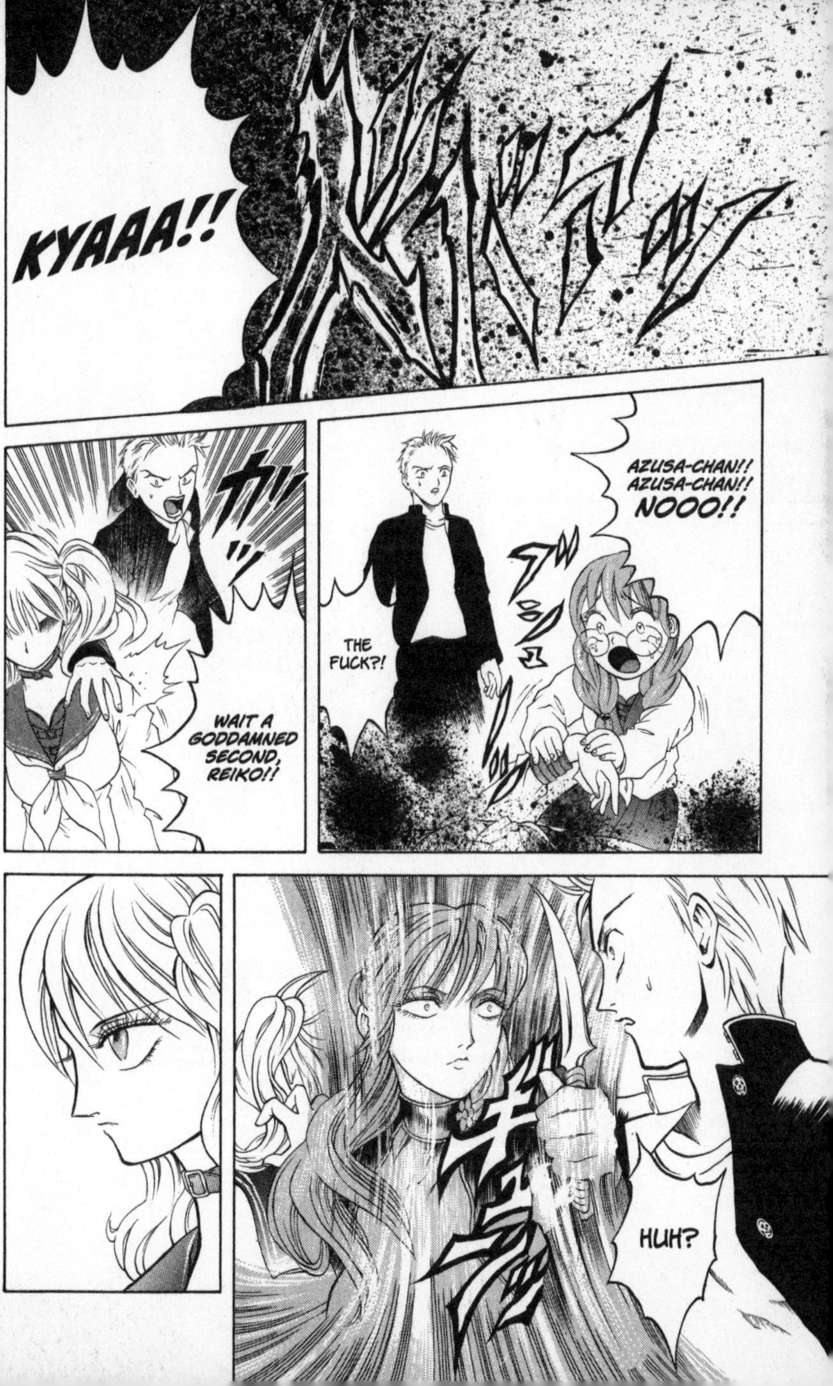
KYAAA!!
AZUSA-CHAN!! AZUSA-CHAN!! NOOO!!
THE FUCK?!
WAIT A GODDAMNED SECOND, REIKO!!
HUH?

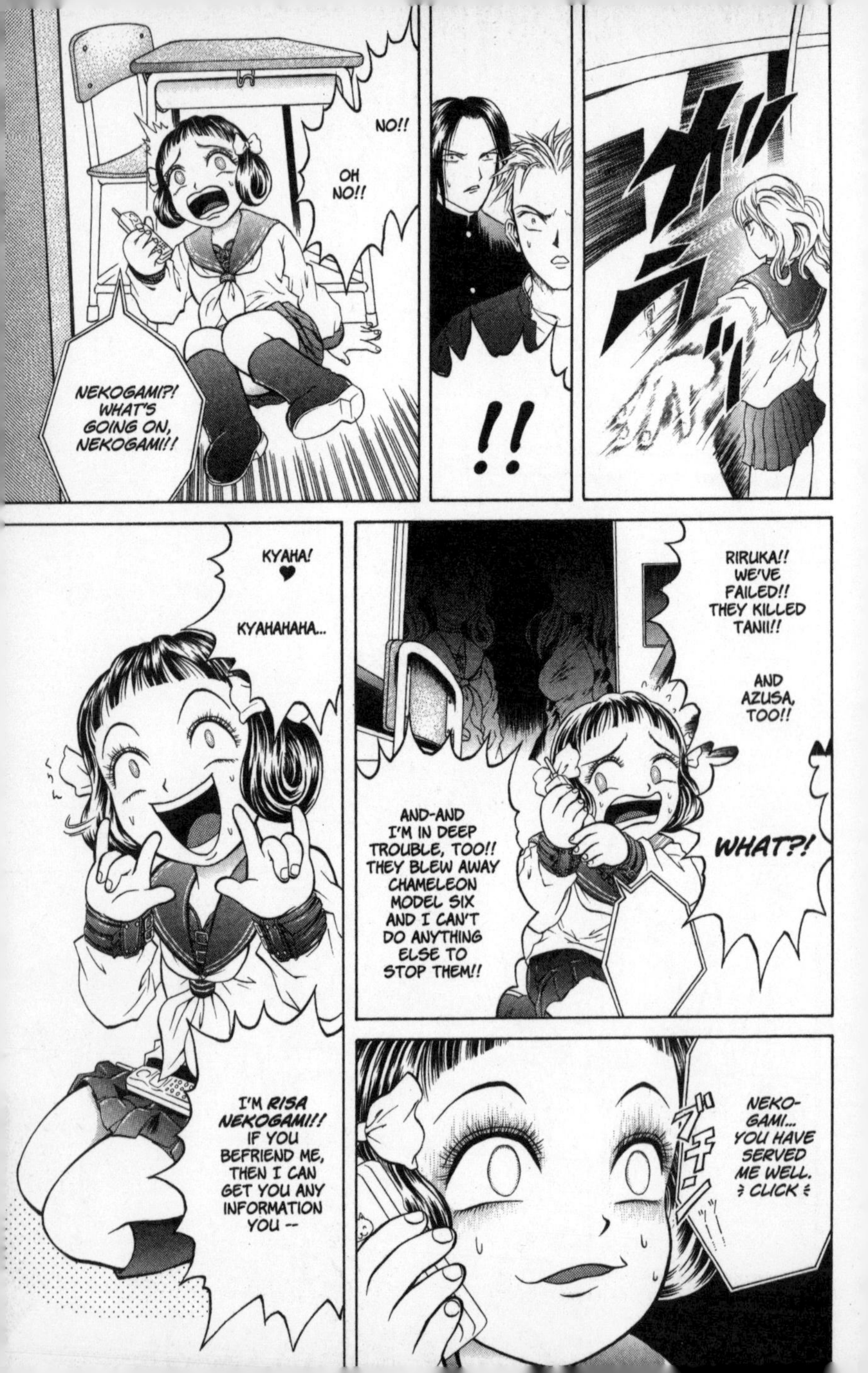
!!
NO!!
OH NO!!
NEKOGAMI?! WHAT'S GOING ON, NEKOGAMI!!
RIRUKA!! WE'VE FAILED!! THEY KILLED TANI!!
AND AZUSA, TOO!!
AND-AND I'M IN DEEP TROUBLE, TOO!! THEY BLEW AWAY CHAMELEON MODEL SIX AND I CAN'T DO ANYTHING ELSE TO STOP THEM!!
WHAT?!
NEKO-GAMI... YOU HAVE SERVED ME WELL.
≷ CLICK ≶
KYAHA! ♥
KYAHAHAHA...
I'M RISA NEKOGAMI!! IF YOU BEFRIEND ME, THEN I CAN GET YOU ANY INFORMATION YOU --

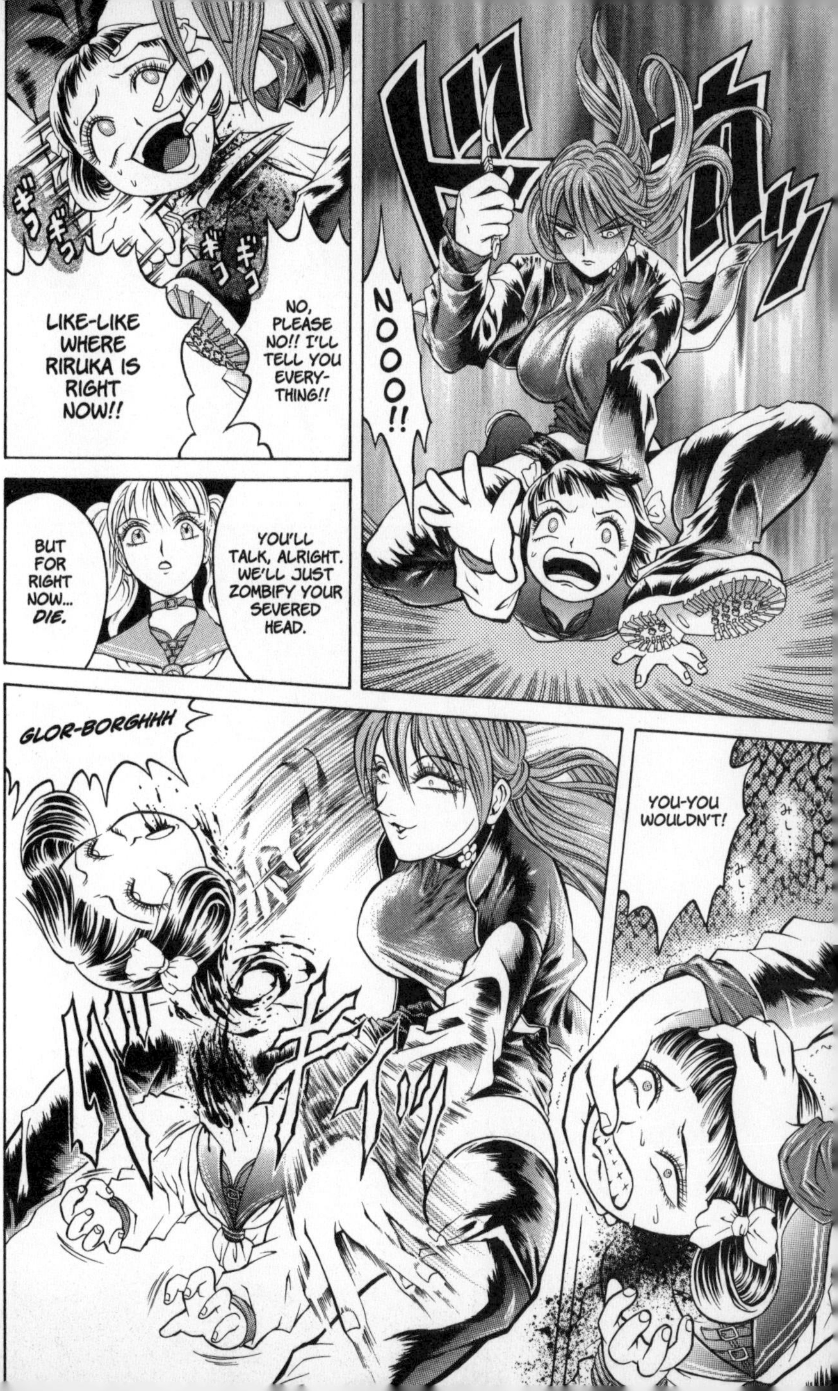
NOOOO!!
NO, PLEASE NO!! I'LL TELL YOU EVERY-THING!!
LIKE-LIKE WHERE RIRUKA IS RIGHT NOW!!
YOU'LL TALK, ALRIGHT. WE'LL JUST ZOMBIFY YOUR SEVERED HEAD.
BUT FOR RIGHT NOW... *DIE.*
YOU-YOU WOULDN'T!
GLOR-BORGHHH

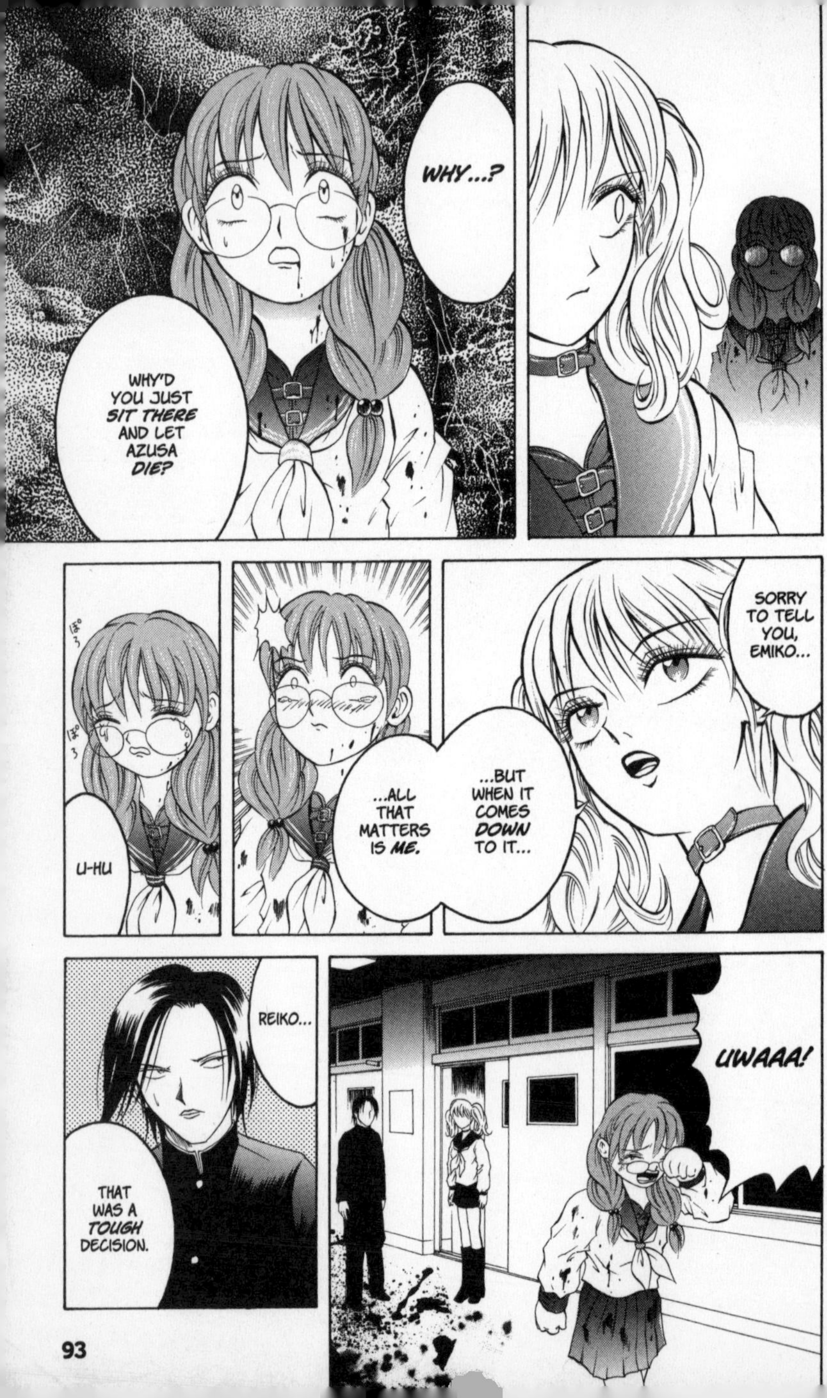

WHY...?
WHY'D YOU JUST SIT THERE AND LET AZUSA DIE?
SORRY TO TELL YOU, EMIKO...
...BUT WHEN IT COMES DOWN TO IT...
...ALL THAT MATTERS IS ME.
ぽろ
ぽろ
U-HU
UWAAA!
REIKO...
THAT WAS A TOUGH DECISION.

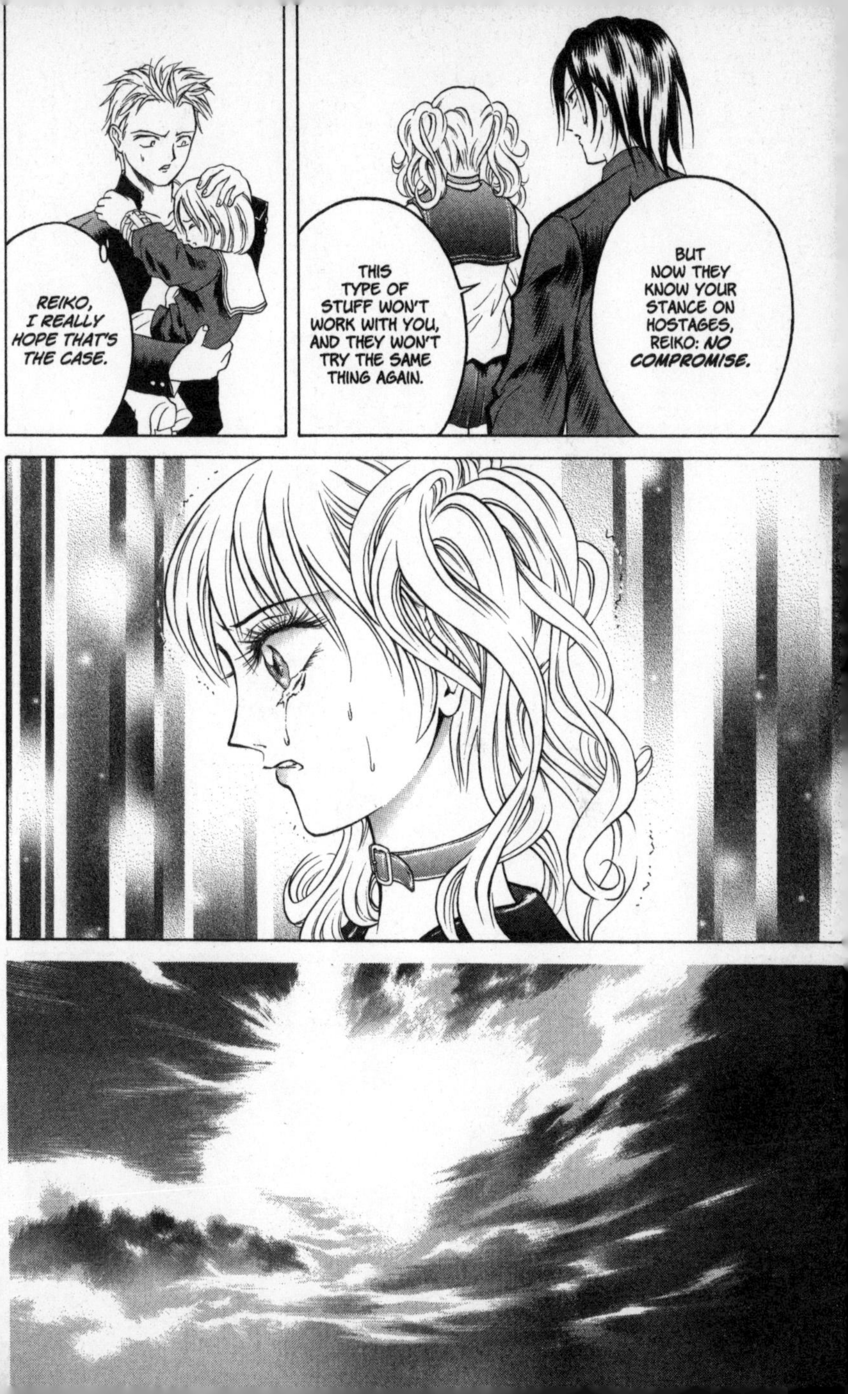
BUT NOW THEY KNOW YOUR STANCE ON HOSTAGES, REIKO: *NO COMPROMISE.*
THIS TYPE OF STUFF WON'T WORK WITH YOU, AND THEY WON'T TRY THE SAME THING AGAIN.
REIKO, I REALLY HOPE THAT'S THE CASE.

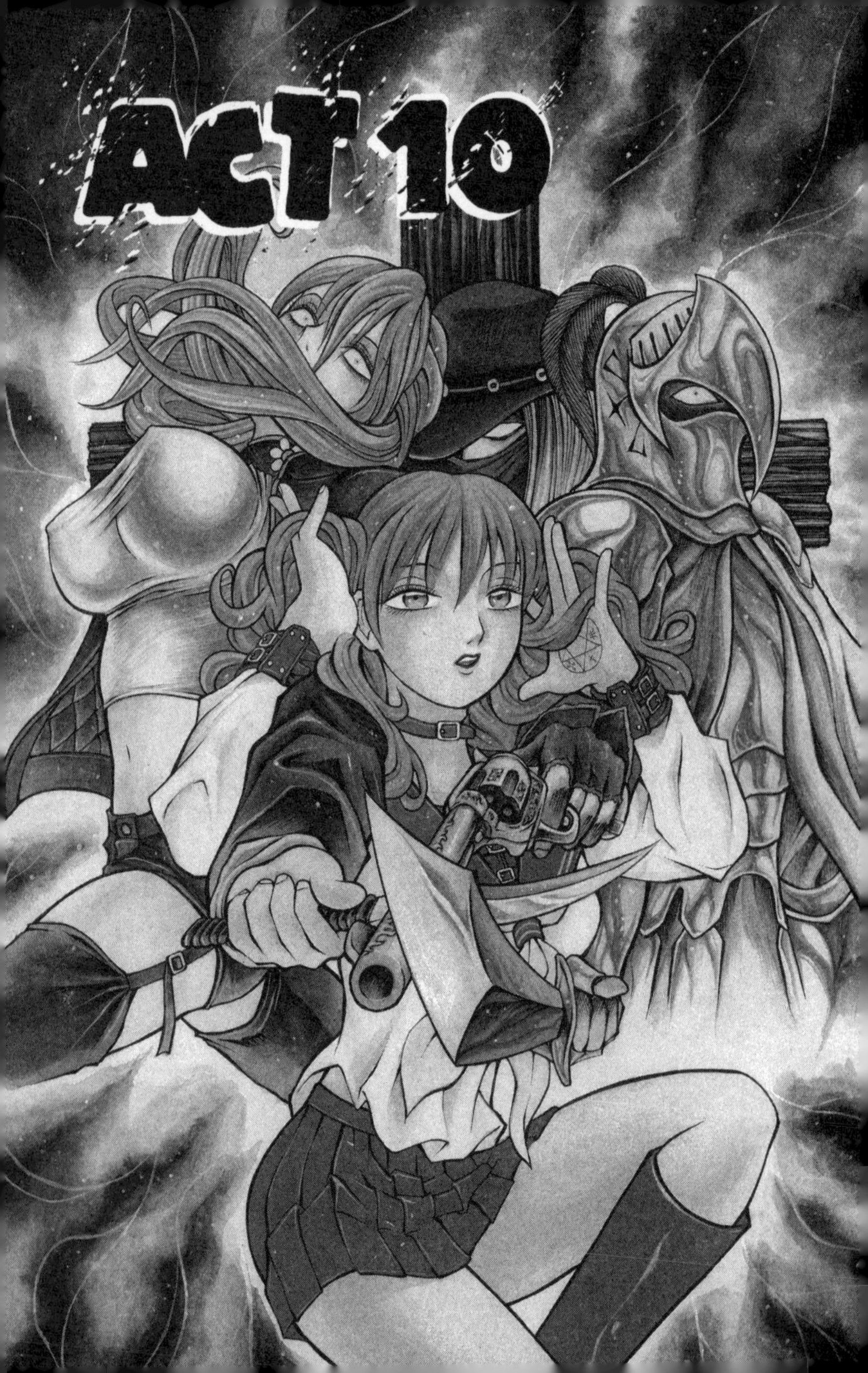
ACT 10

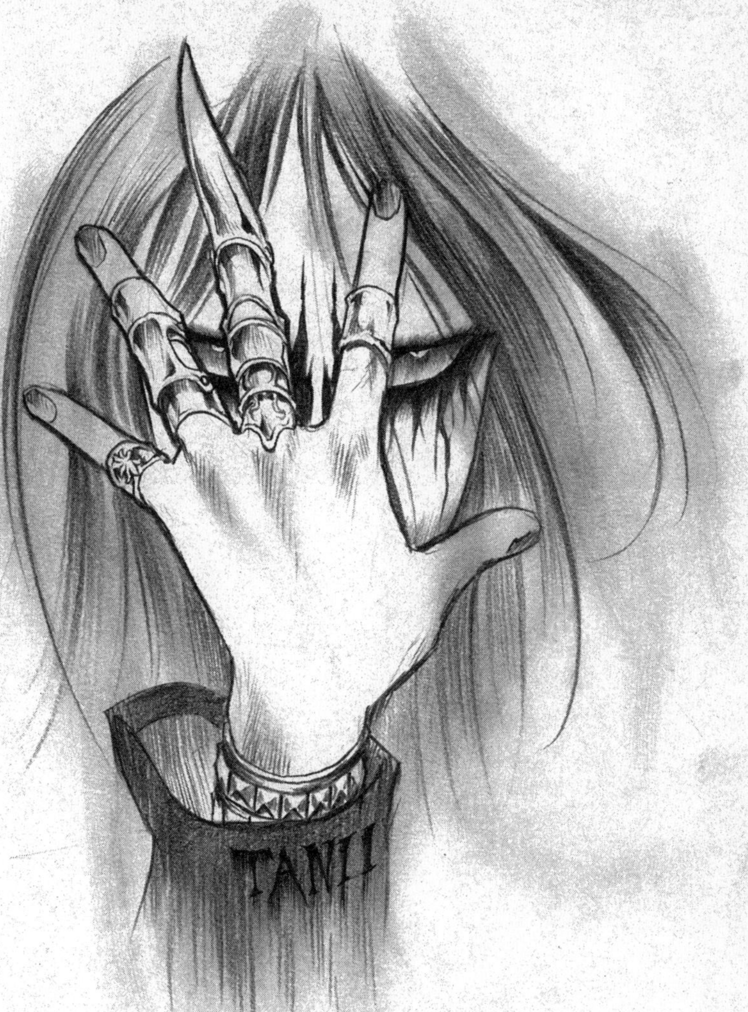
TANII

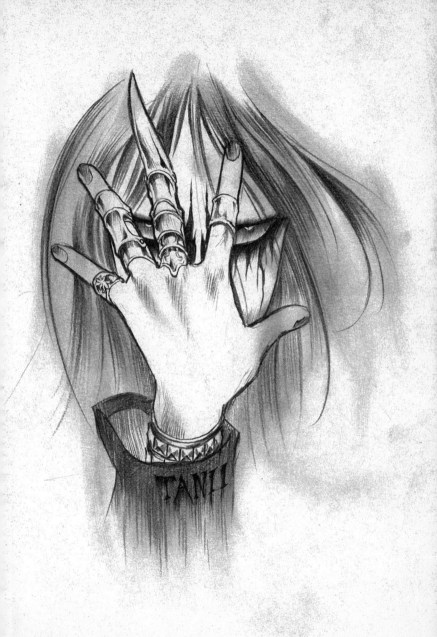

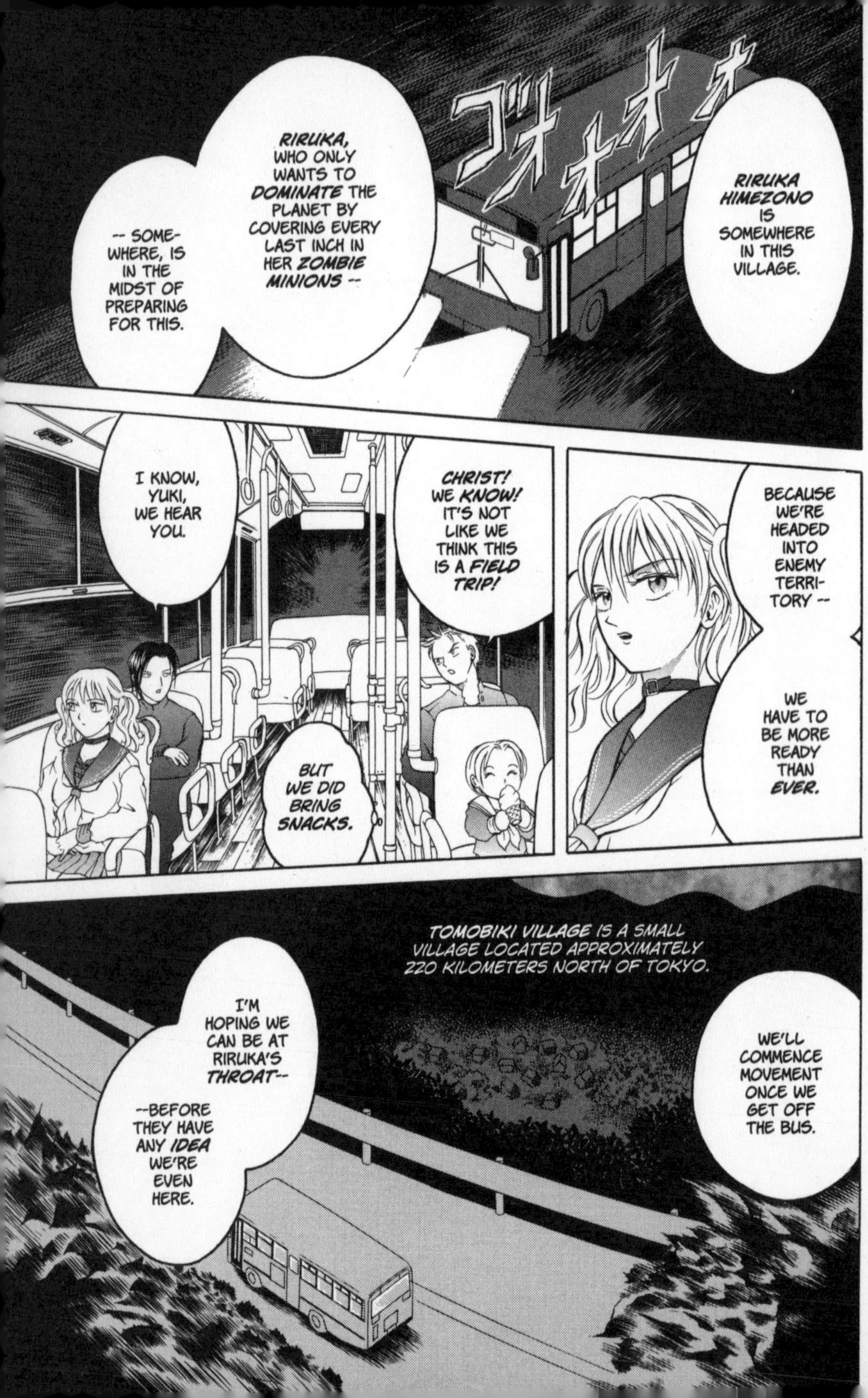
ゴオオオオ
RIRUKA HIMEZONO IS SOMEWHERE IN THIS VILLAGE.
RIRUKA, WHO ONLY WANTS TO DOMINATE THE PLANET BY COVERING EVERY LAST INCH IN HER ZOMBIE MINIONS --
-- SOMEWHERE, IS IN THE MIDST OF PREPARING FOR THIS.
BECAUSE WE'RE HEADED INTO ENEMY TERRITORY --
WE HAVE TO BE MORE READY THAN EVER.
CHRIST! WE KNOW! IT'S NOT LIKE WE THINK THIS IS A FIELD TRIP!
I KNOW, YUKI, WE HEAR YOU.
BUT WE DID BRING SNACKS.
TOMOBIKI VILLAGE IS A SMALL VILLAGE LOCATED APPROXIMATELY 220 KILOMETERS NORTH OF TOKYO.
WE'LL COMMENCE MOVEMENT ONCE WE GET OFF THE BUS.
I'M HOPING WE CAN BE AT RIRUKA'S THROAT--
--BEFORE THEY HAVE ANY IDEA WE'RE EVEN HERE.

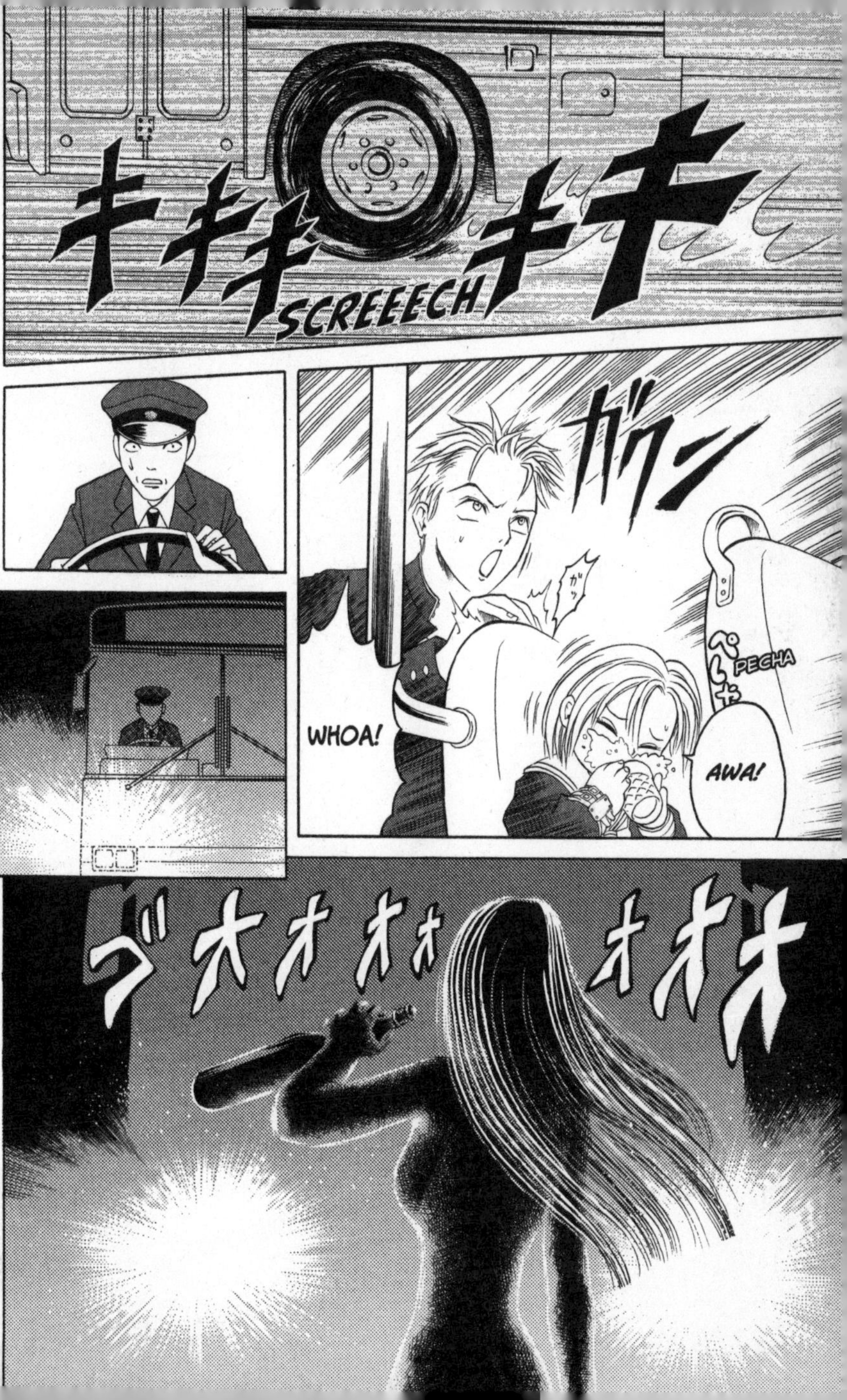
キキキキキ
SCREEECH
ガクン
ガッ
ぺしゃ
PECHA
AWA!
WHOA!
ゴオオオォ
オオオ

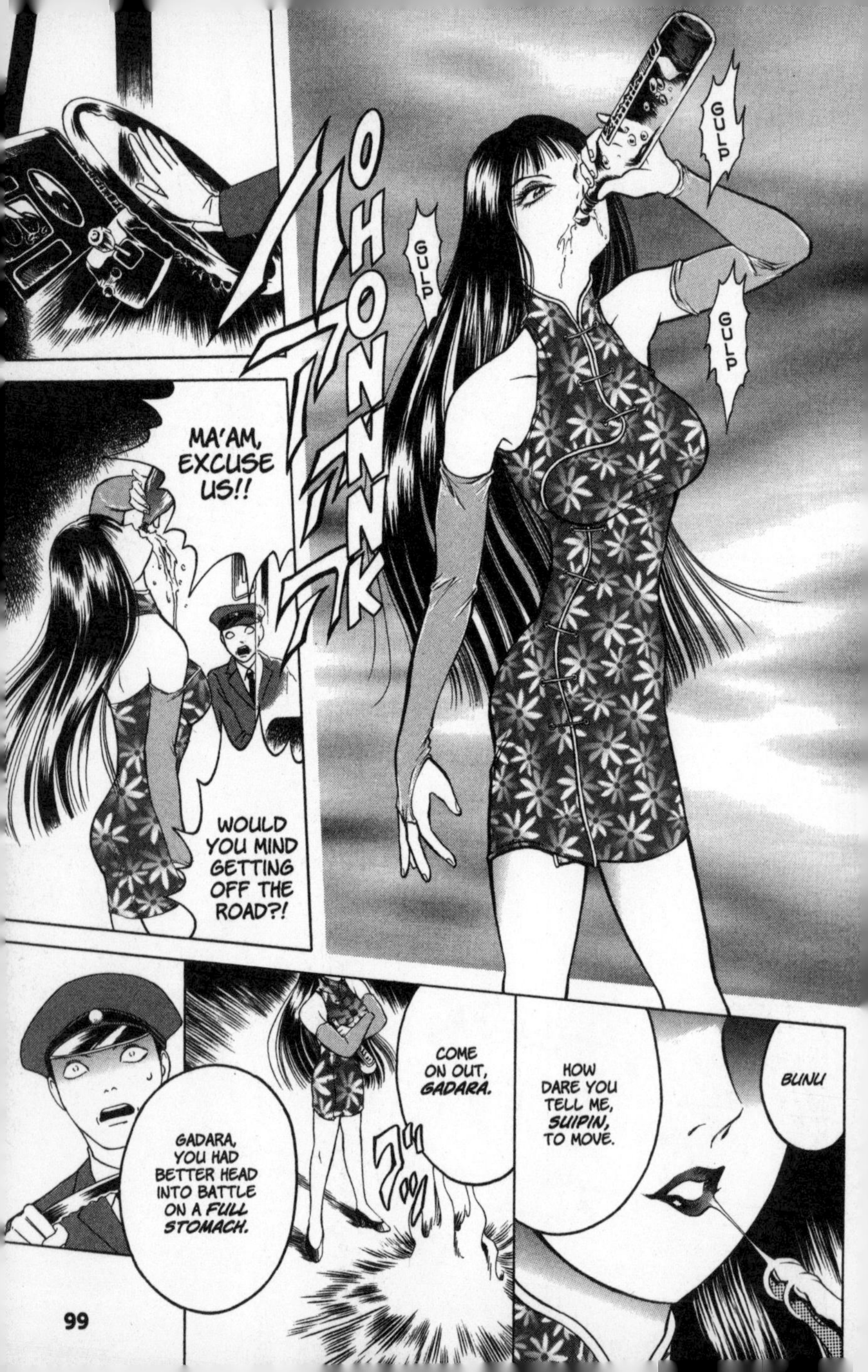
GULP
GULP
GULP
OHONNNK
MA'AM, EXCUSE US!!
WOULD YOU MIND GETTING OFF THE ROAD?!
BUNU
HOW DARE YOU TELL ME, *SUIPIN*, TO MOVE.
COME ON OUT, *GADARA.*
GADARA, YOU HAD BETTER HEAD INTO BATTLE ON A *FULL STOMACH.*

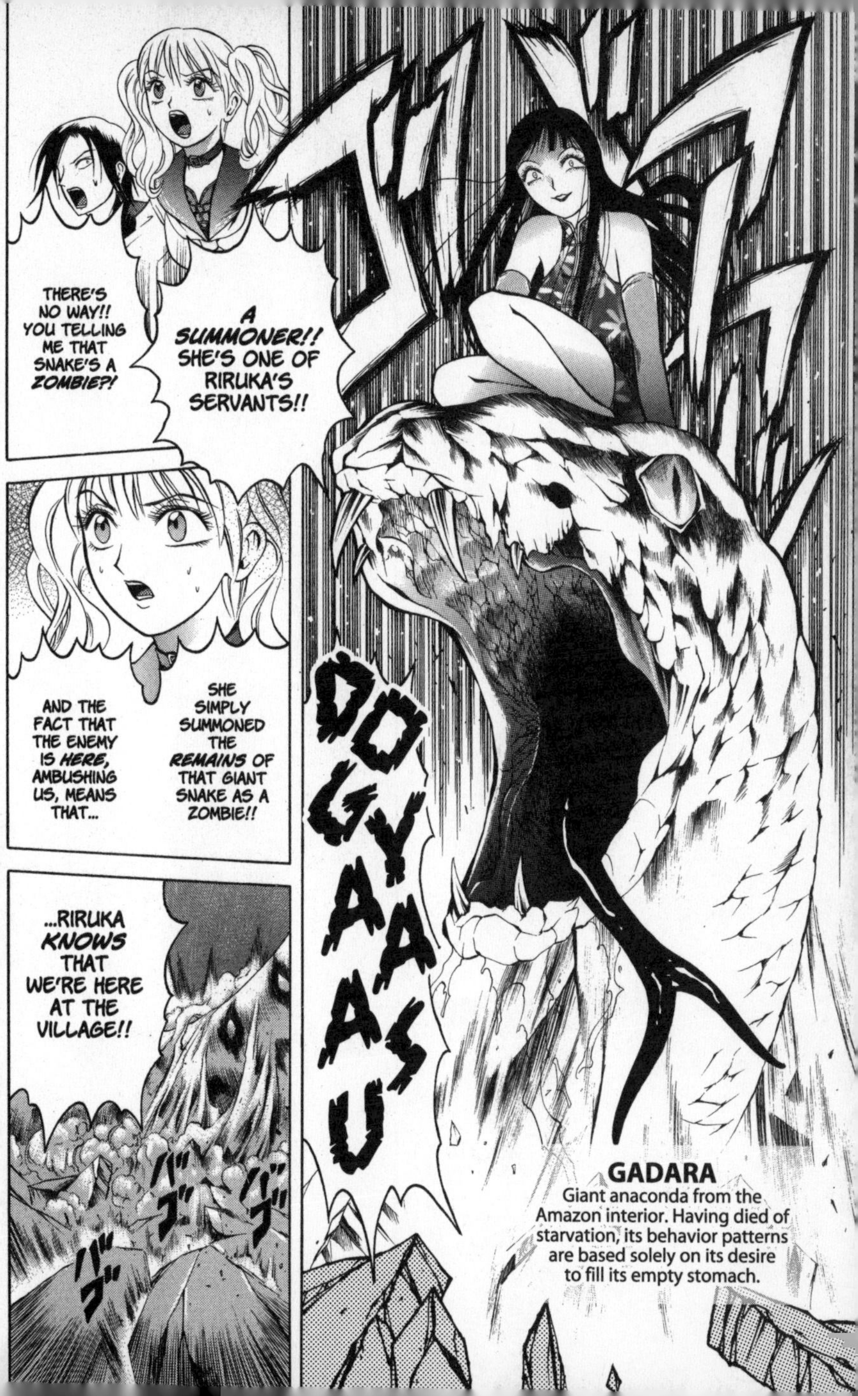
DOGYAAASU
GADARA
Giant anaconda from the Amazon interior. Having died of starvation, its behavior patterns are based solely on its desire to fill its empty stomach.
A SUMMONER!! SHE'S ONE OF RIRUKA'S SERVANTS!!
THERE'S NO WAY!! YOU TELLING ME THAT SNAKE'S A ZOMBIE?!
SHE SIMPLY SUMMONED THE REMAINS OF THAT GIANT SNAKE AS A ZOMBIE!!
AND THE FACT THAT THE ENEMY IS HERE, AMBUSHING US, MEANS THAT...
...RIRUKA KNOWS THAT WE'RE HERE AT THE VILLAGE!!

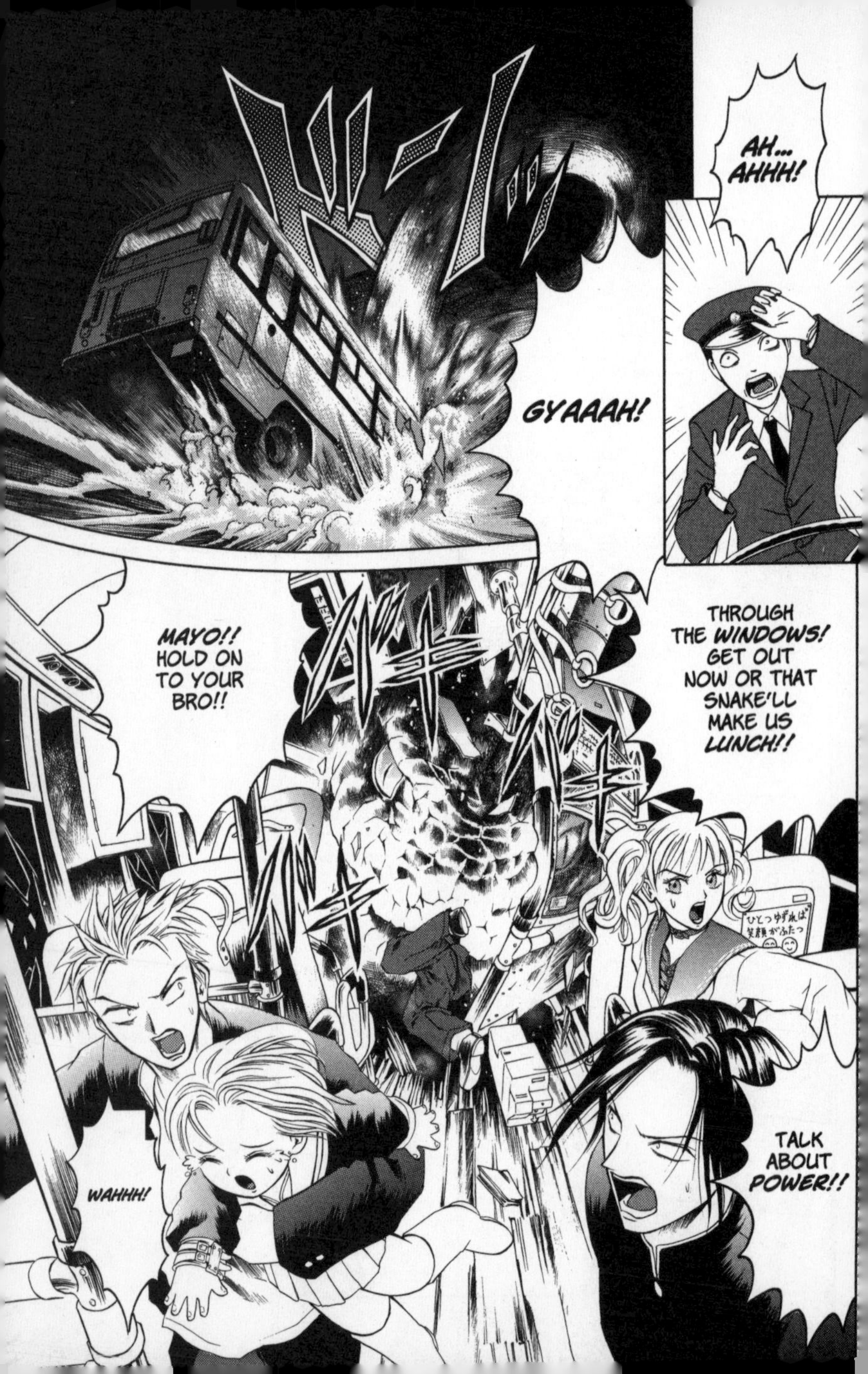
AH... AHHH!
GYAAAH!
THROUGH THE WINDOWS! GET OUT NOW OR THAT SNAKE'LL MAKE US LUNCH!!
MAYO!! HOLD ON TO YOUR BRO!!
TALK ABOUT POWER!!
WAHHH!

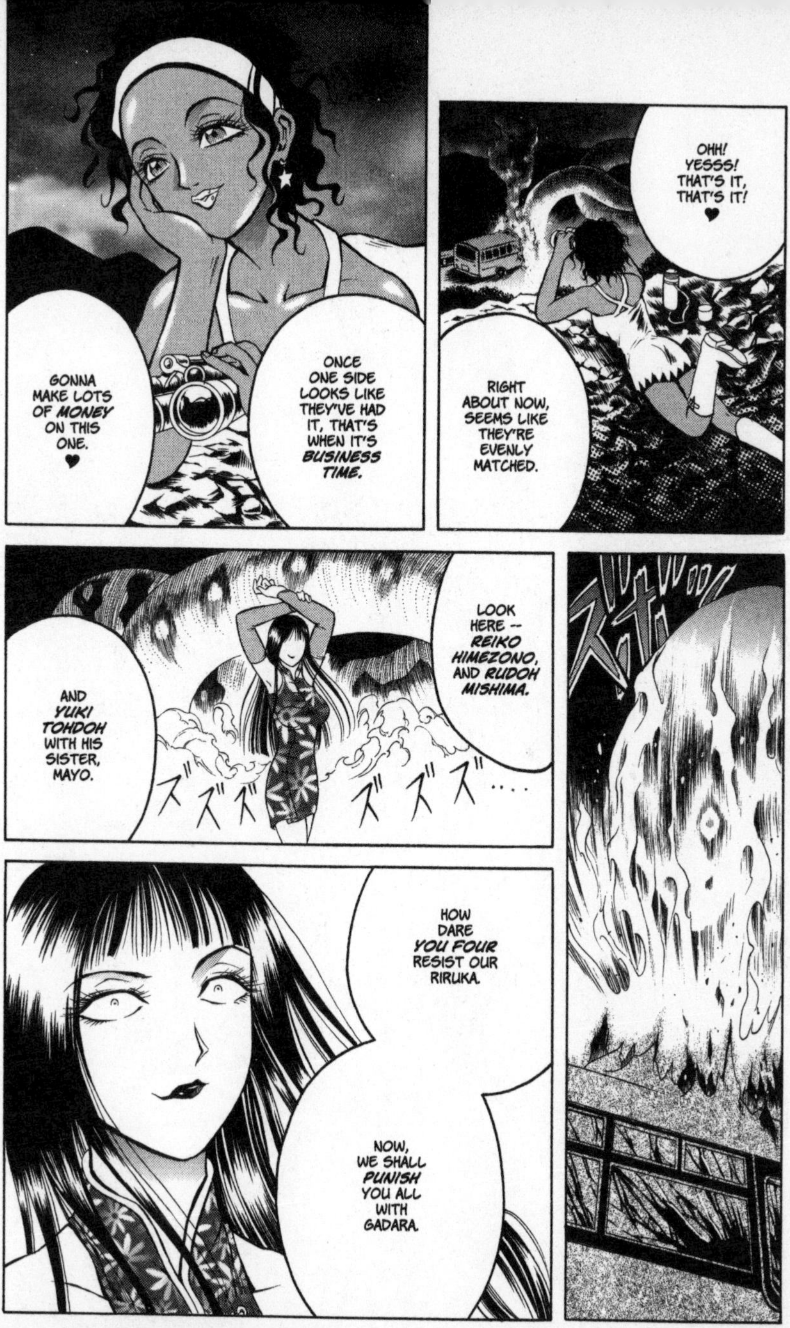
OHH! YESSS! THAT'S IT, THAT'S IT! ♥
RIGHT ABOUT NOW, SEEMS LIKE THEY'RE EVENLY MATCHED.
ONCE ONE SIDE LOOKS LIKE THEY'VE HAD IT, THAT'S WHEN IT'S *BUSINESS TIME.*
GONNA MAKE LOTS OF *MONEY* ON THIS ONE. ♥
LOOK HERE -- *REIKO HIMEZONO,* AND *RUDOH MISHIMA.*
AND *YUKI TOHDOH* WITH HIS SISTER, MAYO.
ズズズ ズズズ....
HOW DARE *YOU FOUR* RESIST OUR RIRUKA.
NOW, WE SHALL *PUNISH* YOU ALL WITH GADARA.

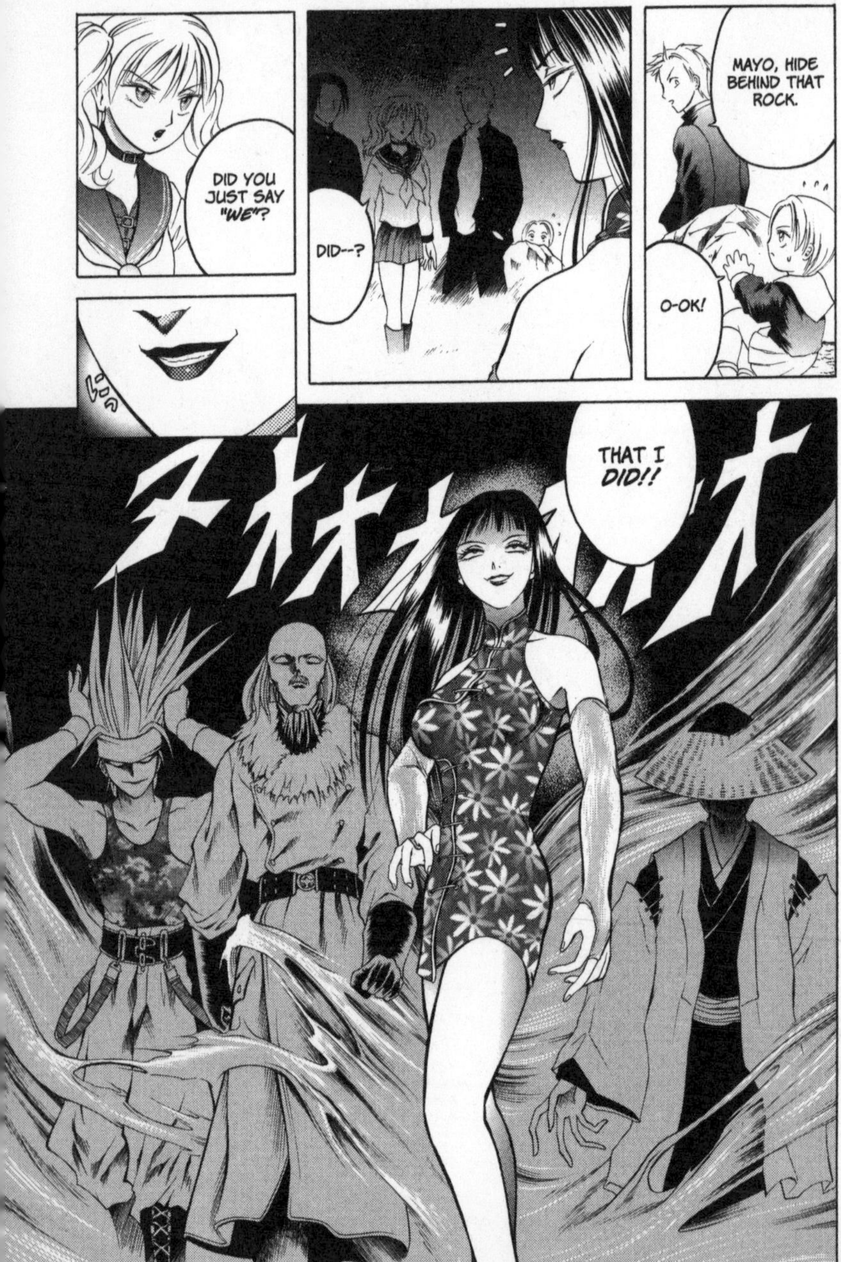
MAYO, HIDE BEHIND THAT ROCK.
O-OK!
DID--?
DID YOU JUST SAY "WE"?
THAT I DID!!

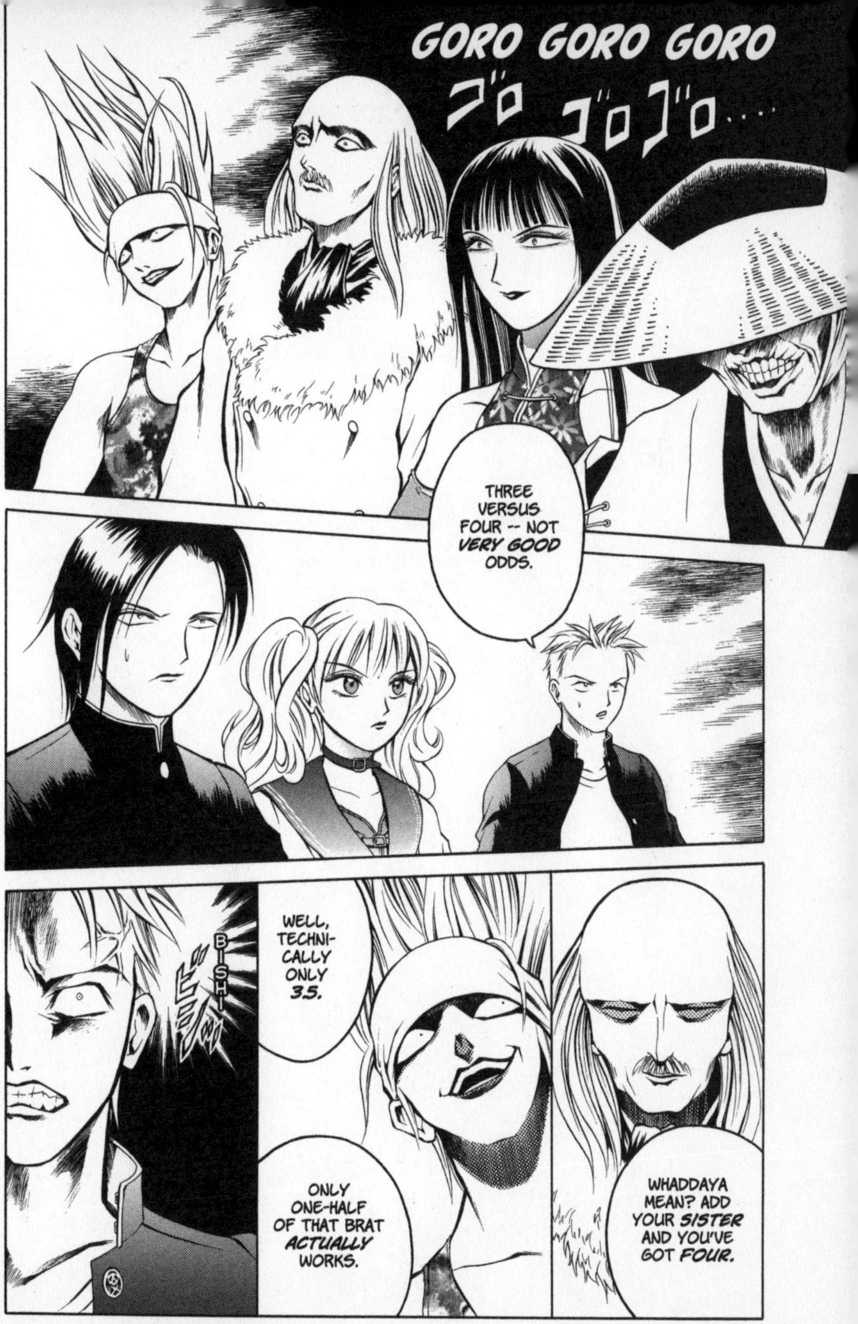
GORO GORO GORO
ゴロ ゴロゴロ……
THREE VERSUS FOUR -- NOT VERY GOOD ODDS.
WHADDAYA MEAN? ADD YOUR SISTER AND YOU'VE GOT FOUR.
WELL, TECHNICALLY ONLY 3.5.
ONLY ONE-HALF OF THAT BRAT ACTUALLY WORKS.
BISHI
ビシッ

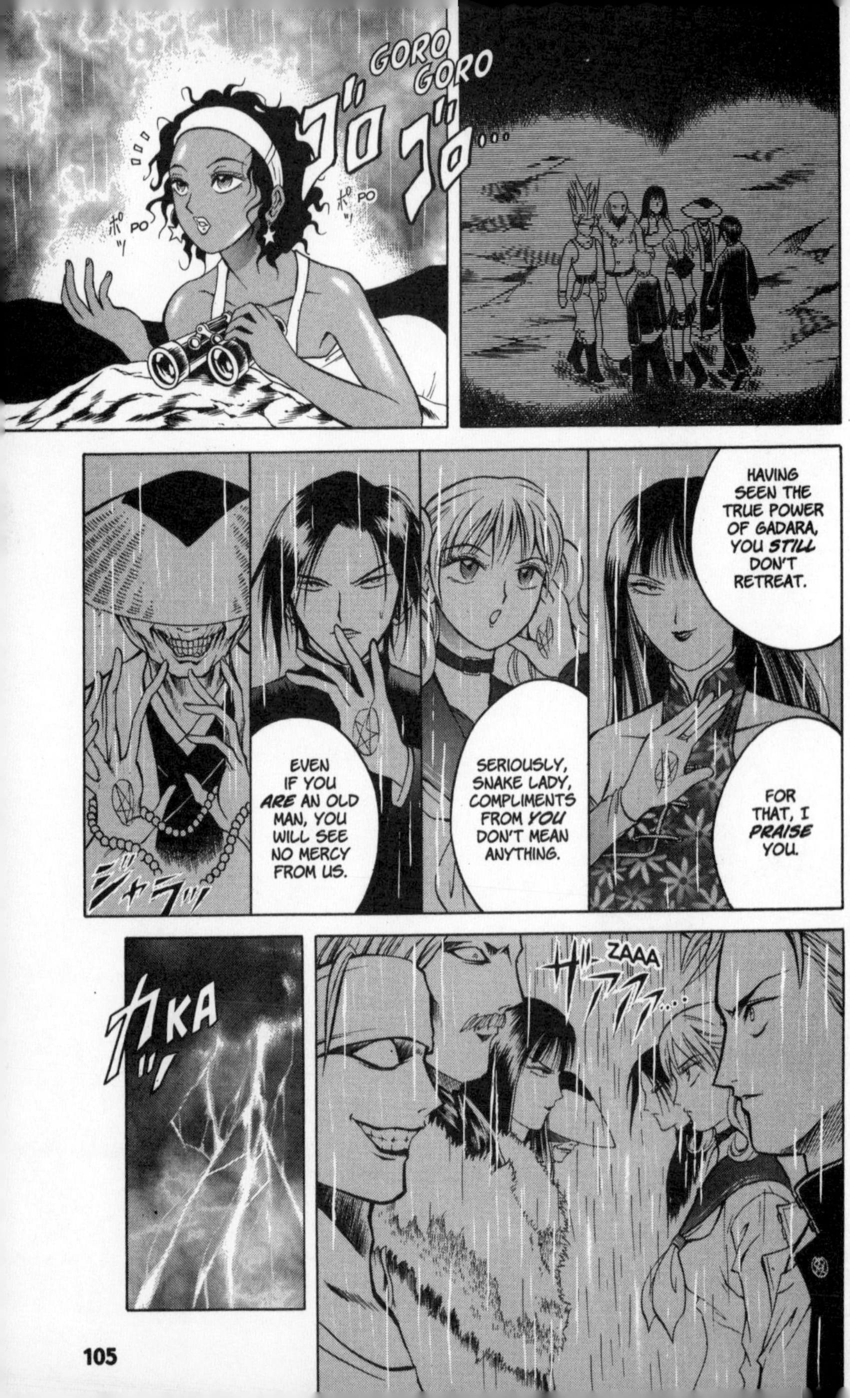
GORO GORO
ゴロゴロ…
PO
PO
HAVING SEEN THE TRUE POWER OF GADARA, YOU *STILL* DON'T RETREAT.
FOR THAT, I *PRAISE* YOU.
SERIOUSLY, SNAKE LADY, COMPLIMENTS FROM *YOU* DON'T MEAN ANYTHING.
EVEN IF YOU *ARE* AN OLD MAN, YOU WILL SEE NO MERCY FROM US.
ジャラッ
ZAAA
ザァァァ…
KA
カッ

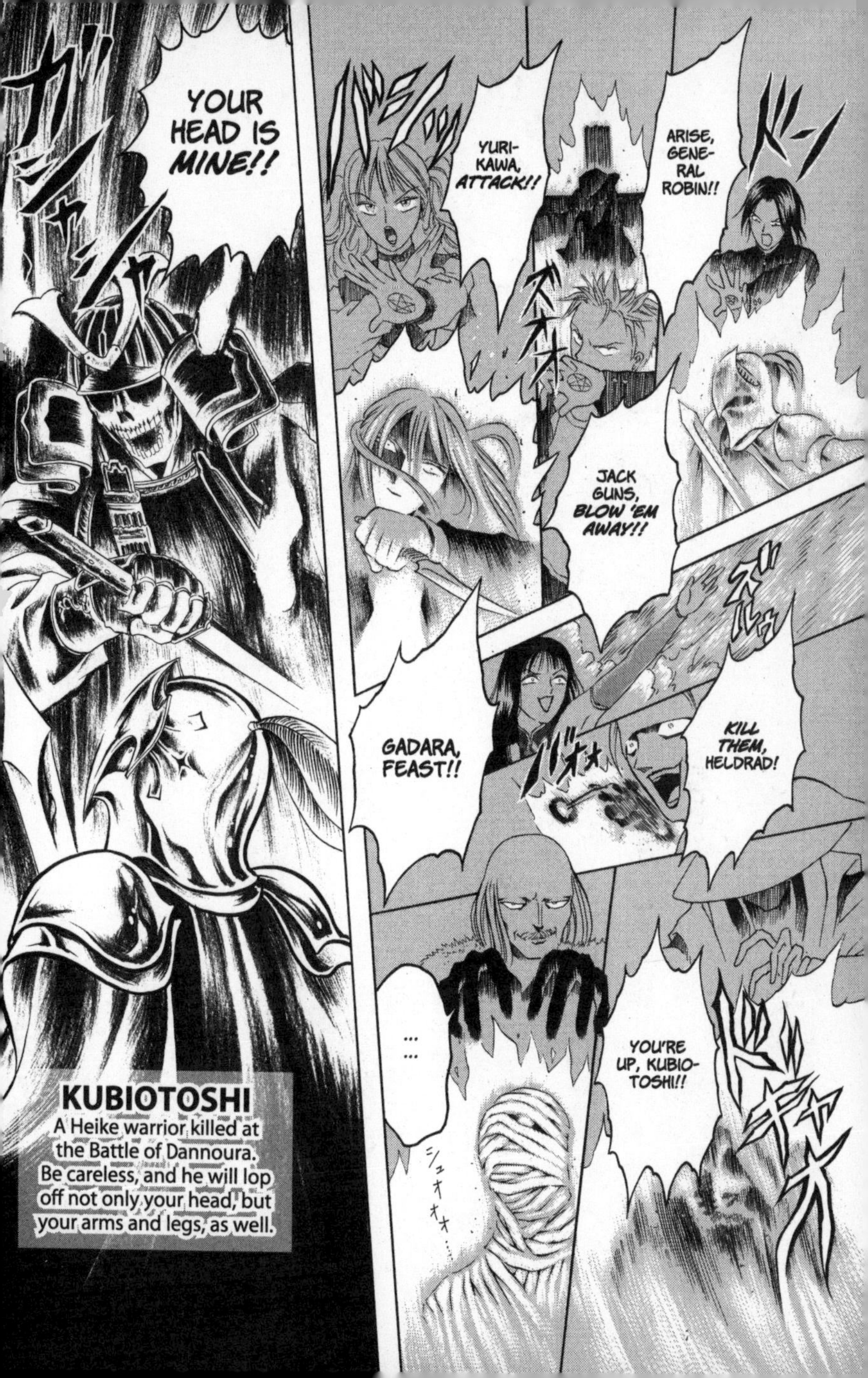
ARISE, GENERAL ROBIN!!
JACK GUNS, BLOW 'EM AWAY!!
YURI-KAWA, ATTACK!!
KILL THEM, HELDRAD!
GADARA, FEAST!!
YOU'RE UP, KUBIO-TOSHI!!
...
...
YOUR HEAD IS MINE!!
KUBIOTOSHI
A Heike warrior killed at the Battle of Dannoura. Be careless, and he will lop off not only your head, but your arms and legs, as well.

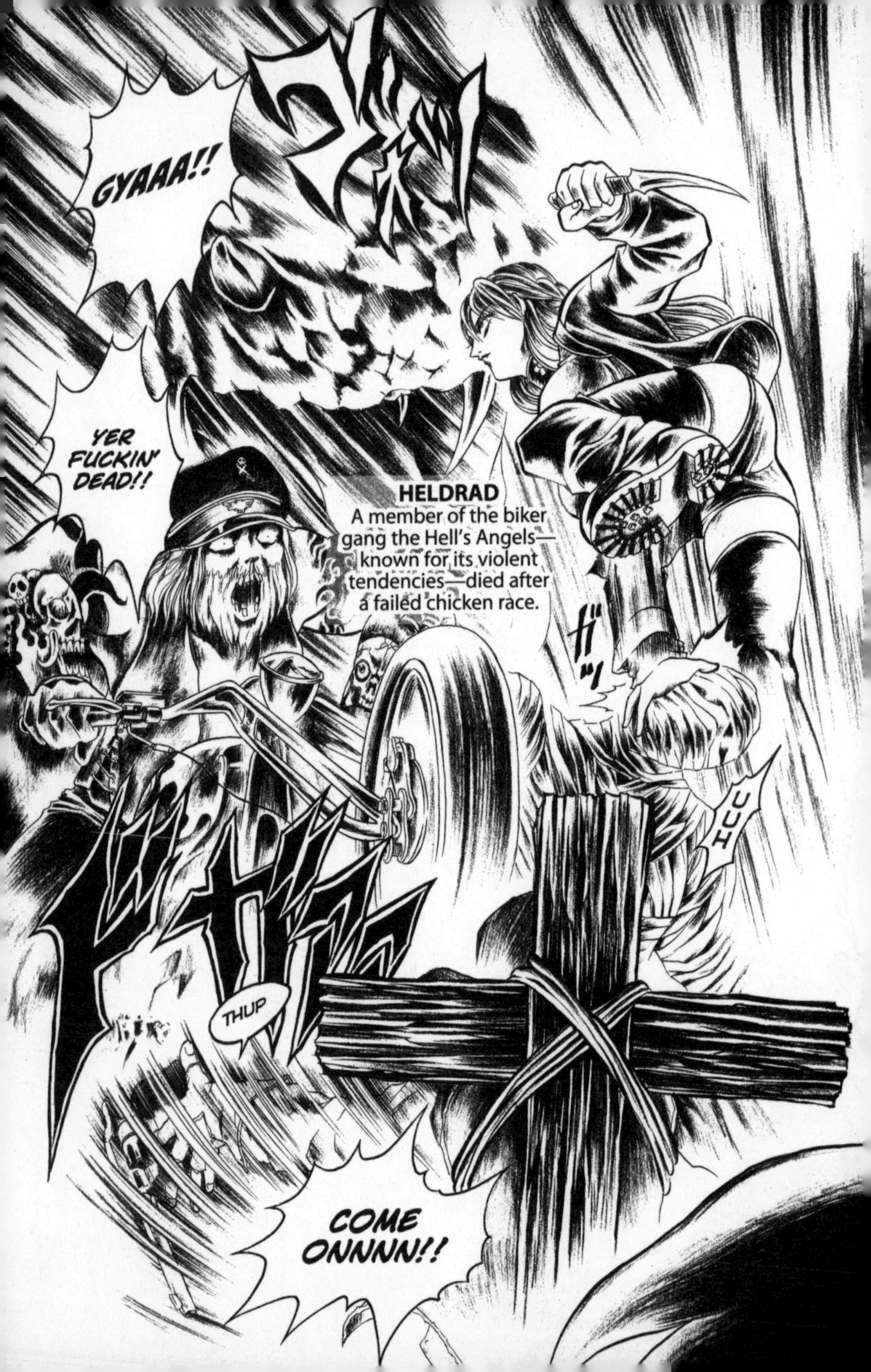
GYAAA!!
YER FUCKIN' DEAD!!
HELDRAD
A member of the biker gang the Hell's Angels—known for its violent tendencies—died after a failed chicken race.
UUH
THUP
COME ONNNN!!

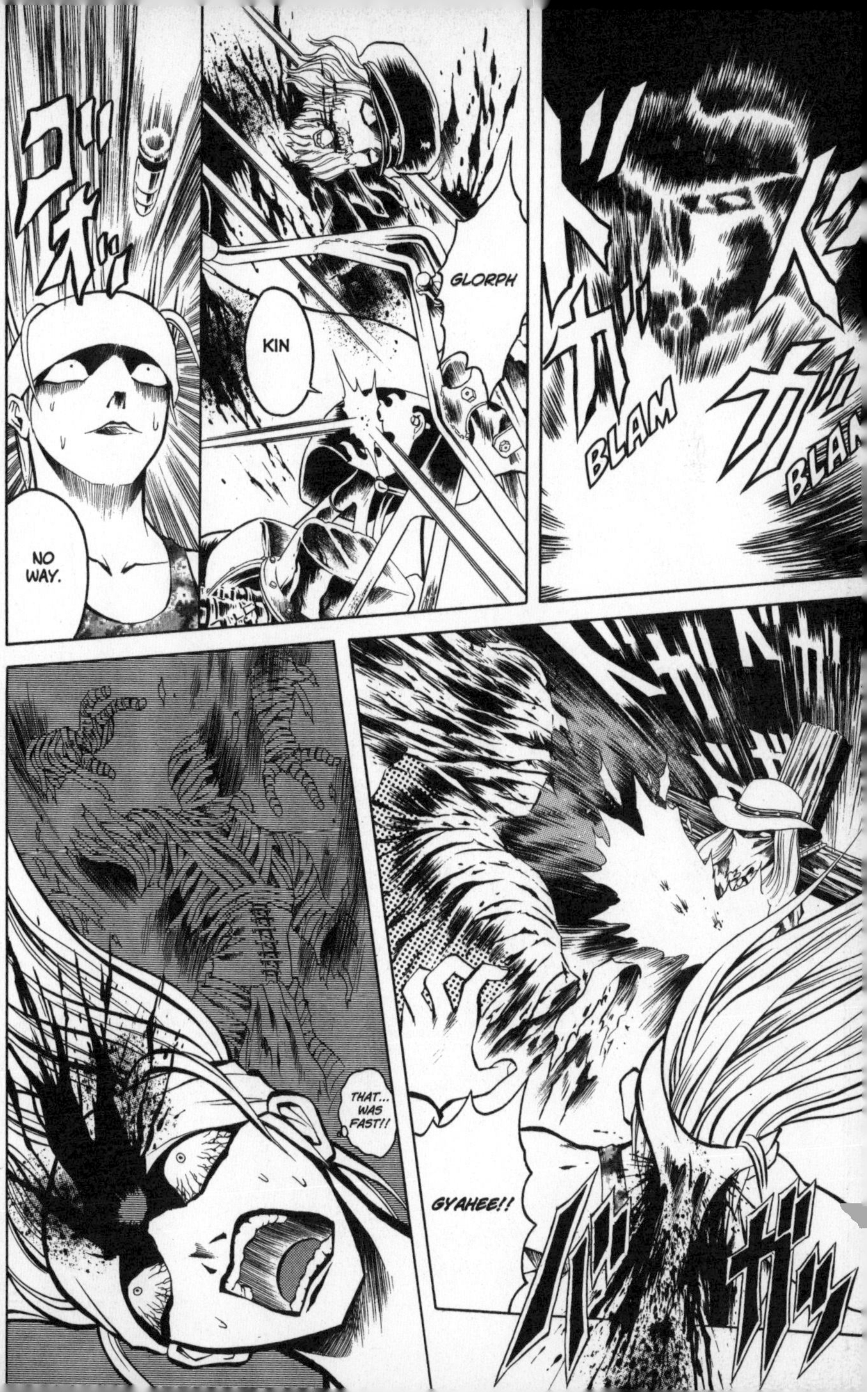
BLAM
GLORPH
KIN
NO WAY.
GYAHEE!!
THAT... WAS FAST!!

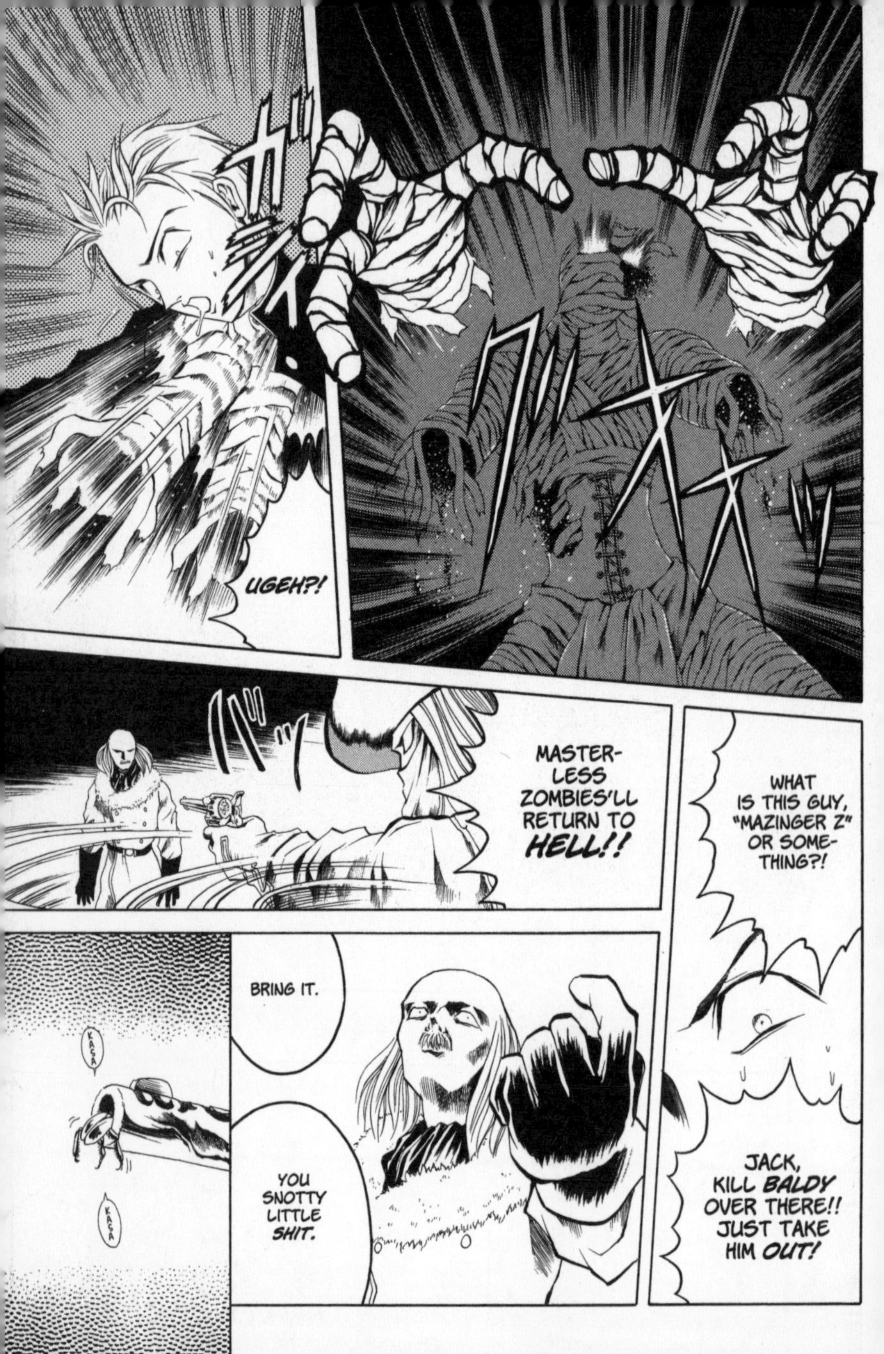
UGEH?!
WHAT IS THIS GUY, "MAZINGER Z" OR SOME-THING?!
JACK, KILL *BALDY* OVER THERE!! JUST TAKE HIM *OUT!*
MASTER-LESS ZOMBIES'LL RETURN TO ***HELL!!***
BRING IT.
YOU SNOTTY LITTLE *SHIT.*
KASA
KASA

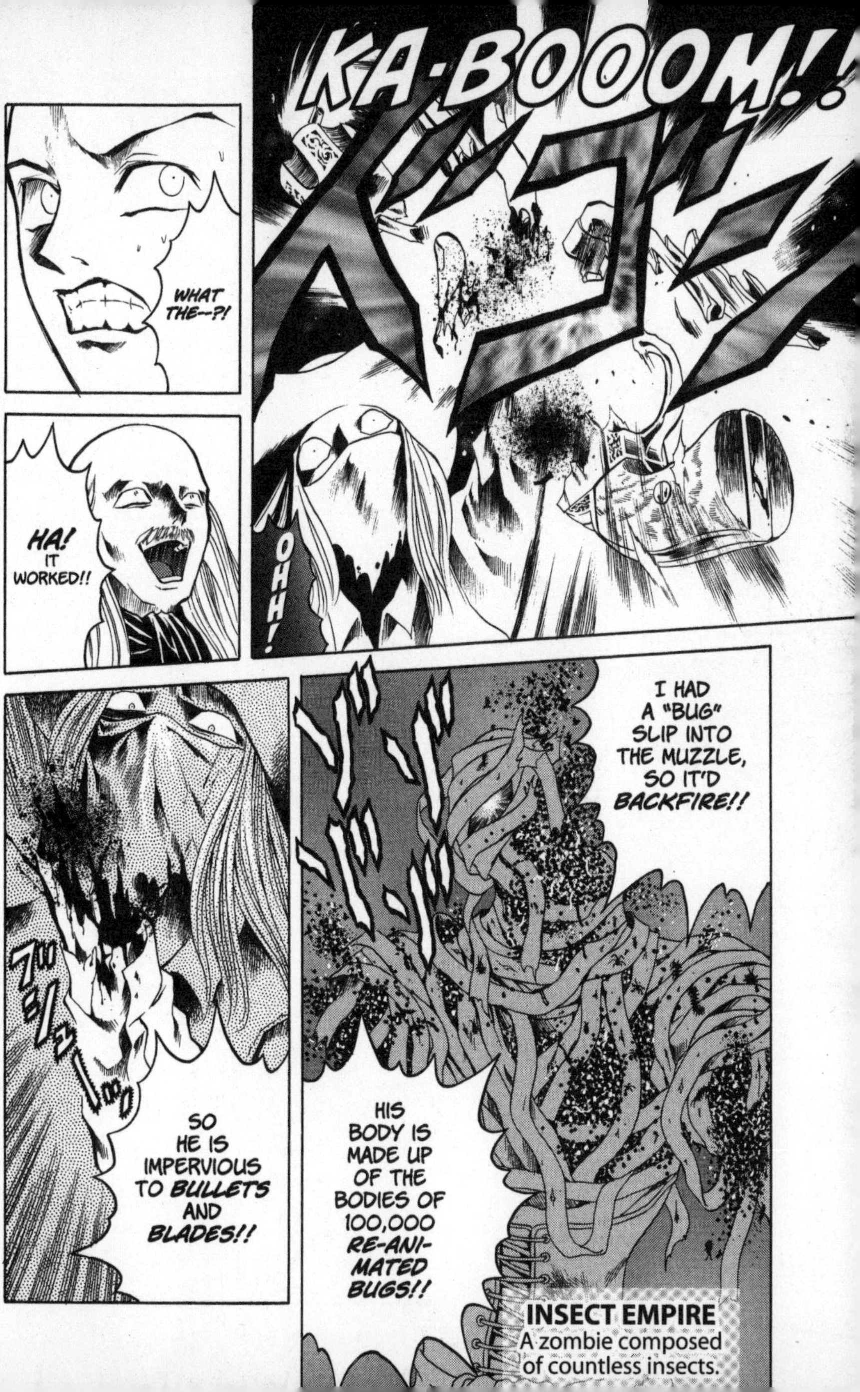
KA-BOOOM!!
OHHH!
WHAT THE--?!
HA! IT WORKED!!
I HAD A "BUG" SLIP INTO THE MUZZLE, SO IT'D BACKFIRE!!
HIS BODY IS MADE UP OF THE BODIES OF 100,000 RE-ANIMATED BUGS!!
INSECT EMPIRE
A zombie composed of countless insects.
SO HE IS IMPERVIOUS TO BULLETS AND BLADES!!

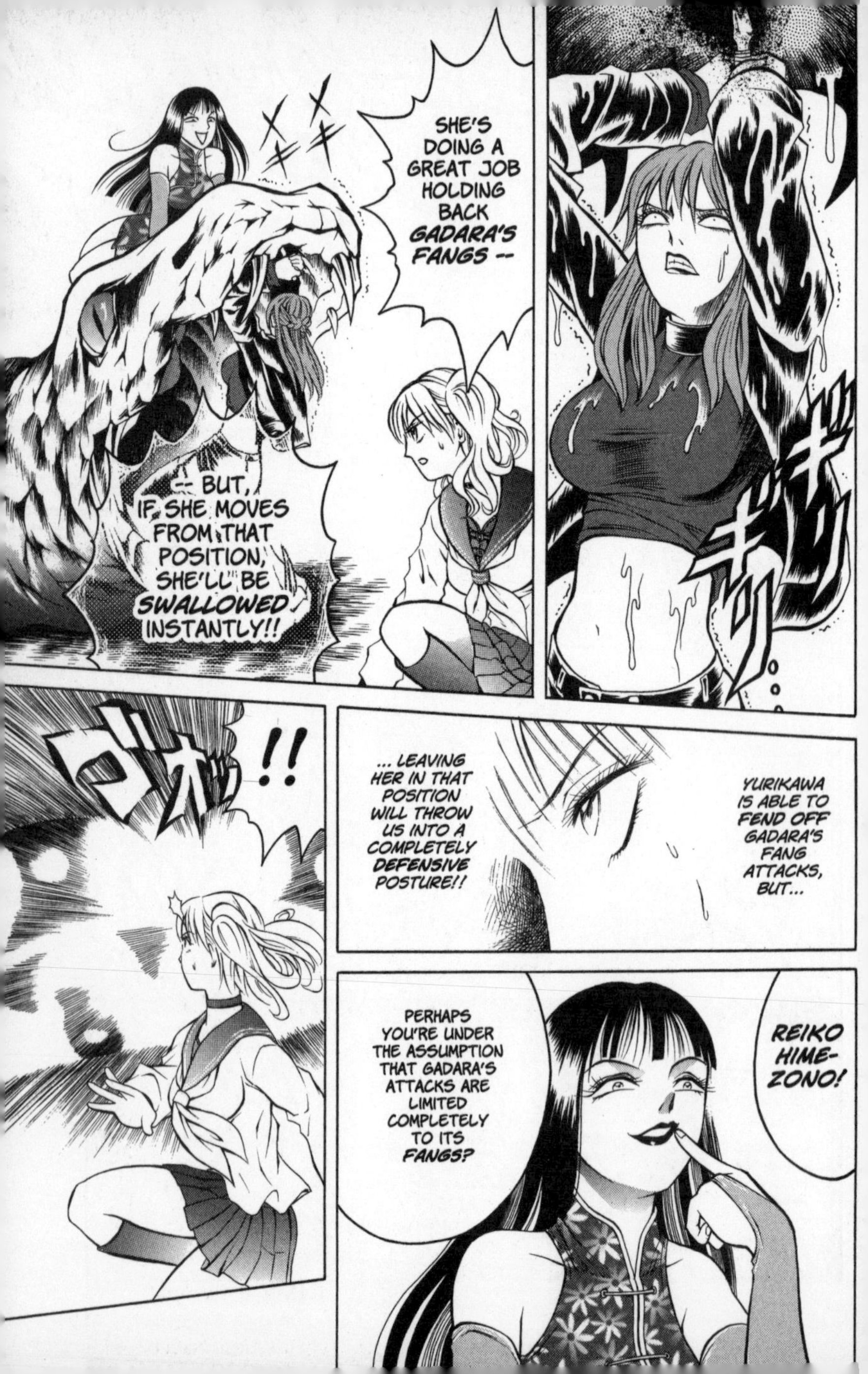
SHE'S DOING A GREAT JOB HOLDING BACK GADARA'S FANGS --
-- BUT, IF SHE MOVES FROM THAT POSITION, SHE'LL BE SWALLOWED INSTANTLY!!
YURIKAWA IS ABLE TO FEND OFF GADARA'S FANG ATTACKS, BUT...
... LEAVING HER IN THAT POSITION WILL THROW US INTO A COMPLETELY DEFENSIVE POSTURE!!
REIKO HIME-ZONO!
PERHAPS YOU'RE UNDER THE ASSUMPTION THAT GADARA'S ATTACKS ARE LIMITED COMPLETELY TO ITS FANGS?

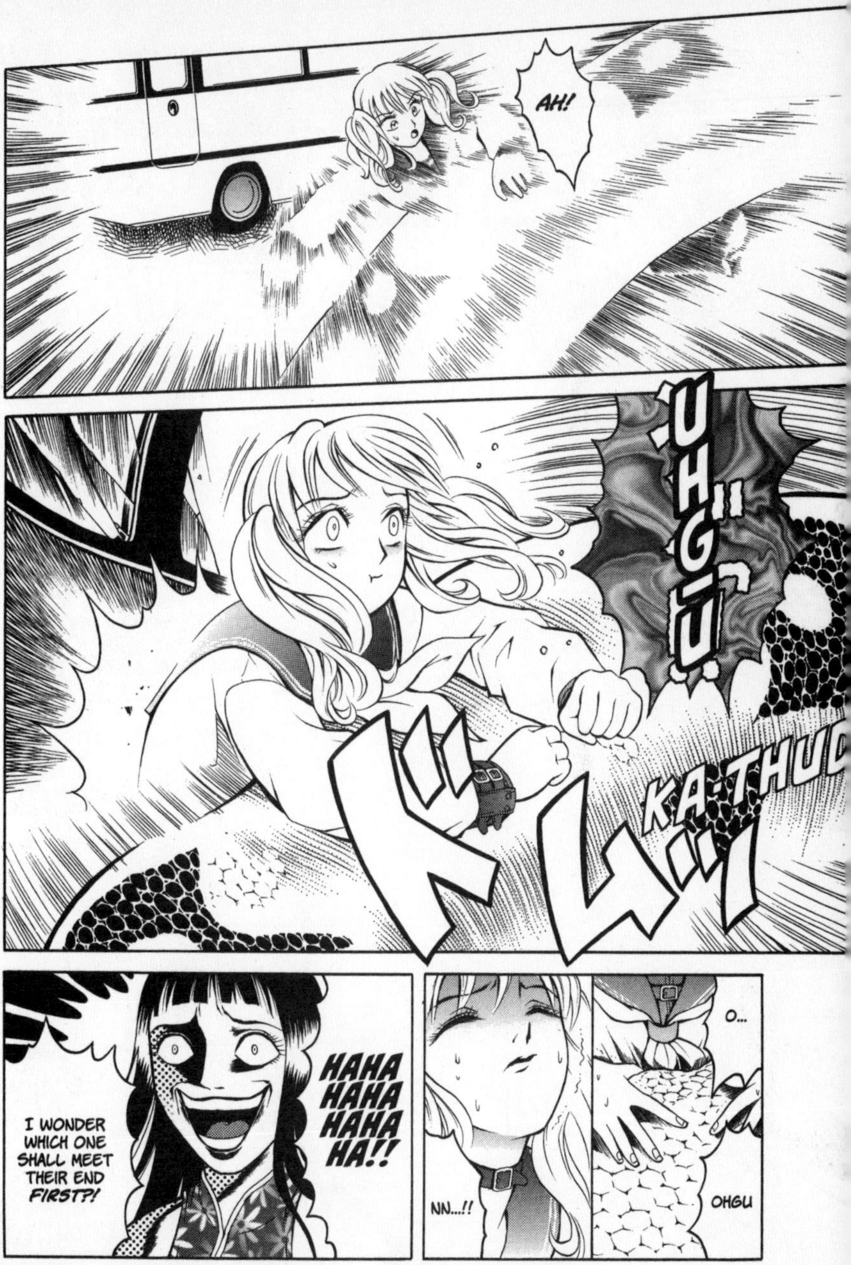
AH!
UHGŪ!!
KA-THUD
O...
OHGU
NN...!!
HAHA HAHA HAHA HA!!
I WONDER WHICH ONE SHALL MEET THEIR END *FIRST?!*

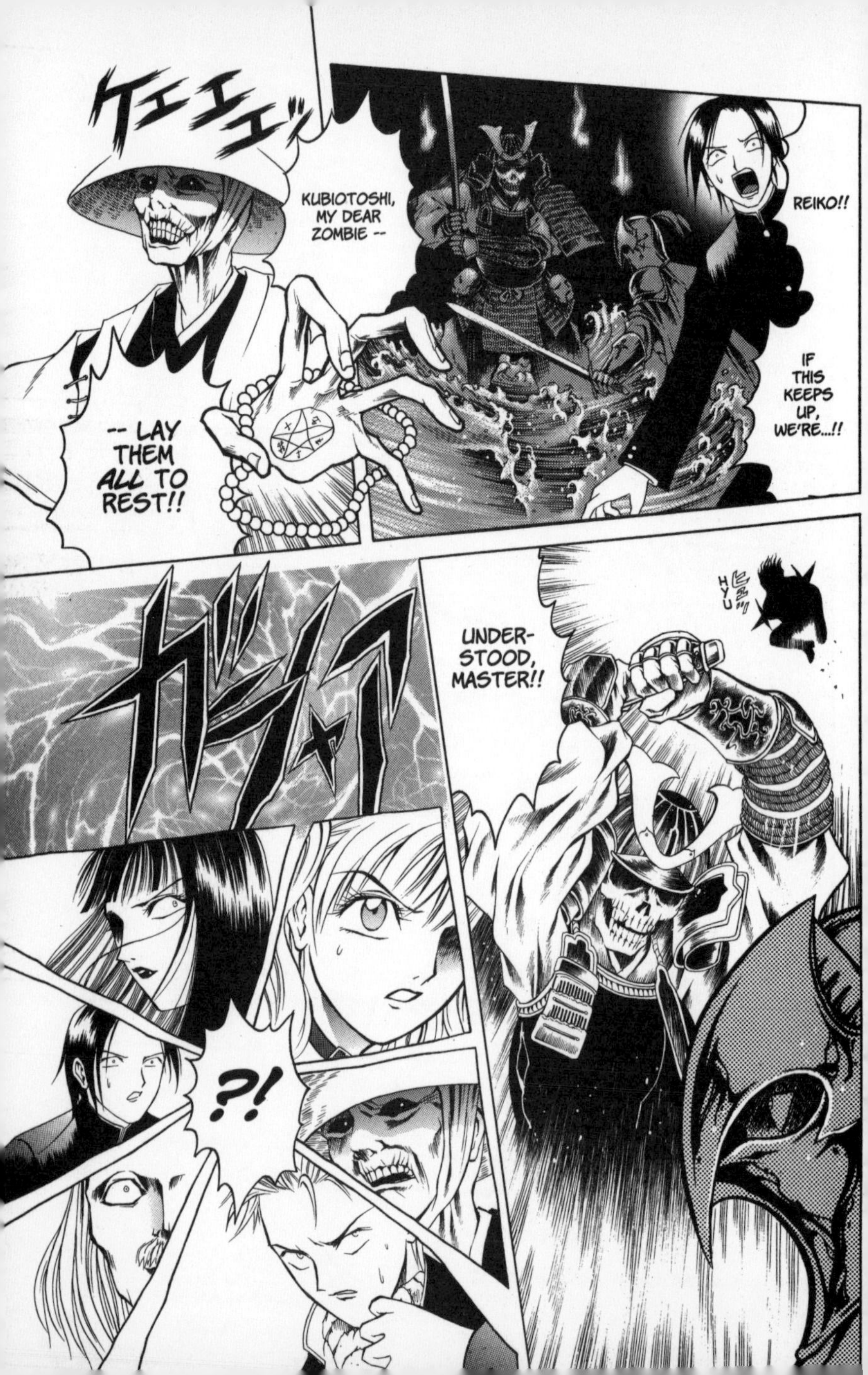
REIKO!!
IF THIS KEEPS UP, WE'RE...!!
ケエエエ
KUBIOTOSHI, MY DEAR ZOMBIE --
-- LAY THEM ALL TO REST!!
ヒュ HYU
UNDER-STOOD, MASTER!!
?!

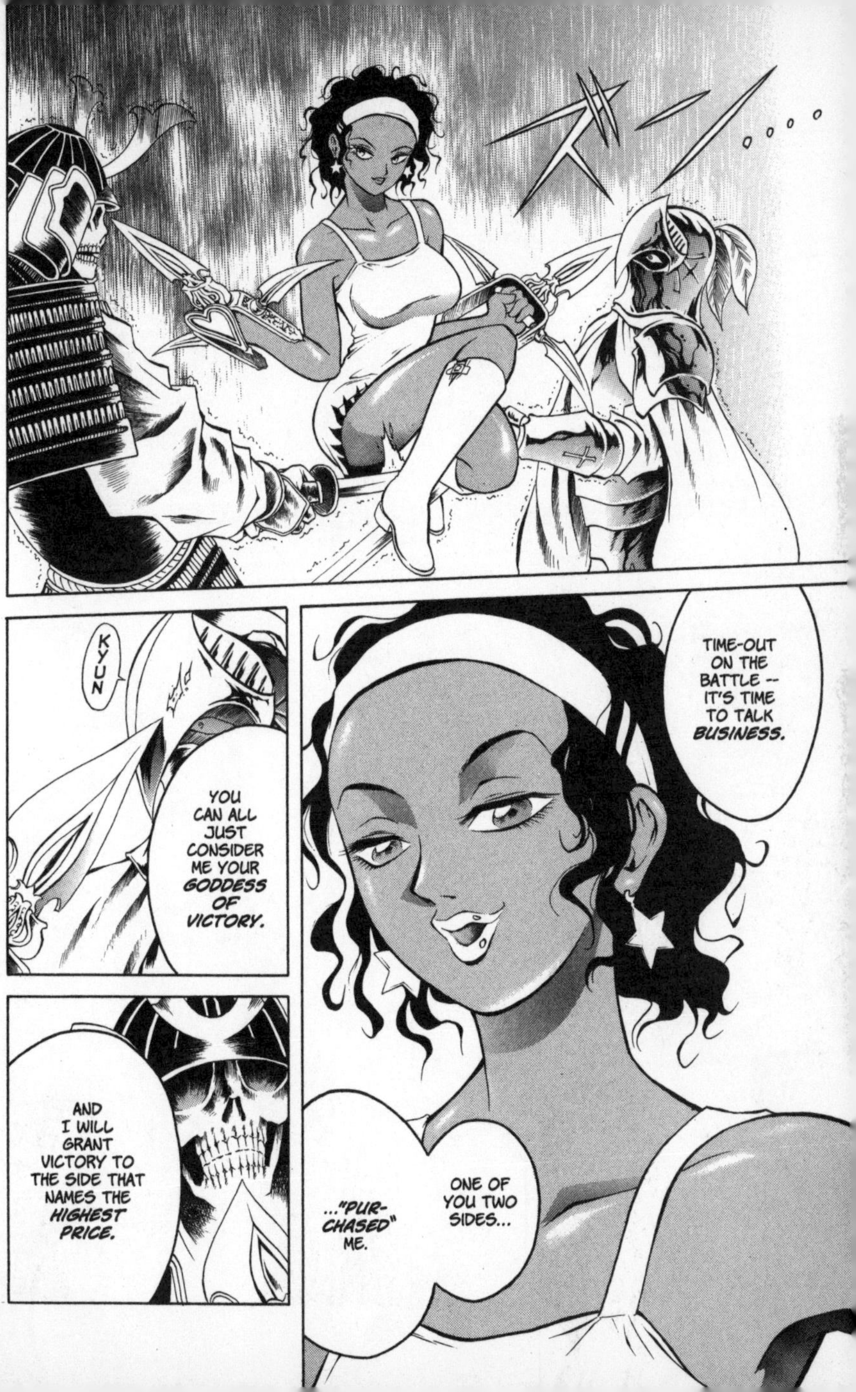

TIME-OUT ON THE BATTLE -- IT'S TIME TO TALK BUSINESS.
ONE OF YOU TWO SIDES...
..."PURCHASED" ME.
KYUN
YOU CAN ALL JUST CONSIDER ME YOUR GODDESS OF VICTORY.
AND I WILL GRANT VICTORY TO THE SIDE THAT NAMES THE HIGHEST PRICE.

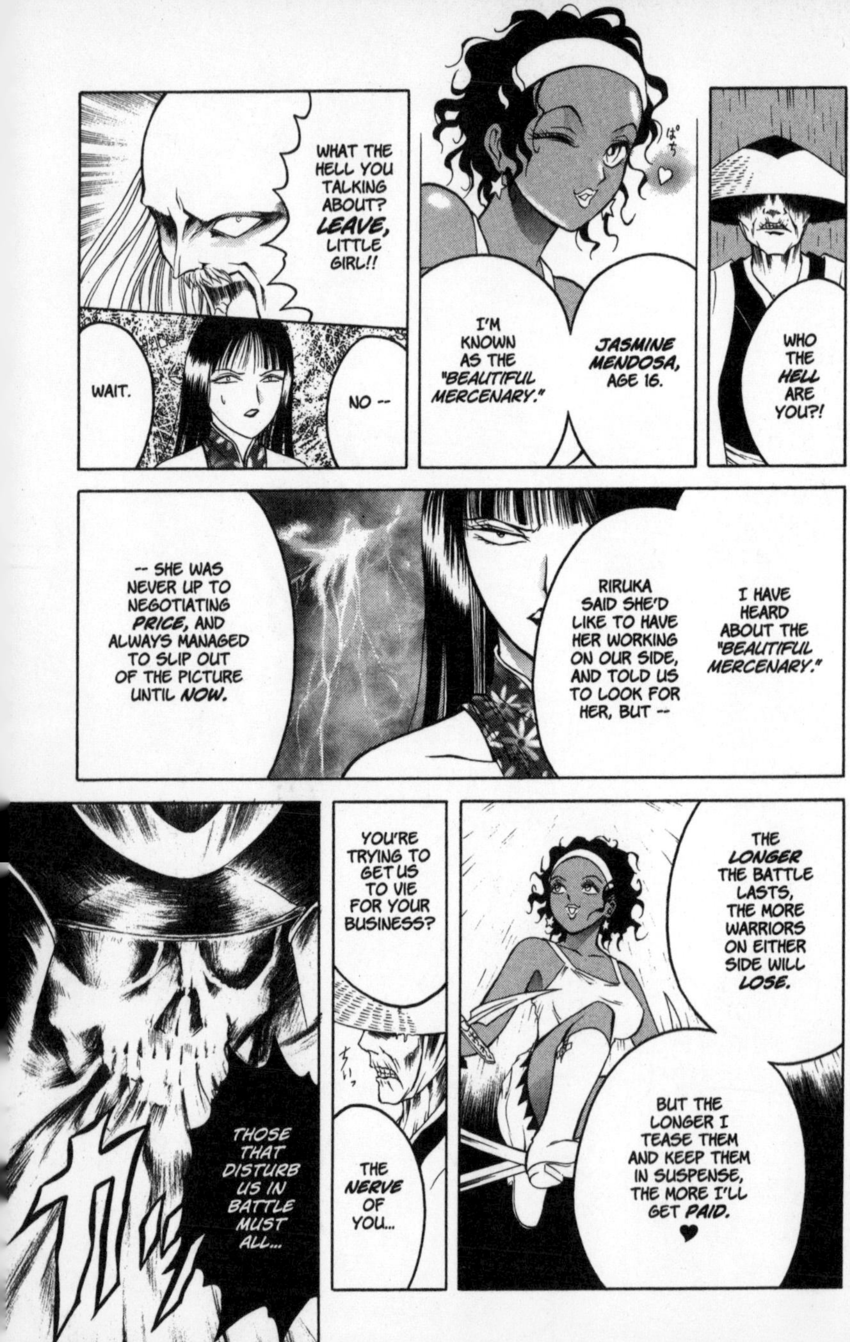
WHO THE HELL ARE YOU?!
ぱち
JASMINE MENDOSA, AGE 16.
I'M KNOWN AS THE "BEAUTIFUL MERCENARY."
WHAT THE HELL YOU TALKING ABOUT? LEAVE, LITTLE GIRL!!
NO --
WAIT.
I HAVE HEARD ABOUT THE "BEAUTIFUL MERCENARY."
RIRUKA SAID SHE'D LIKE TO HAVE HER WORKING ON OUR SIDE, AND TOLD US TO LOOK FOR HER, BUT --
-- SHE WAS NEVER UP TO NEGOTIATING PRICE, AND ALWAYS MANAGED TO SLIP OUT OF THE PICTURE UNTIL NOW.
THE LONGER THE BATTLE LASTS, THE MORE WARRIORS ON EITHER SIDE WILL LOSE.
BUT THE LONGER I TEASE THEM AND KEEP THEM IN SUSPENSE, THE MORE I'LL GET PAID. ♥
YOU'RE TRYING TO GET US TO VIE FOR YOUR BUSINESS?
THE NERVE OF YOU...
THOSE THAT DISTURB US IN BATTLE MUST ALL...

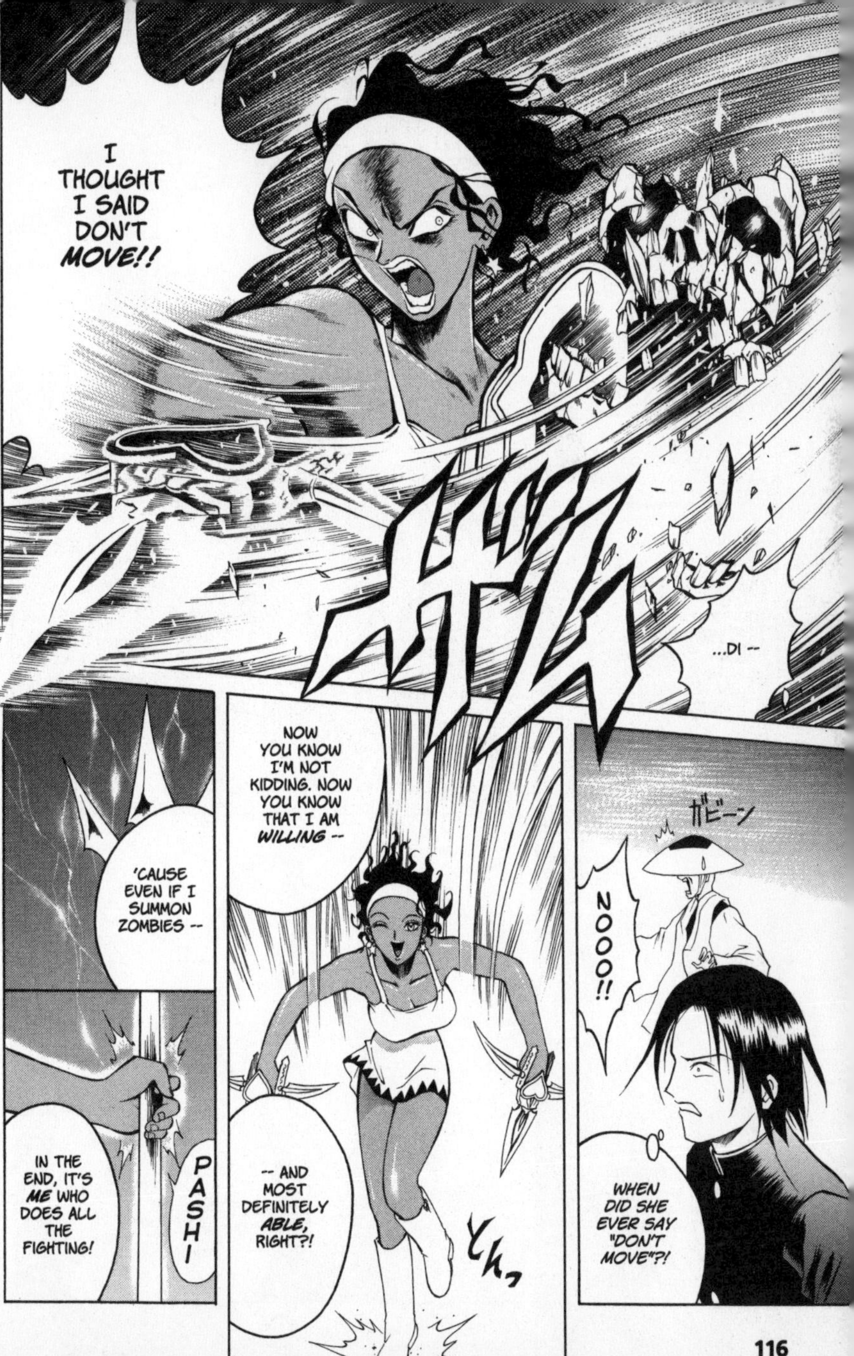
I THOUGHT I SAID DON'T *MOVE!!*
...DI --
ガビーン
NOOOO!!
WHEN DID SHE EVER SAY "DON'T MOVE"?!
NOW YOU KNOW I'M NOT KIDDING. NOW YOU KNOW THAT I AM *WILLING* --
-- AND MOST DEFINITELY *ABLE,* RIGHT?!
'CAUSE EVEN IF I SUMMON ZOMBIES --
IN THE END, IT'S *ME* WHO DOES ALL THE FIGHTING!
PASHI

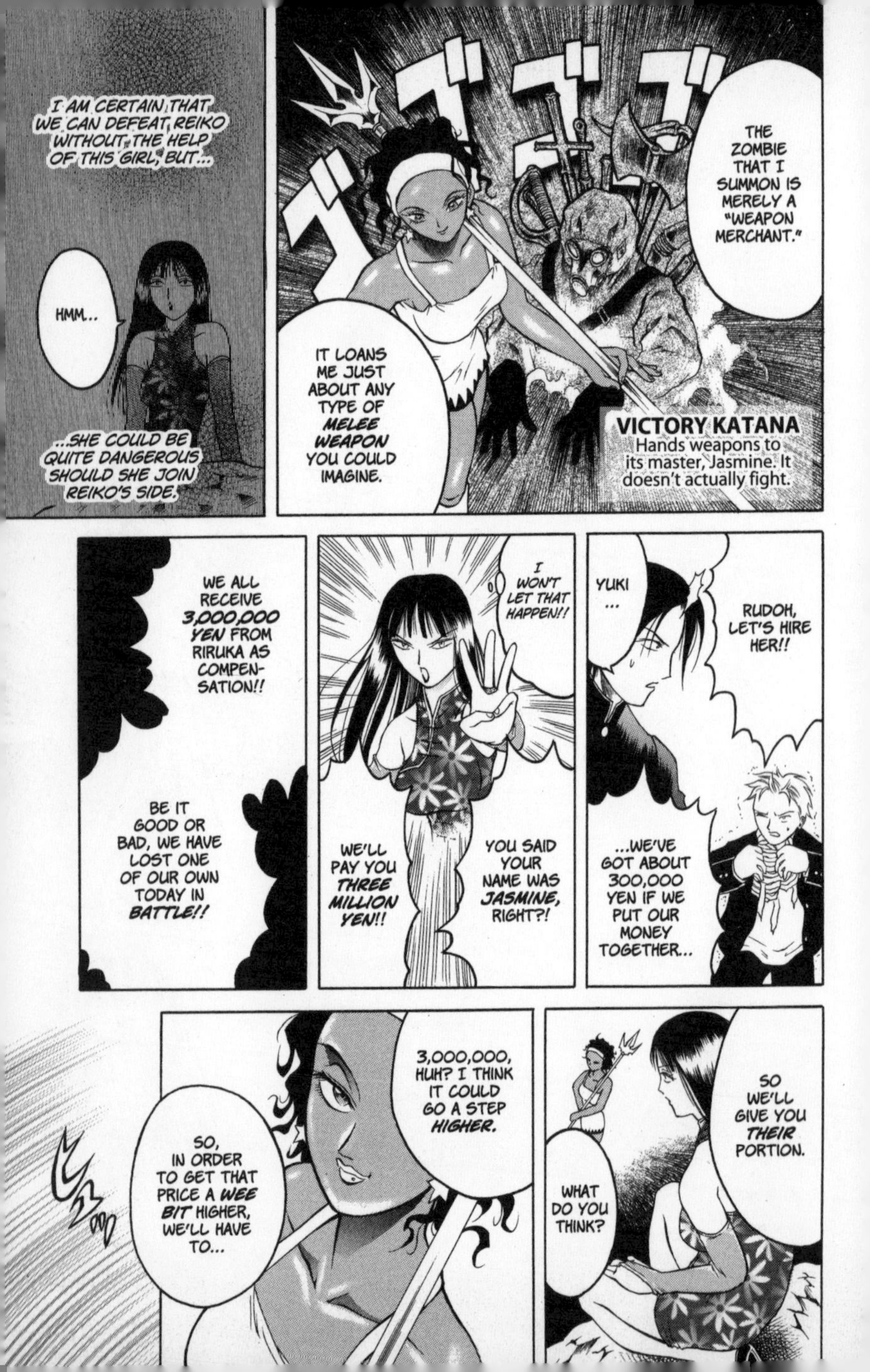
THE ZOMBIE THAT I SUMMON IS MERELY A "WEAPON MERCHANT."
IT LOANS ME JUST ABOUT ANY TYPE OF MELEE WEAPON YOU COULD IMAGINE.
VICTORY KATANA
Hands weapons to its master, Jasmine. It doesn't actually fight.
I AM CERTAIN THAT WE CAN DEFEAT REIKO WITHOUT THE HELP OF THIS GIRL, BUT...
HMM...
...SHE COULD BE QUITE DANGEROUS SHOULD SHE JOIN REIKO'S SIDE.
RUDOH, LET'S HIRE HER!!
YUKI ...
...WE'VE GOT ABOUT 300,000 YEN IF WE PUT OUR MONEY TOGETHER...
I WON'T LET THAT HAPPEN!!
YOU SAID YOUR NAME WAS JASMINE, RIGHT?!
WE'LL PAY YOU THREE MILLION YEN!!
WE ALL RECEIVE 3,000,000 YEN FROM RIRUKA AS COMPENSATION!!
BE IT GOOD OR BAD, WE HAVE LOST ONE OF OUR OWN TODAY IN BATTLE!!
SO WE'LL GIVE YOU THEIR PORTION.
WHAT DO YOU THINK?
3,000,000, HUH? I THINK IT COULD GO A STEP HIGHER.
SO, IN ORDER TO GET THAT PRICE A WEE BIT HIGHER, WE'LL HAVE TO...

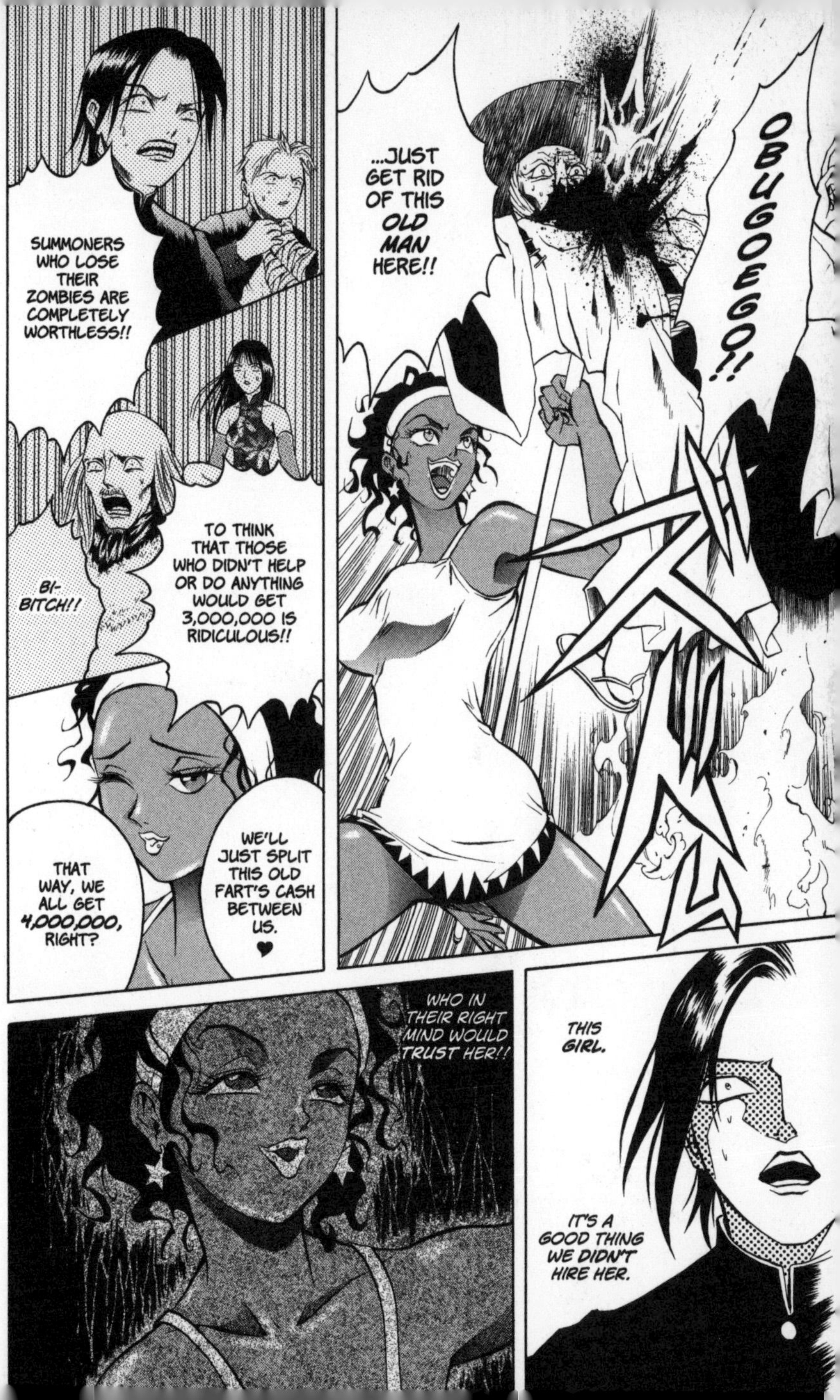
OBUGOEGGO!!
...JUST GET RID OF THIS OLD MAN HERE!!
SUMMONERS WHO LOSE THEIR ZOMBIES ARE COMPLETELY WORTHLESS!!
TO THINK THAT THOSE WHO DIDN'T HELP OR DO ANYTHING WOULD GET 3,000,000 IS RIDICULOUS!!
BI-BITCH!!
WE'LL JUST SPLIT THIS OLD FART'S CASH BETWEEN US. ♥
THAT WAY, WE ALL GET 4,000,000, RIGHT?
THIS GIRL.
IT'S A GOOD THING WE DIDN'T HIRE HER.
WHO IN THEIR RIGHT MIND WOULD TRUST HER!!

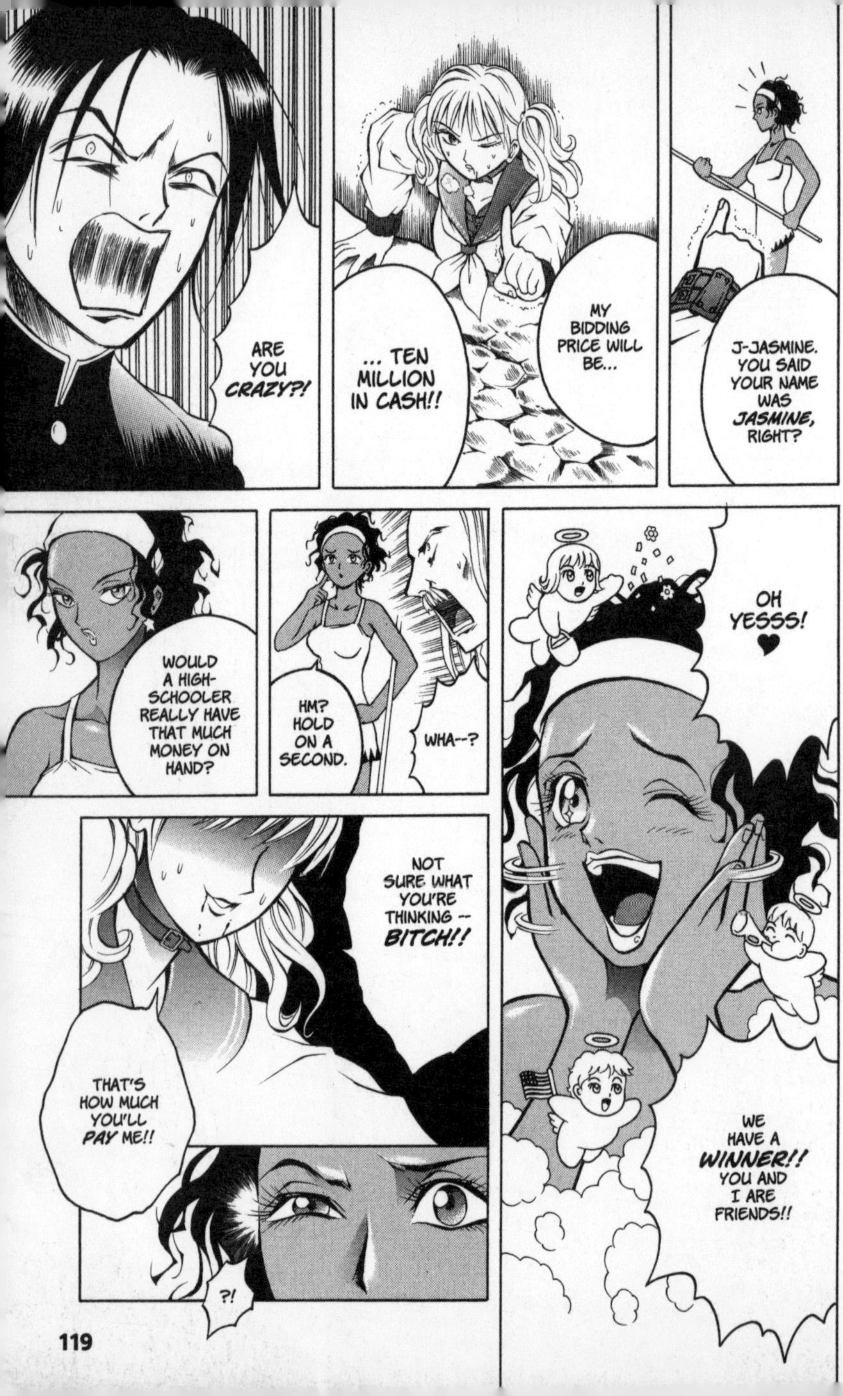

J-JASMINE. YOU SAID YOUR NAME WAS *JASMINE*, RIGHT?
MY BIDDING PRICE WILL BE...
... TEN MILLION IN CASH!!
ARE YOU *CRAZY?!*
OH YESSS! ♥
WE HAVE A *WINNER!!* YOU AND I ARE FRIENDS!!
WHA--?
HM? HOLD ON A SECOND.
WOULD A HIGH-SCHOOLER REALLY HAVE THAT MUCH MONEY ON HAND?
NOT SURE WHAT YOU'RE THINKING -- *BITCH!!*
THAT'S HOW MUCH YOU'LL *PAY* ME!!
?!

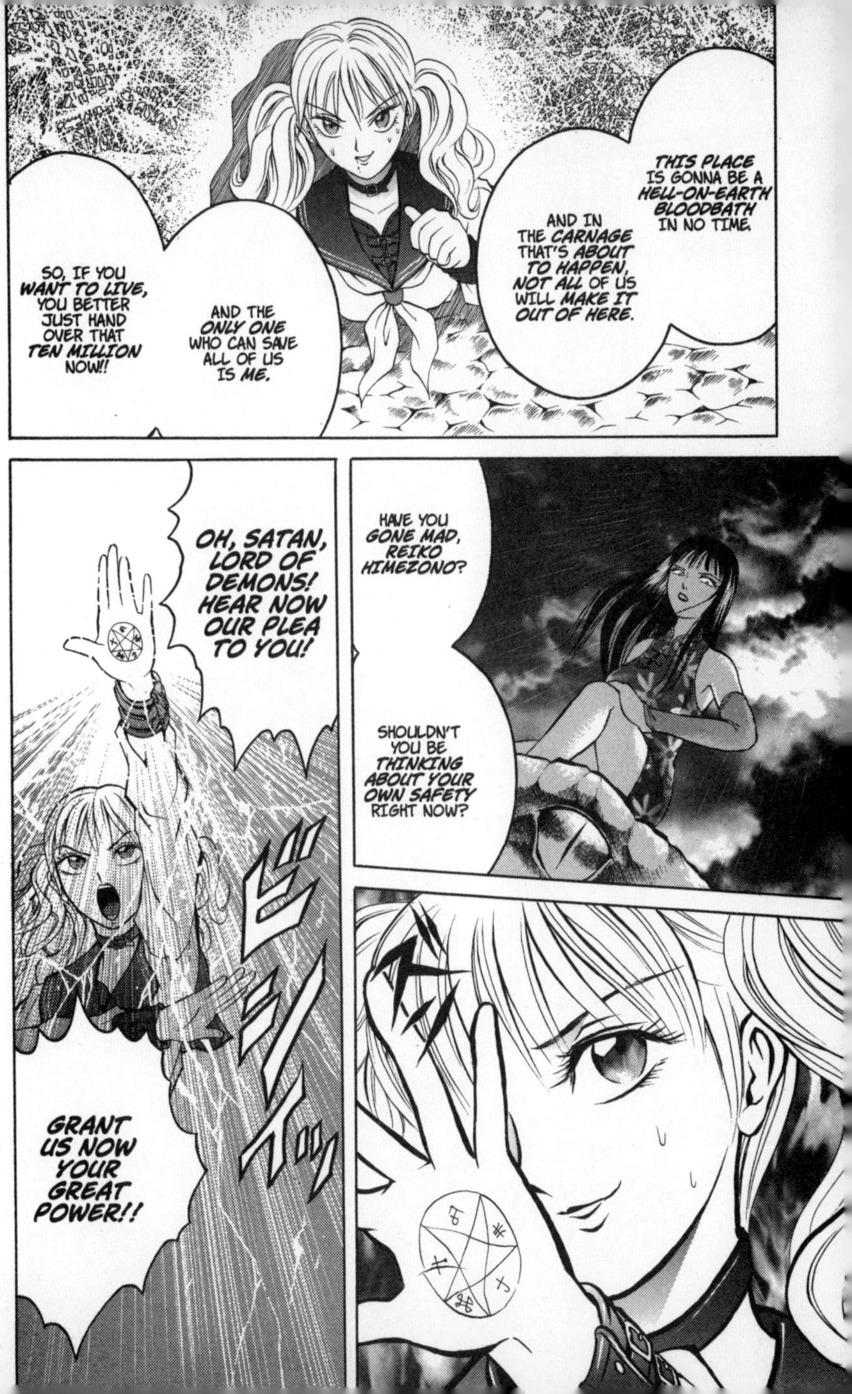
THIS PLACE IS GONNA BE A HELL-ON-EARTH BLOODBATH IN NO TIME.
AND IN THE CARNAGE THAT'S ABOUT TO HAPPEN, NOT ALL OF US WILL MAKE IT OUT OF HERE.
AND THE ONLY ONE WHO CAN SAVE ALL OF US IS ME.
SO, IF YOU WANT TO LIVE, YOU BETTER JUST HAND OVER THAT TEN MILLION NOW!!
HAVE YOU GONE MAD, REIKO HIMEZONO?
SHOULDN'T YOU BE THINKING ABOUT YOUR OWN SAFETY RIGHT NOW?
OH, SATAN, LORD OF DEMONS! HEAR NOW OUR PLEA TO YOU!
GRANT US NOW YOUR GREAT POWER!!

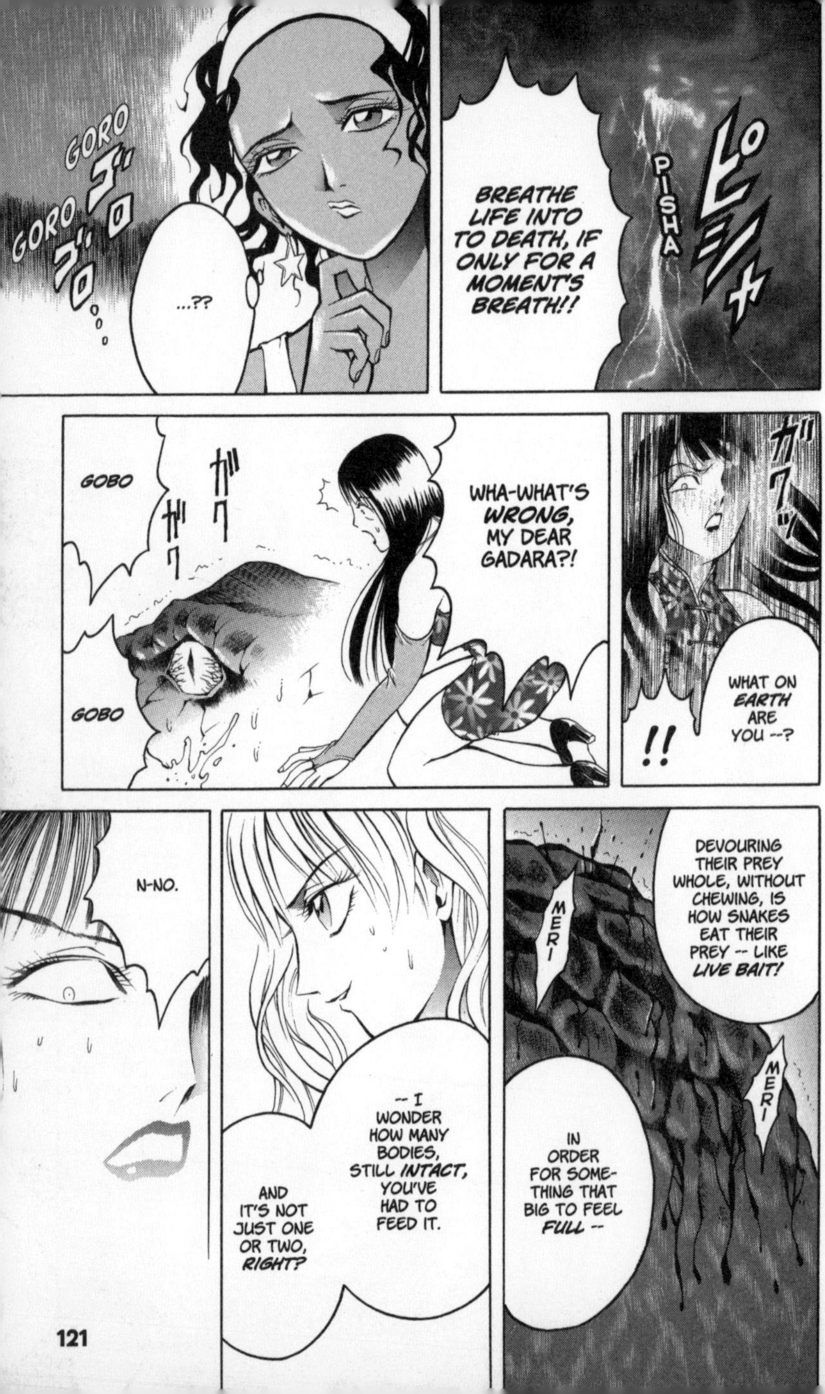

PISHA
ピシャ
BREATHE LIFE INTO TO DEATH, IF ONLY FOR A MOMENT'S BREATH!!
GORO GORO
ゴロゴロ
...??
ガクッ
WHAT ON EARTH ARE YOU --?
!!
WHA-WHAT'S *WRONG*, MY DEAR GADARA?!
GOBO
ガク ガク
GOBO
DEVOURING THEIR PREY WHOLE, WITHOUT CHEWING, IS HOW SNAKES EAT THEIR PREY -- LIKE *LIVE BAIT!*
MERI
MERI
IN ORDER FOR SOME-THING THAT BIG TO FEEL *FULL* --
-- I WONDER HOW MANY BODIES, STILL *INTACT*, YOU'VE HAD TO FEED IT.
AND IT'S NOT JUST ONE OR TWO, *RIGHT?*
N-NO.

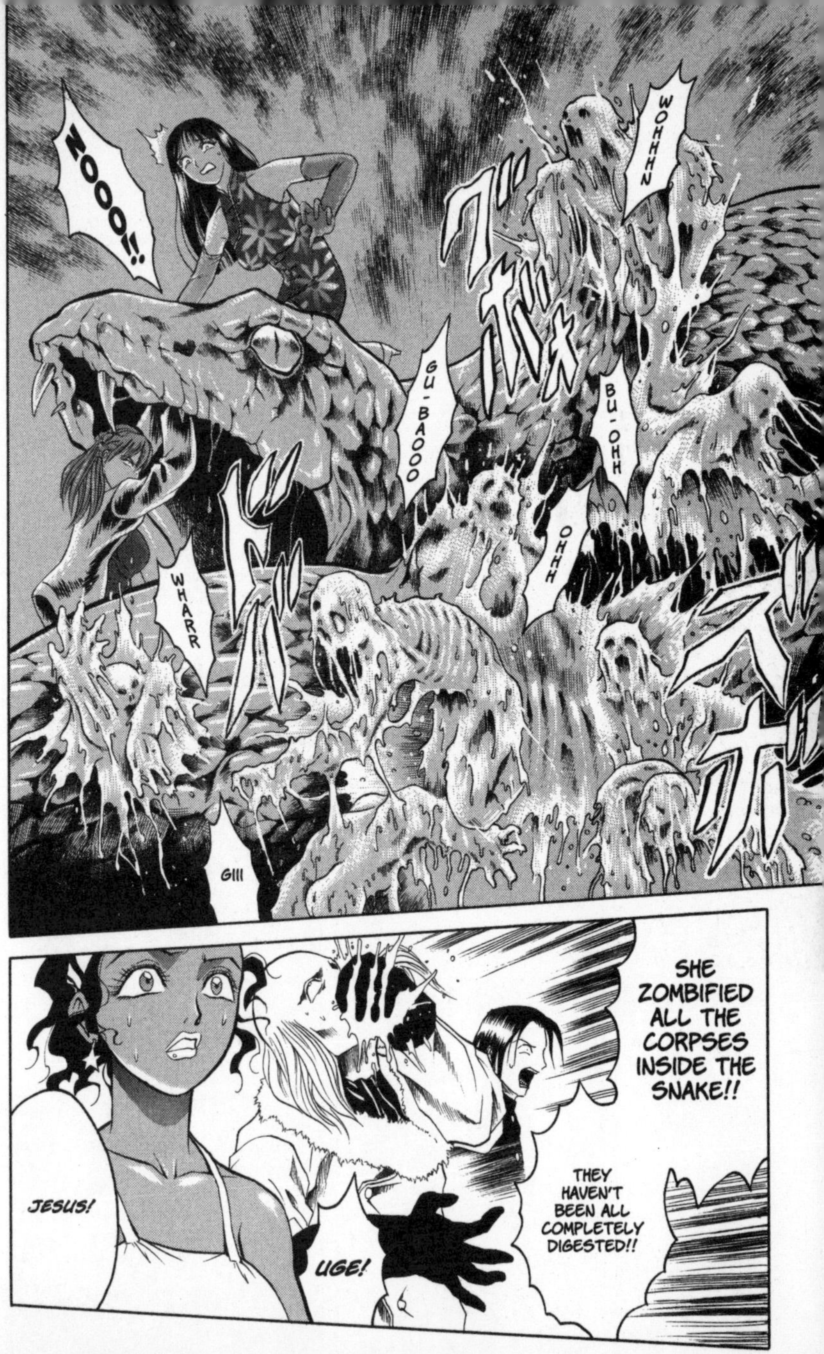
WOHHHN
BU-OHH
GU-BAOOO
ZOOOO!!
OHHH
WHARR
GIII
SHE ZOMBIFIED ALL THE CORPSES INSIDE THE SNAKE!!
THEY HAVEN'T BEEN ALL COMPLETELY DIGESTED!!
UGE!
JESUS!

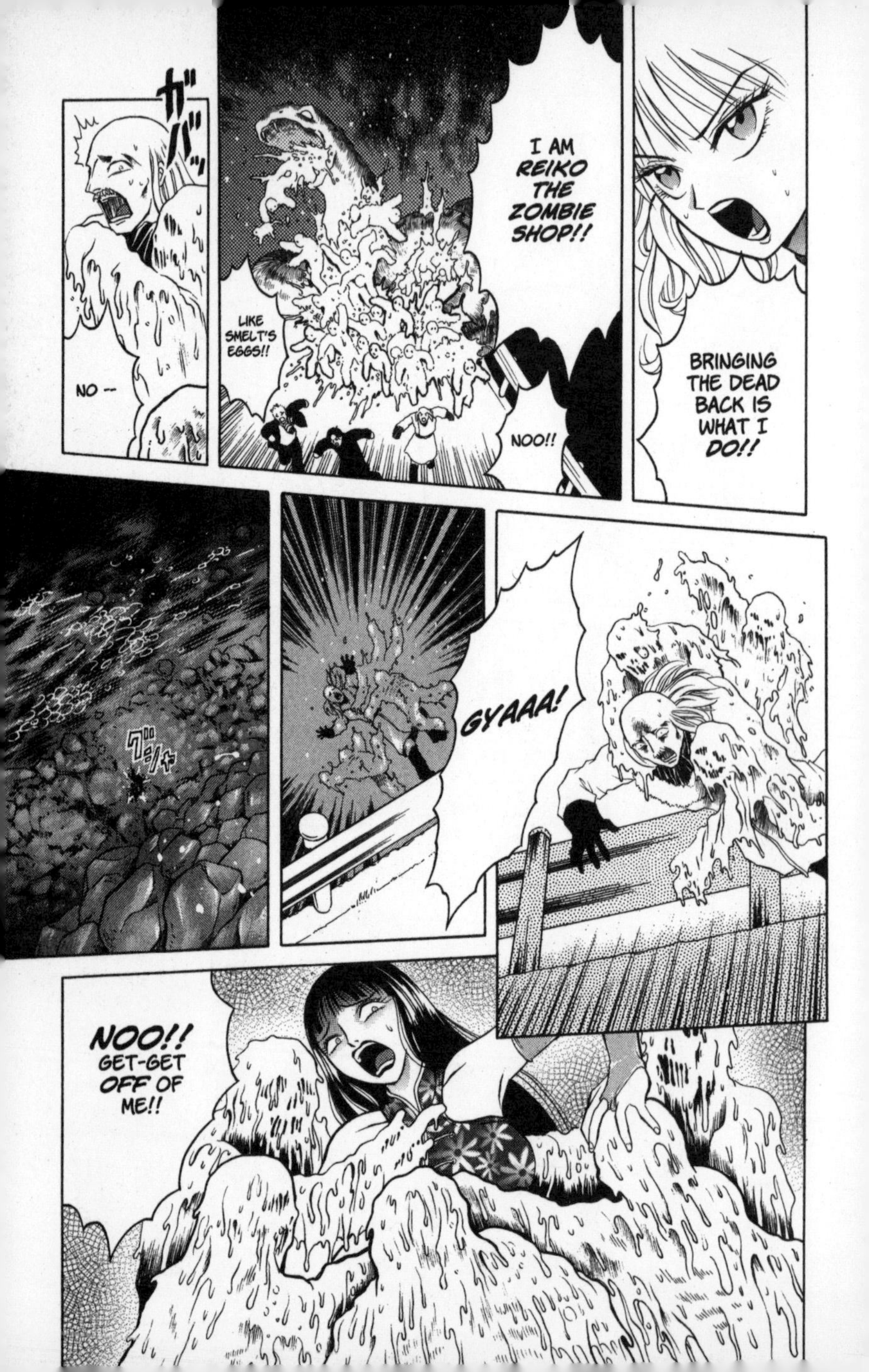
BRINGING THE DEAD BACK IS WHAT I DO!!
I AM REIKO THE ZOMBIE SHOP!!
LIKE SMELT'S EGGS!!
NOO!!
ガバッ
NO --
GYAAA!
グシャ
NOO!! GET-GET OFF OF ME!!

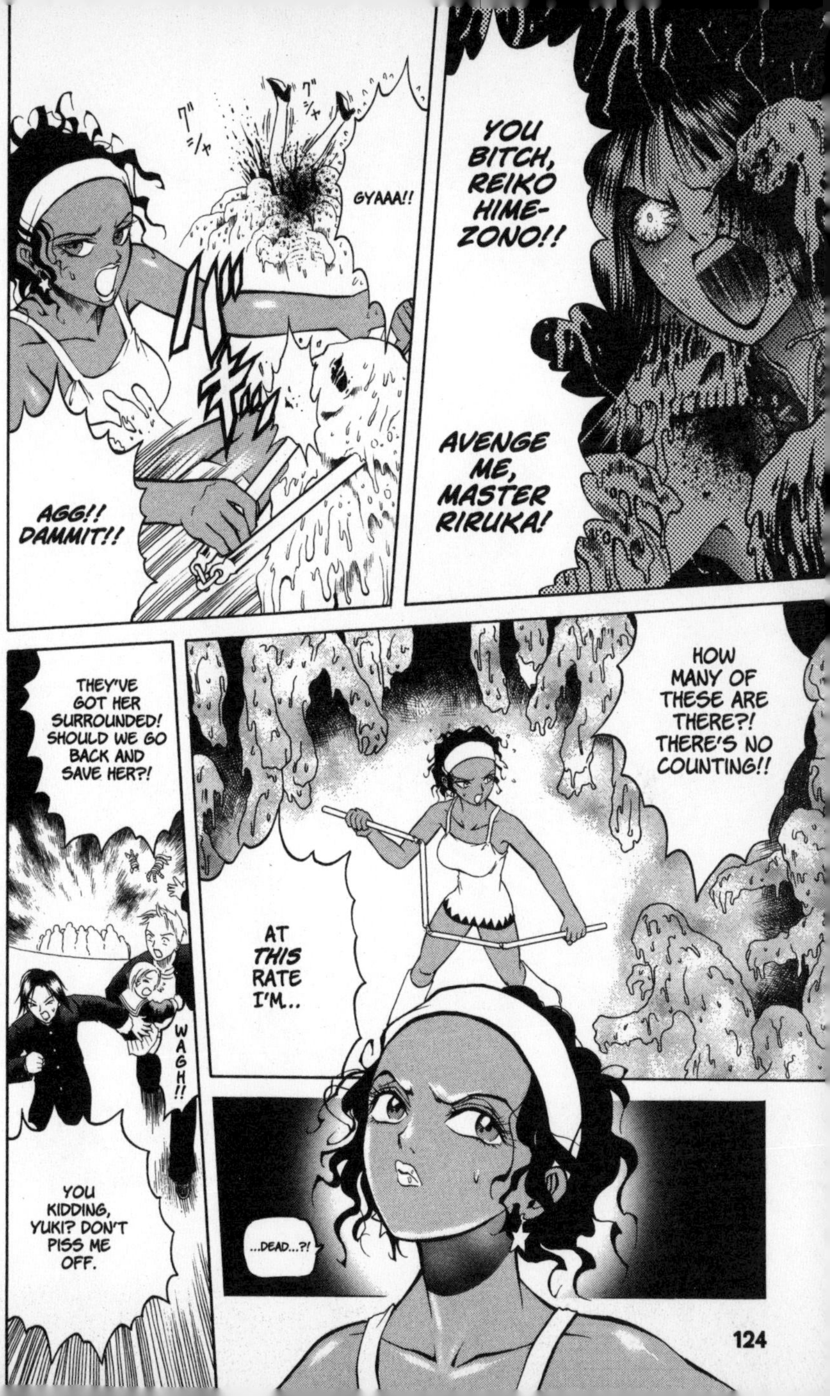
YOU BITCH, REIKO HIME-ZONO!!
AVENGE ME, MASTER RIRUKA!
GYAAA!!
AGG!! DAMMIT!!
HOW MANY OF THESE ARE THERE?! THERE'S NO COUNTING!!
AT *THIS* RATE I'M...
...DEAD...?!
THEY'VE GOT HER SURROUNDED! SHOULD WE GO BACK AND SAVE HER?!
WAGH!!
YOU KIDDING, YUKI? DON'T PISS ME OFF.

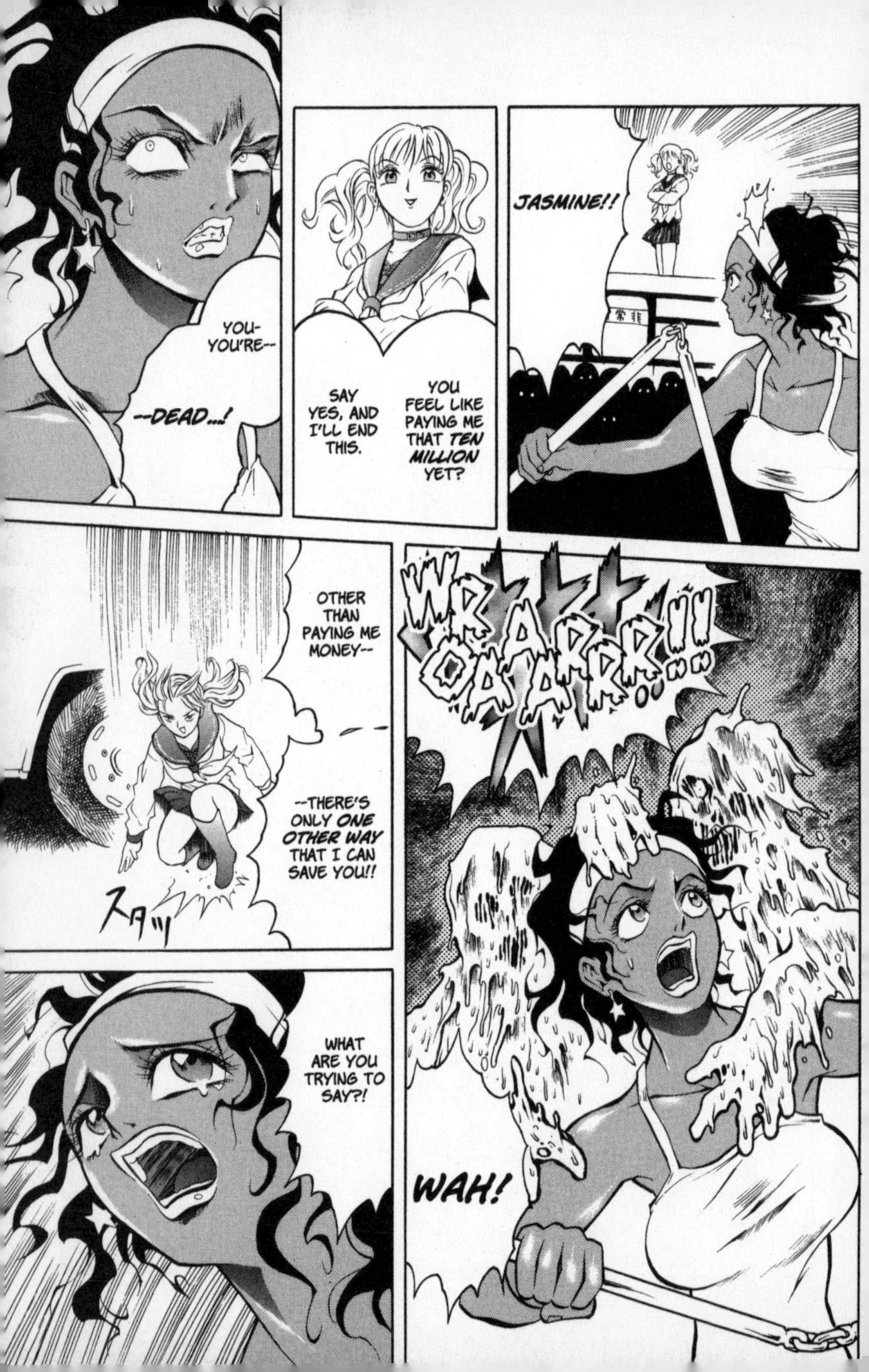
JASMINE!!
YOU FEEL LIKE PAYING ME THAT *TEN MILLION* YET?
SAY YES, AND I'LL END THIS.
YOU- YOU'RE--
--DEAD...!
WRARR!!
OAARR!!
WAH!
OTHER THAN PAYING ME MONEY--
--THERE'S ONLY *ONE OTHER WAY* THAT I CAN SAVE YOU!!
スタッ
WHAT ARE YOU TRYING TO SAY?!

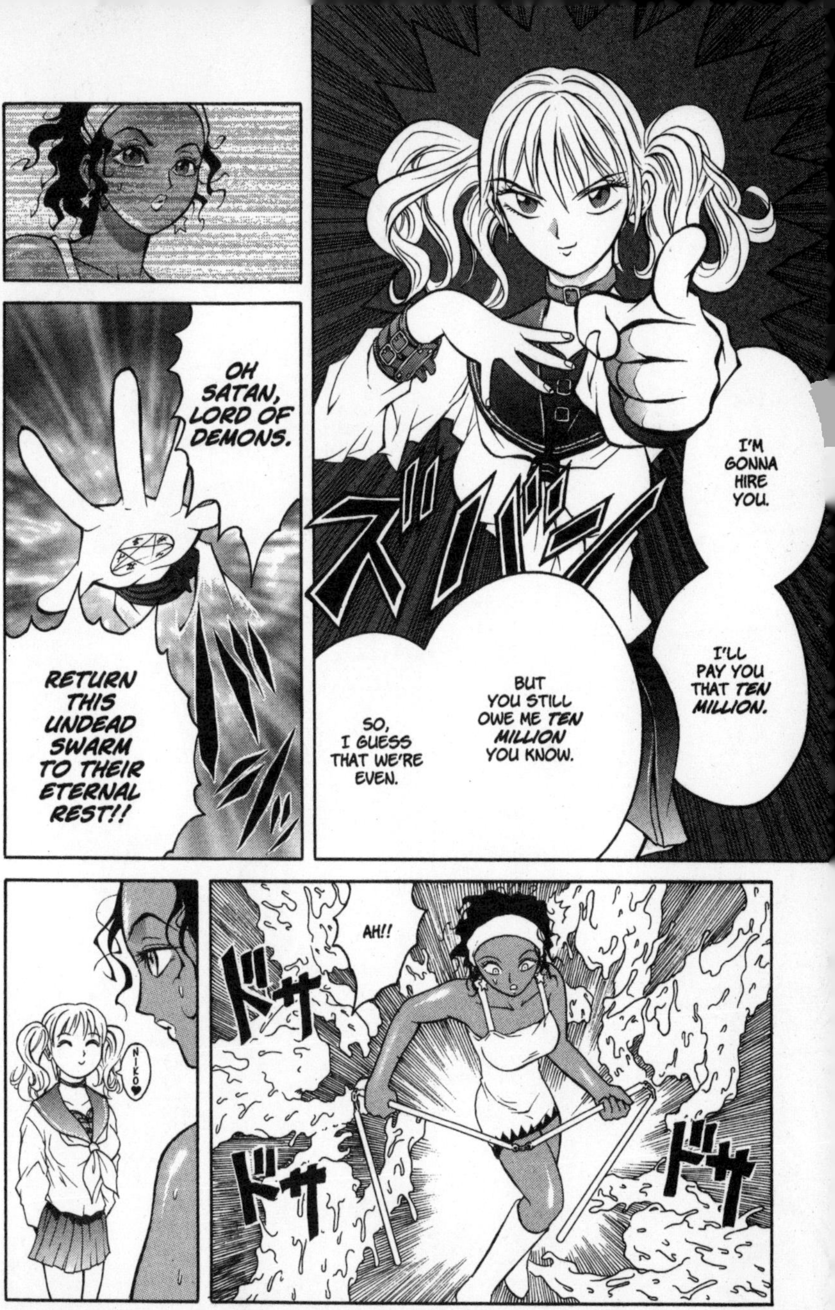
I'M GONNA HIRE YOU.
I'LL PAY YOU THAT *TEN MILLION.*
BUT YOU STILL OWE ME *TEN MILLION* YOU KNOW.
SO, I GUESS THAT WE'RE EVEN.
OH SATAN, LORD OF DEMONS.
RETURN THIS UNDEAD SWARM TO THEIR ETERNAL REST!!
AH!!
ドサ
ドサ
ドサ
NIKO♥

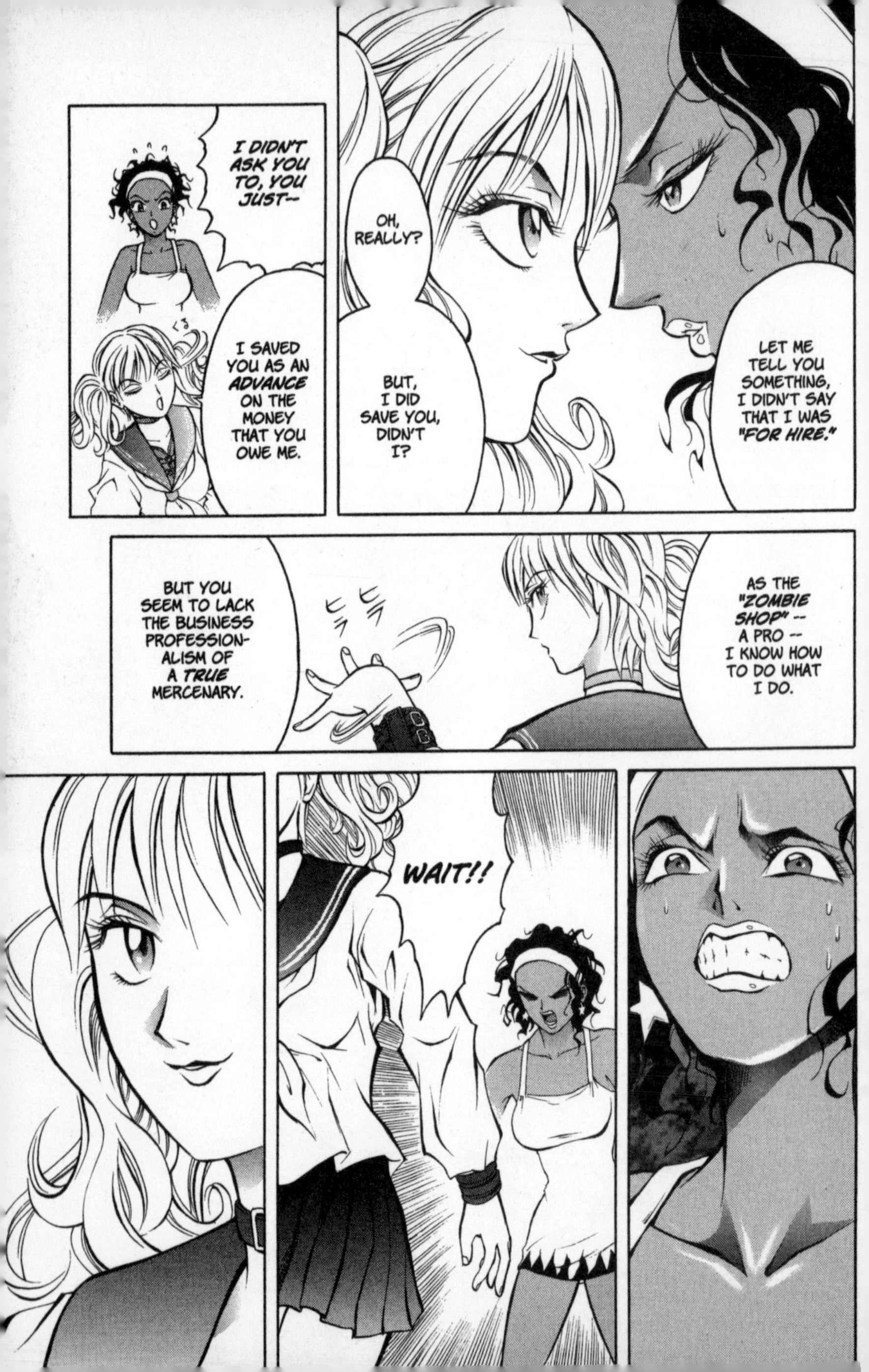
LET ME TELL YOU SOMETHING, I DIDN'T SAY THAT I WAS "FOR HIRE."
OH, REALLY?
BUT, I DID SAVE YOU, DIDN'T I?
I DIDN'T ASK YOU TO, YOU JUST--
I SAVED YOU AS AN ADVANCE ON THE MONEY THAT YOU OWE ME.
AS THE "ZOMBIE SHOP" -- A PRO -- I KNOW HOW TO DO WHAT I DO.
ヒラ ヒラ
BUT YOU SEEM TO LACK THE BUSINESS PROFESSION-ALISM OF A TRUE MERCENARY.
WAIT!!

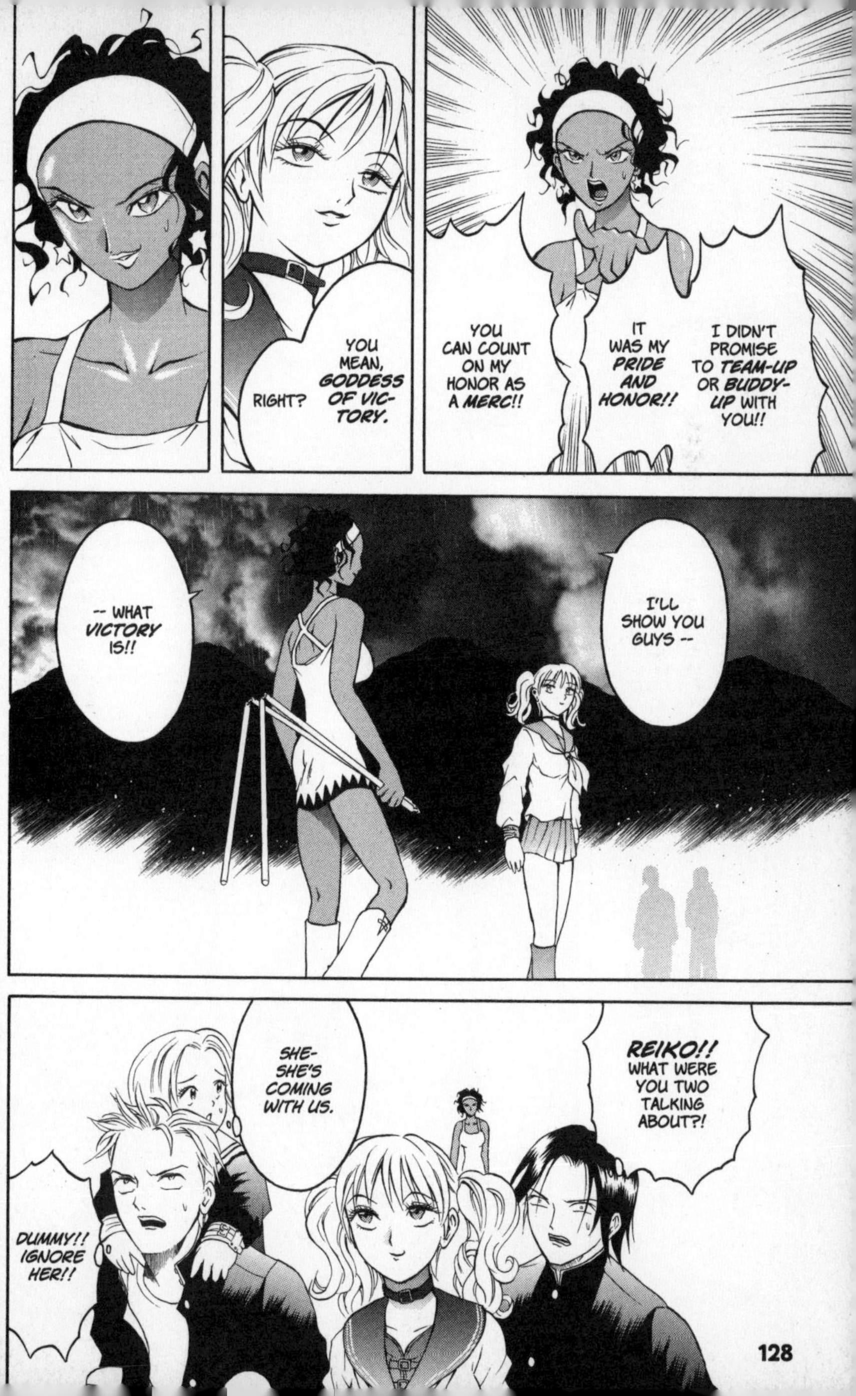
I DIDN'T PROMISE TO TEAM-UP OR BUDDY-UP WITH YOU!!
IT WAS MY PRIDE AND HONOR!!
YOU CAN COUNT ON MY HONOR AS A MERC!!
YOU MEAN, GODDESS OF VICTORY.
RIGHT?
I'LL SHOW YOU GUYS --
-- WHAT VICTORY IS!!
REIKO!! WHAT WERE YOU TWO TALKING ABOUT?!
SHE- SHE'S COMING WITH US.
DUMMY!! IGNORE HER!!

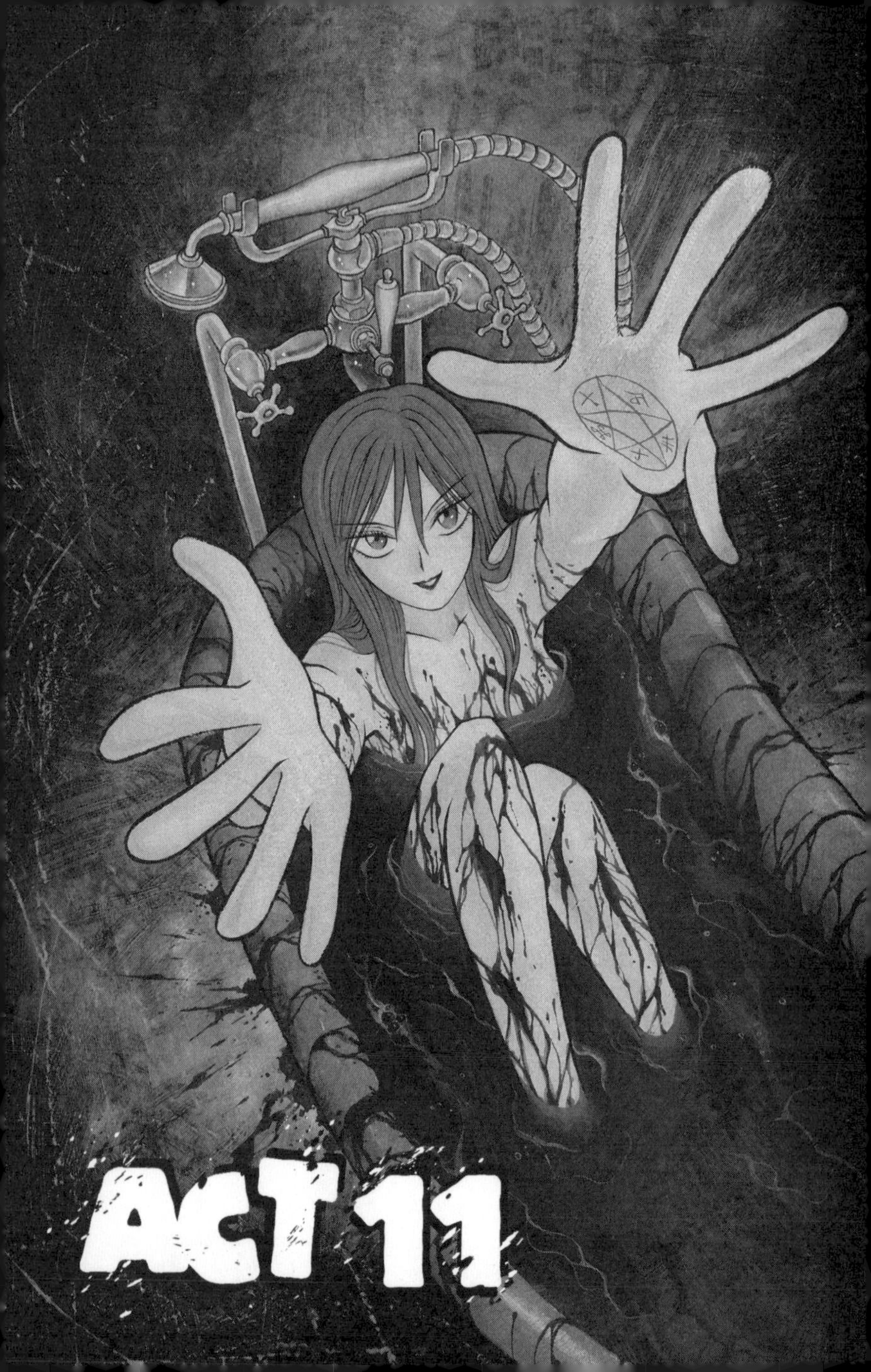
ACT 11

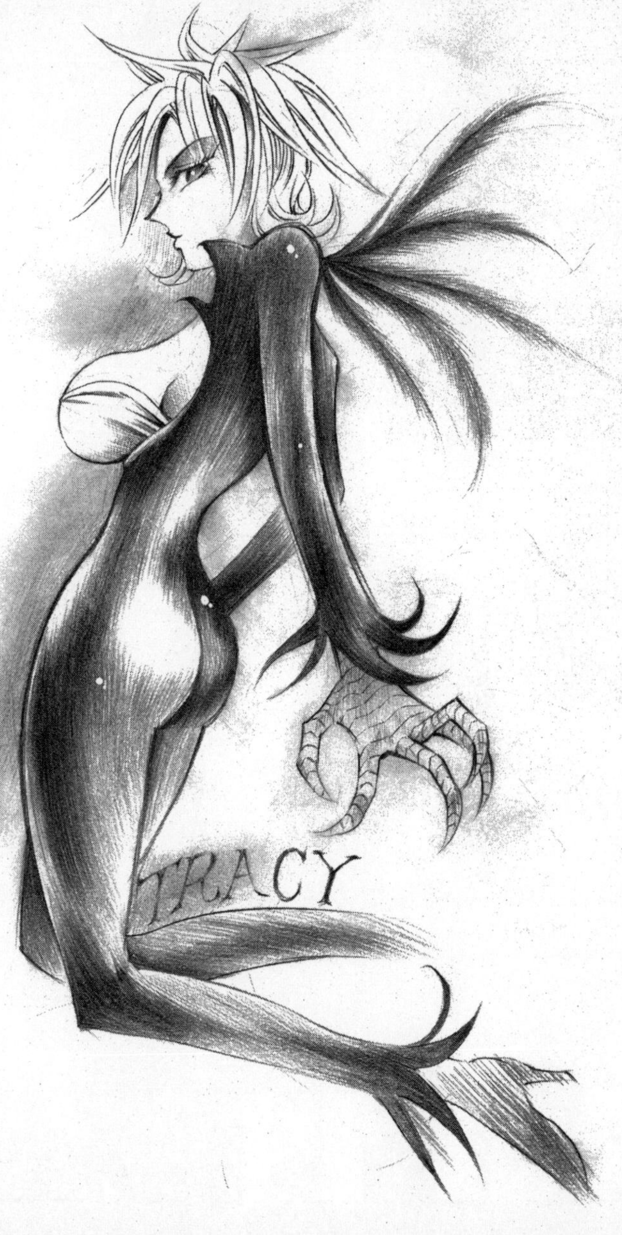
TRACY

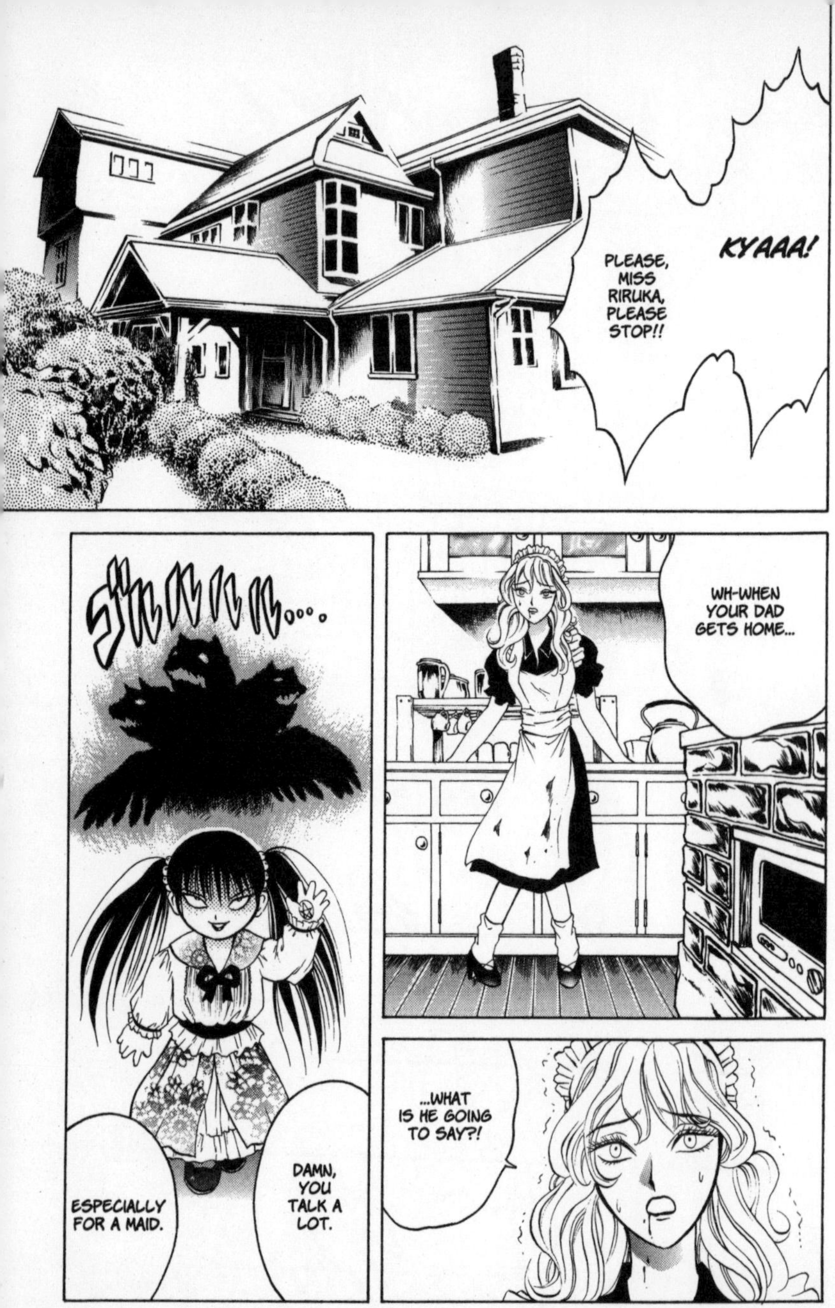
KYAAA!
PLEASE, MISS RIRUKA, PLEASE STOP!!
WH-WHEN YOUR DAD GETS HOME...
...WHAT IS HE GOING TO SAY?!
ジルハハハ…。
DAMN, YOU TALK A LOT.
ESPECIALLY FOR A MAID.

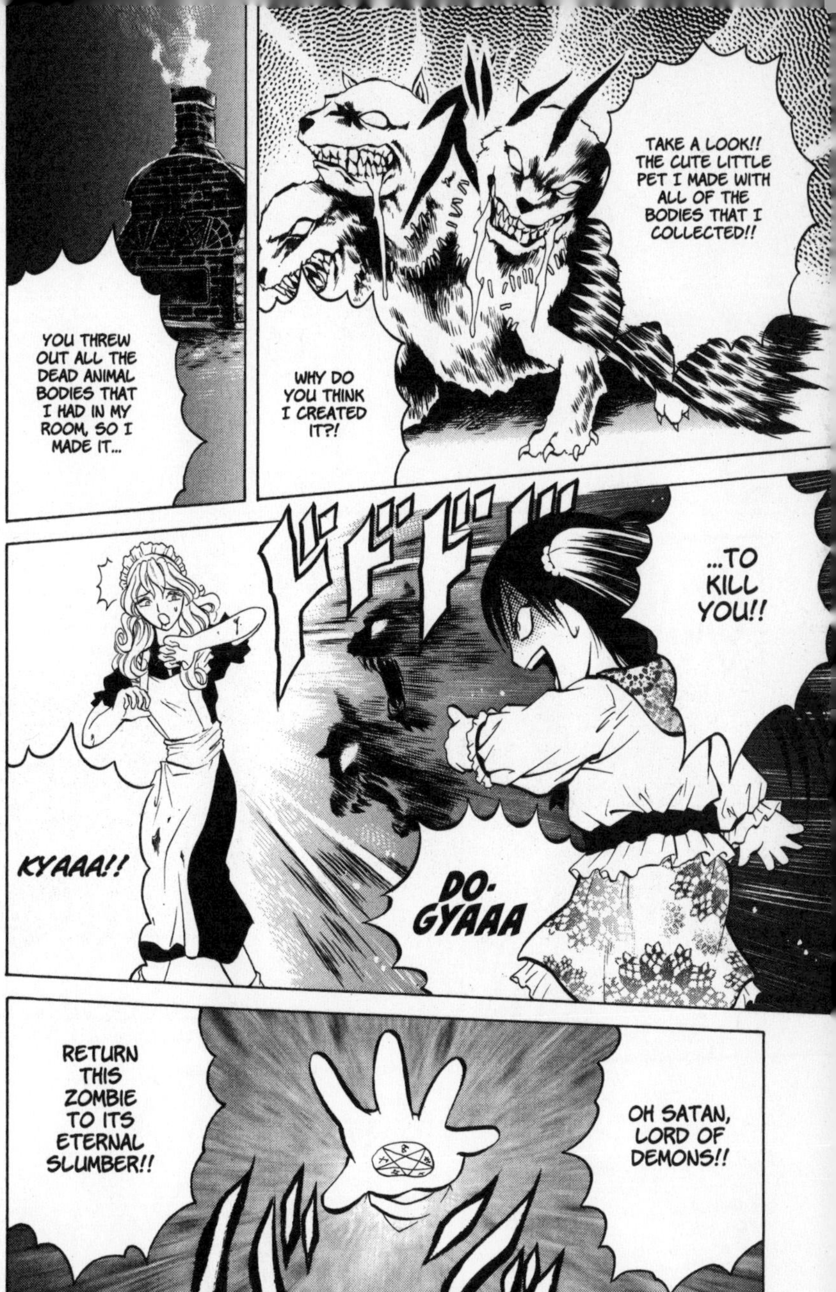
TAKE A LOOK!! THE CUTE LITTLE PET I MADE WITH ALL OF THE BODIES THAT I COLLECTED!!
WHY DO YOU THINK I CREATED IT?!
YOU THREW OUT ALL THE DEAD ANIMAL BODIES THAT I HAD IN MY ROOM, SO I MADE IT...
...TO KILL YOU!!
DO-GYAAA
KYAAA!!
OH SATAN, LORD OF DEMONS!!
RETURN THIS ZOMBIE TO ITS ETERNAL SLUMBER!!

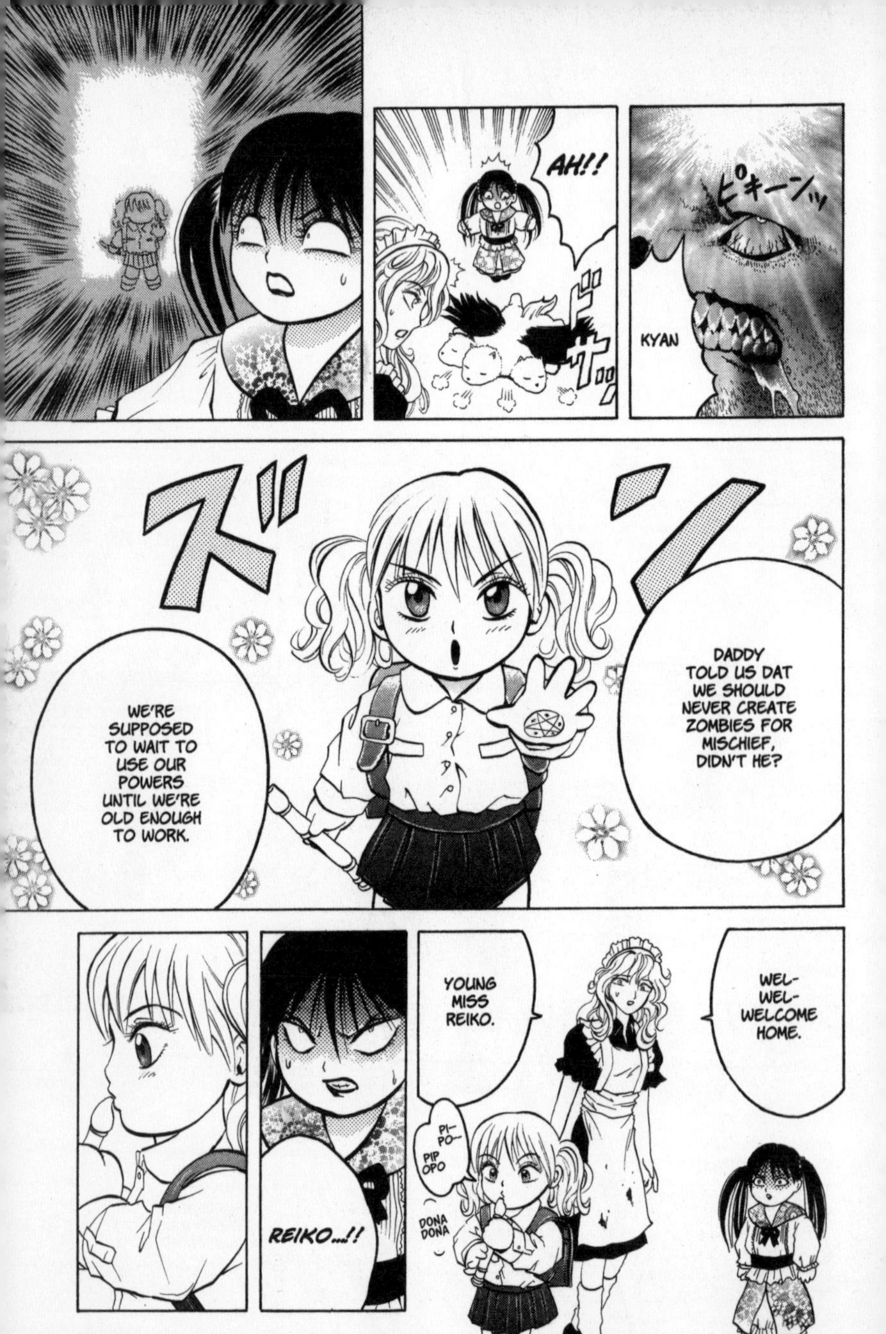
ピキーンッ
KYAN
AH!!
ドサッ
ズン
DADDY TOLD US DAT WE SHOULD NEVER CREATE ZOMBIES FOR MISCHIEF, DIDN'T HE?
WE'RE SUPPOSED TO WAIT TO USE OUR POWERS UNTIL WE'RE OLD ENOUGH TO WORK.
WEL- WEL- WELCOME HOME.
YOUNG MISS REIKO.
PI- PO- PIP OPO
DONA DONA
REIKO...!!

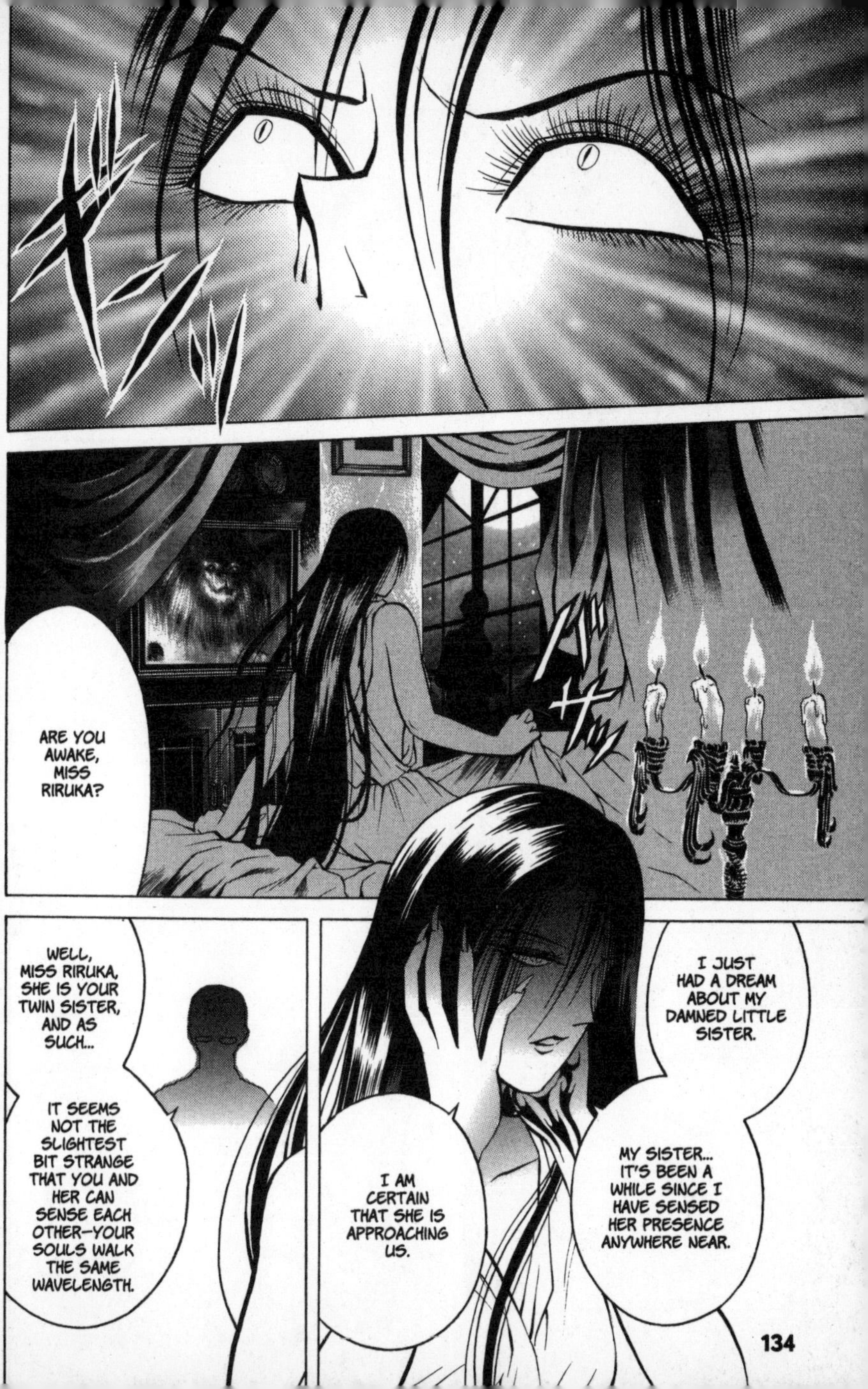
ARE YOU AWAKE, MISS RIRUKA?
I JUST HAD A DREAM ABOUT MY DAMNED LITTLE SISTER.
MY SISTER... IT'S BEEN A WHILE SINCE I HAVE SENSED HER PRESENCE ANYWHERE NEAR.
I AM CERTAIN THAT SHE IS APPROACHING US.
WELL, MISS RIRUKA, SHE IS YOUR TWIN SISTER, AND AS SUCH...
IT SEEMS NOT THE SLIGHTEST BIT STRANGE THAT YOU AND HER CAN SENSE EACH OTHER—YOUR SOULS WALK THE SAME WAVELENGTH.

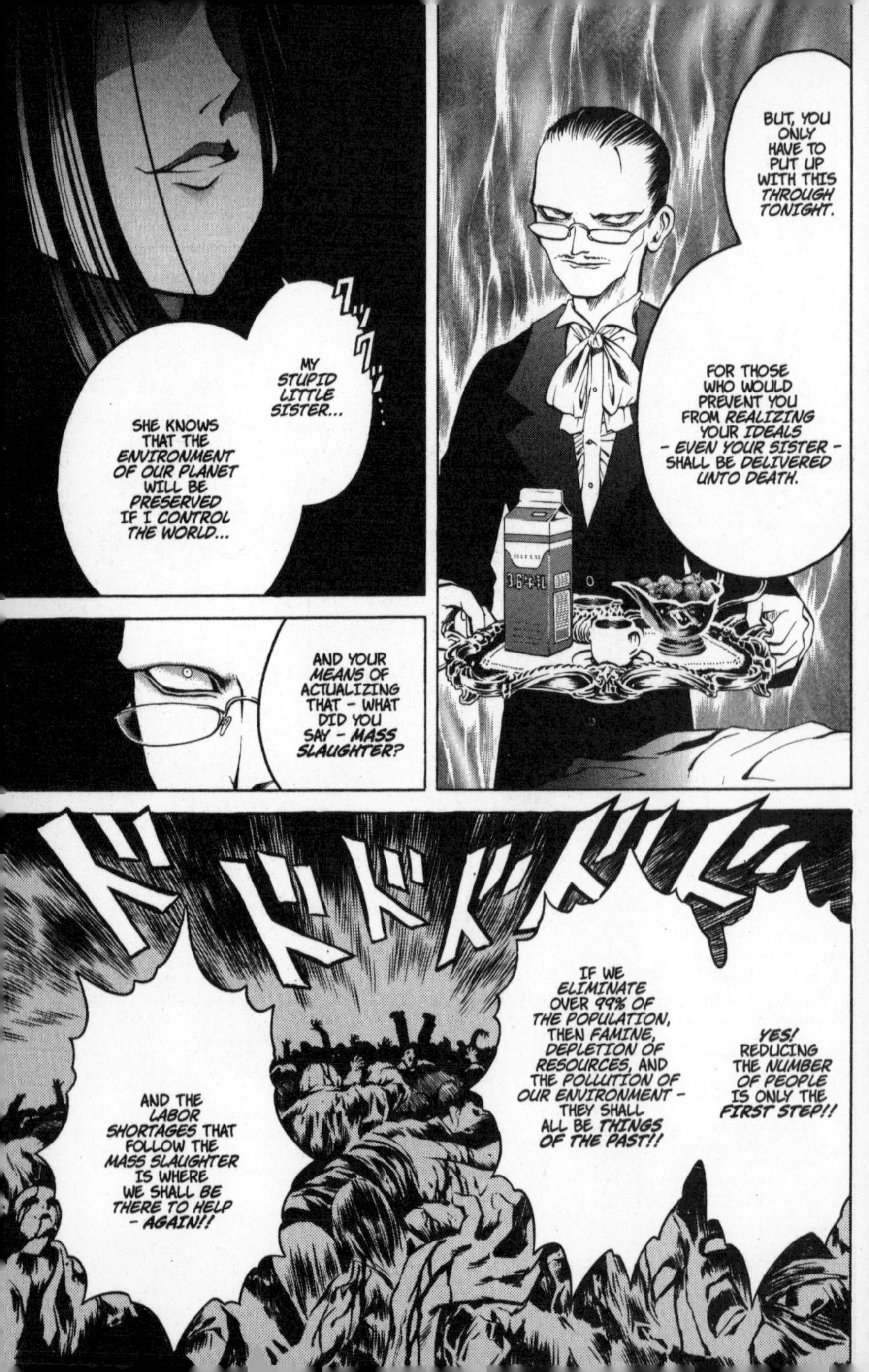
BUT, YOU ONLY HAVE TO PUT UP WITH THIS THROUGH TONIGHT.
FOR THOSE WHO WOULD PREVENT YOU FROM REALIZING YOUR IDEALS - EVEN YOUR SISTER - SHALL BE DELIVERED UNTO DEATH.
MY STUPID LITTLE SISTER...
SHE KNOWS THAT THE ENVIRONMENT OF OUR PLANET WILL BE PRESERVED IF I CONTROL THE WORLD...
AND YOUR MEANS OF ACTUALIZING THAT - WHAT DID YOU SAY - MASS SLAUGHTER?
YES! REDUCING THE NUMBER OF PEOPLE IS ONLY THE FIRST STEP!!
IF WE ELIMINATE OVER 99% OF THE POPULATION, THEN FAMINE, DEPLETION OF RESOURCES, AND THE POLLUTION OF OUR ENVIRONMENT - THEY SHALL ALL BE THINGS OF THE PAST!!
AND THE LABOR SHORTAGES THAT FOLLOW THE MASS SLAUGHTER IS WHERE WE SHALL BE THERE TO HELP - AGAIN!!

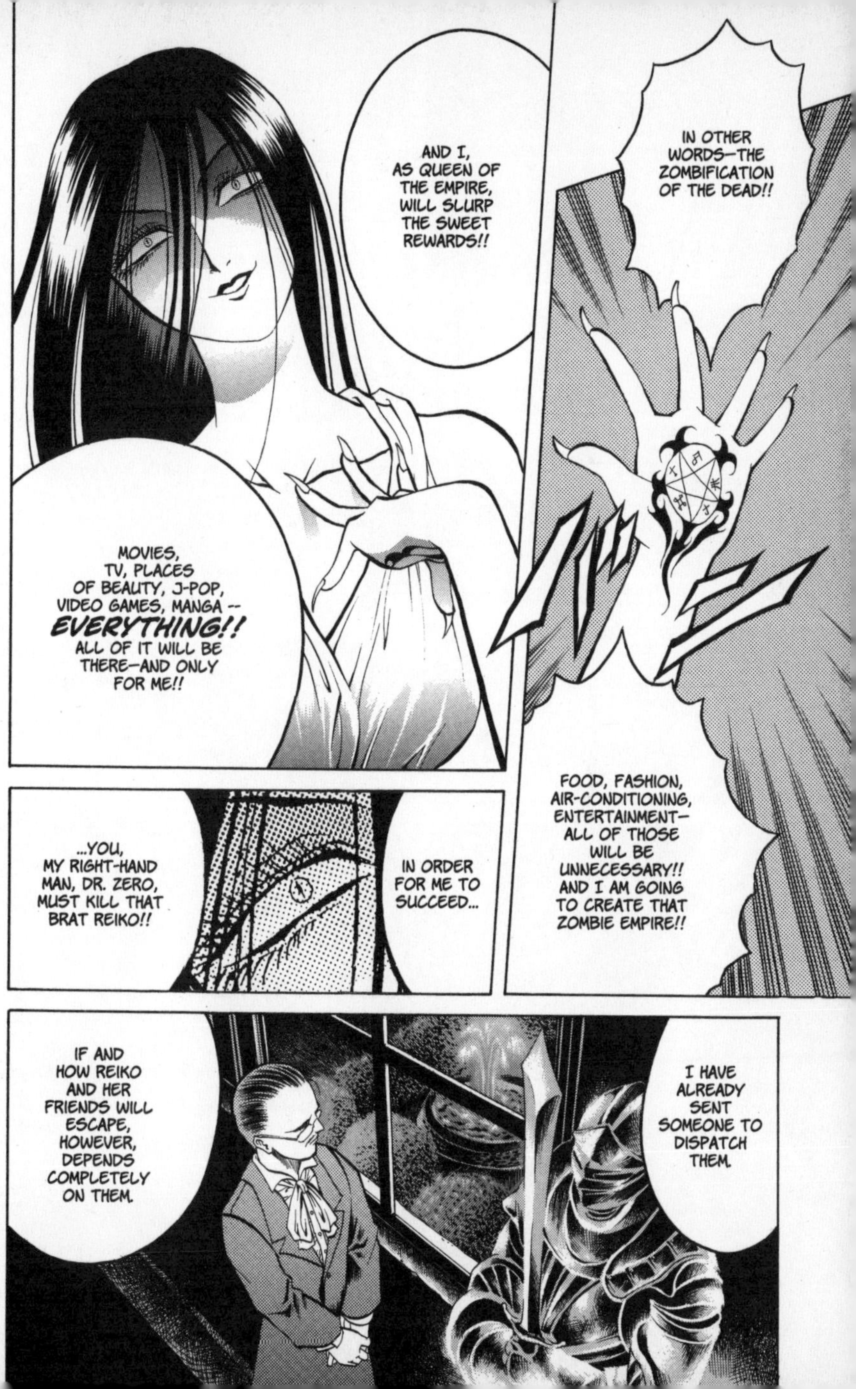
IN OTHER WORDS—THE ZOMBIFICATION OF THE DEAD!!
FOOD, FASHION, AIR-CONDITIONING, ENTERTAINMENT— ALL OF THOSE WILL BE UNNECESSARY!! AND I AM GOING TO CREATE THAT ZOMBIE EMPIRE!!
AND I, AS QUEEN OF THE EMPIRE, WILL SLURP THE SWEET REWARDS!!
MOVIES, TV, PLACES OF BEAUTY, J-POP, VIDEO GAMES, MANGA -- *EVERYTHING!!* ALL OF IT WILL BE THERE—AND ONLY FOR ME!!
IN ORDER FOR ME TO SUCCEED...
...YOU, MY RIGHT-HAND MAN, DR. ZERO, MUST KILL THAT BRAT REIKO!!
I HAVE ALREADY SENT SOMEONE TO DISPATCH THEM.
IF AND HOW REIKO AND HER FRIENDS WILL ESCAPE, HOWEVER, DEPENDS COMPLETELY ON THEM.

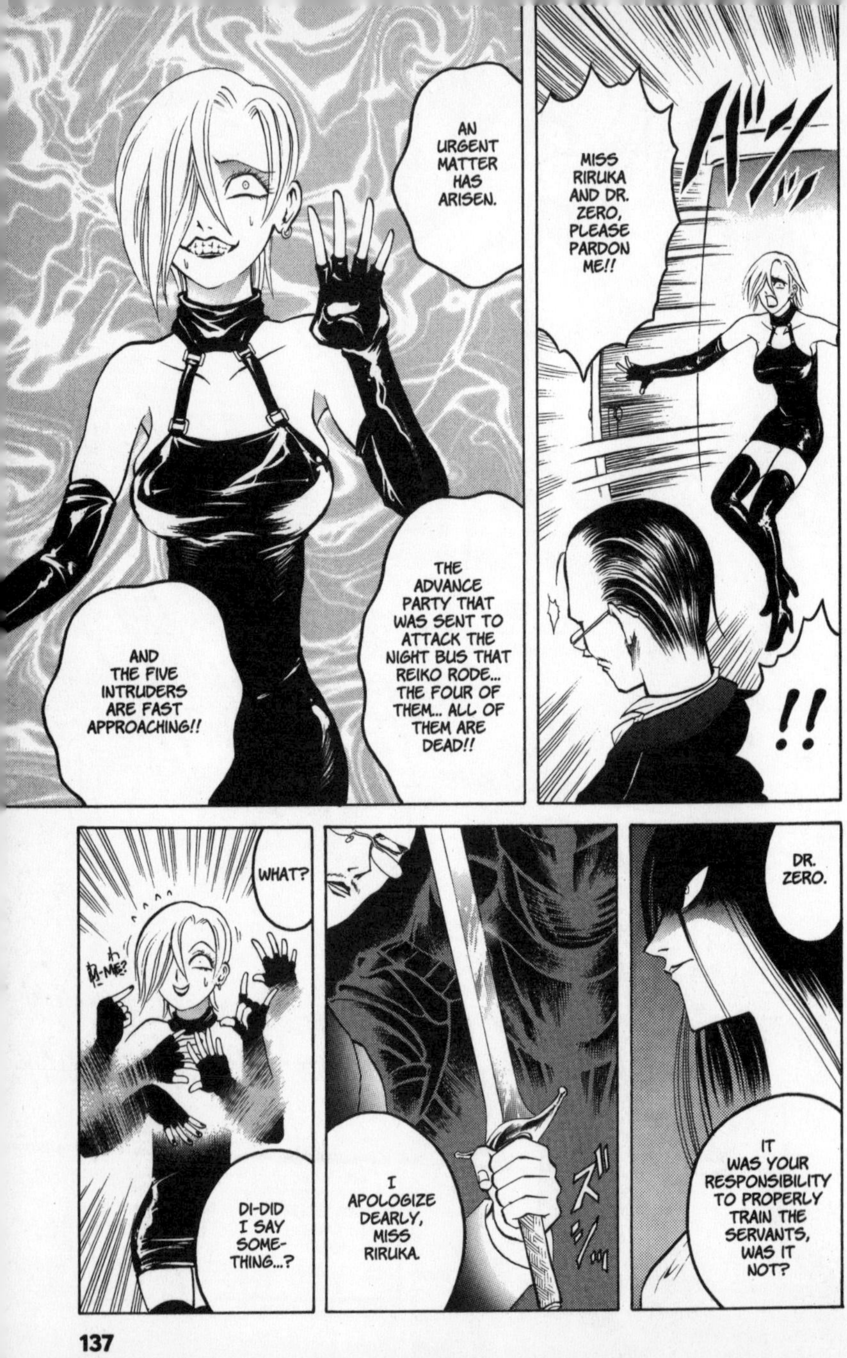
MISS RIRUKA AND DR. ZERO, PLEASE PARDON ME!!
!!
AN URGENT MATTER HAS ARISEN.
THE ADVANCE PARTY THAT WAS SENT TO ATTACK THE NIGHT BUS THAT REIKO RODE... THE FOUR OF THEM... ALL OF THEM ARE DEAD!!
AND THE FIVE INTRUDERS ARE FAST APPROACHING!!
DR. ZERO.
IT WAS YOUR RESPONSIBILITY TO PROPERLY TRAIN THE SERVANTS, WAS IT NOT?
I APOLOGIZE DEARLY, MISS RIRUKA.
WHAT?
M-ME?
DI-DID I SAY SOME-THING...?

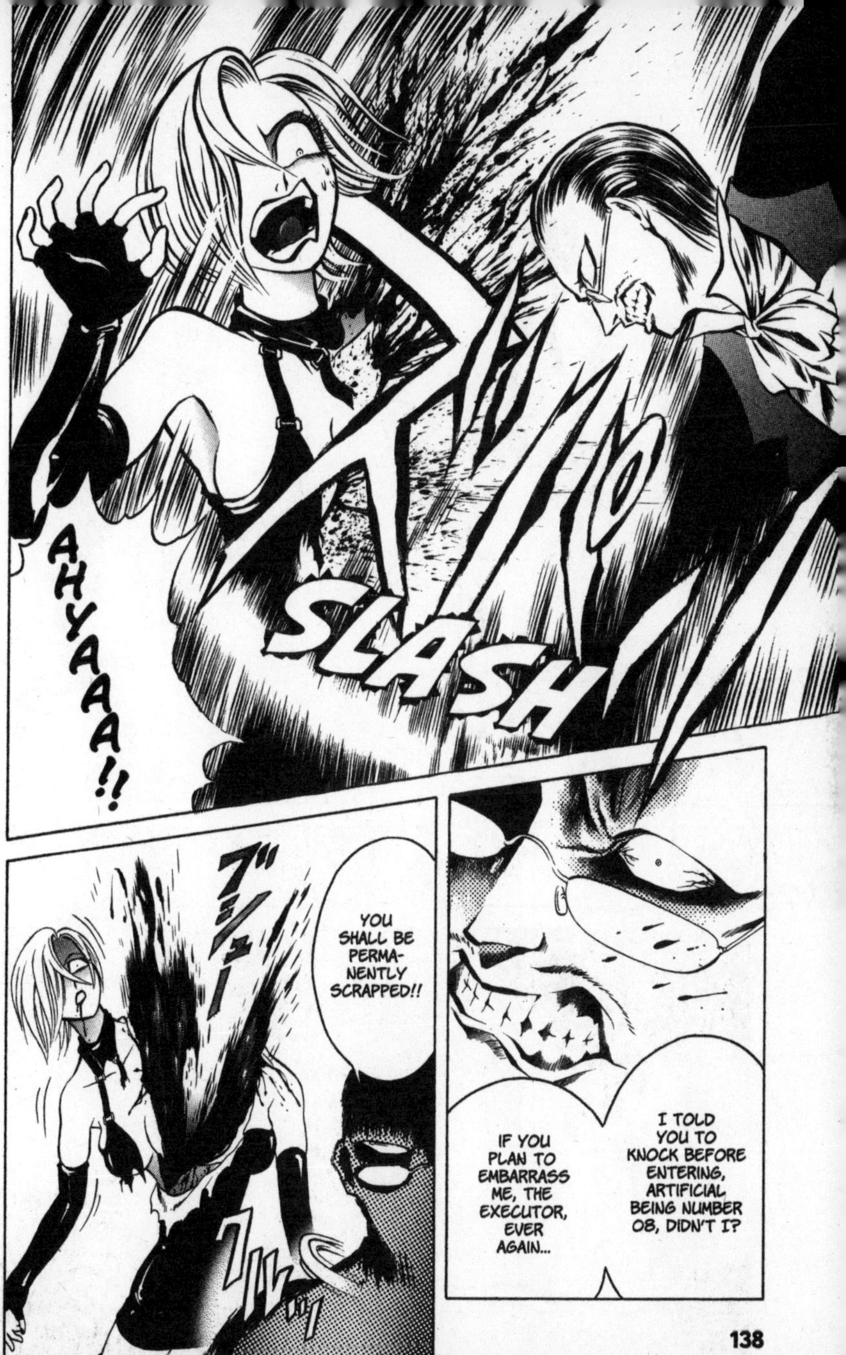
AHYAAAA!!
SLASH
I TOLD YOU TO KNOCK BEFORE ENTERING, ARTIFICIAL BEING NUMBER 08, DIDN'T I?
IF YOU PLAN TO EMBARRASS ME, THE EXECUTOR, EVER AGAIN...
YOU SHALL BE PERMA-NENTLY SCRAPPED!!

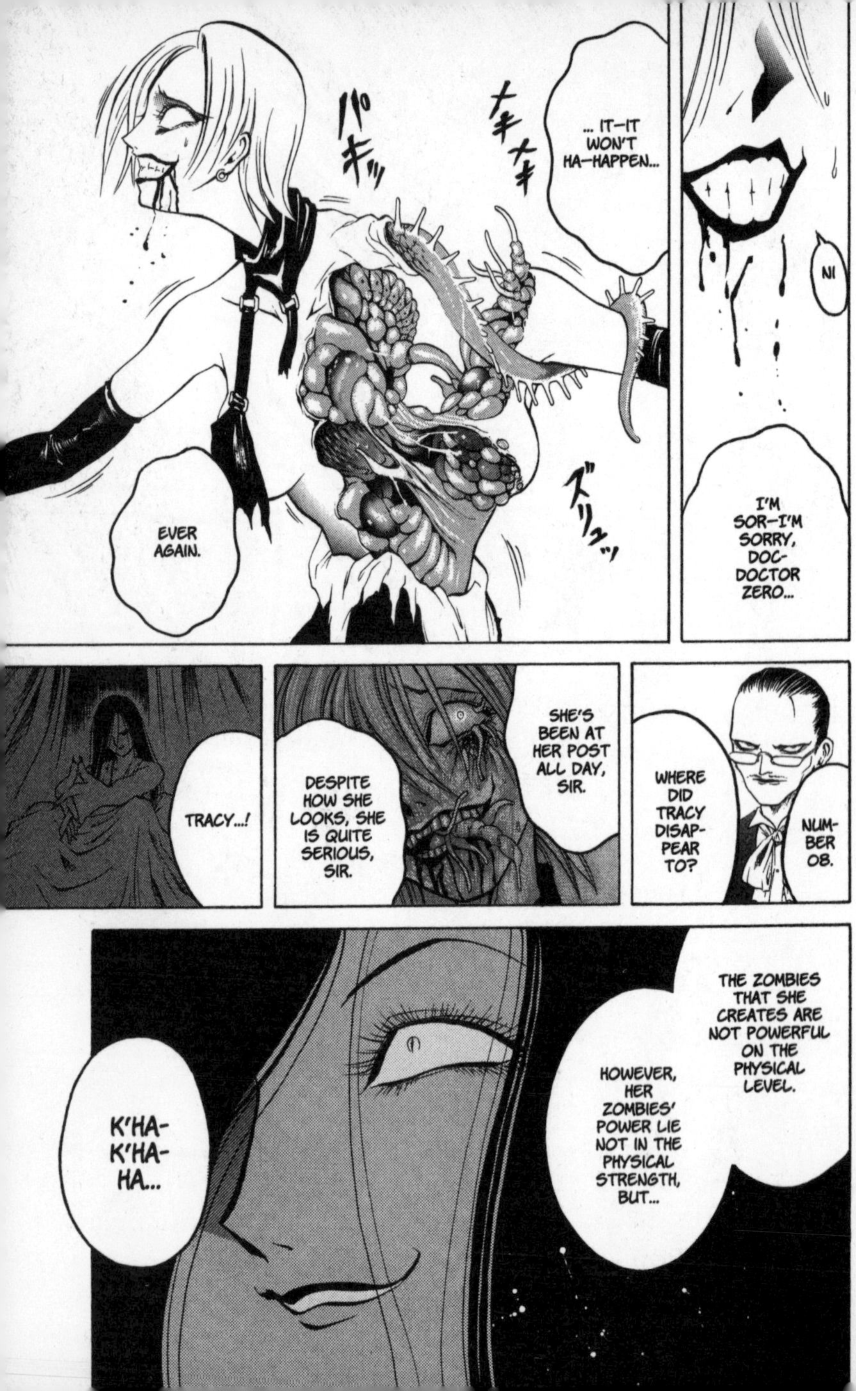
NI
I'M SOR—I'M SORRY, DOC-DOCTOR ZERO...
... IT—IT WON'T HA—HAPPEN...
メキメキ
パキッ
ズリュッ
EVER AGAIN.
NUMBER 08.
WHERE DID TRACY DISAPPEAR TO?
SHE'S BEEN AT HER POST ALL DAY, SIR.
DESPITE HOW SHE LOOKS, SHE IS QUITE SERIOUS, SIR.
TRACY...!
THE ZOMBIES THAT SHE CREATES ARE NOT POWERFUL ON THE PHYSICAL LEVEL.
HOWEVER, HER ZOMBIES' POWER LIE NOT IN THE PHYSICAL STRENGTH, BUT...
K'HA-K'HA-HA...

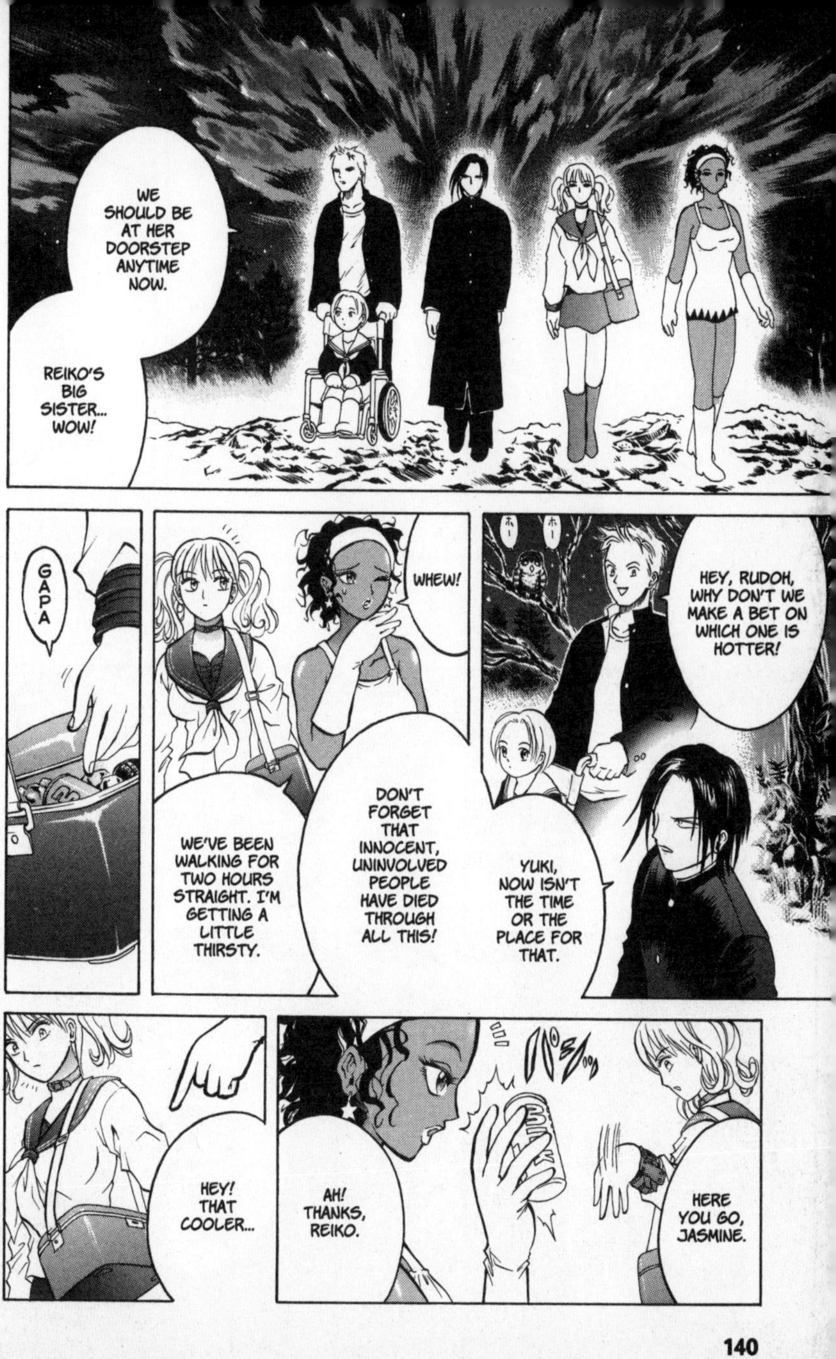
WE SHOULD BE AT HER DOORSTEP ANYTIME NOW.
REIKO'S BIG SISTER... WOW!
ホー
ホー
HEY, RUDOH, WHY DON'T WE MAKE A BET ON WHICH ONE IS HOTTER!
YUKI, NOW ISN'T THE TIME OR THE PLACE FOR THAT.
WHEW!
DON'T FORGET THAT INNOCENT, UNINVOLVED PEOPLE HAVE DIED THROUGH ALL THIS!
WE'VE BEEN WALKING FOR TWO HOURS STRAIGHT. I'M GETTING A LITTLE THIRSTY.
GAPA
HERE YOU GO, JASMINE.
AH! THANKS, REIKO.
HEY! THAT COOLER...

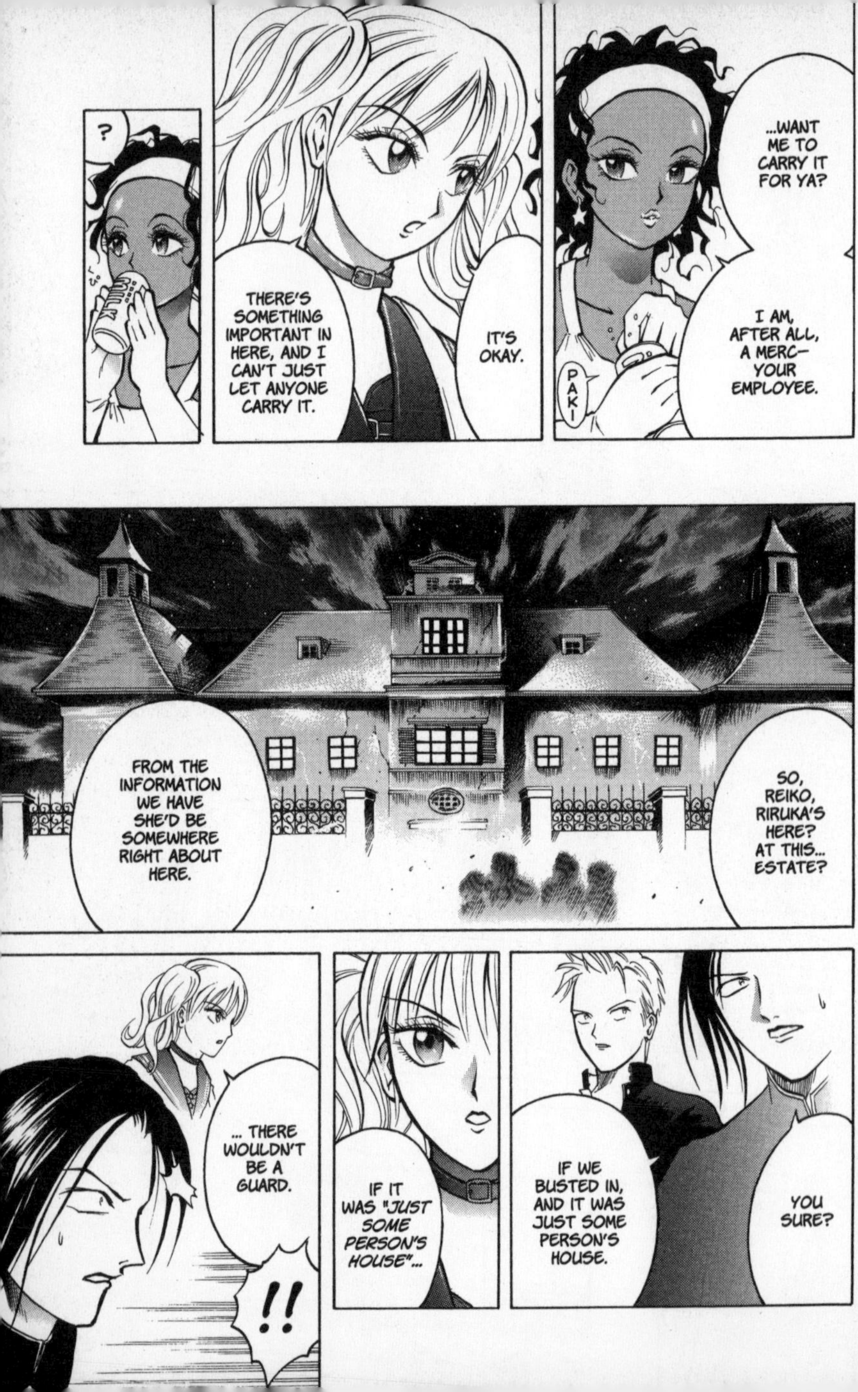
...WANT ME TO CARRY IT FOR YA?
I AM, AFTER ALL, A MERC— YOUR EMPLOYEE.
PAKI
IT'S OKAY.
THERE'S SOMETHING IMPORTANT IN HERE, AND I CAN'T JUST LET ANYONE CARRY IT.
?
SO, REIKO, RIRUKA'S HERE? AT THIS... ESTATE?
FROM THE INFORMATION WE HAVE SHE'D BE SOMEWHERE RIGHT ABOUT HERE.
YOU SURE?
IF WE BUSTED IN, AND IT WAS JUST SOME PERSON'S HOUSE.
IF IT WAS "JUST SOME PERSON'S HOUSE"...
... THERE WOULDN'T BE A GUARD.
!!

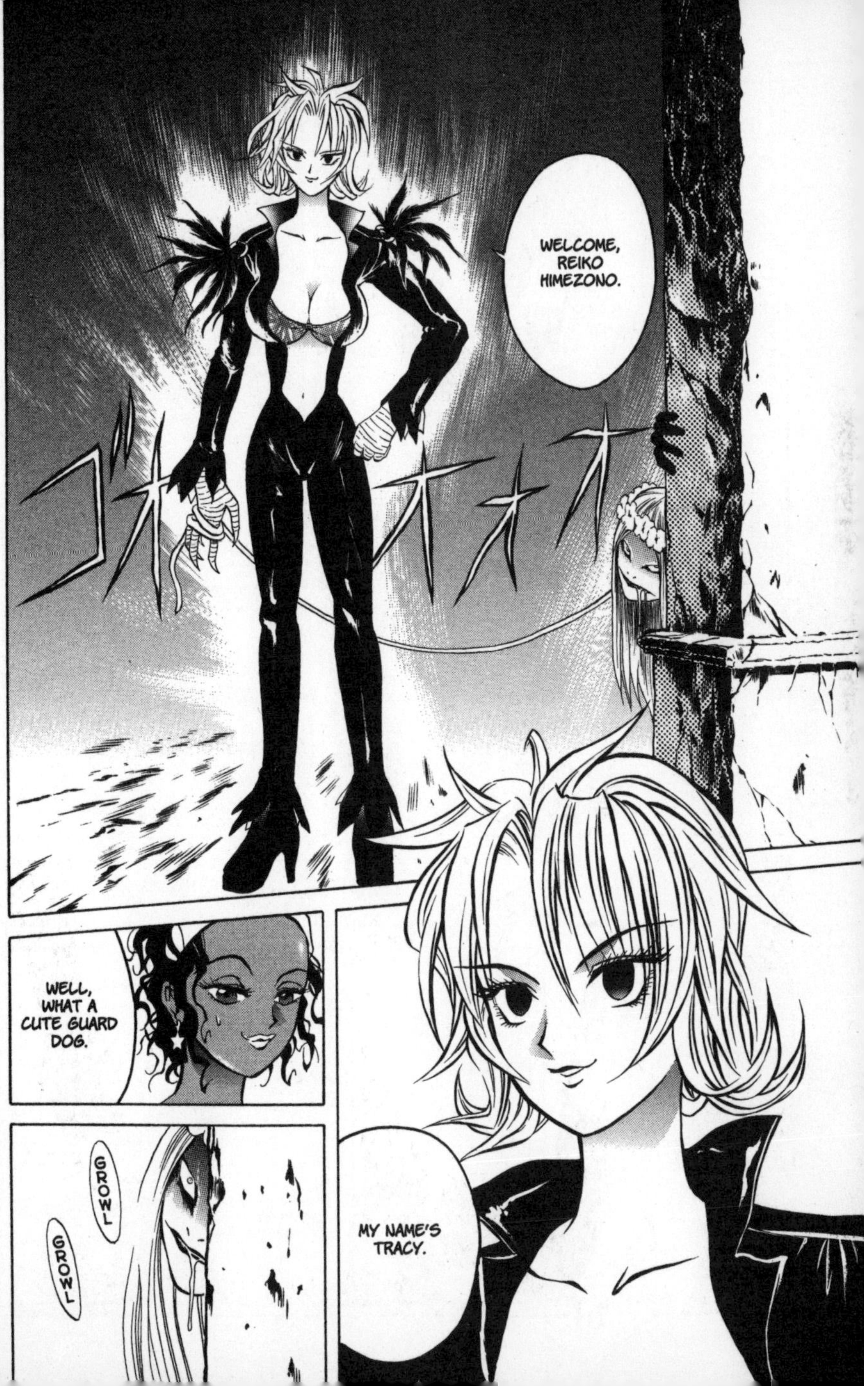
WELCOME, REIKO HIMEZONO.
ゴオオオオ
MY NAME'S TRACY.
WELL, WHAT A CUTE GUARD DOG.
GROWL
GROWL

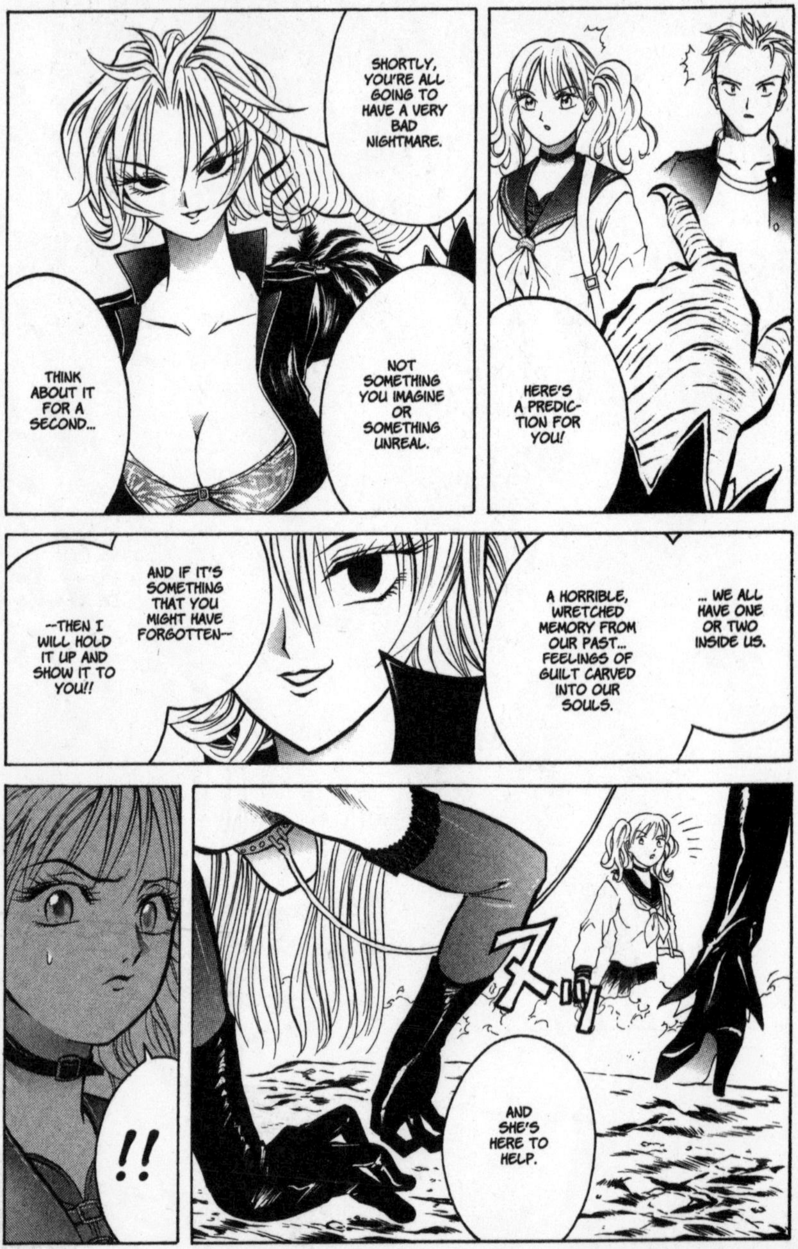
HERE'S A PREDICTION FOR YOU!
SHORTLY, YOU'RE ALL GOING TO HAVE A VERY BAD NIGHTMARE.
NOT SOMETHING YOU IMAGINE OR SOMETHING UNREAL.
THINK ABOUT IT FOR A SECOND...
... WE ALL HAVE ONE OR TWO INSIDE US.
A HORRIBLE, WRETCHED MEMORY FROM OUR PAST... FEELINGS OF GUILT CARVED INTO OUR SOULS.
AND IF IT'S SOMETHING THAT YOU MIGHT HAVE FORGOTTEN--
--THEN I WILL HOLD IT UP AND SHOW IT TO YOU!!
スッ
AND SHE'S HERE TO HELP.
!!

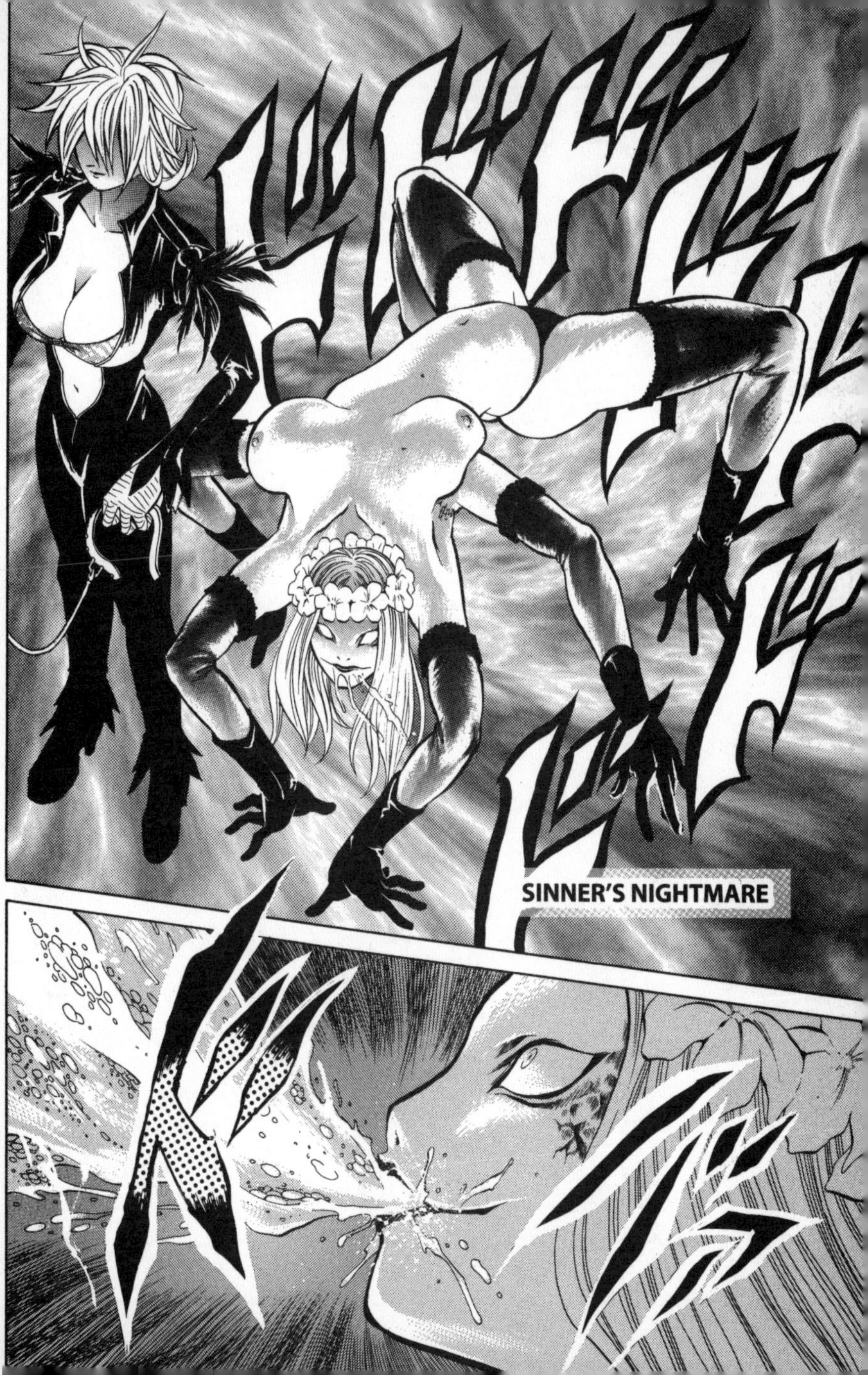
SINNER'S NIGHTMARE

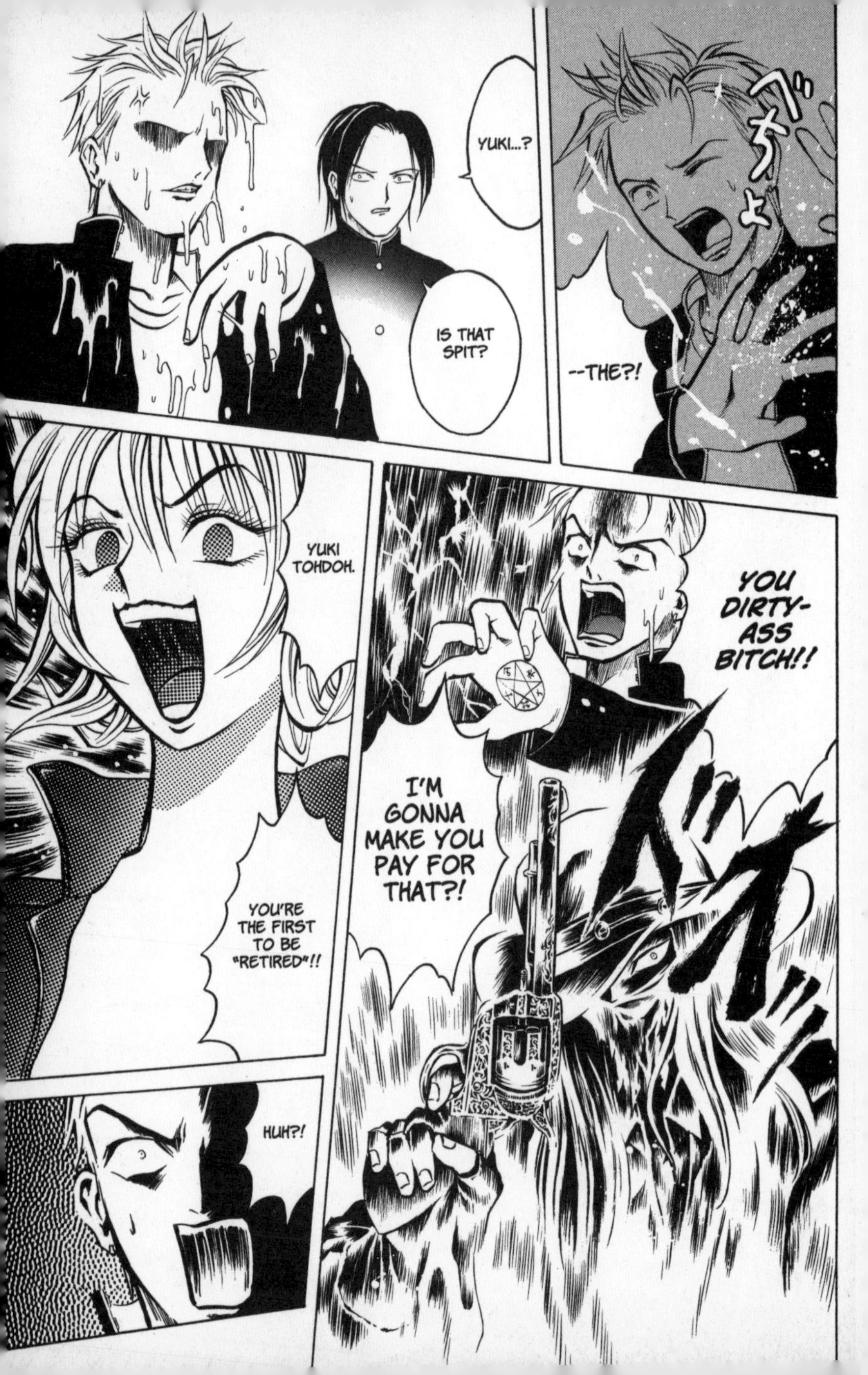
べちょ
--THE?!
YUKI...?
IS THAT SPIT?
YOU DIRTY-ASS BITCH!!
I'M GONNA MAKE YOU PAY FOR THAT?!
YUKI TOHDOH.
YOU'RE THE FIRST TO BE "RETIRED"!!
HUH?!

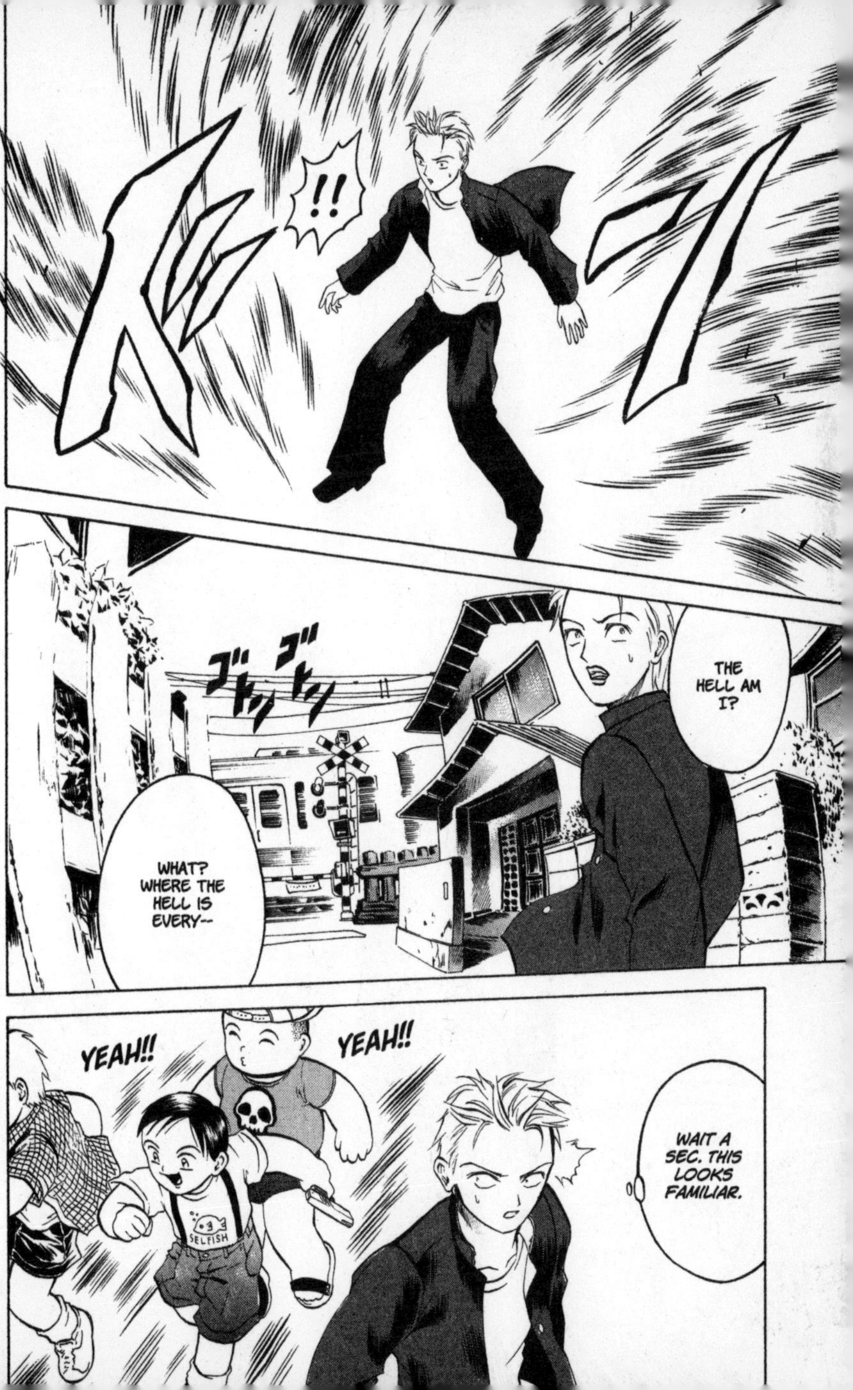
!!
THE HELL AM I?
ゴトン ゴトン
WHAT? WHERE THE HELL IS EVERY--
WAIT A SEC. THIS LOOKS FAMILIAR.
YEAH!!
YEAH!!

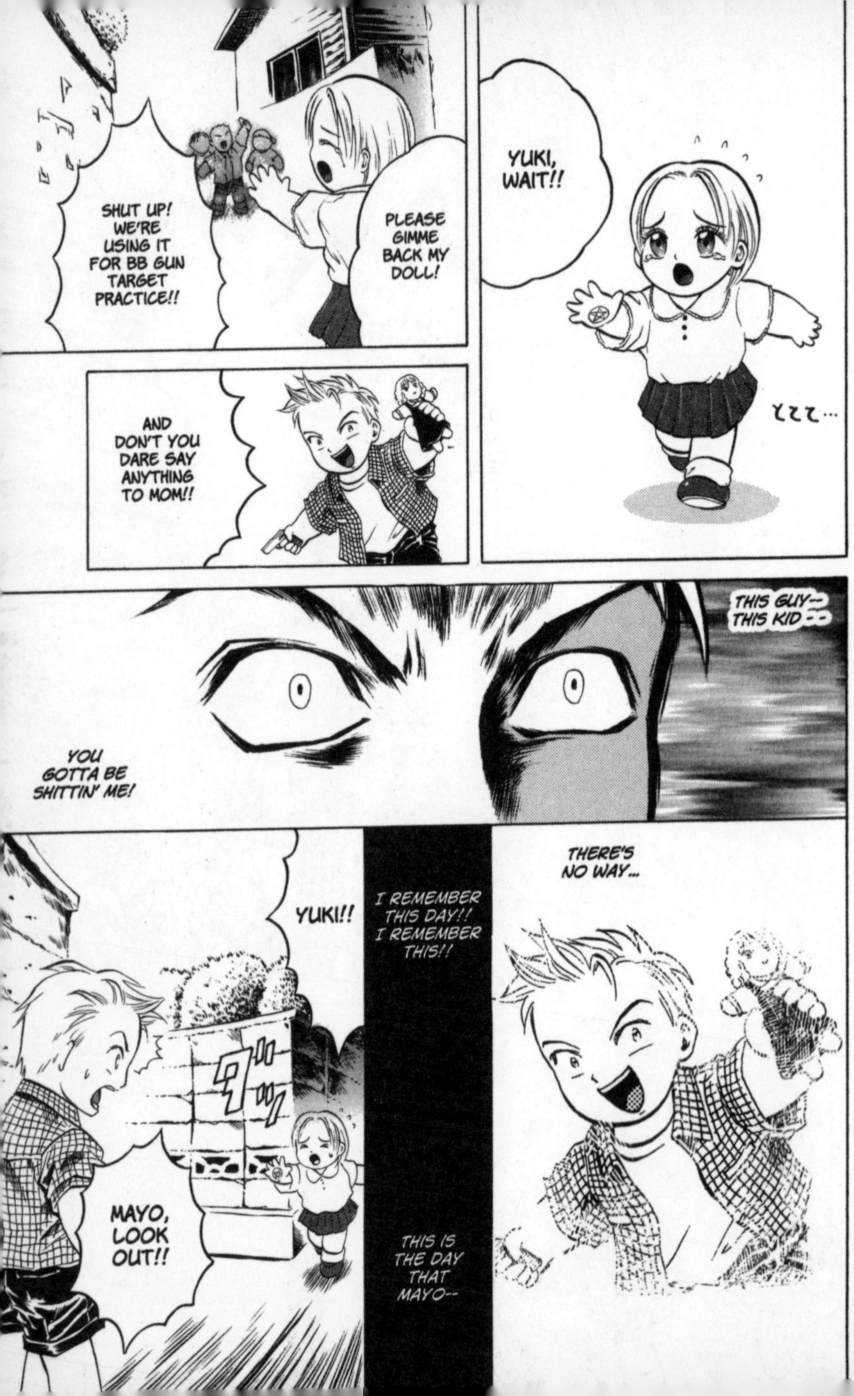

YUKI, WAIT!!
とてて…
PLEASE GIMME BACK MY DOLL!
SHUT UP! WE'RE USING IT FOR BB GUN TARGET PRACTICE!!
AND DON'T YOU DARE SAY ANYTHING TO MOM!!
THIS GUY-- THIS KID--
YOU GOTTA BE SHITTIN' ME!
THERE'S NO WAY...
I REMEMBER THIS DAY!! I REMEMBER THIS!!
THIS IS THE DAY THAT MAYO--
YUKI!!
MAYO, LOOK OUT!!

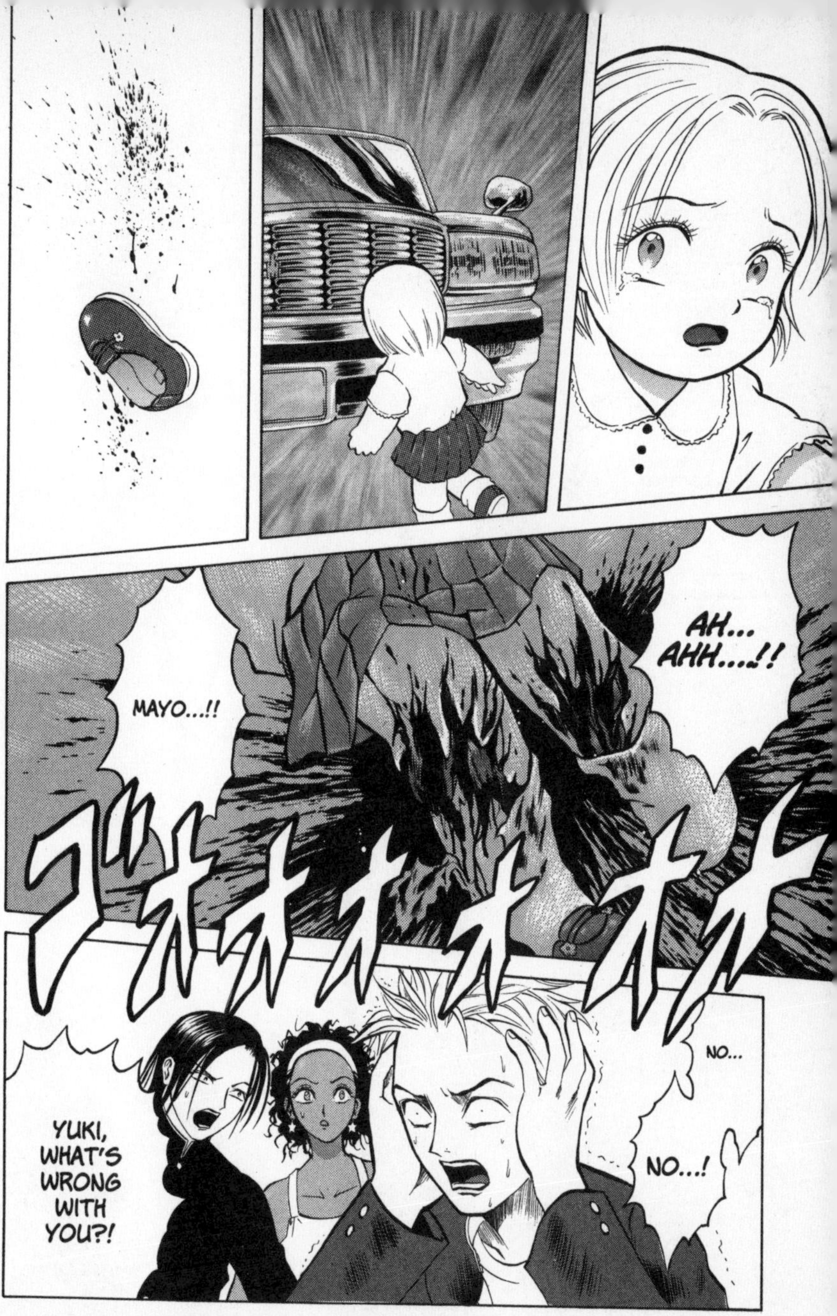
AH... AHH...!!
MAYO...!!
ブオオオオオッ
NO...
NO...!
YUKI, WHAT'S WRONG WITH YOU?!

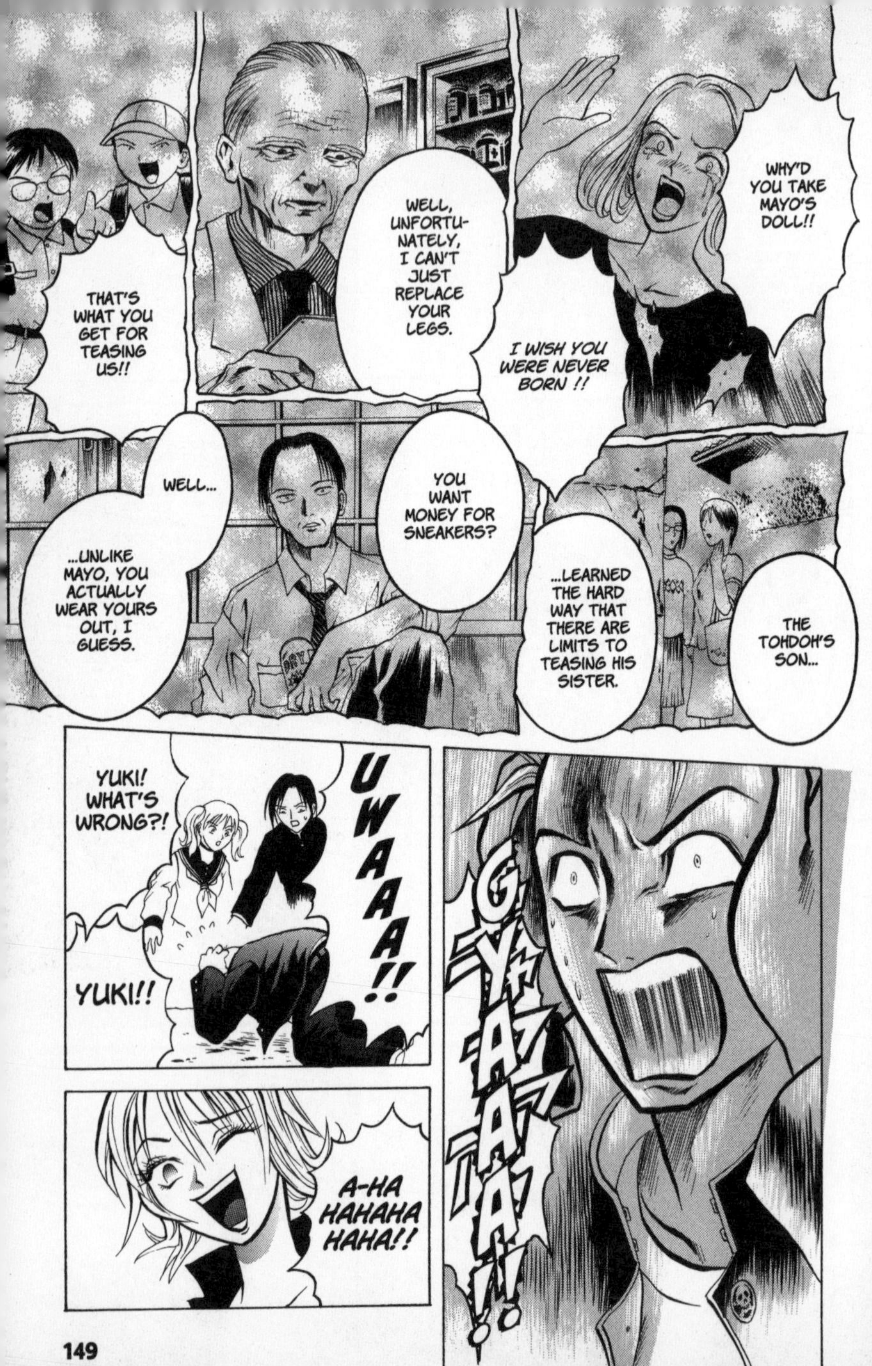
WHY'D YOU TAKE MAYO'S DOLL!!
I WISH YOU WERE NEVER BORN !!
WELL, UNFORTU- NATELY, I CAN'T JUST REPLACE YOUR LEGS.
THAT'S WHAT YOU GET FOR TEASING US!!
THE TOHDOH'S SON...
...LEARNED THE HARD WAY THAT THERE ARE LIMITS TO TEASING HIS SISTER.
YOU WANT MONEY FOR SNEAKERS?
WELL...
...UNLIKE MAYO, YOU ACTUALLY WEAR YOURS OUT, I GUESS.
GYAAAAA!!
UWAAAA!!
YUKI! WHAT'S WRONG?!
YUKI!!
A-HA HAHAHA HAHA!!

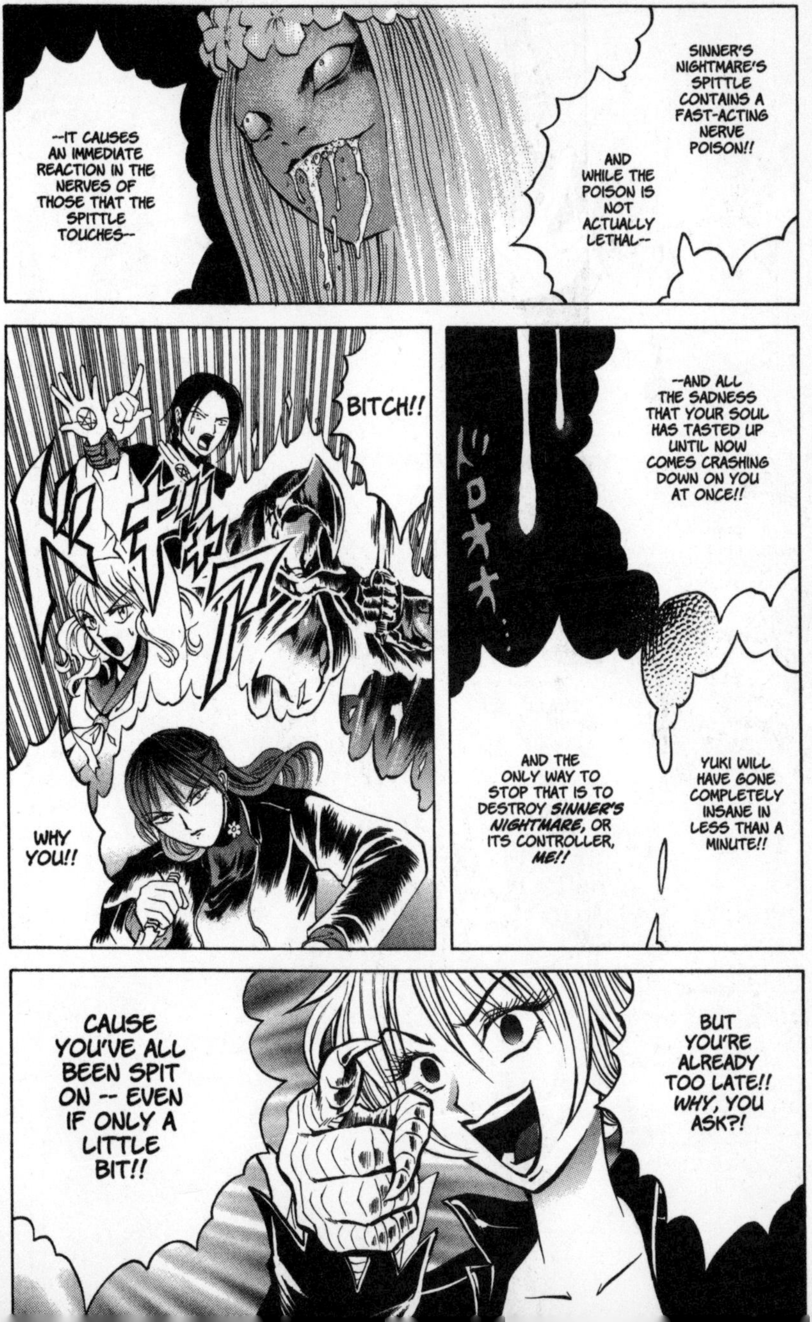
SINNER'S NIGHTMARE'S SPITTLE CONTAINS A FAST-ACTING NERVE POISON!!
AND WHILE THE POISON IS NOT ACTUALLY LETHAL--
--IT CAUSES AN IMMEDIATE REACTION IN THE NERVES OF THOSE THAT THE SPITTLE TOUCHES--
--AND ALL THE SADNESS THAT YOUR SOUL HAS TASTED UP UNTIL NOW COMES CRASHING DOWN ON YOU AT ONCE!!
YUKI WILL HAVE GONE COMPLETELY INSANE IN LESS THAN A MINUTE!!
AND THE ONLY WAY TO STOP THAT IS TO DESTROY *SINNER'S NIGHTMARE*, OR ITS CONTROLLER, *ME!!*
BITCH!!
WHY YOU!!
BUT YOU'RE ALREADY TOO LATE!! *WHY*, YOU ASK?!
CAUSE YOU'VE ALL BEEN SPIT ON -- EVEN IF ONLY A LITTLE BIT!!

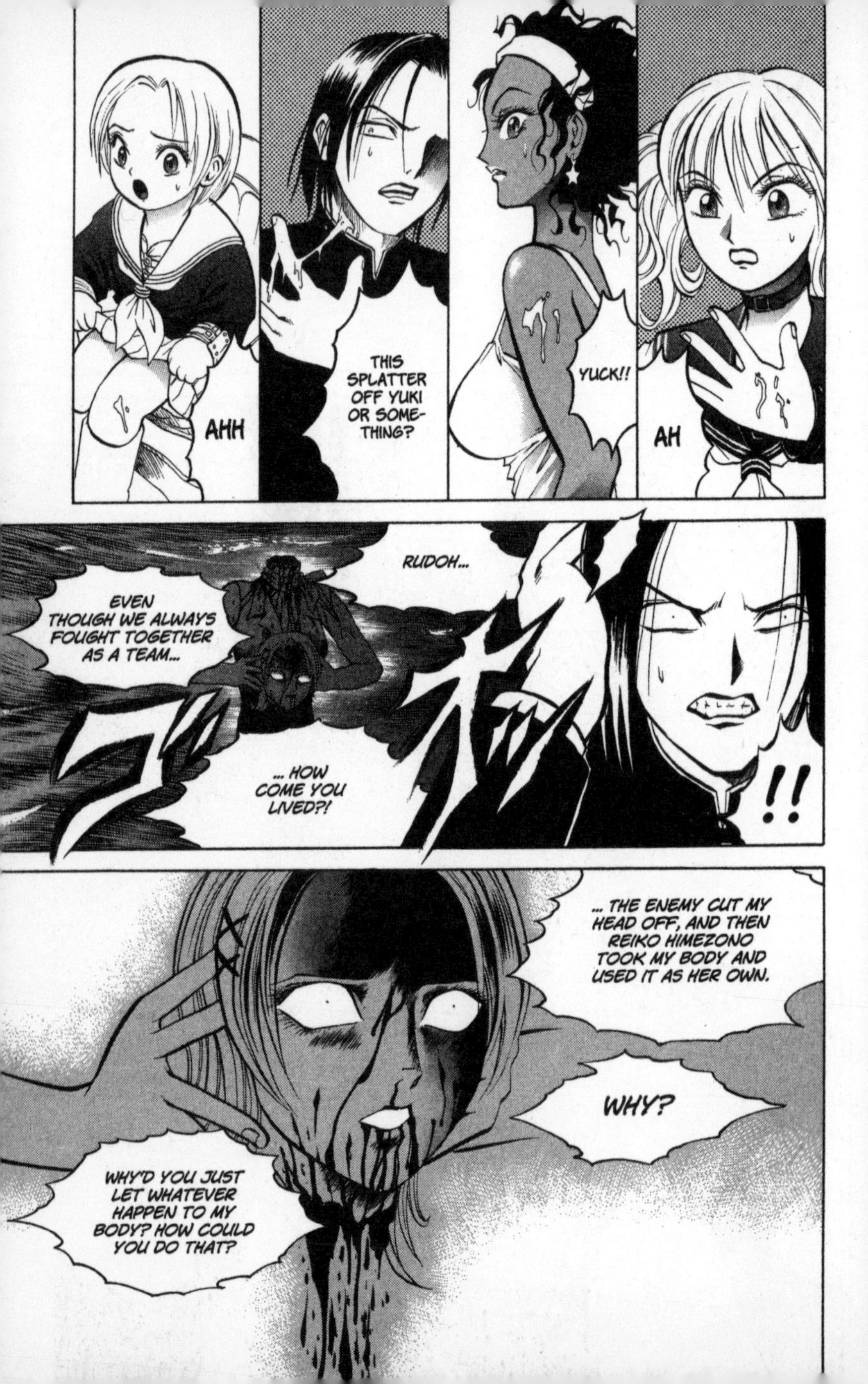
AH
YUCK!!
THIS SPLATTER OFF YUKI OR SOMETHING?
AHH
RUDOH...
EVEN THOUGH WE ALWAYS FOUGHT TOGETHER AS A TEAM...
... HOW COME YOU LIVED?!
!!
... THE ENEMY CUT MY HEAD OFF, AND THEN REIKO HIMEZONO TOOK MY BODY AND USED IT AS HER OWN.
WHY?
WHY'D YOU JUST LET WHATEVER HAPPEN TO MY BODY? HOW COULD YOU DO THAT?

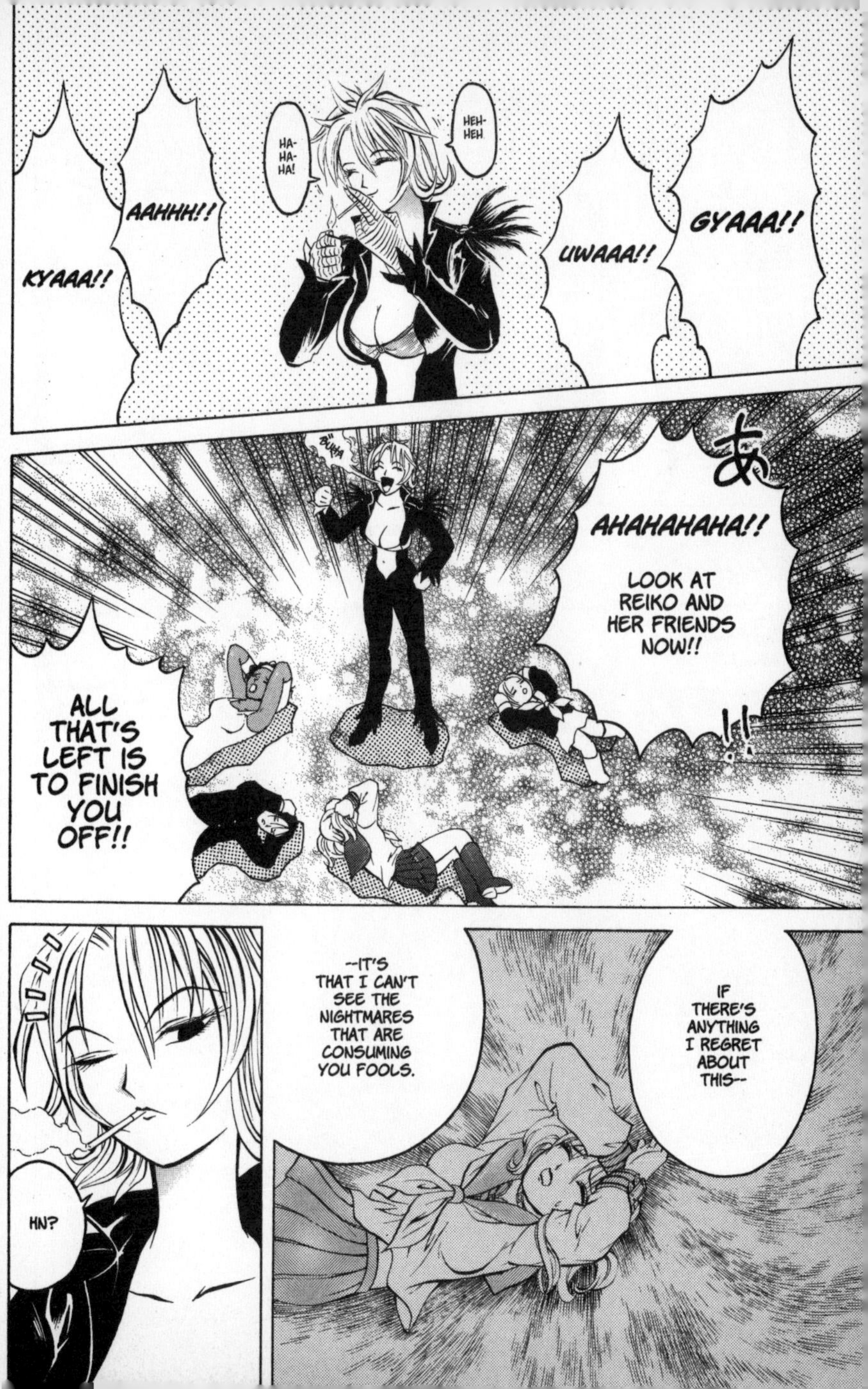
GYAAA!!
UWAAA!!
HEH-HEH
HA-HA-HA!
AAHHH!!
KYAAA!!
あ
AHAHAHAHA!!
LOOK AT REIKO AND HER FRIENDS NOW!!
!!
ALL THAT'S LEFT IS TO FINISH YOU OFF!!
IF THERE'S ANYTHING I REGRET ABOUT THIS--
--IT'S THAT I CAN'T SEE THE NIGHTMARES THAT ARE CONSUMING YOU FOOLS.
HN?

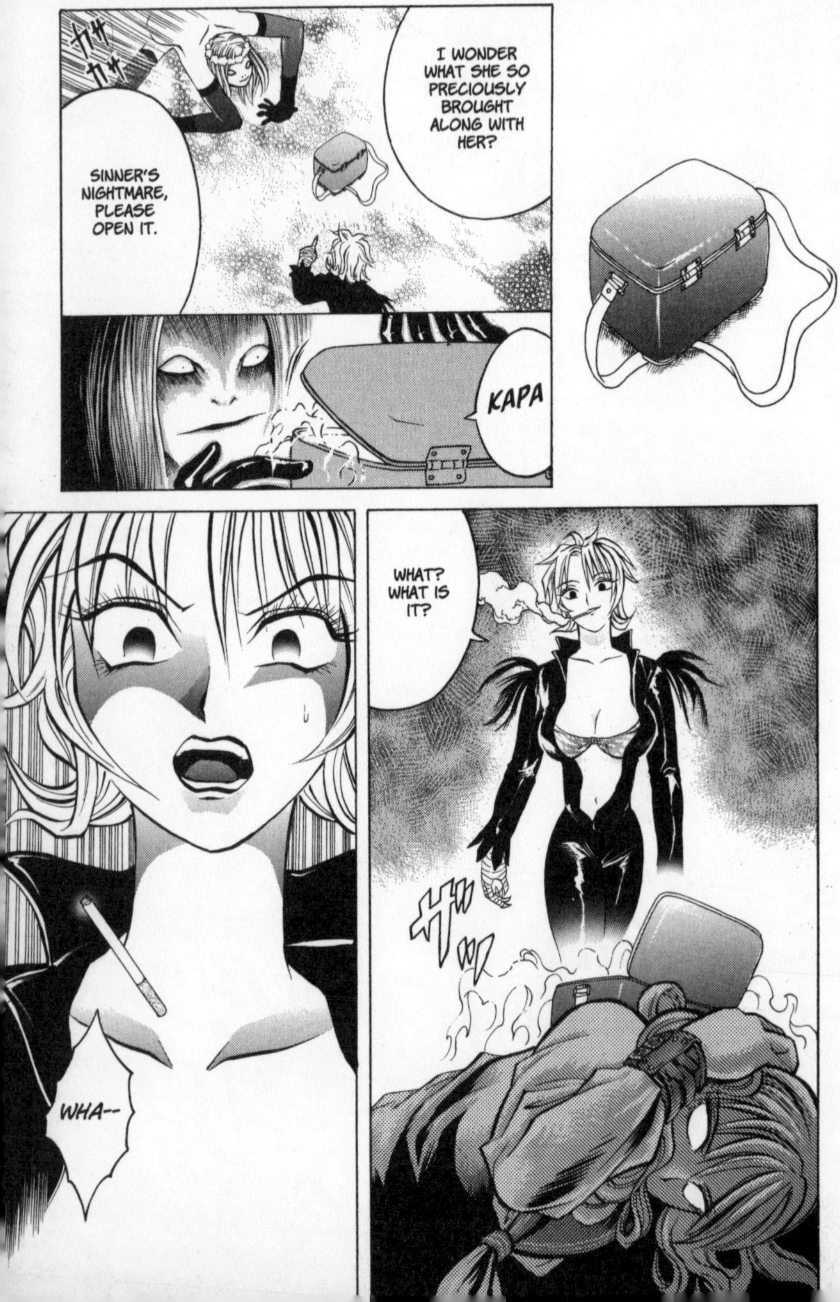
I WONDER WHAT SHE SO PRECIOUSLY BROUGHT ALONG WITH HER?
SINNER'S NIGHTMARE, PLEASE OPEN IT.
カサ
カサ
KAPA
WHAT? WHAT IS IT?
ザッ
WHA--

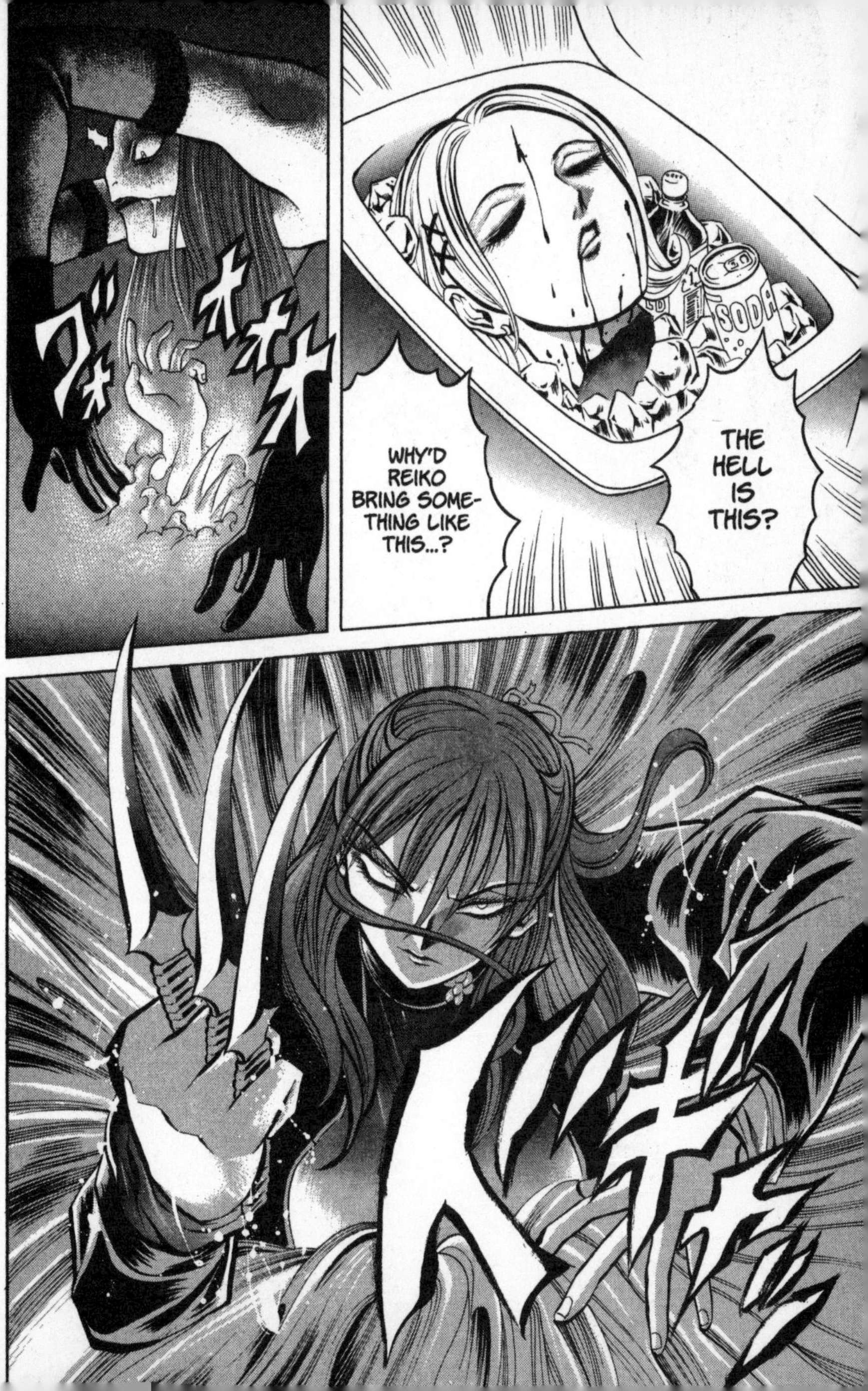
THE HELL IS THIS?
WHY'D REIKO BRING SOME-THING LIKE THIS...?

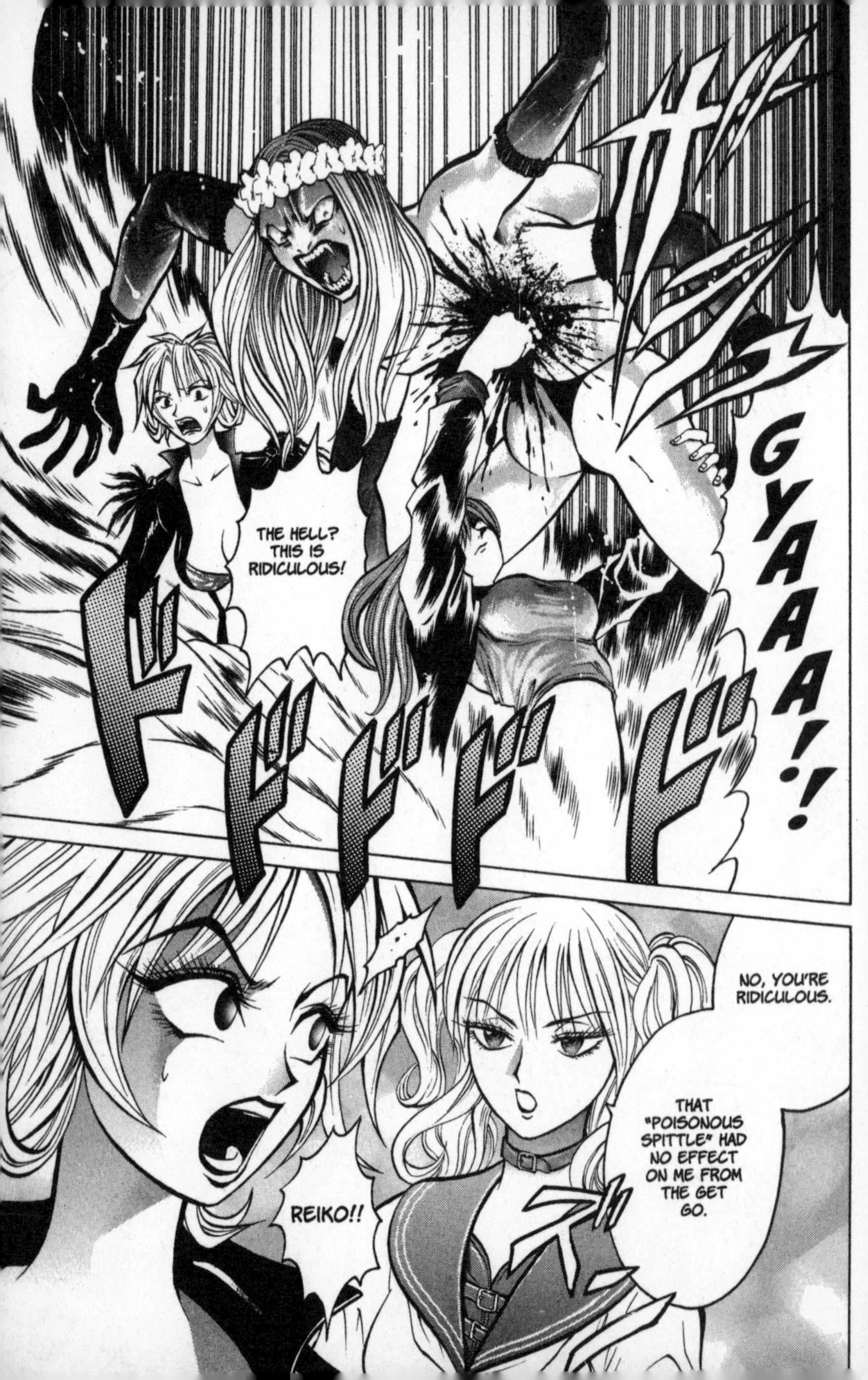
GYAAAA!!
THE HELL? THIS IS RIDICULOUS!
NO, YOU'RE RIDICULOUS.
THAT "POISONOUS SPITTLE" HAD NO EFFECT ON ME FROM THE GET GO.
REIKO!!

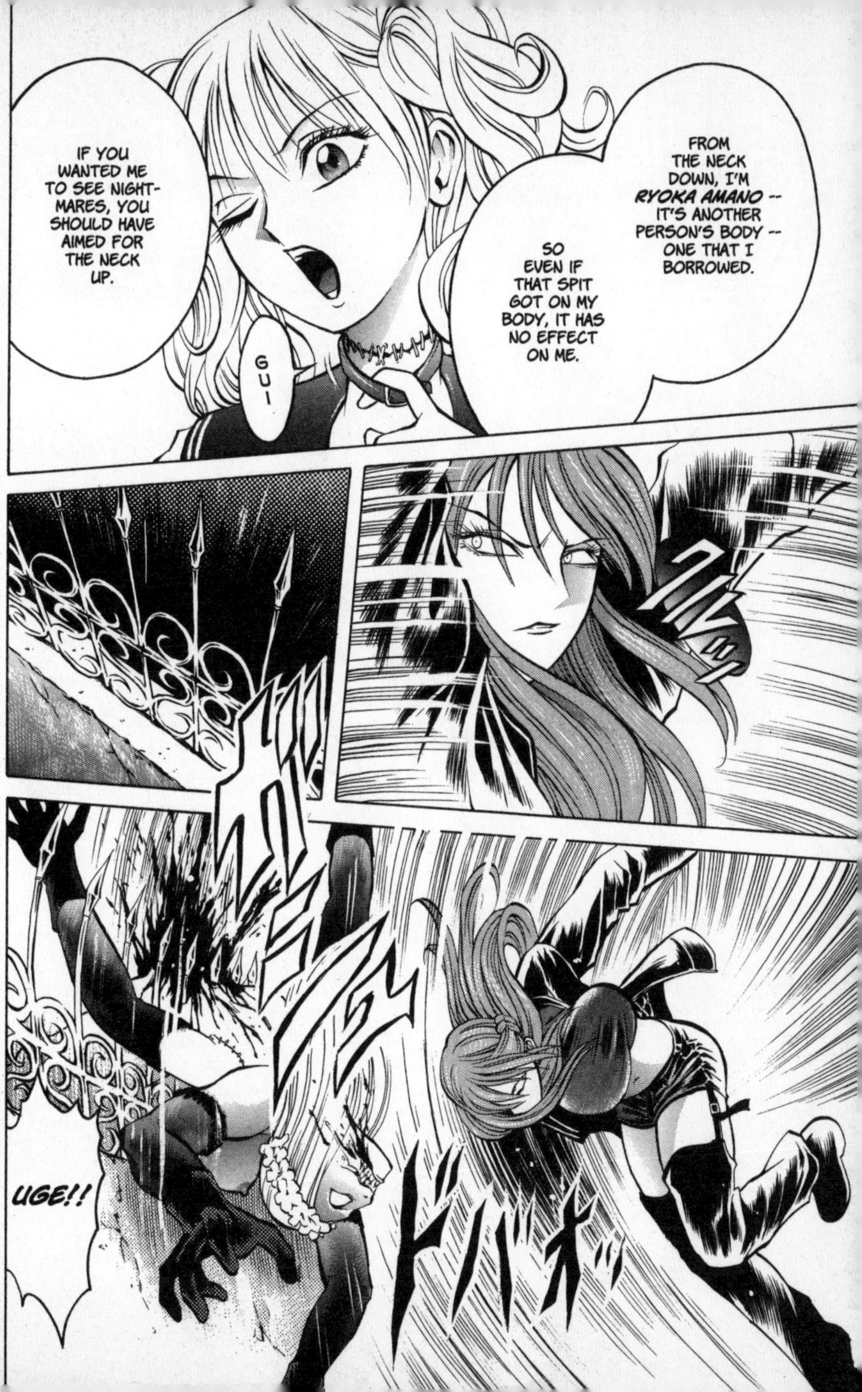
FROM THE NECK DOWN, I'M *RYOKA AMANO* -- IT'S ANOTHER PERSON'S BODY -- ONE THAT I BORROWED.
SO EVEN IF THAT SPIT GOT ON MY BODY, IT HAS NO EFFECT ON ME.
GUI
IF YOU WANTED ME TO SEE NIGHT-MARES, YOU SHOULD HAVE AIMED FOR THE NECK UP.
UGE!!

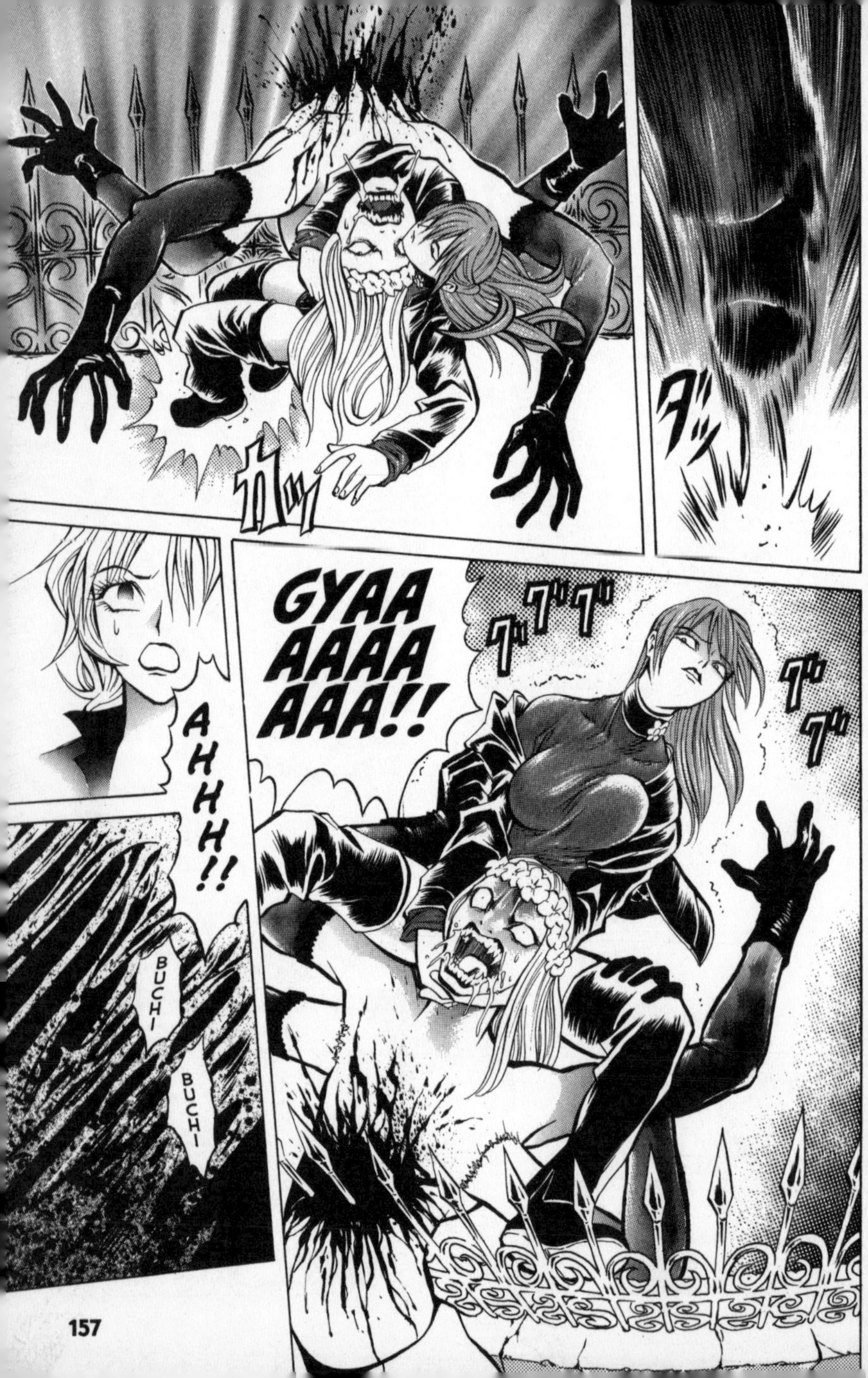
ダッ
ガッ
GYAA AAAA AAA!!
AHHHH!!
BUCHI
BUCHI

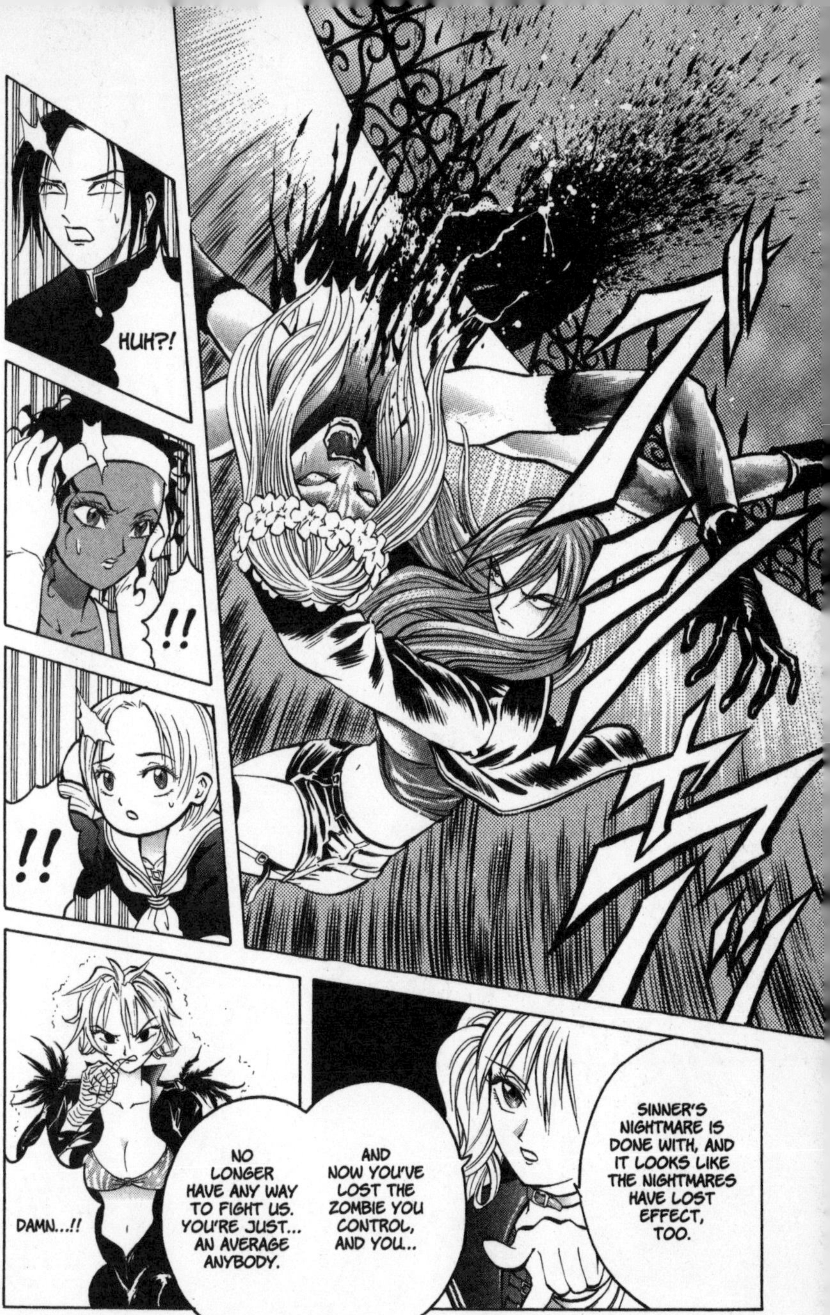
HUH?!
!!
!!
SINNER'S NIGHTMARE IS DONE WITH, AND IT LOOKS LIKE THE NIGHTMARES HAVE LOST EFFECT, TOO.
AND NOW YOU'VE LOST THE ZOMBIE YOU CONTROL, AND YOU..
NO LONGER HAVE ANY WAY TO FIGHT US. YOU'RE JUST... AN AVERAGE ANYBODY.
DAMN...!!

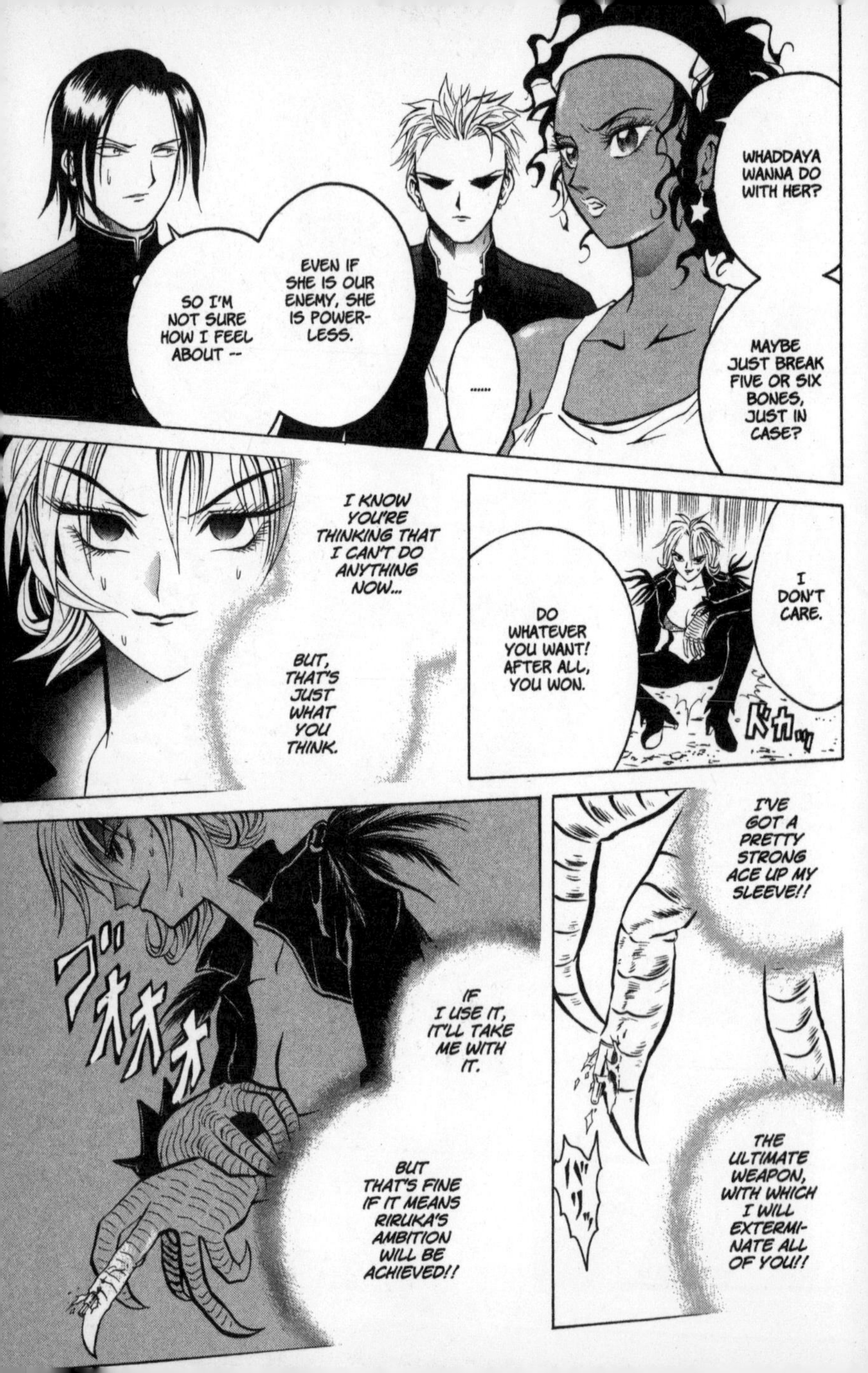
WHADDAYA WANNA DO WITH HER?
MAYBE JUST BREAK FIVE OR SIX BONES, JUST IN CASE?
......
EVEN IF SHE IS OUR ENEMY, SHE IS POWER-LESS.
SO I'M NOT SURE HOW I FEEL ABOUT --
I DON'T CARE.
DO WHATEVER YOU WANT! AFTER ALL, YOU WON.
ドカッ
I KNOW YOU'RE THINKING THAT I CAN'T DO ANYTHING NOW...
BUT, THAT'S JUST WHAT YOU THINK.
I'VE GOT A PRETTY STRONG ACE UP MY SLEEVE!!
THE ULTIMATE WEAPON, WITH WHICH I WILL EXTERMI-NATE ALL OF YOU!!
IF I USE IT, IT'LL TAKE ME WITH IT.
BUT THAT'S FINE IF IT MEANS RIRUKA'S AMBITION WILL BE ACHIEVED!!

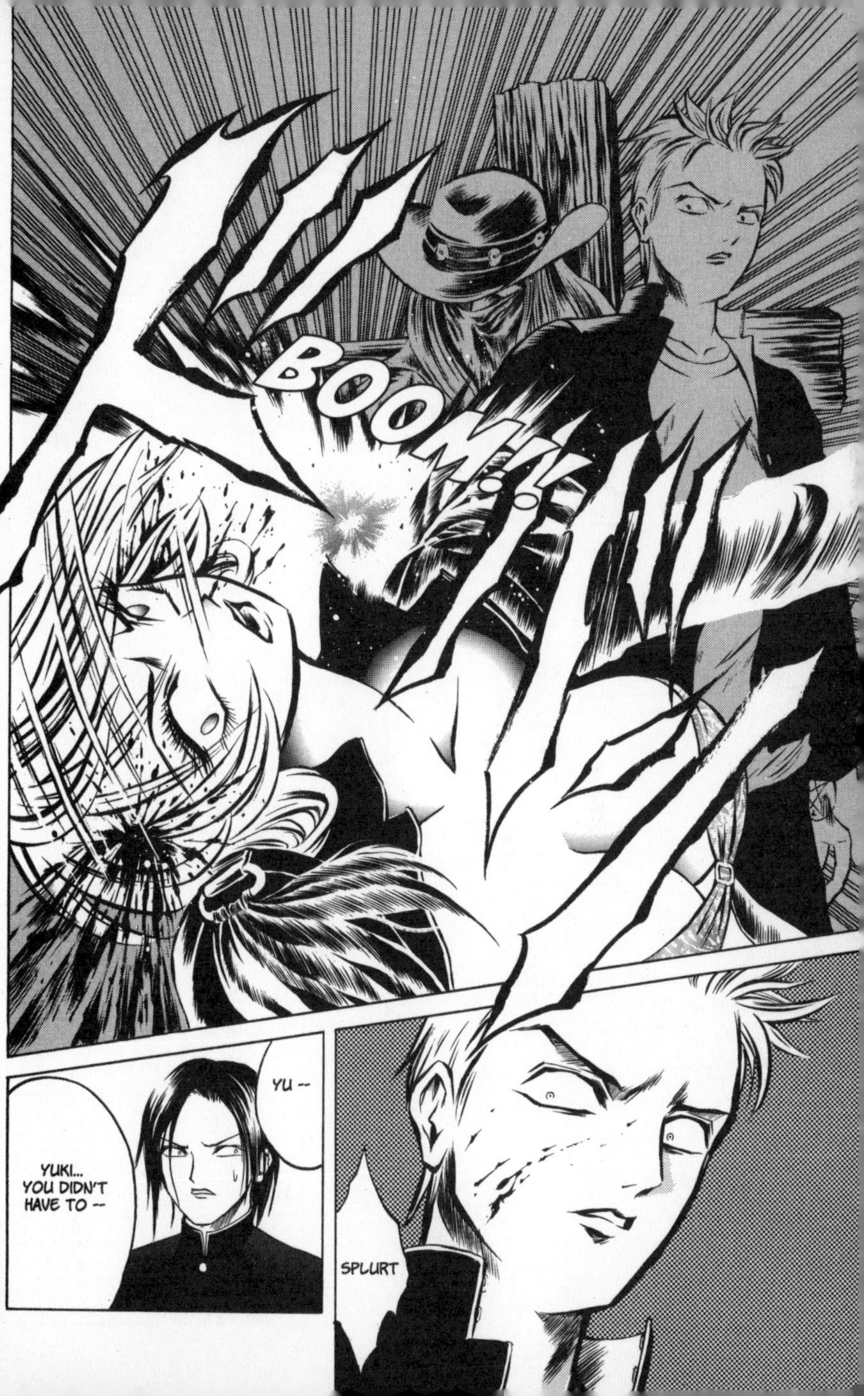
BOOM!!
SPLURT
YU --
YUKI... YOU DIDN'T HAVE TO --

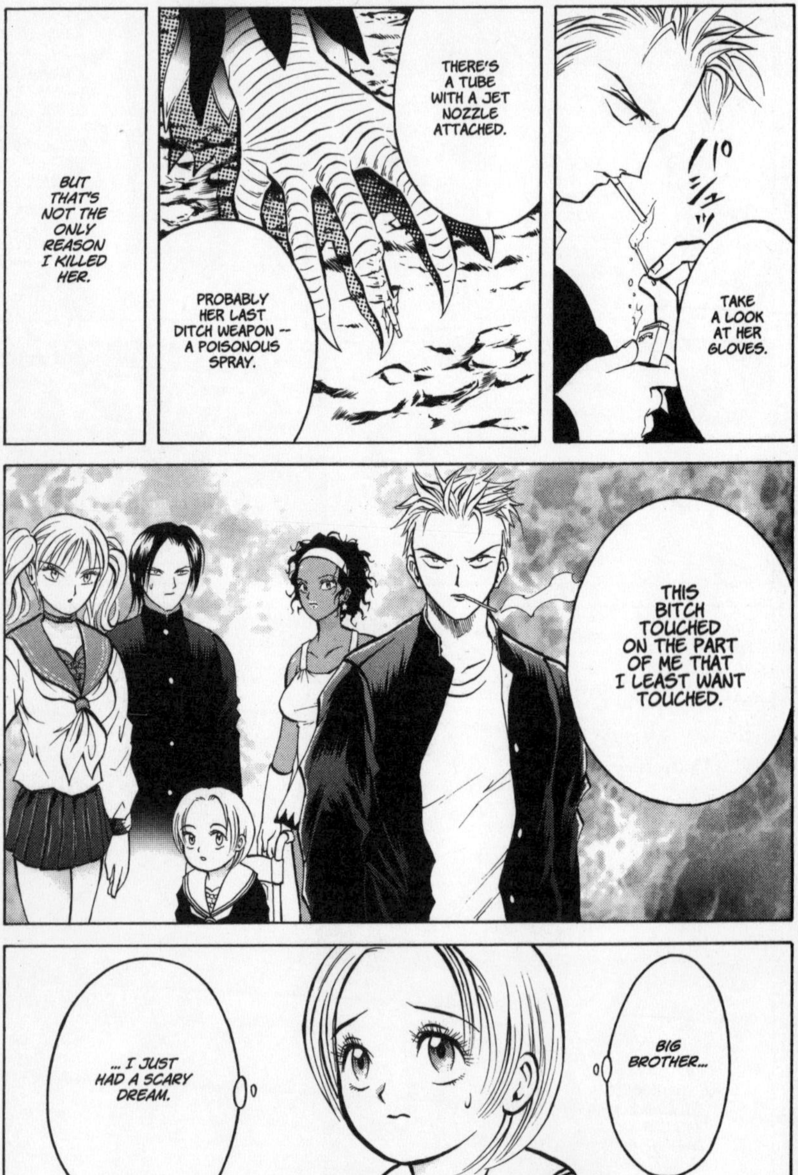
TAKE A LOOK AT HER GLOVES.
THERE'S A TUBE WITH A JET NOZZLE ATTACHED.
PROBABLY HER LAST DITCH WEAPON -- A POISONOUS SPRAY.
BUT THAT'S NOT THE ONLY REASON I KILLED HER.
THIS BITCH TOUCHED ON THE PART OF ME THAT I LEAST WANT TOUCHED.
BIG BROTHER...
... I JUST HAD A SCARY DREAM.

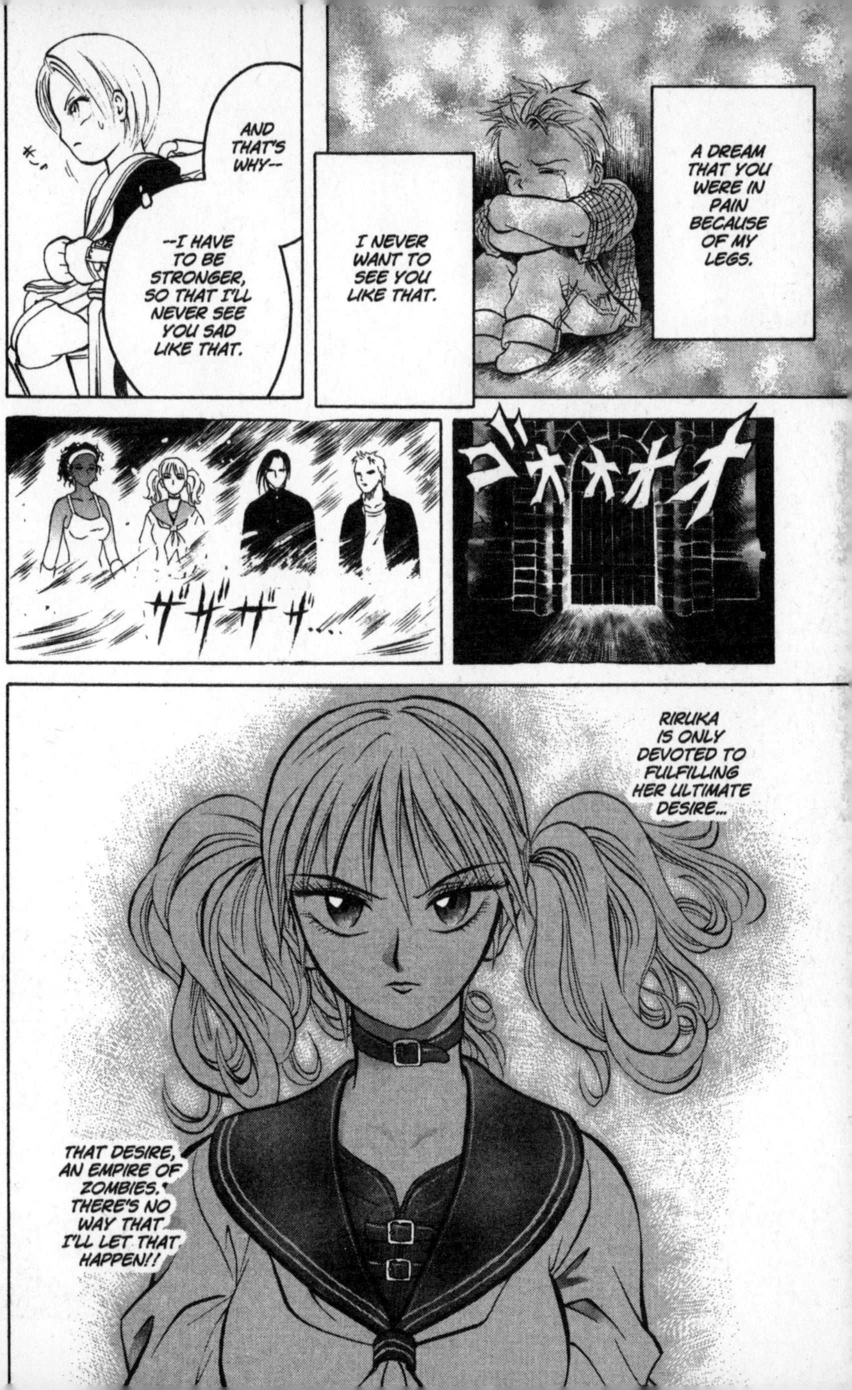

A DREAM THAT YOU WERE IN PAIN BECAUSE OF MY LEGS.
I NEVER WANT TO SEE YOU LIKE THAT.
AND THAT'S WHY--
--I HAVE TO BE STRONGER, SO THAT I'LL NEVER SEE YOU SAD LIKE THAT.
ゴォォオオ
ザザザザ....
RIRUKA IS ONLY DEVOTED TO FULFILLING HER ULTIMATE DESIRE...
THAT DESIRE, AN EMPIRE OF ZOMBIES. THERE'S NO WAY THAT I'LL LET THAT HAPPEN!!

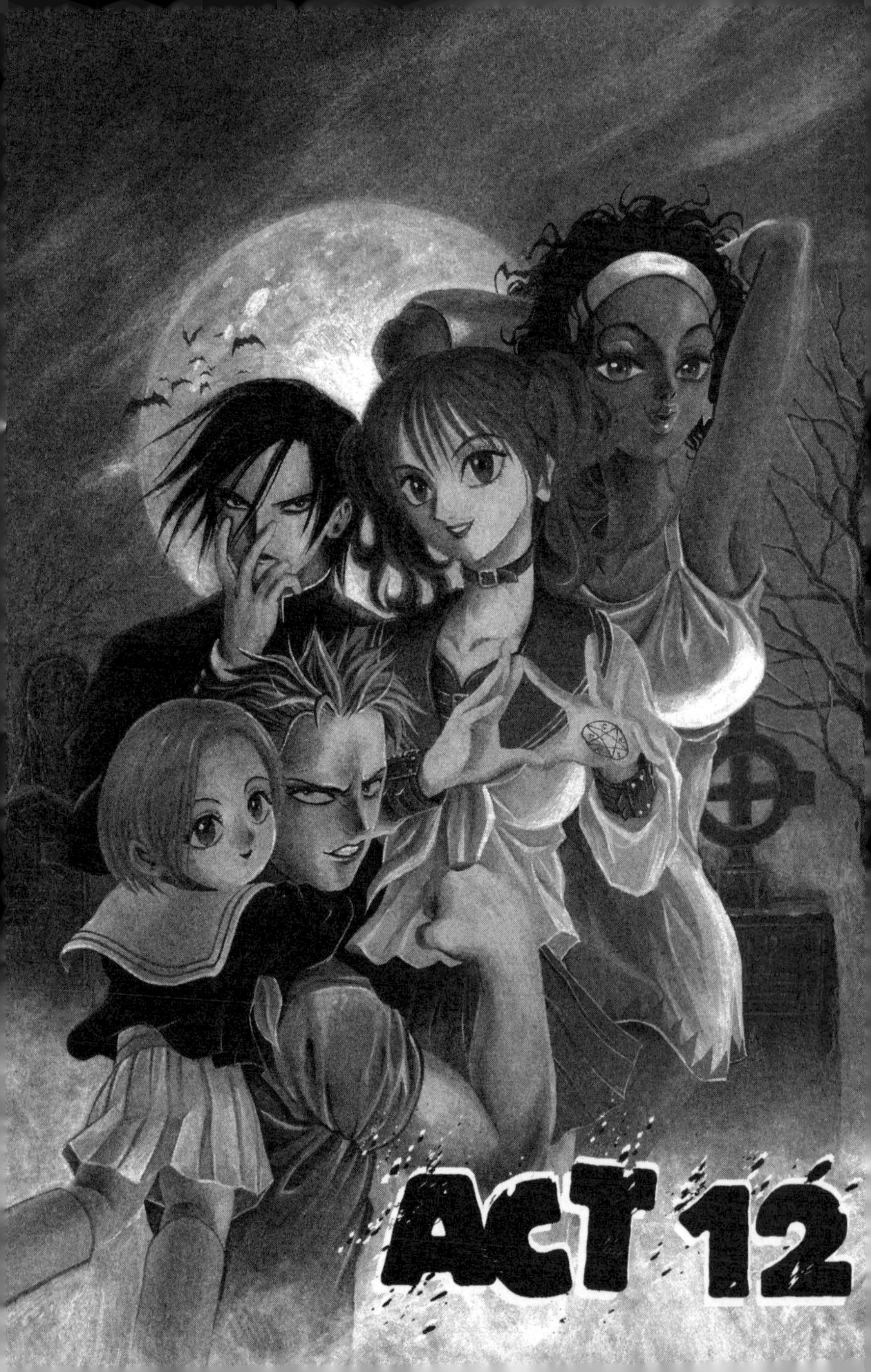
ACT 12

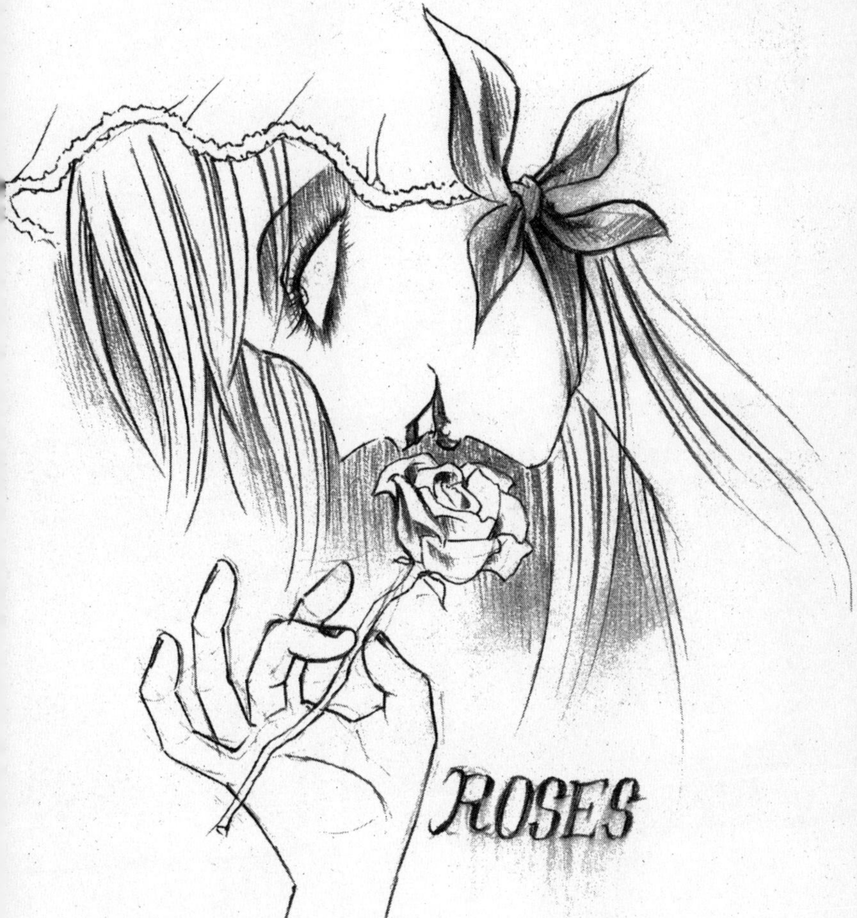
ROSES

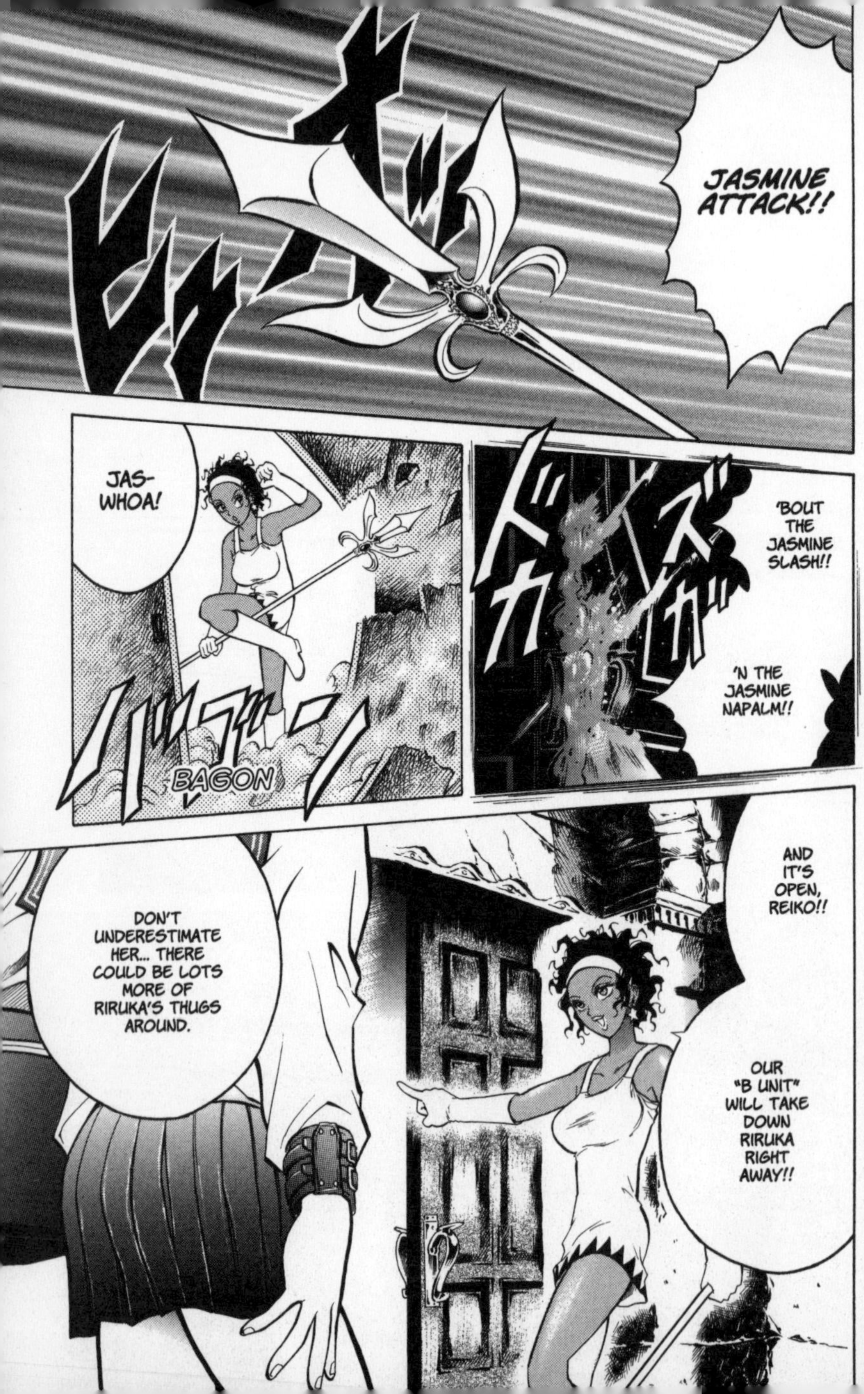
JASMINE ATTACK!!
'BOUT THE JASMINE SLASH!!
'N THE JASMINE NAPALM!!
JAS-WHOA!
BAGON
AND IT'S OPEN, REIKO!!
OUR "B UNIT" WILL TAKE DOWN RIRUKA RIGHT AWAY!!
DON'T UNDERESTIMATE HER... THERE COULD BE LOTS MORE OF RIRUKA'S THUGS AROUND.

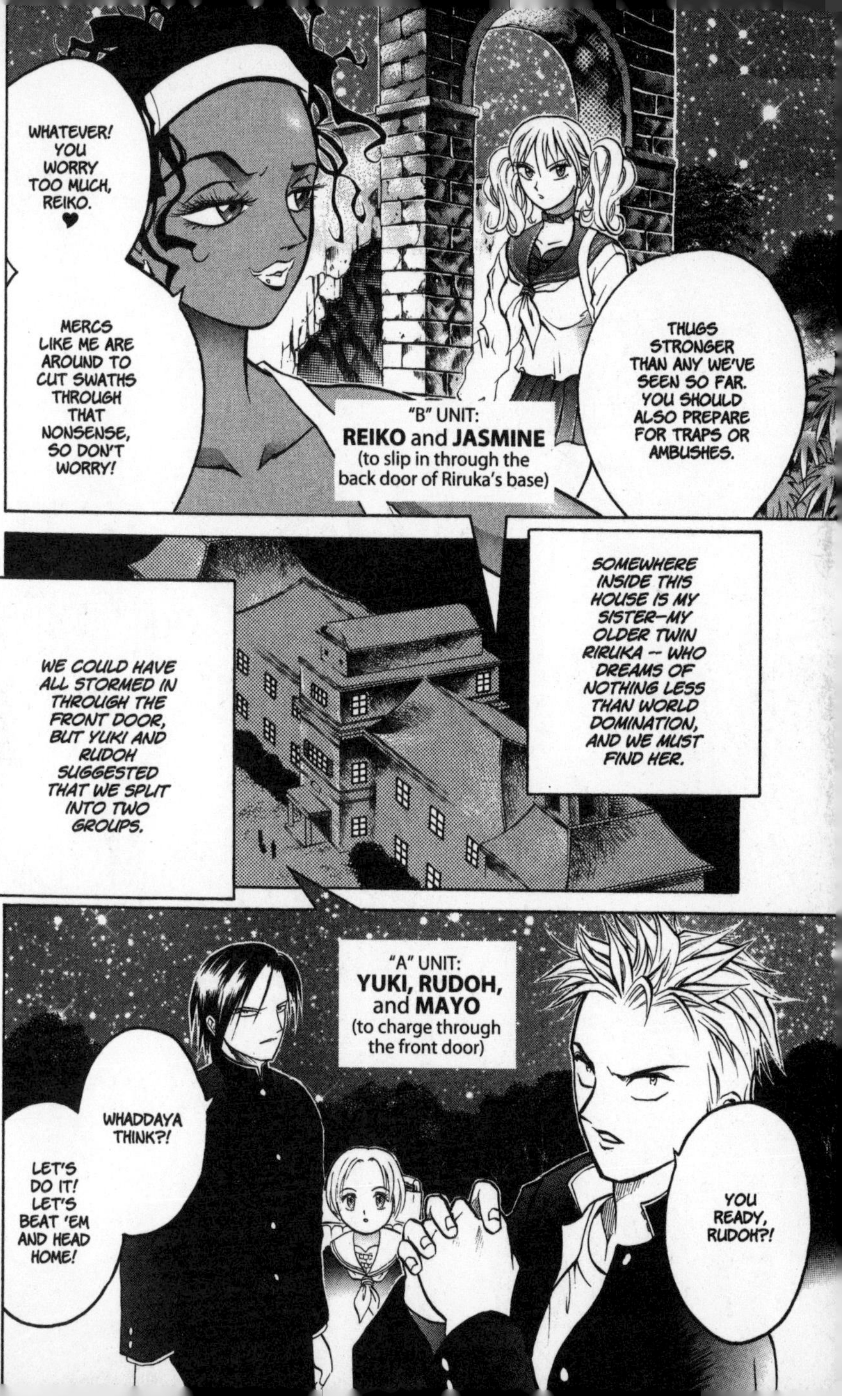

THUGS STRONGER THAN ANY WE'VE SEEN SO FAR. YOU SHOULD ALSO PREPARE FOR TRAPS OR AMBUSHES.
"B" UNIT: REIKO and JASMINE (to slip in through the back door of Riruka's base)
WHATEVER! YOU WORRY TOO MUCH, REIKO. ♥
MERCS LIKE ME ARE AROUND TO CUT SWATHS THROUGH THAT NONSENSE, SO DON'T WORRY!
SOMEWHERE INSIDE THIS HOUSE IS MY SISTER—MY OLDER TWIN RIRUKA -- WHO DREAMS OF NOTHING LESS THAN WORLD DOMINATION, AND WE MUST FIND HER.
WE COULD HAVE ALL STORMED IN THROUGH THE FRONT DOOR, BUT YUKI AND RUDOH SUGGESTED THAT WE SPLIT INTO TWO GROUPS.
"A" UNIT: YUKI, RUDOH, and MAYO (to charge through the front door)
YOU READY, RUDOH?!
WHADDAYA THINK?!
LET'S DO IT! LET'S BEAT 'EM AND HEAD HOME!

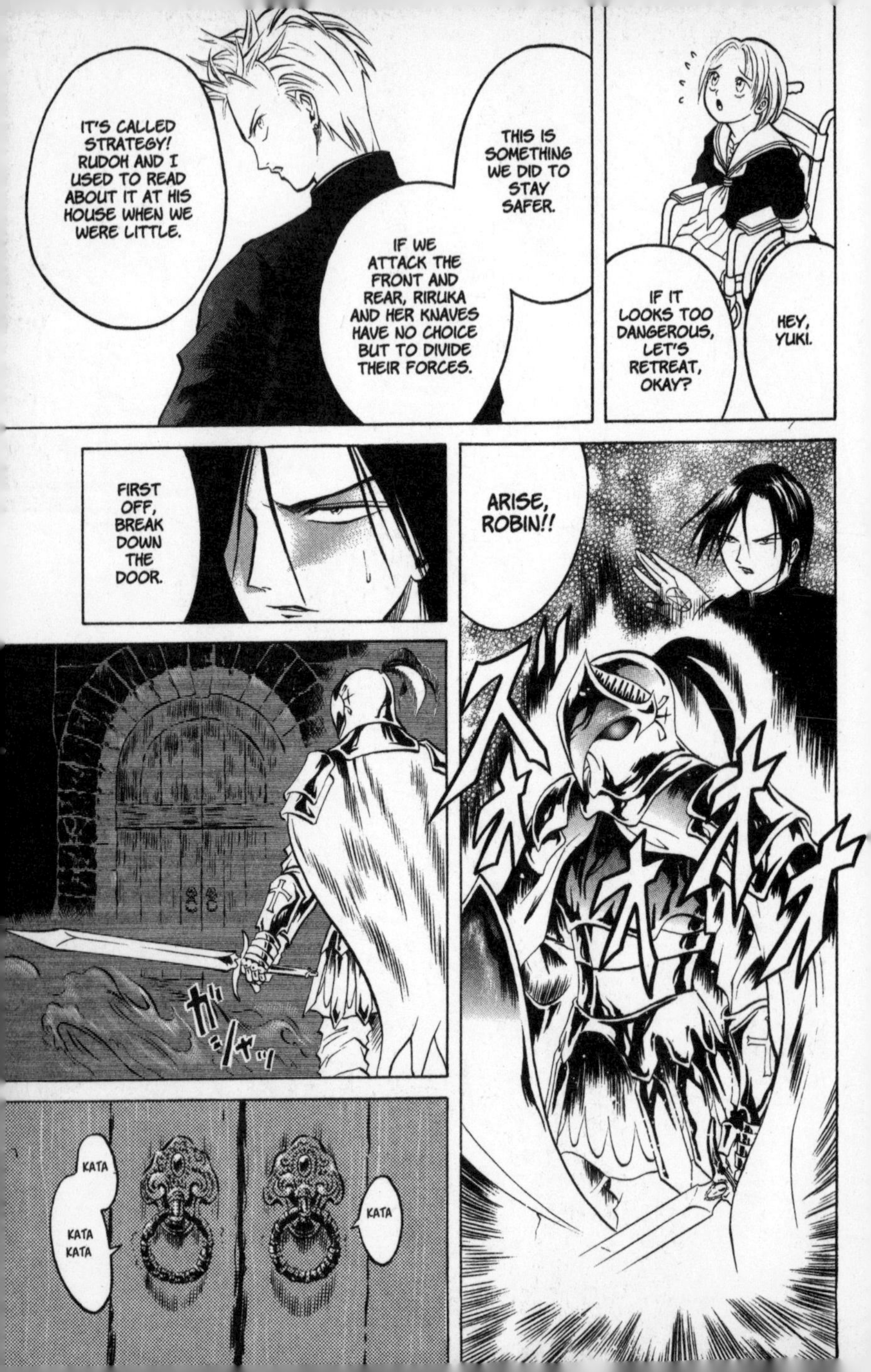
HEY, YUKI.
IF IT LOOKS TOO DANGEROUS, LET'S RETREAT, OKAY?
THIS IS SOMETHING WE DID TO STAY SAFER.
IF WE ATTACK THE FRONT AND REAR, RIRUKA AND HER KNAVES HAVE NO CHOICE BUT TO DIVIDE THEIR FORCES.
IT'S CALLED STRATEGY! RUDOH AND I USED TO READ ABOUT IT AT HIS HOUSE WHEN WE WERE LITTLE.
ARISE, ROBIN!!
FIRST OFF, BREAK DOWN THE DOOR.
KATA
KATA
KATA KATA

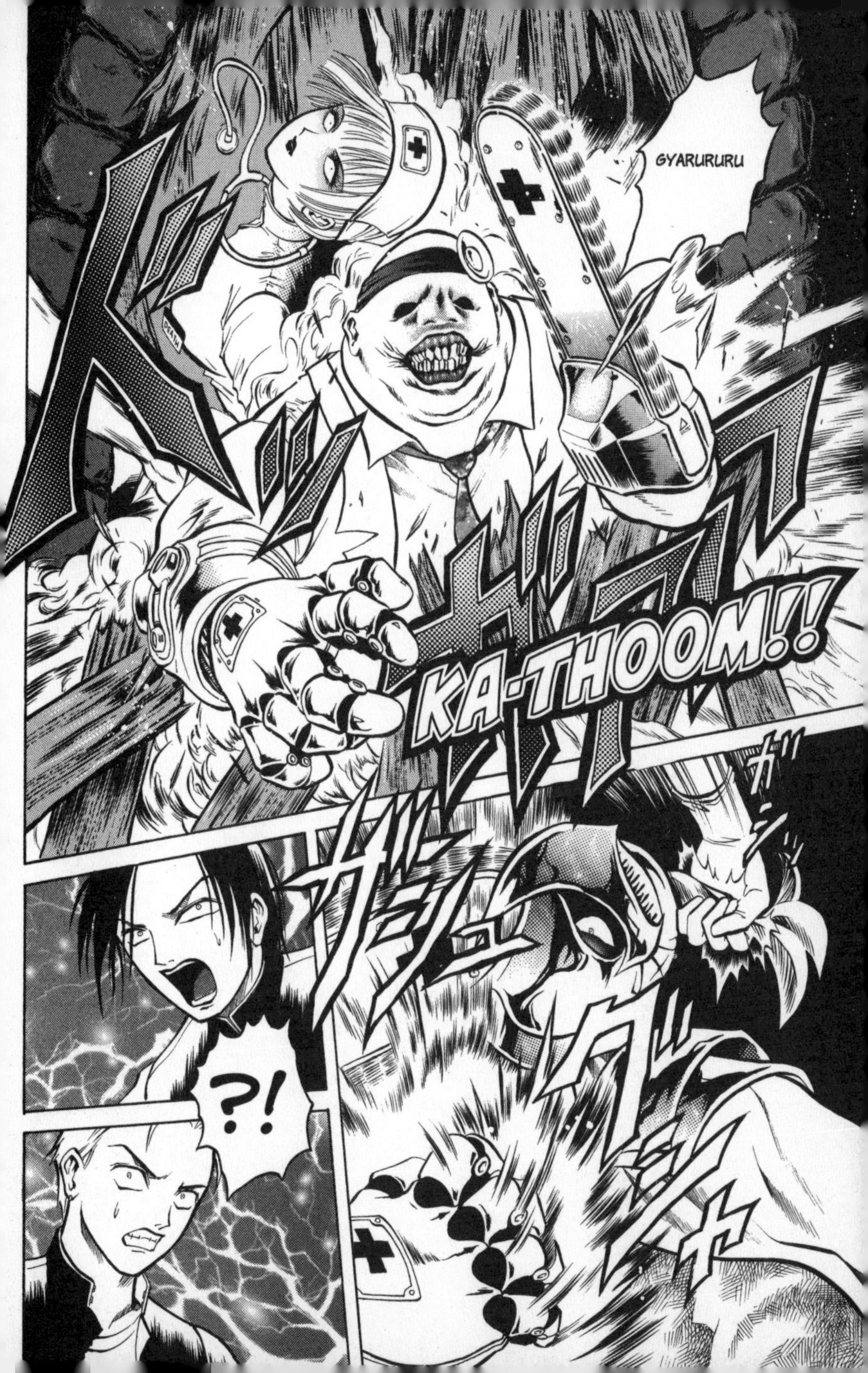
GYARURURU
DEATH
KA-THOOM!!
?!

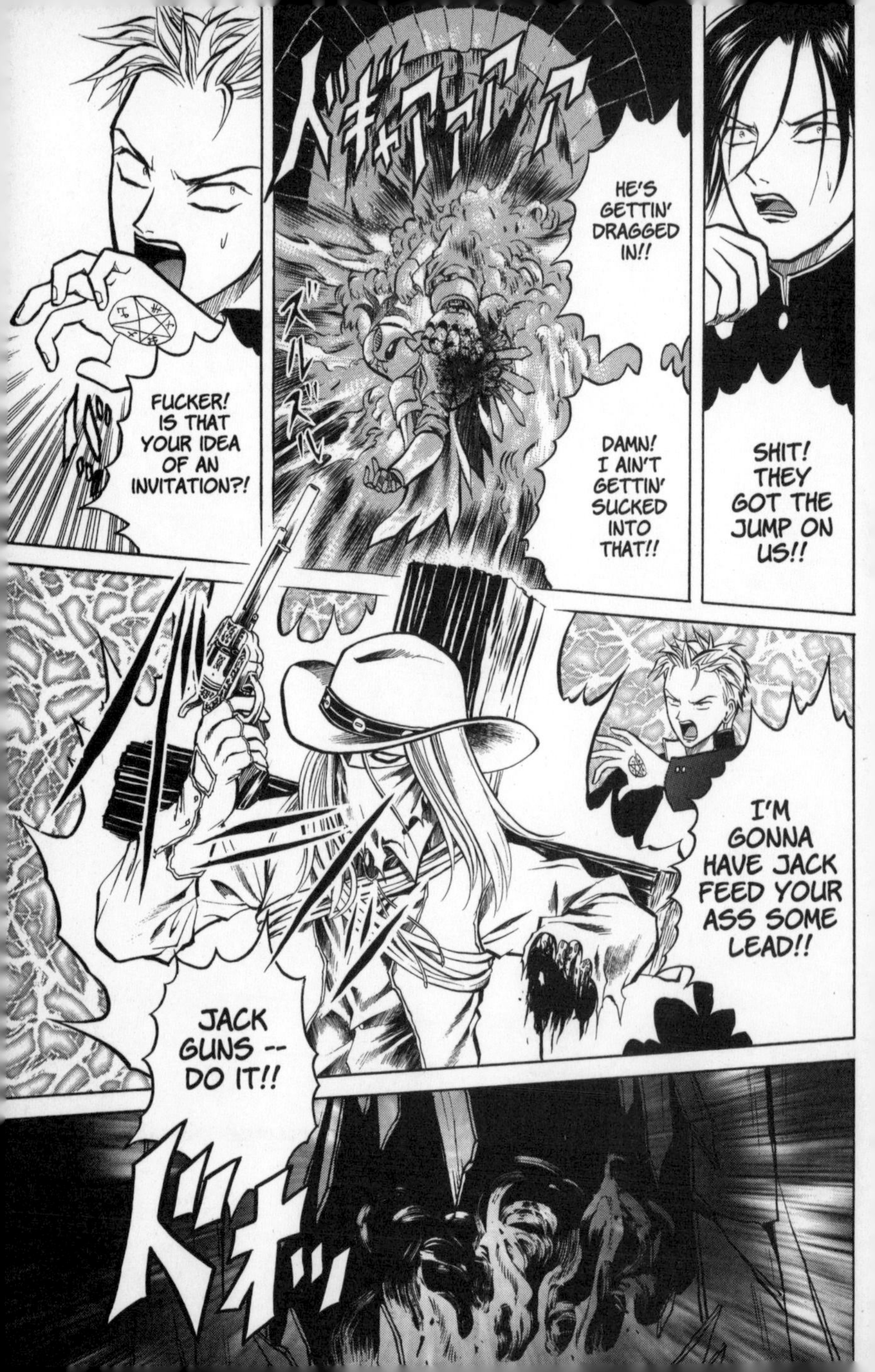
SHIT! THEY GOT THE JUMP ON US!!
HE'S GETTIN' DRAGGED IN!!
DAMN! I AIN'T GETTIN' SUCKED INTO THAT!!
FUCKER! IS THAT YOUR IDEA OF AN INVITATION?!
I'M GONNA HAVE JACK FEED YOUR ASS SOME LEAD!!
JACK GUNS -- DO IT!!

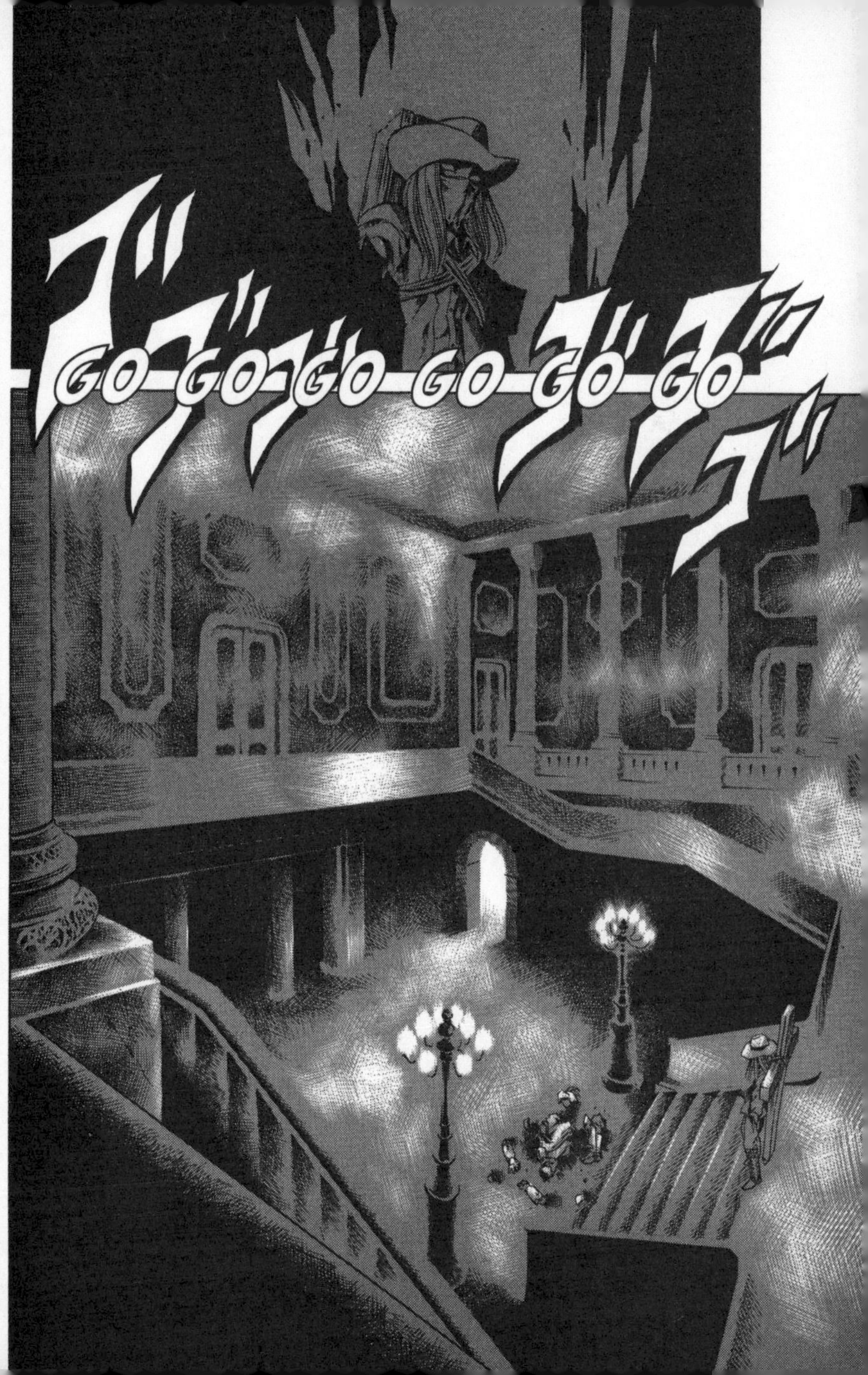
ゴゴゴゴゴゴ
GO GO GO GO GO GO

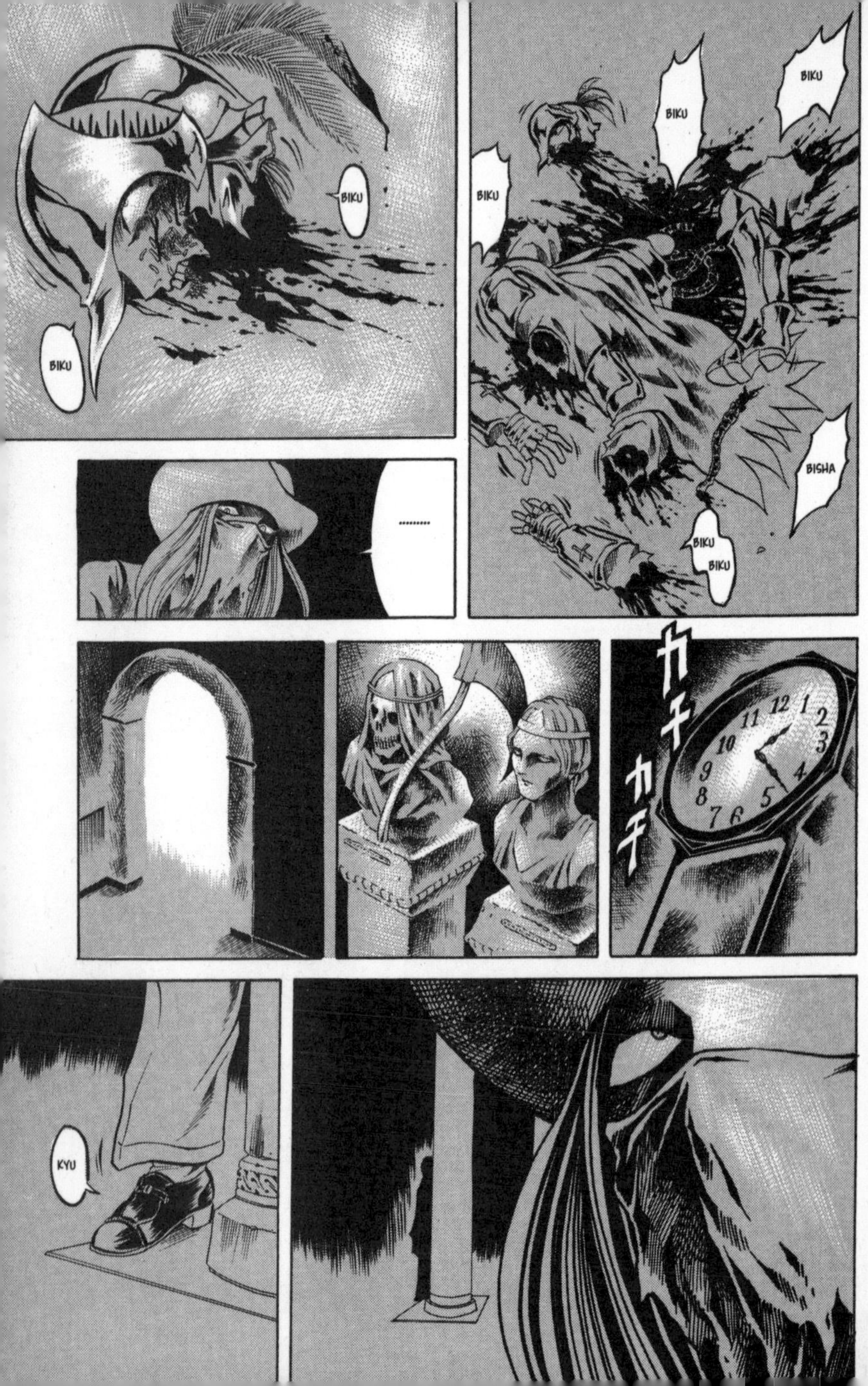
BIKU
BIKU
BIKU
BISHA
BIKU
BIKU
BIKU
BIKU
....
カチ
カチ
KYU

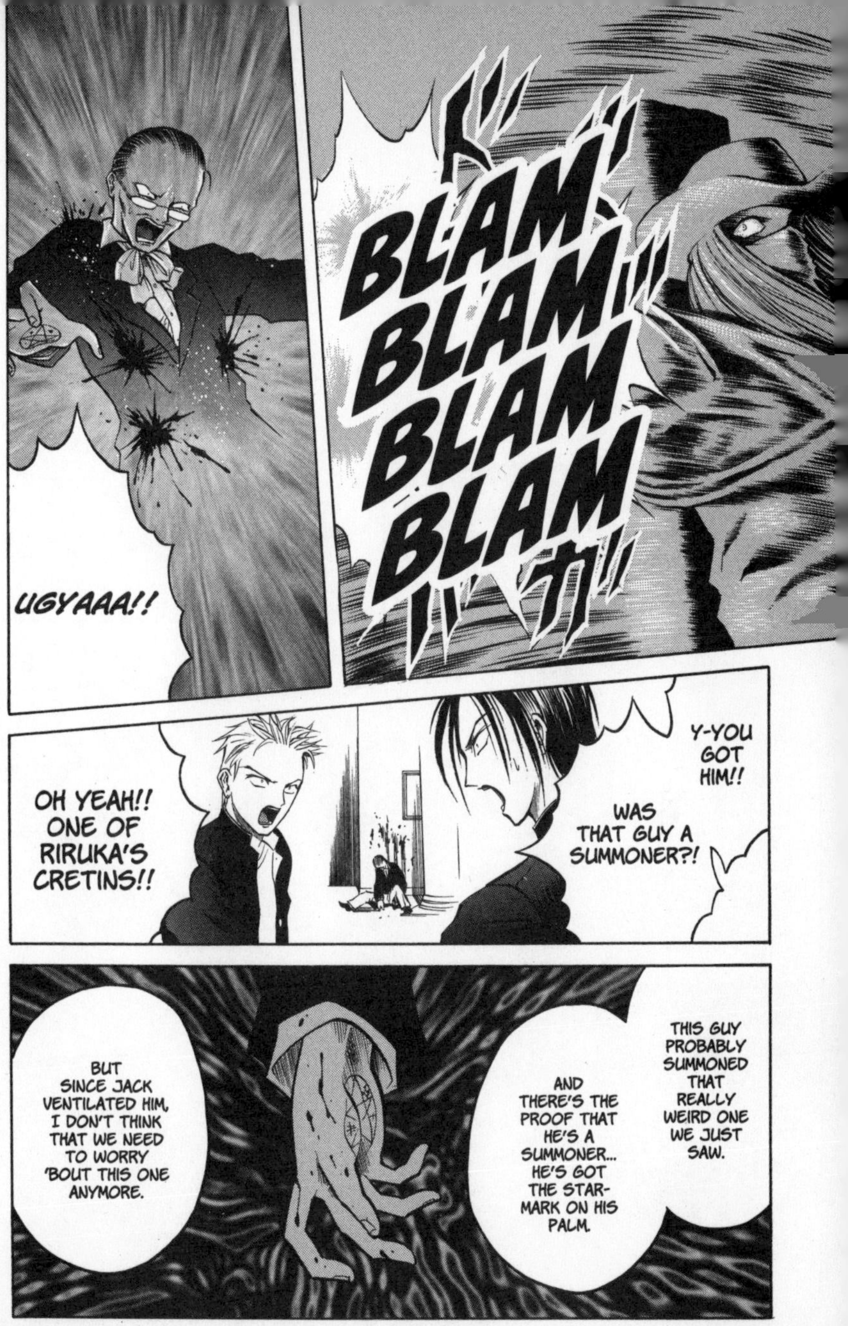
BLAM BLAM BLAM BLAM BLAM
UGYAAA!!
Y-YOU GOT HIM!!
WAS THAT GUY A SUMMONER?!
OH YEAH!! ONE OF RIRUKA'S CRETINS!!
THIS GUY PROBABLY SUMMONED THAT REALLY WEIRD ONE WE JUST SAW.
AND THERE'S THE PROOF THAT HE'S A SUMMONER... HE'S GOT THE STAR-MARK ON HIS PALM.
BUT SINCE JACK VENTILATED HIM, I DON'T THINK THAT WE NEED TO WORRY 'BOUT THIS ONE ANYMORE.

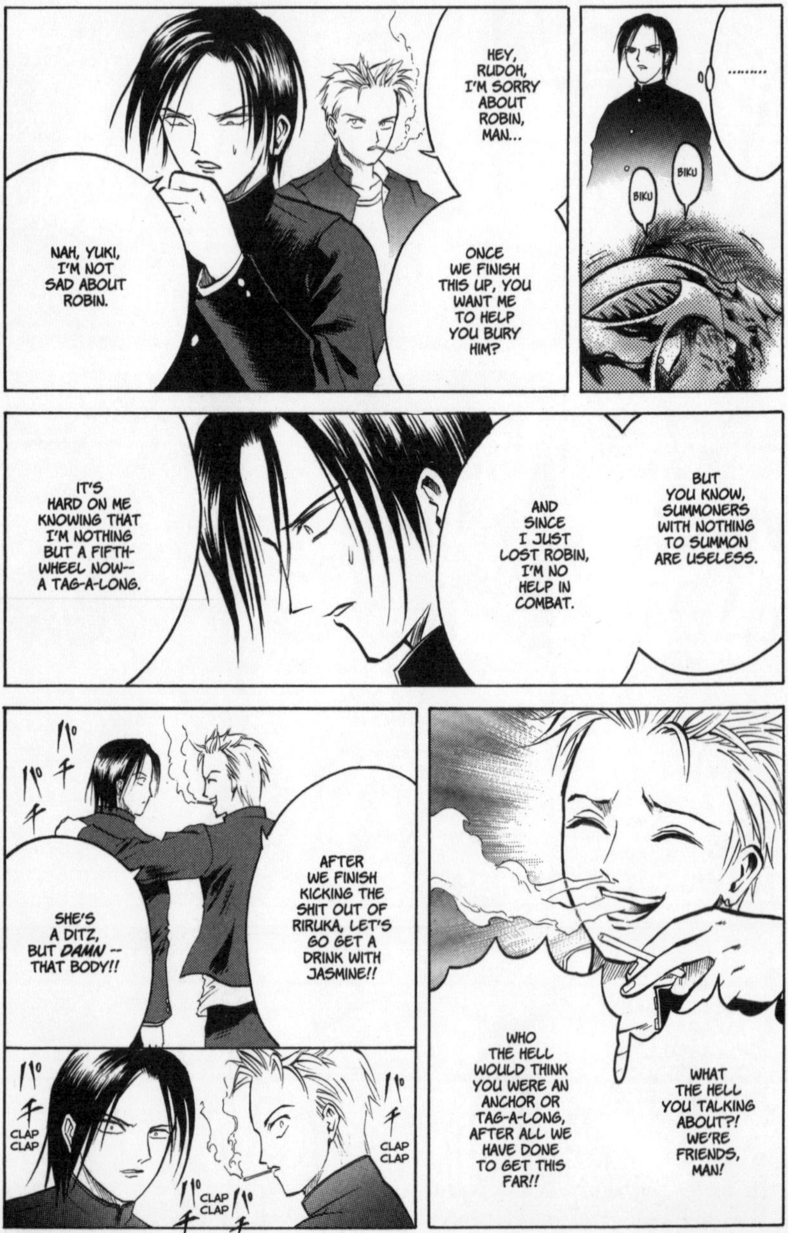
....
BIKU
BIKU
HEY, RUDOH, I'M SORRY ABOUT ROBIN, MAN...
ONCE WE FINISH THIS UP, YOU WANT ME TO HELP YOU BURY HIM?
NAH, YUKI, I'M NOT SAD ABOUT ROBIN.
BUT YOU KNOW, SUMMONERS WITH NOTHING TO SUMMON ARE USELESS.
AND SINCE I JUST LOST ROBIN, I'M NO HELP IN COMBAT.
IT'S HARD ON ME KNOWING THAT I'M NOTHING BUT A FIFTH-WHEEL NOW--A TAG-A-LONG.
WHAT THE HELL YOU TALKING ABOUT?! WE'RE FRIENDS, MAN!
WHO THE HELL WOULD THINK YOU WERE AN ANCHOR OR TAG-A-LONG, AFTER ALL WE HAVE DONE TO GET THIS FAR!!
パチ
パチ
AFTER WE FINISH KICKING THE SHIT OUT OF RIRUKA, LET'S GO GET A DRINK WITH JASMINE!!
SHE'S A DITZ, BUT *DAMN* -- THAT BODY!!
パチ
CLAP CLAP
パチ
CLAP CLAP
パチ
CLAP CLAP
パチ

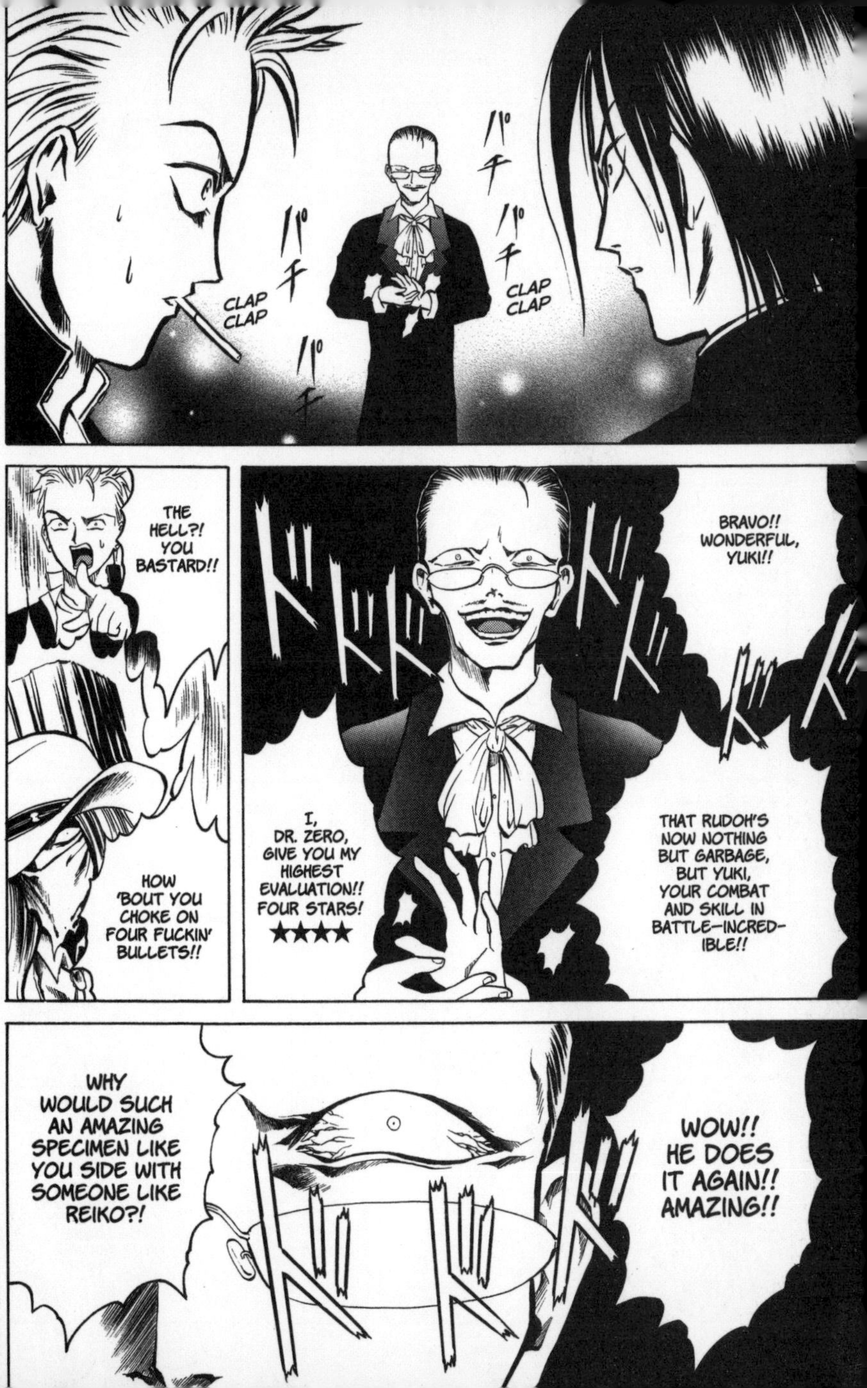
パチ パチ
CLAP CLAP
パチ パチ
CLAP CLAP
BRAVO!! WONDERFUL, YUKI!!
THAT RUDOH'S NOW NOTHING BUT GARBAGE, BUT YUKI, YOUR COMBAT AND SKILL IN BATTLE—INCRED-IBLE!!
I, DR. ZERO, GIVE YOU MY HIGHEST EVALUATION!! FOUR STARS! ★★★★
THE HELL?! YOU BASTARD!!
HOW 'BOUT YOU CHOKE ON FOUR FUCKIN' BULLETS!!
WOW!! HE DOES IT AGAIN!! AMAZING!!
WHY WOULD SUCH AN AMAZING SPECIMEN LIKE YOU SIDE WITH SOMEONE LIKE REIKO?!

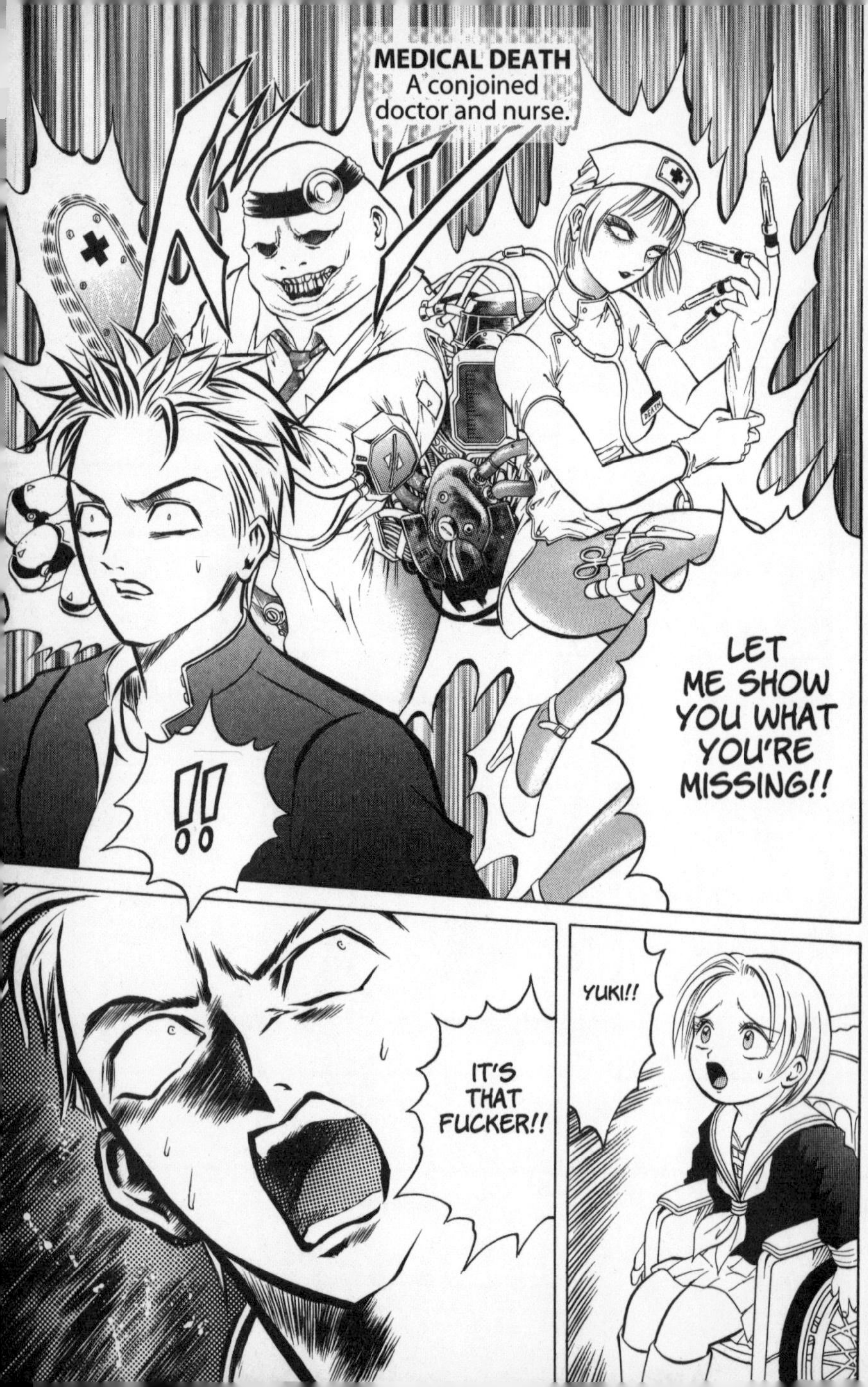
MEDICAL DEATH
A conjoined doctor and nurse.
LET ME SHOW YOU WHAT YOU'RE MISSING!!
!!
YUKI!!
IT'S THAT FUCKER!!

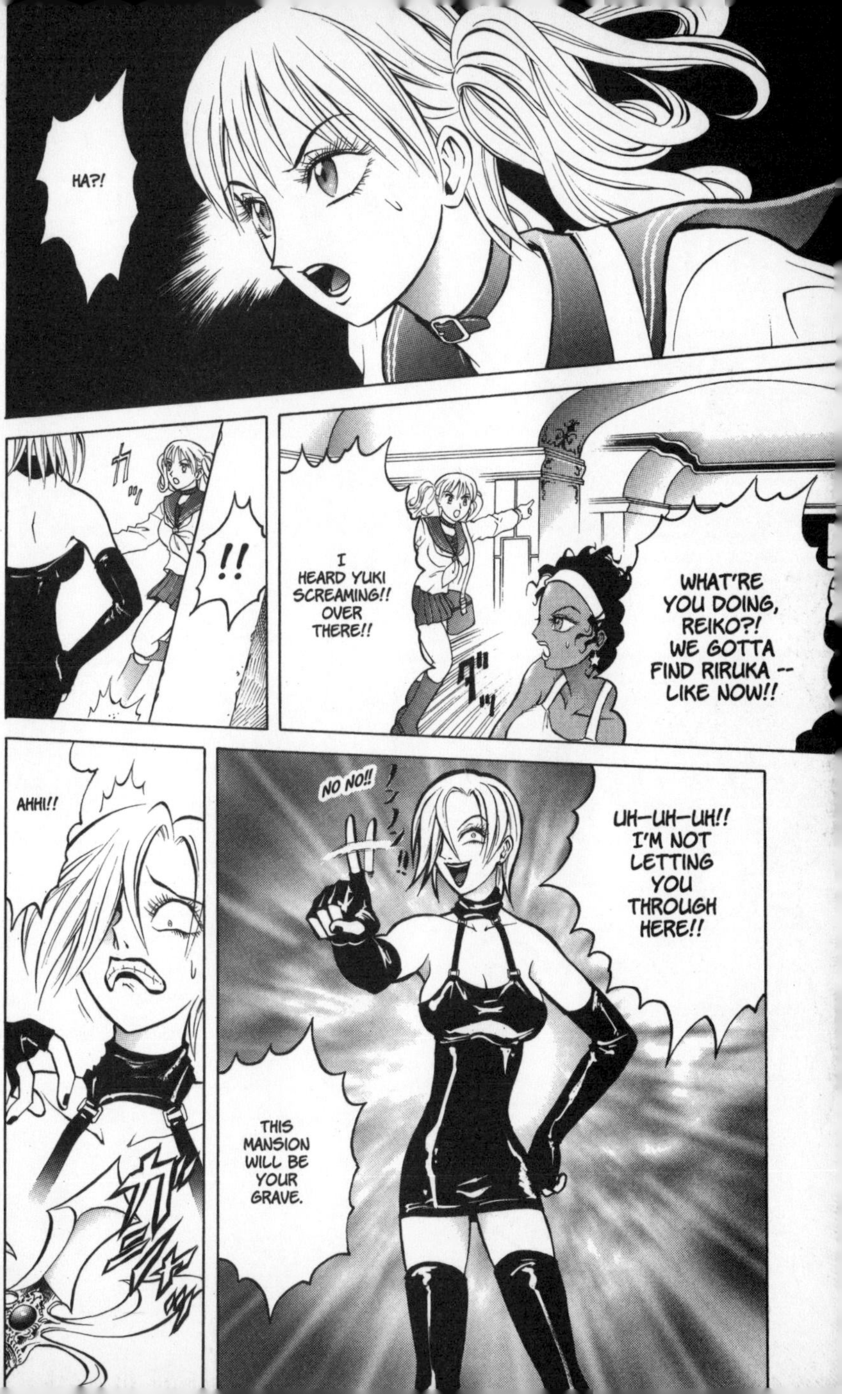
HA?!
WHAT'RE YOU DOING, REIKO?! WE GOTTA FIND RIRUKA -- LIKE NOW!!
I HEARD YUKI SCREAMING!! OVER THERE!!
!!
NO NO!!
UH-UH-UH!! I'M NOT LETTING YOU THROUGH HERE!!
THIS MANSION WILL BE YOUR GRAVE.
AHH!!

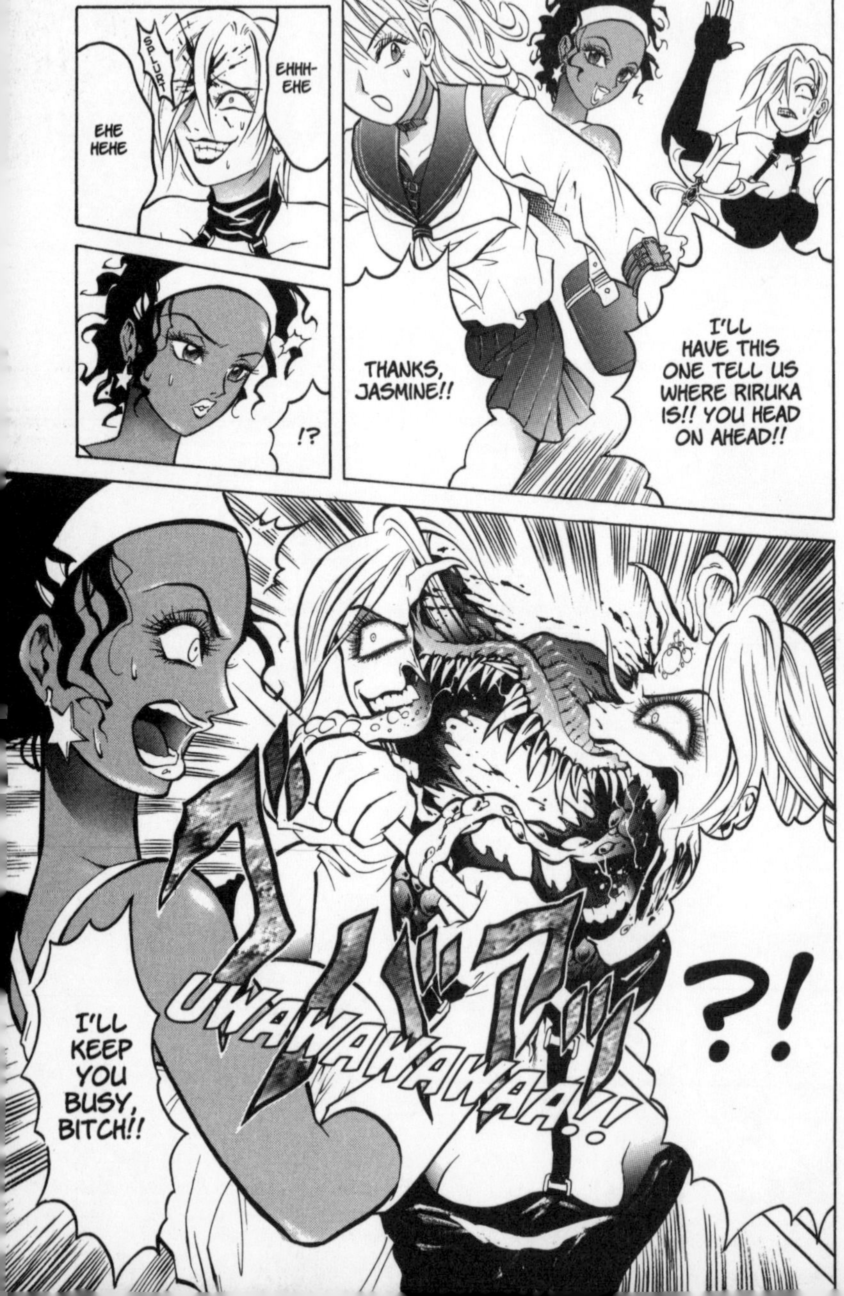

I'LL HAVE THIS ONE TELL US WHERE RIRUKA IS!! YOU HEAD ON AHEAD!!
THANKS, JASMINE!!
EHHH-EHE
SPLURT
EHE HEHE
!?
?!
UWAWAWAWAWAA!!
I'LL KEEP YOU BUSY, BITCH!!

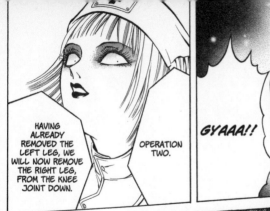

GYAAA!!
OPERATION TWO.
HAVING ALREADY REMOVED THE LEFT LEG, WE WILL NOW REMOVE THE RIGHT LEG, FROM THE KNEE JOINT DOWN.
THE POINT OF THIS SERIES OF OPERATIONS IS TO ACCENTUATE THE FEELING OF PAIN IN THE PATIENT.
THEREFORE, THE OPERATION WILL COMMENCE WITHOUT USING EVEN THE SLIGHTEST BIT OF ANESTHETIC.
AAAH!!
SH-SHIT!!
I GOTTA HELP YUKI...!
AND THE NEXT DOSE OF MUSCLE RELAXANT SHALL BE FOR RUDOH.

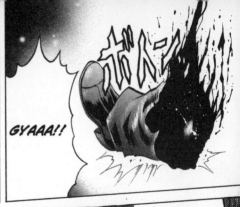

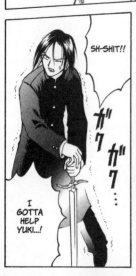

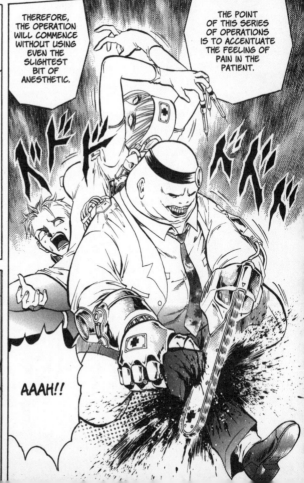

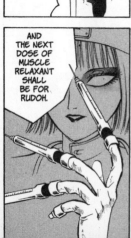

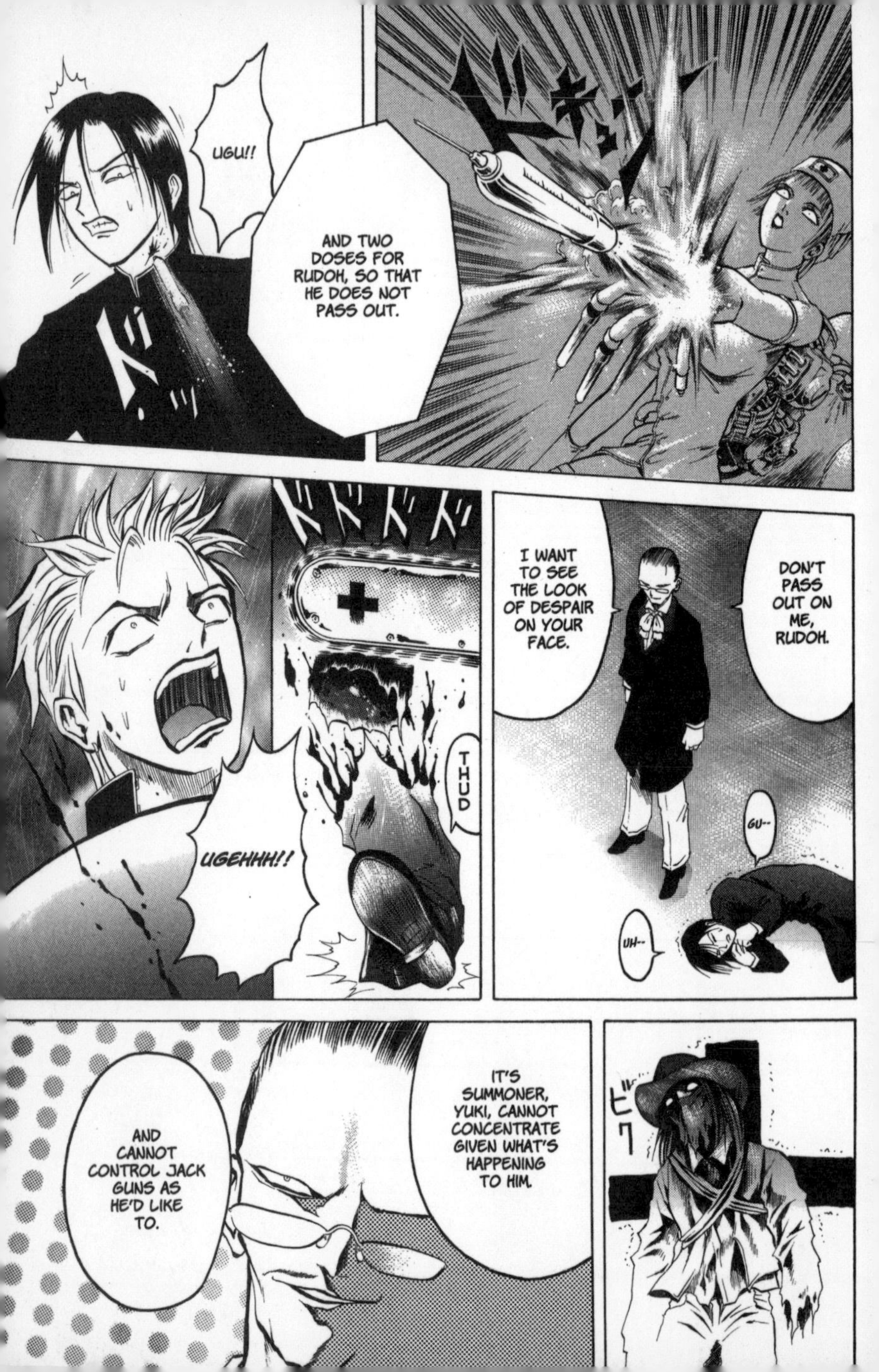
AND TWO DOSES FOR RUDOH, SO THAT HE DOES NOT PASS OUT.
UGU!!
DON'T PASS OUT ON ME, RUDOH.
I WANT TO SEE THE LOOK OF DESPAIR ON YOUR FACE.
GU--
UH--
THUD
UGEHHH!!
IT'S SUMMONER, YUKI, CANNOT CONCENTRATE GIVEN WHAT'S HAPPENING TO HIM.
AND CANNOT CONTROL JACK GUNS AS HE'D LIKE TO.

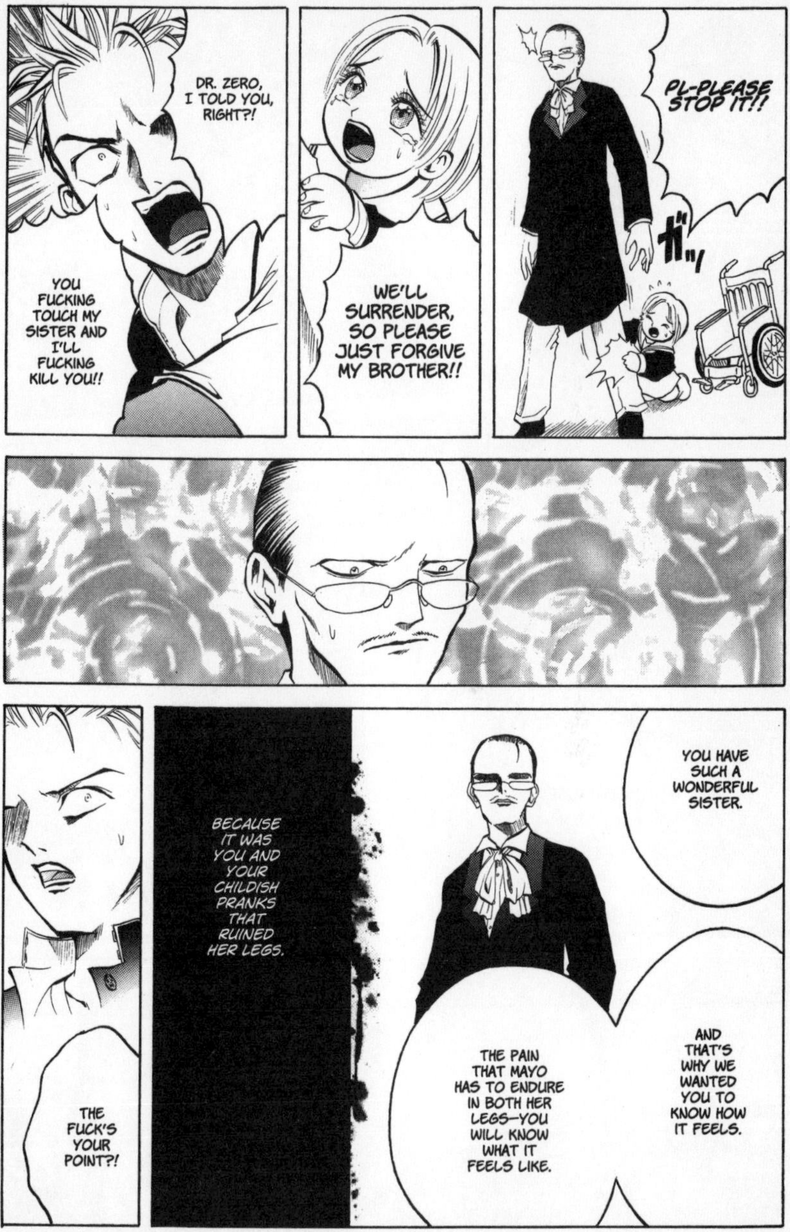
PL-PLEASE STOP IT!!
ガッ
WE'LL SURRENDER, SO PLEASE JUST FORGIVE MY BROTHER!!
DR. ZERO, I TOLD YOU, RIGHT?!
YOU FUCKING TOUCH MY SISTER AND I'LL FUCKING KILL YOU!!
YOU HAVE SUCH A WONDERFUL SISTER.
BECAUSE IT WAS YOU AND YOUR CHILDISH PRANKS THAT RUINED HER LEGS.
AND THAT'S WHY WE WANTED YOU TO KNOW HOW IT FEELS.
THE PAIN THAT MAYO HAS TO ENDURE IN BOTH HER LEGS—YOU WILL KNOW WHAT IT FEELS LIKE.
THE FUCK'S YOUR POINT?!

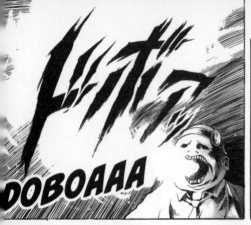

DOBOAAA

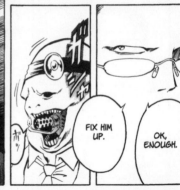

FIX HIM UP.

OK, ENOUGH.

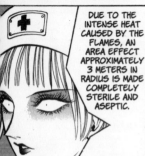

DUE TO THE INTENSE HEAT CAUSED BY THE FLAMES, AN AREA EFFECT APPROXIMATELY 3 METERS IN RADIUS IS MADE COMPLETELY STERILE AND ASEPTIC.

AND, HENCEFORTH, THE LEGS RE-ATTACHED. NOW STARTING OPERATION THREE.

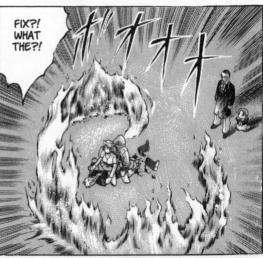

FIX?! WHAT THE?!

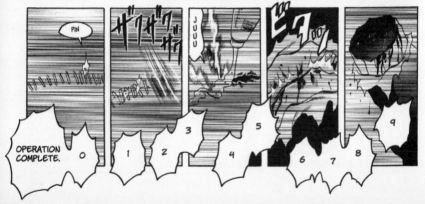

PIN

JUUU

OPERATION COMPLETE.

0   1   2   3   4   5   6   7   8   9

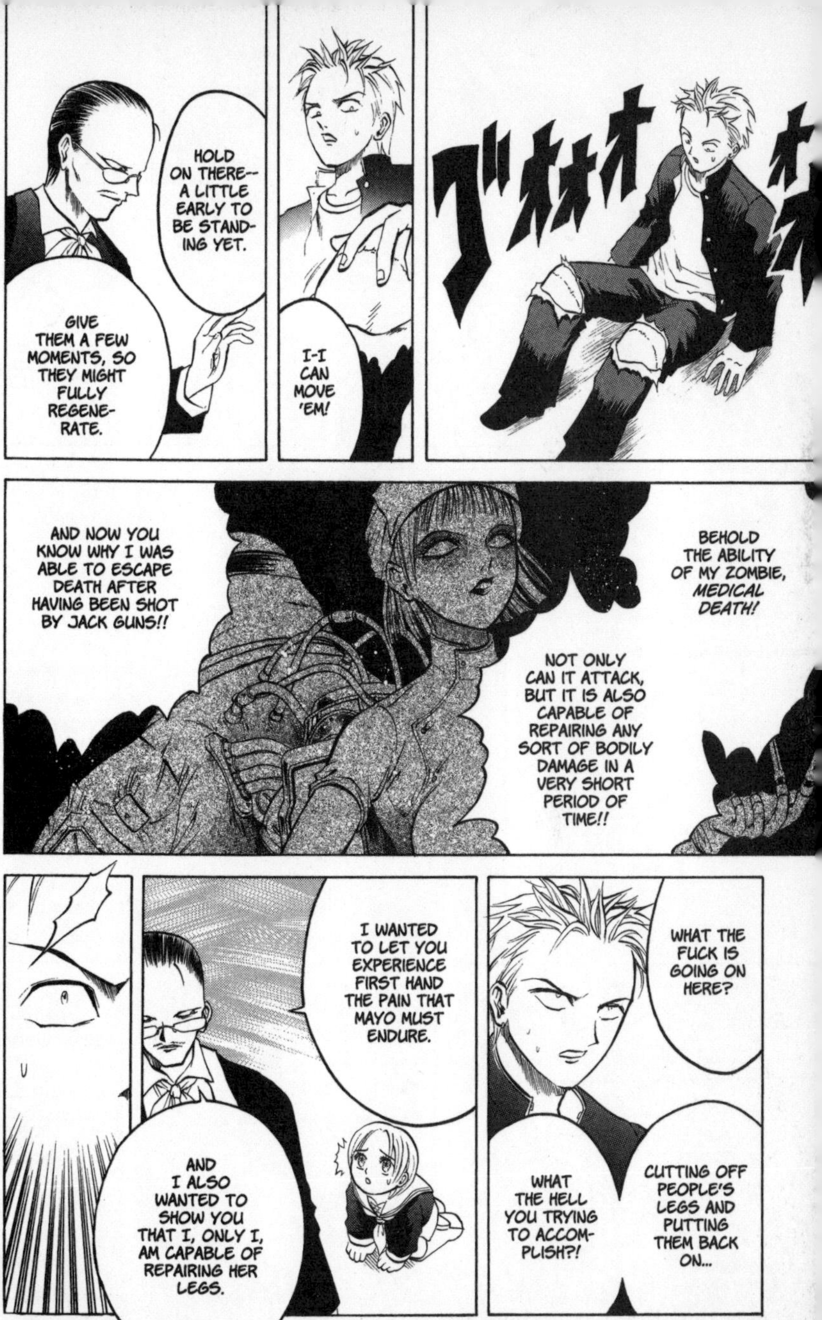

ブォォオ
I-I CAN MOVE 'EM!
HOLD ON THERE-- A LITTLE EARLY TO BE STAND-ING YET.
GIVE THEM A FEW MOMENTS, SO THEY MIGHT FULLY REGENE-RATE.
BEHOLD THE ABILITY OF MY ZOMBIE, *MEDICAL DEATH!*
NOT ONLY CAN IT ATTACK, BUT IT IS ALSO CAPABLE OF REPAIRING ANY SORT OF BODILY DAMAGE IN A VERY SHORT PERIOD OF TIME!!
AND NOW YOU KNOW WHY I WAS ABLE TO ESCAPE DEATH AFTER HAVING BEEN SHOT BY JACK GUNS!!
WHAT THE FUCK IS GOING ON HERE?
CUTTING OFF PEOPLE'S LEGS AND PUTTING THEM BACK ON...
WHAT THE HELL YOU TRYING TO ACCOM-PLISH?!
I WANTED TO LET YOU EXPERIENCE FIRST HAND THE PAIN THAT MAYO MUST ENDURE.
AND I ALSO WANTED TO SHOW YOU THAT I, ONLY I, AM CAPABLE OF REPAIRING HER LEGS.

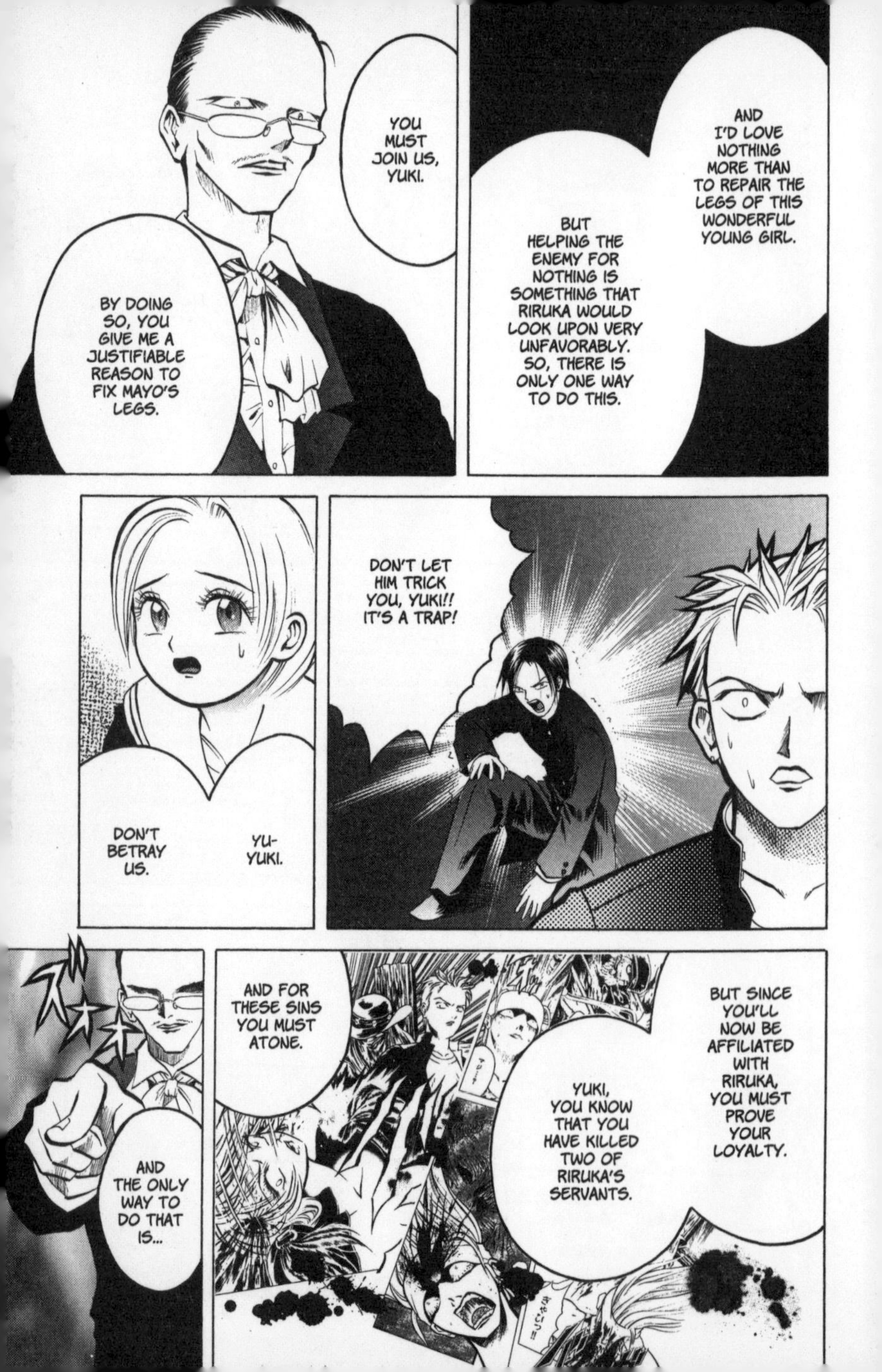
AND I'D LOVE NOTHING MORE THAN TO REPAIR THE LEGS OF THIS WONDERFUL YOUNG GIRL.
BUT HELPING THE ENEMY FOR NOTHING IS SOMETHING THAT RIRUKA WOULD LOOK UPON VERY UNFAVORABLY. SO, THERE IS ONLY ONE WAY TO DO THIS.
YOU MUST JOIN US, YUKI.
BY DOING SO, YOU GIVE ME A JUSTIFIABLE REASON TO FIX MAYO'S LEGS.
DON'T LET HIM TRICK YOU, YUKI!! IT'S A TRAP!
YU-YUKI.
DON'T BETRAY US.
BUT SINCE YOU'LL NOW BE AFFILIATED WITH RIRUKA, YOU MUST PROVE YOUR LOYALTY.
YUKI, YOU KNOW THAT YOU HAVE KILLED TWO OF RIRUKA'S SERVANTS.
AND FOR THESE SINS YOU MUST ATONE.
AND THE ONLY WAY TO DO THAT IS...

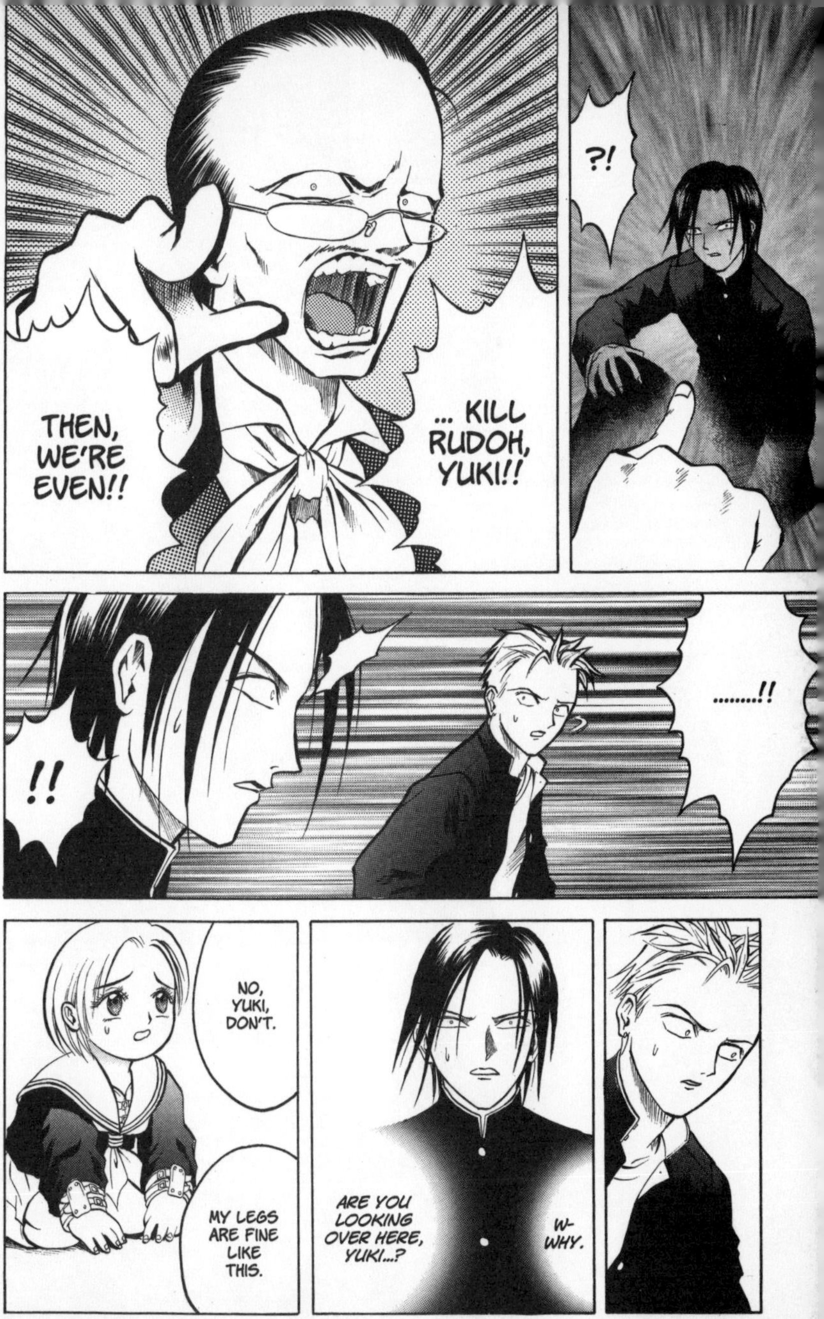
?!
... KILL RUDOH, YUKI!!
THEN, WE'RE EVEN!!
........!!
!!
W- WHY.
ARE YOU LOOKING OVER HERE, YUKI...?
NO, YUKI, DON'T.
MY LEGS ARE FINE LIKE THIS.

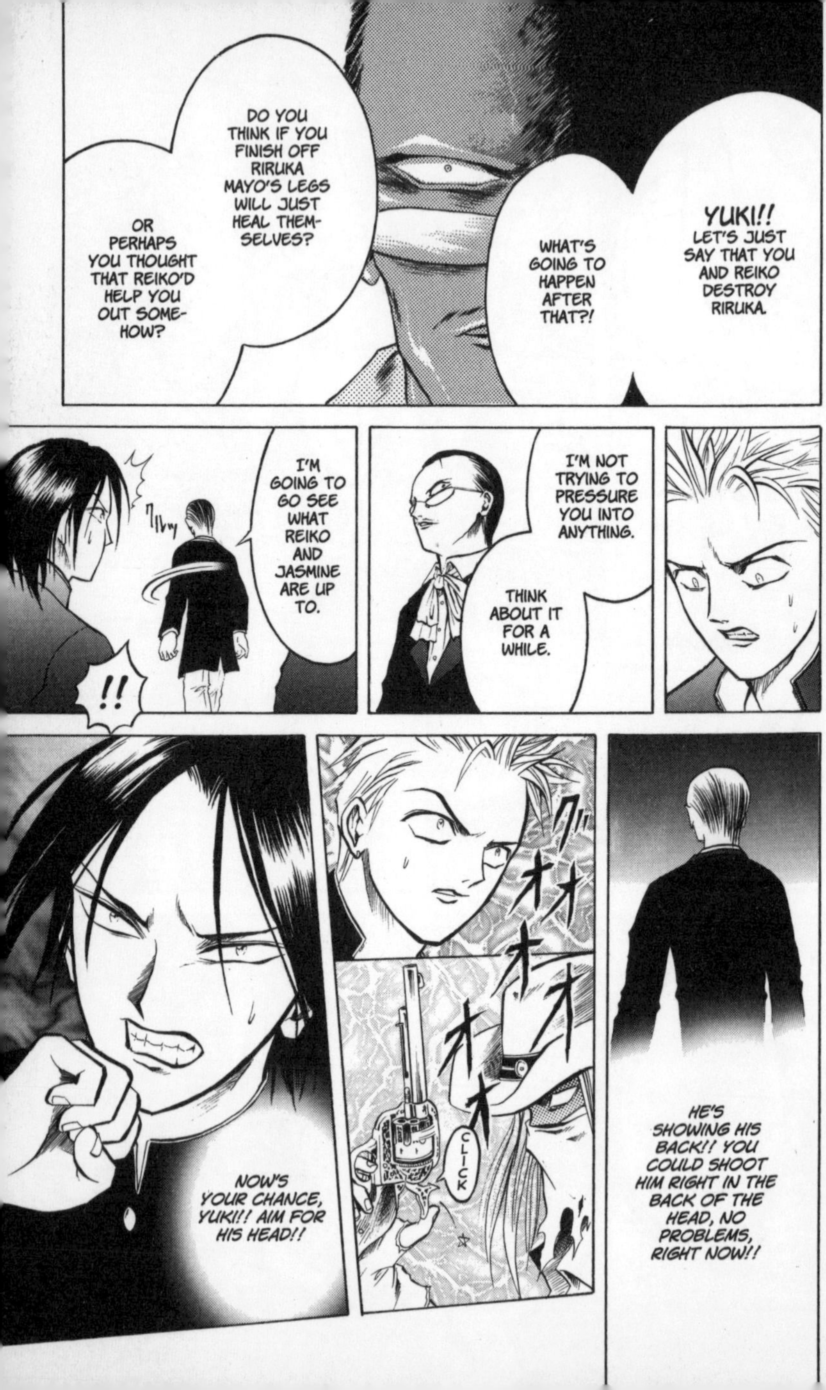
YUKI!! LET'S JUST SAY THAT YOU AND REIKO DESTROY RIRUKA.
WHAT'S GOING TO HAPPEN AFTER THAT?!
DO YOU THINK IF YOU FINISH OFF RIRUKA MAYO'S LEGS WILL JUST HEAL THEM-SELVES?
OR PERHAPS YOU THOUGHT THAT REIKO'D HELP YOU OUT SOME-HOW?
I'M NOT TRYING TO PRESSURE YOU INTO ANYTHING.
THINK ABOUT IT FOR A WHILE.
I'M GOING TO GO SEE WHAT REIKO AND JASMINE ARE UP TO.
!!
HE'S SHOWING HIS BACK!! YOU COULD SHOOT HIM RIGHT IN THE BACK OF THE HEAD, NO PROBLEMS, RIGHT NOW!!
CLICK
NOW'S YOUR CHANCE, YUKI!! AIM FOR HIS HEAD!!

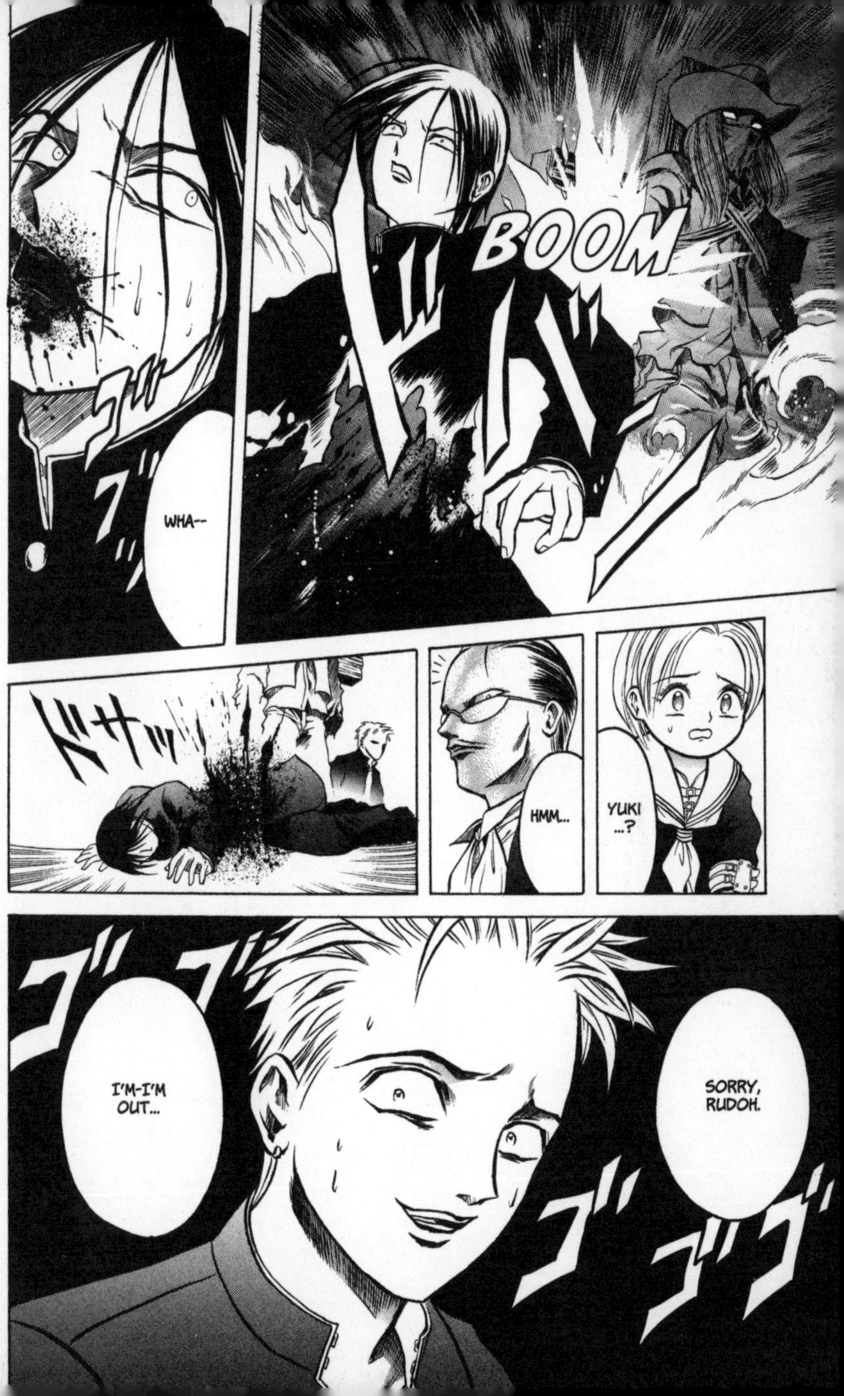
BOOM
WHA--
YUKI ...?
HMM...
SORRY, RUDOH.
I'M-I'M OUT...

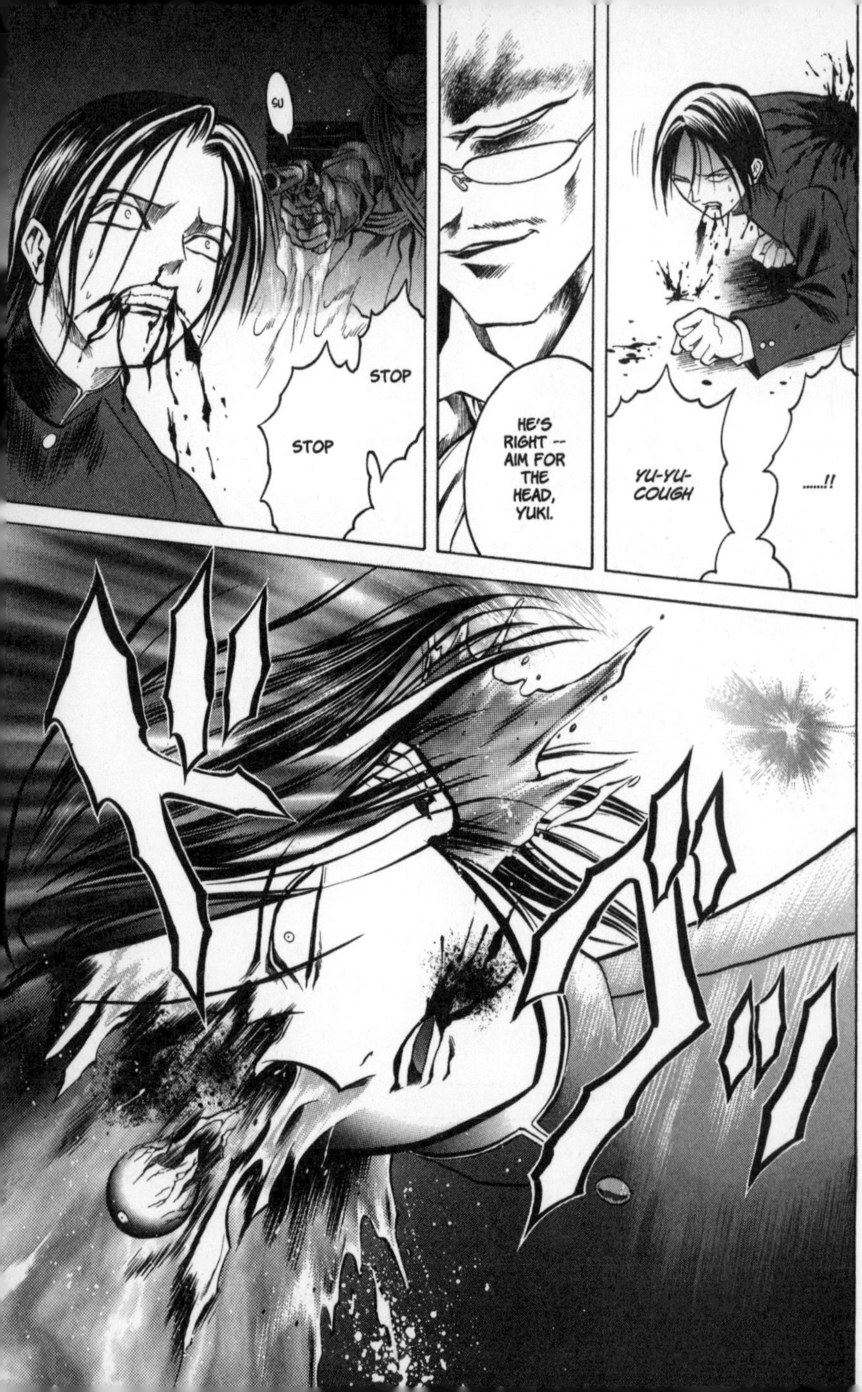
......!!
YU-YU-COUGH
HE'S RIGHT -- AIM FOR THE HEAD, YUKI.
SU
STOP
STOP

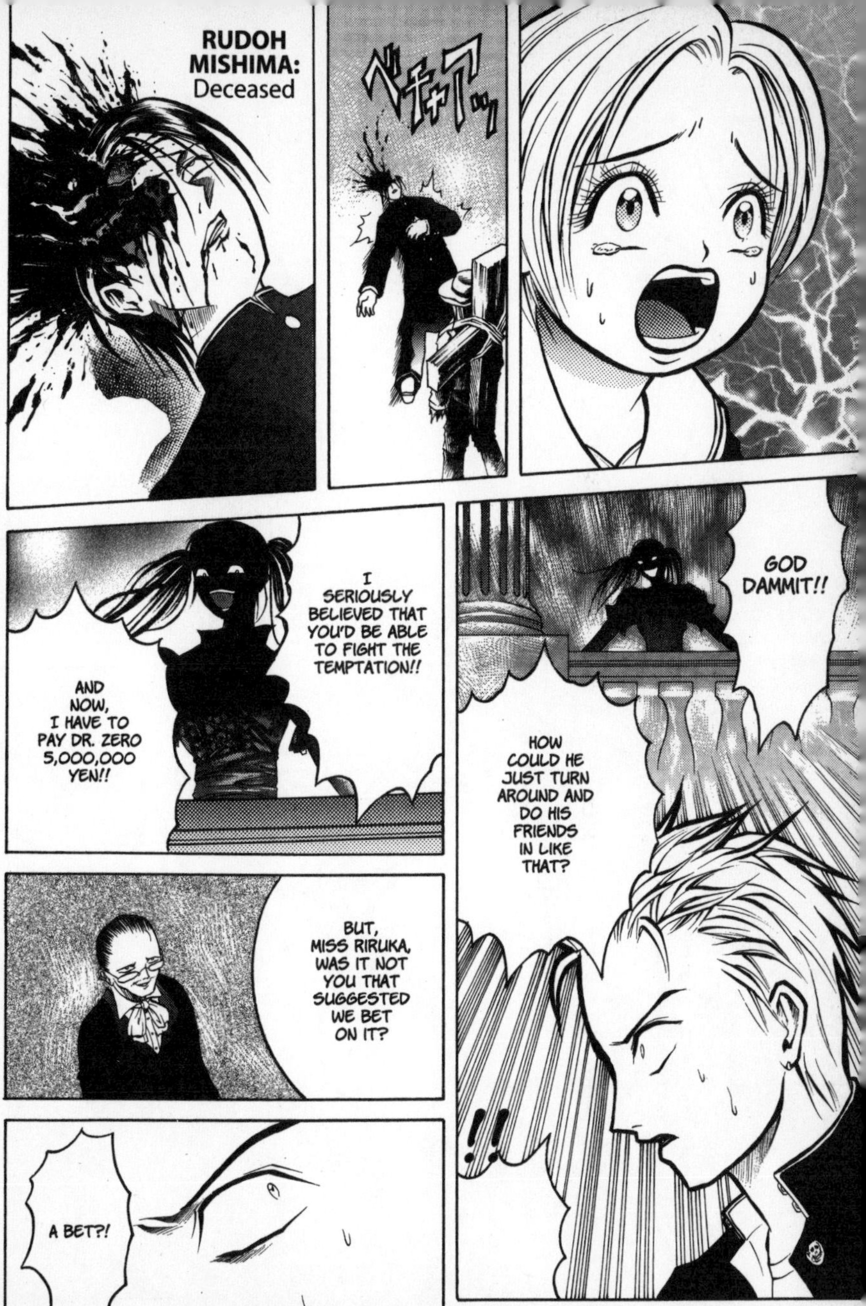
ベチャアッ
RUDOH MISHIMA: Deceased
GOD DAMMIT!!
HOW COULD HE JUST TURN AROUND AND DO HIS FRIENDS IN LIKE THAT?
!!
I SERIOUSLY BELIEVED THAT YOU'D BE ABLE TO FIGHT THE TEMPTATION!!
AND NOW, I HAVE TO PAY DR. ZERO 5,000,000 YEN!!
BUT, MISS RIRUKA, WAS IT NOT YOU THAT SUGGESTED WE BET ON IT?
A BET?!

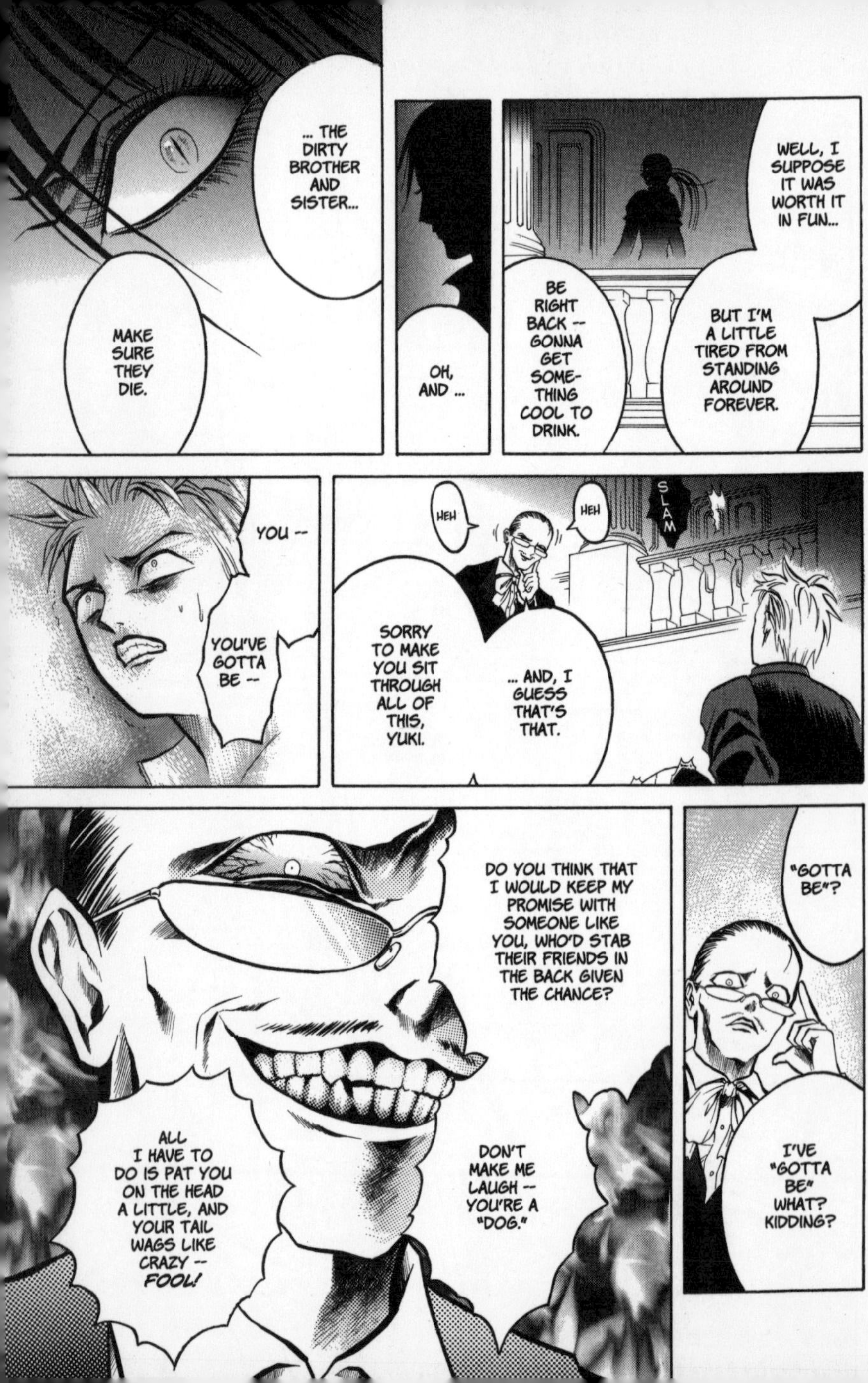
WELL, I SUPPOSE IT WAS WORTH IT IN FUN...
BUT I'M A LITTLE TIRED FROM STANDING AROUND FOREVER.
BE RIGHT BACK -- GONNA GET SOME-THING COOL TO DRINK.
OH, AND ...
... THE DIRTY BROTHER AND SISTER...
MAKE SURE THEY DIE.
SLAM
HEH
HEH
... AND, I GUESS THAT'S THAT.
SORRY TO MAKE YOU SIT THROUGH ALL OF THIS, YUKI.
YOU --
YOU'VE GOTTA BE --
"GOTTA BE"?
I'VE "GOTTA BE" WHAT? KIDDING?
DO YOU THINK THAT I WOULD KEEP MY PROMISE WITH SOMEONE LIKE YOU, WHO'D STAB THEIR FRIENDS IN THE BACK GIVEN THE CHANCE?
DON'T MAKE ME LAUGH -- YOU'RE A "DOG."
ALL I HAVE TO DO IS PAT YOU ON THE HEAD A LITTLE, AND YOUR TAIL WAGS LIKE CRAZY -- *FOOL!*

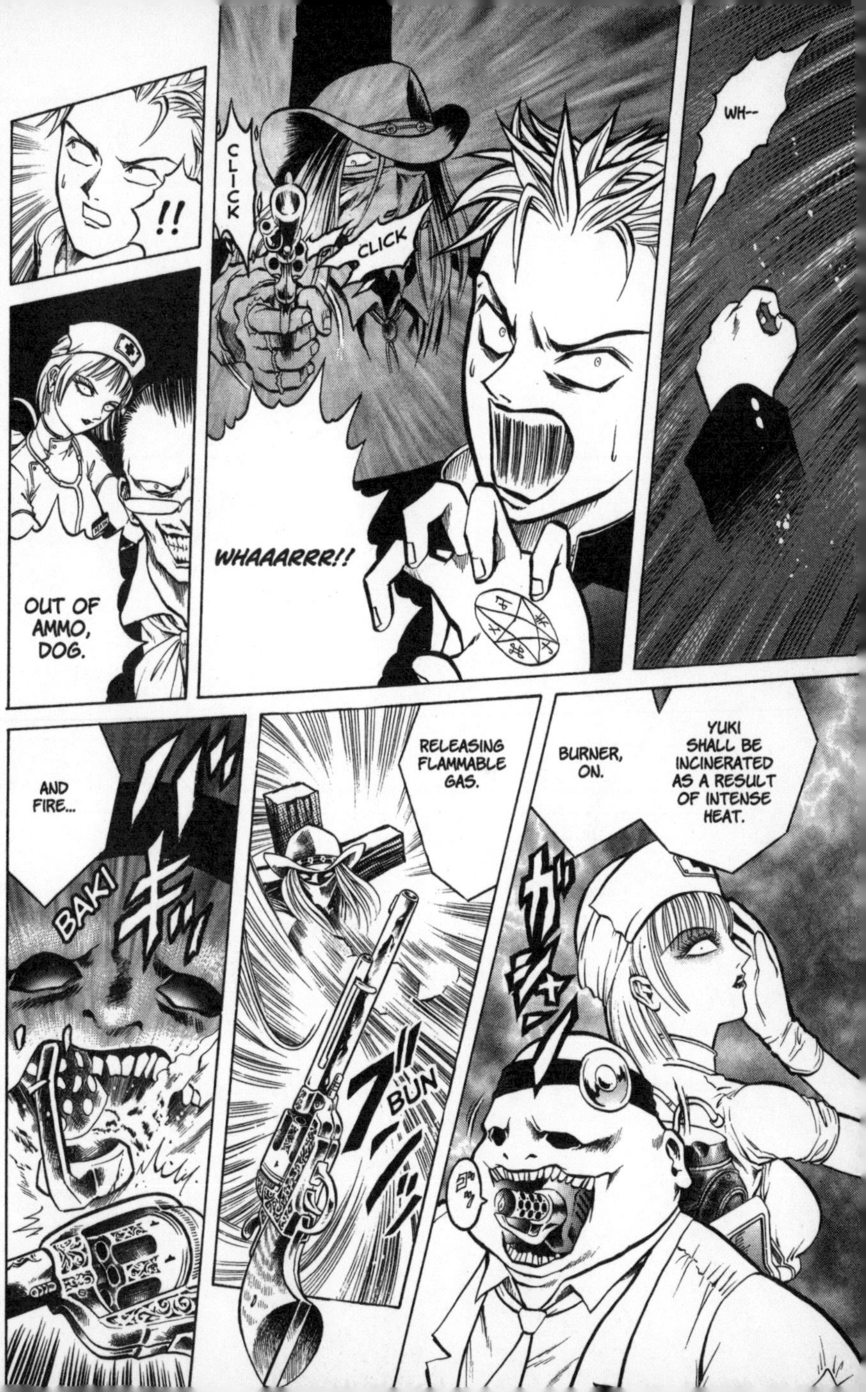

WH--
CLICK
CLICK
WHAAARRR!!
!!
OUT OF AMMO, DOG.
YUKI SHALL BE INCINERATED AS A RESULT OF INTENSE HEAT.
BURNER, ON.
RELEASING FLAMMABLE GAS.
BUN
AND FIRE...
BAKI

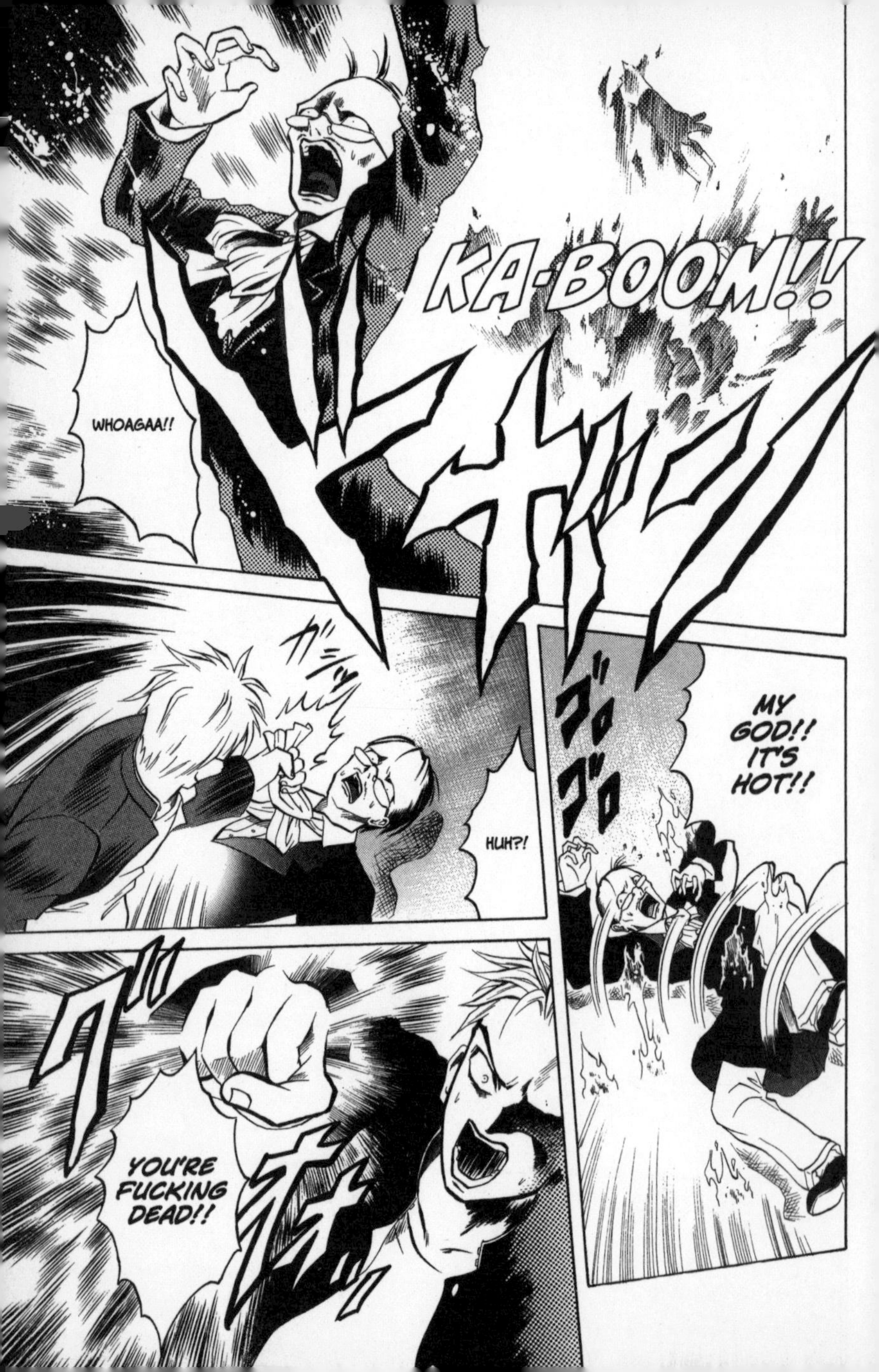
KA-BOOM!!
WHOAGAA!!
ゴロゴロ
MY GOD!! IT'S HOT!!
ガシッ
HUH?!
YOU'RE FUCKING DEAD!!

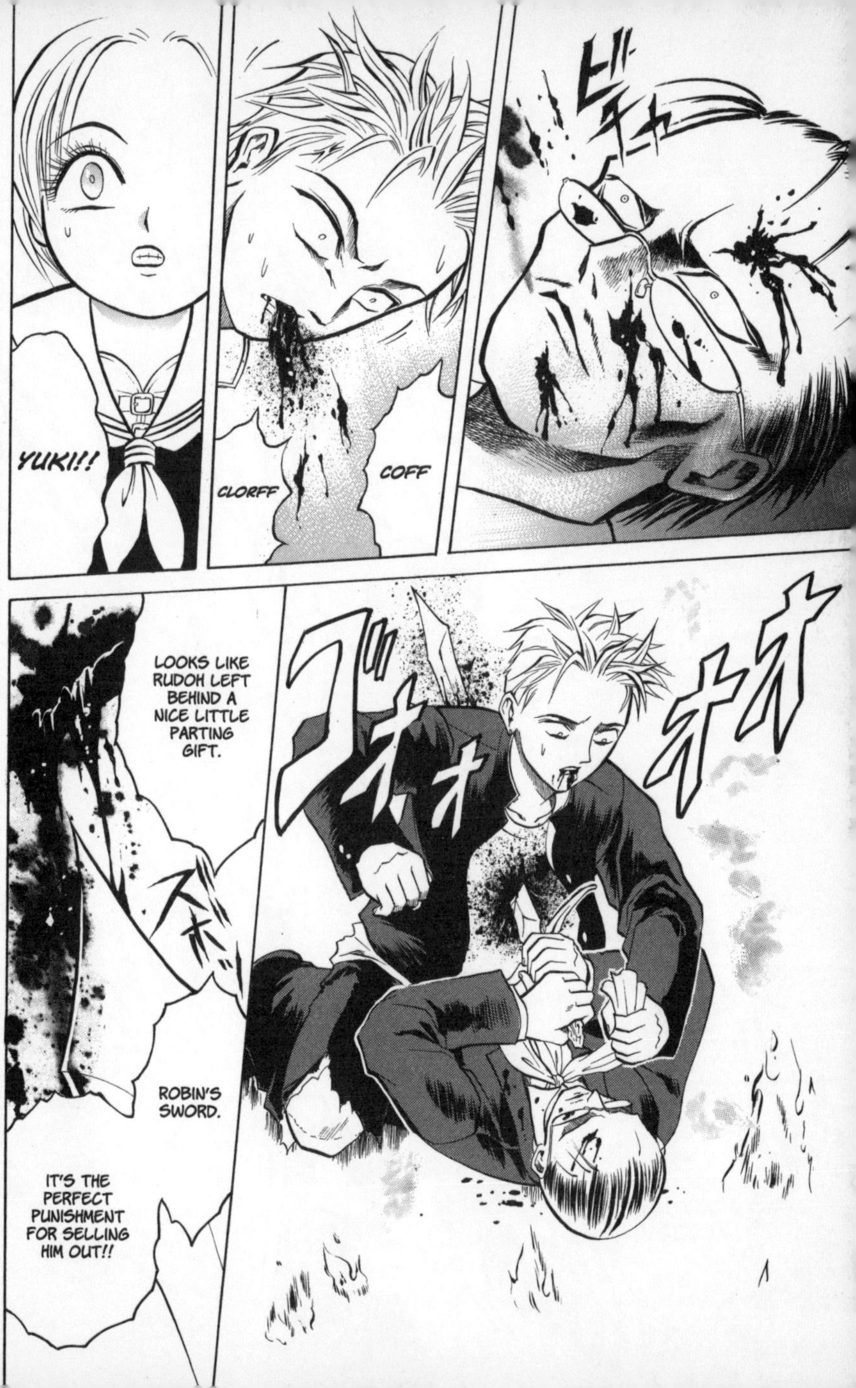
COFF
CLORFF
YUKI!!
LOOKS LIKE RUDOH LEFT BEHIND A NICE LITTLE PARTING GIFT.
ROBIN'S SWORD.
IT'S THE PERFECT PUNISHMENT FOR SELLING HIM OUT!!

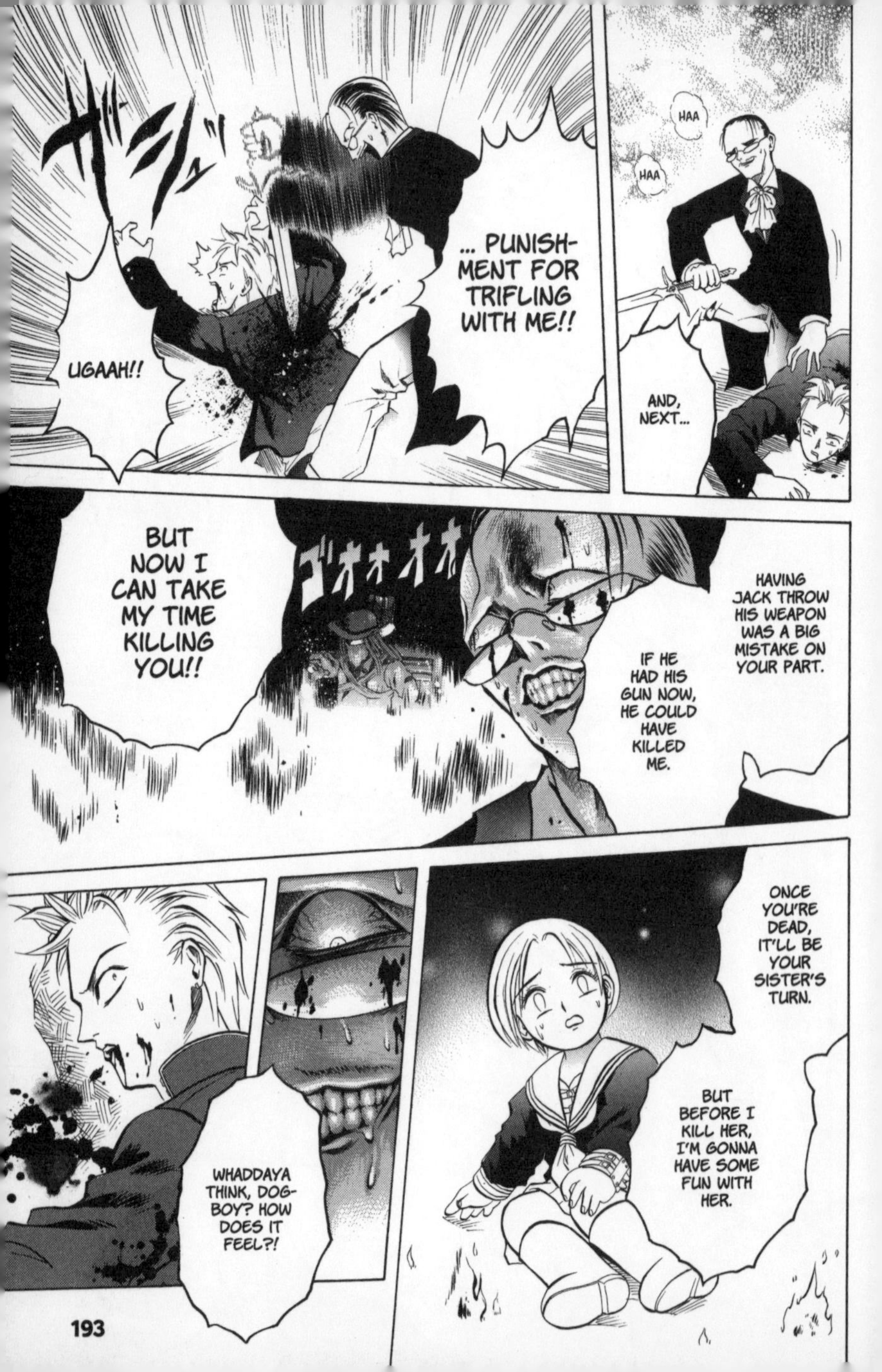
HAA
HAA
AND, NEXT...
... PUNISHMENT FOR TRIFLING WITH ME!!
UGAAH!!
HAVING JACK THROW HIS WEAPON WAS A BIG MISTAKE ON YOUR PART.
IF HE HAD HIS GUN NOW, HE COULD HAVE KILLED ME.
ゴオォオオ
BUT NOW I CAN TAKE MY TIME KILLING YOU!!
ONCE YOU'RE DEAD, IT'LL BE YOUR SISTER'S TURN.
BUT BEFORE I KILL HER, I'M GONNA HAVE SOME FUN WITH HER.
WHADDAYA THINK, DOG-BOY? HOW DOES IT FEEL?!

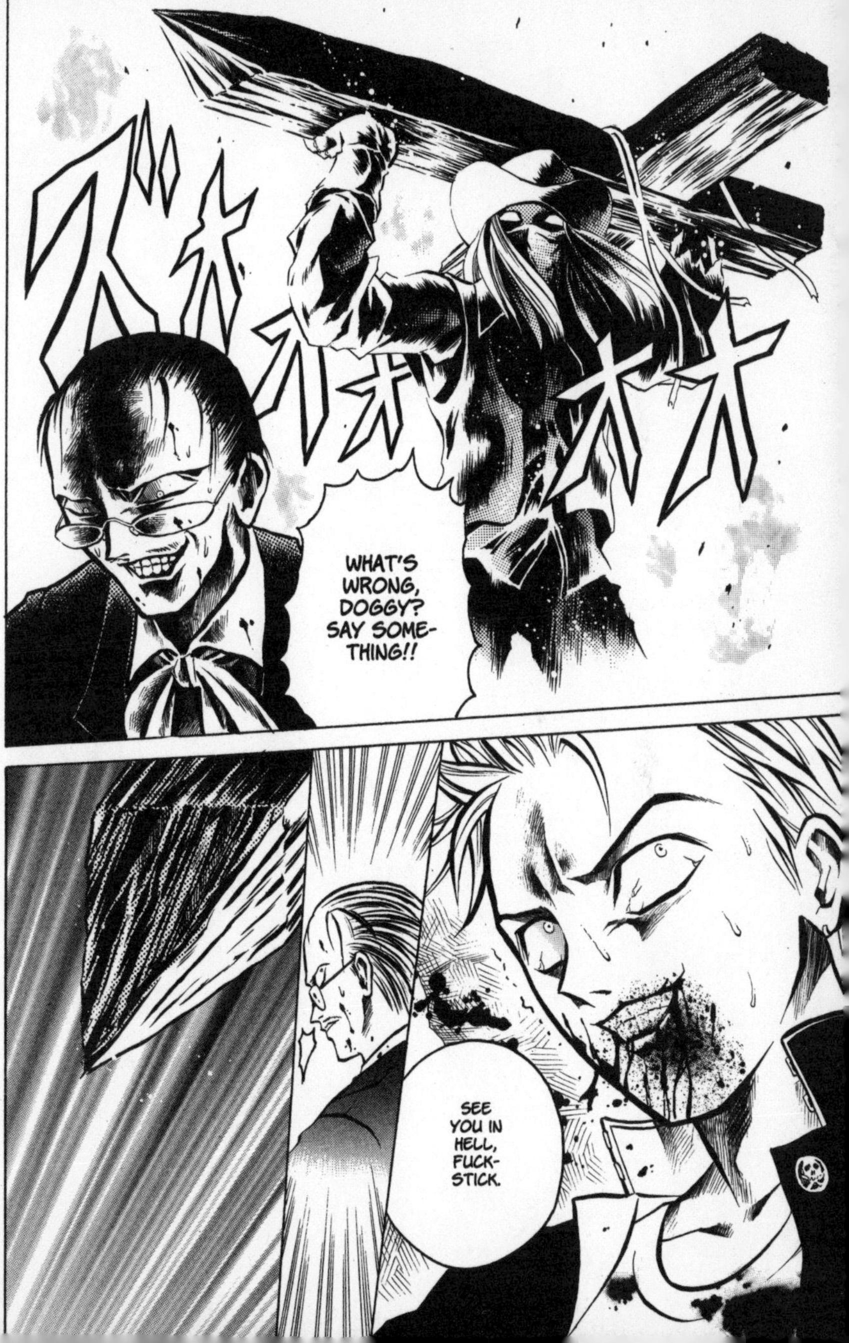
WHAT'S WRONG, DOGGY? SAY SOME-THING!!
SEE YOU IN HELL, FUCK-STICK.

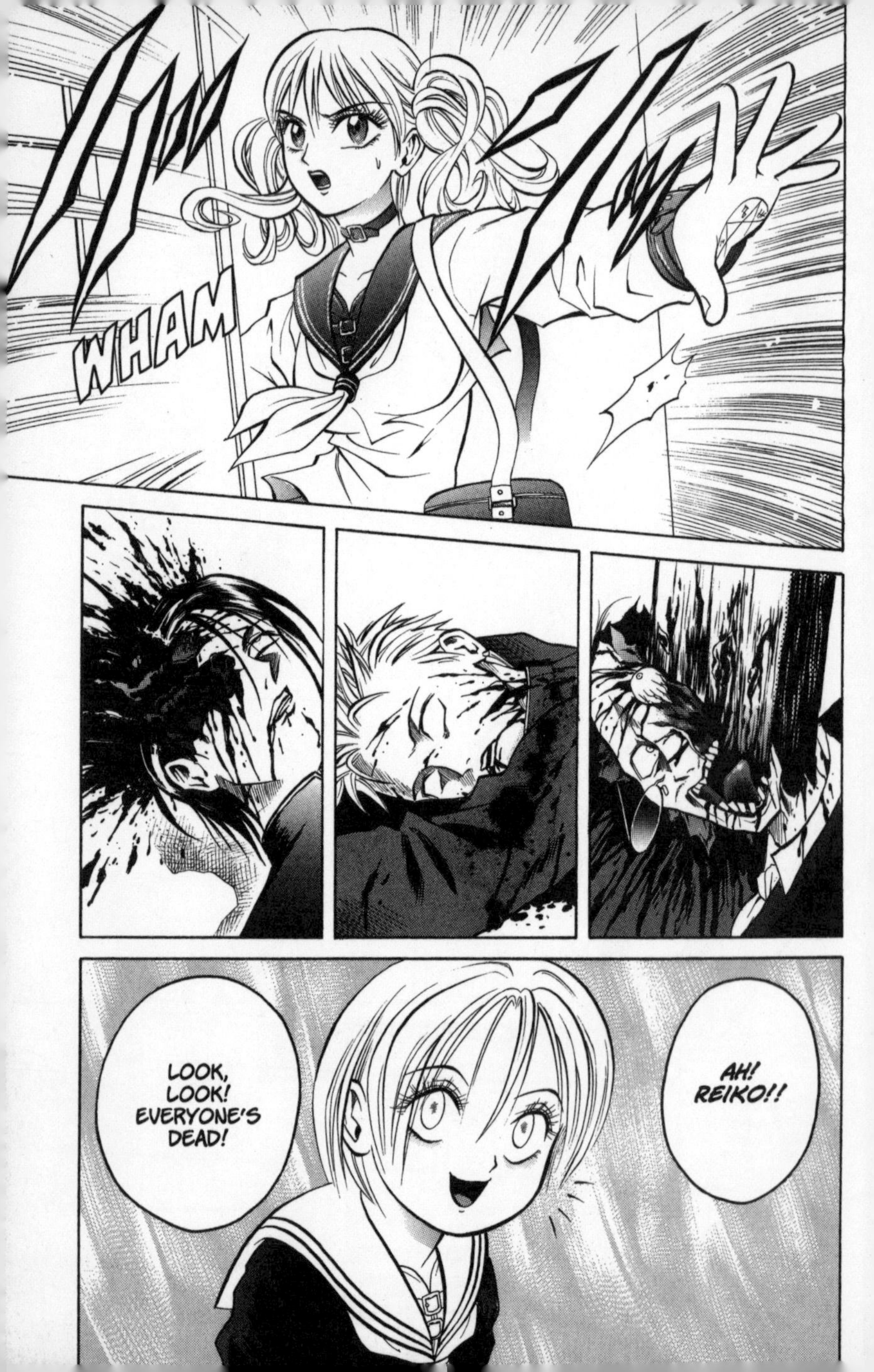
WHAM
AH! REIKO!!
LOOK, LOOK! EVERYONE'S DEAD!

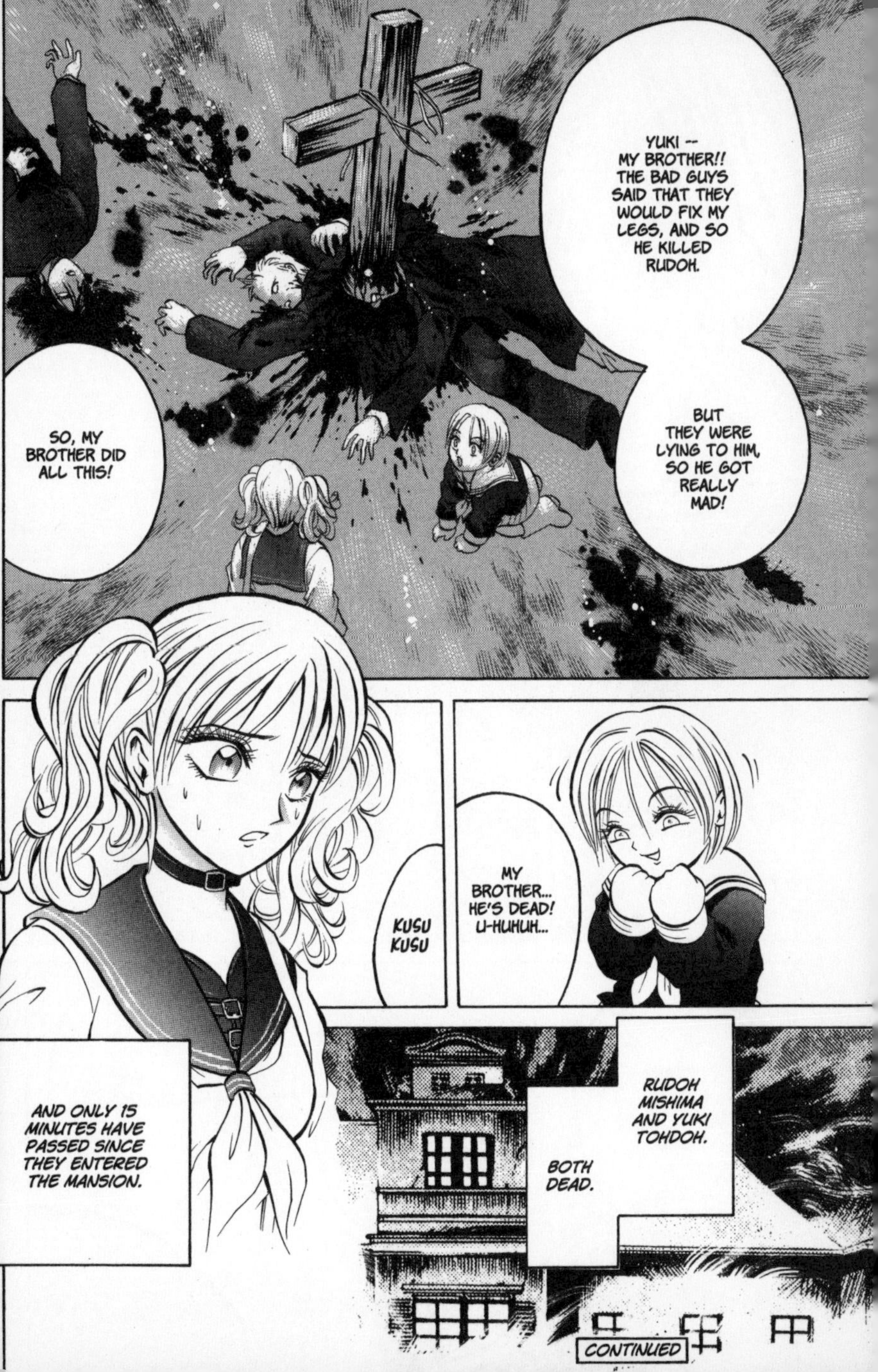
YUKI -- MY BROTHER!! THE BAD GUYS SAID THAT THEY WOULD FIX MY LEGS, AND SO HE KILLED RUDOH.
BUT THEY WERE LYING TO HIM, SO HE GOT REALLY MAD!
SO, MY BROTHER DID ALL THIS!
MY BROTHER... HE'S DEAD! U-HUHUH...
KUSU KUSU
RUDOH MISHIMA AND YUKI TOHDOH.
BOTH DEAD.
AND ONLY 15 MINUTES HAVE PASSED SINCE THEY ENTERED THE MANSION.
CONTINUED

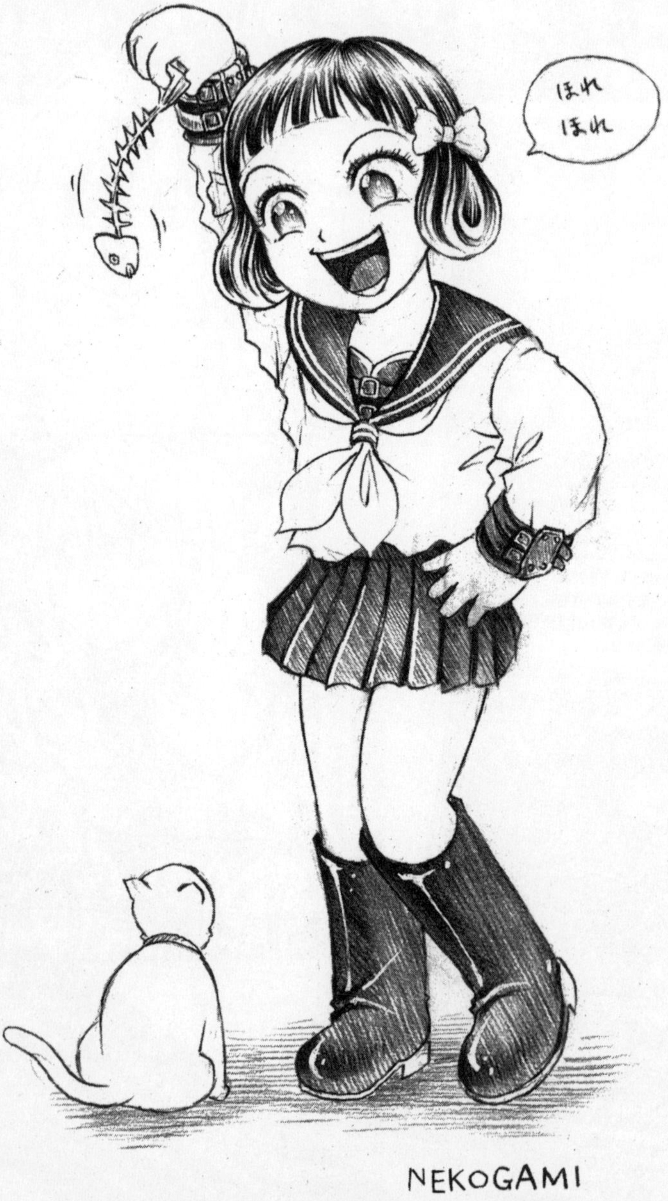
ほれ
ほれ
NEKOGAMI

the ZOMBIE SHOP GALLERY

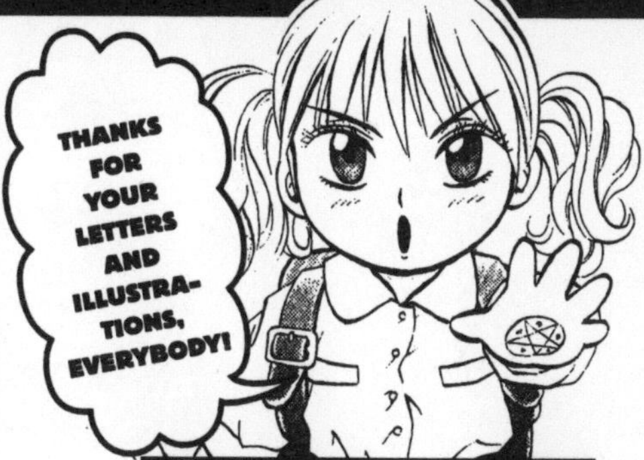
THANKS FOR YOUR LETTERS AND ILLUSTRA-TIONS, EVERYBODY!

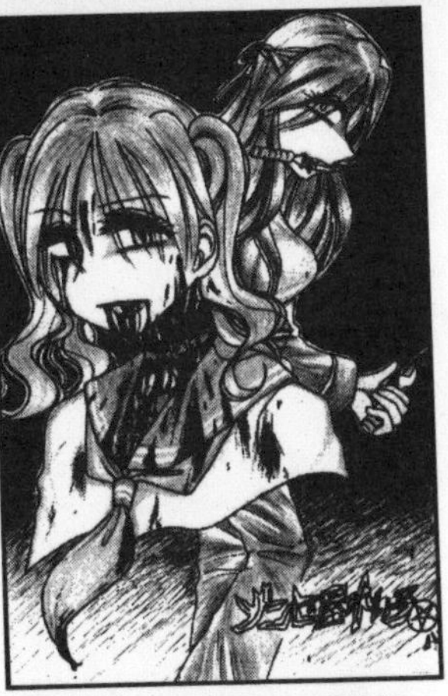

YUKA MARUYAMA • AGE 14
CHIBA PREFECTURE, JAPAN
YOU REALLY CAPTURED REIKO'S NECK PERFECTLY!

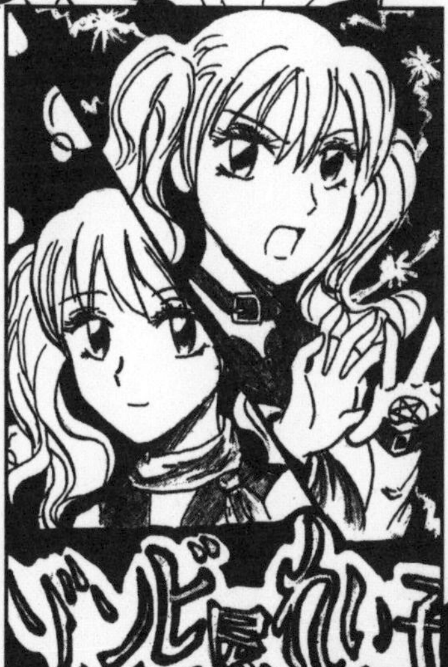
ゾンビ屋れい子

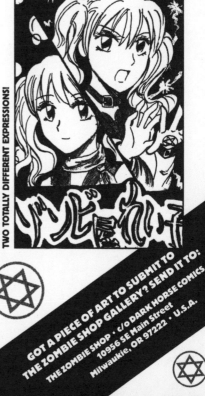

SAYA HIRATA • AGE 12
CHIBA PREFECTURE, JAPAN
TWO TOTALLY DIFFERENT EXPRESSIONS!

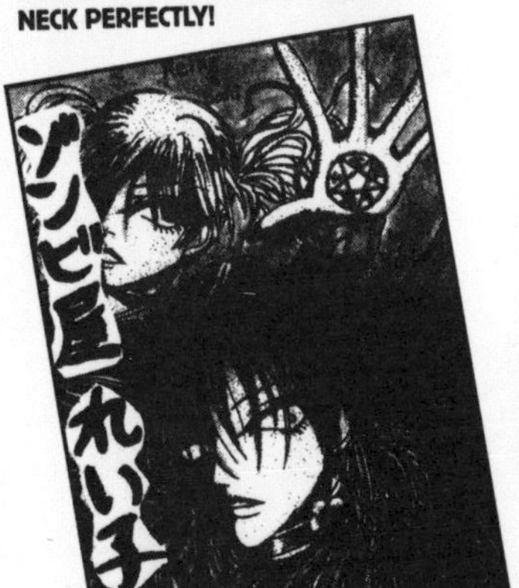
ゾンビ屋れい子

YUKI TAKESHITA • AGE 15
SAPORO, JAPAN
YOUR USE OF COLOR WAS AMAZING! IT'S A SHAME THAT YOU CAN'T SEE IT IN BLACK-AND-WHITE...

GOT A PIECE OF ART TO SUBMIT TO THE ZOMBIE SHOP GALLERY? SEND IT TO:
THE ZOMBIE SHOP • c/o DARK HORSE COMICS
10956 SE Main Street
Milwaukie, OR 97222 • U.S.A.

translation
MICHAEL GOMBOS

lettering
MICHAEL DAVID THOMAS

publisher
MIKE RICHARDSON

collection designer
APRIL GRAY

editor
MICHAEL CARRIGLITTO

art director
LIA RIBACCHI

English-language version produced by DARK HORSE COMICS.

REIKO, THE ZOMBIE SHOP VOL. 2

published by
Dark Horse Manga
a division of Dark Horse Comics, Inc.

Dark Horse Comics, Inc.
10956 S.E. Main Street
Milwaukie, OR 97222

darkhorse.com

To find a comics shop in your area,
call the Comic Shop Locator Service
toll-free at 1-888-266-4226

First edition: March 2006
ISBN: 1-59307-459-X

10 9 8 7 6 5 4 3 2 1
Printed in Canada

THIS IS THE BACK OF THE BOOK

This manga collection is translated into English but oriented in right-to-left reading format at the creator's request, maintaining the artwork's visual orientation as originally published in Japan. If you've never read manga in this way before, take a look at the diagram below to give yourself an idea of how to go about it. Basically, you'll be starting in the upper right corner and will read each balloon and panel moving right to left. It may take some getting used to, but you should get the hang of it very quickly. Have fun!

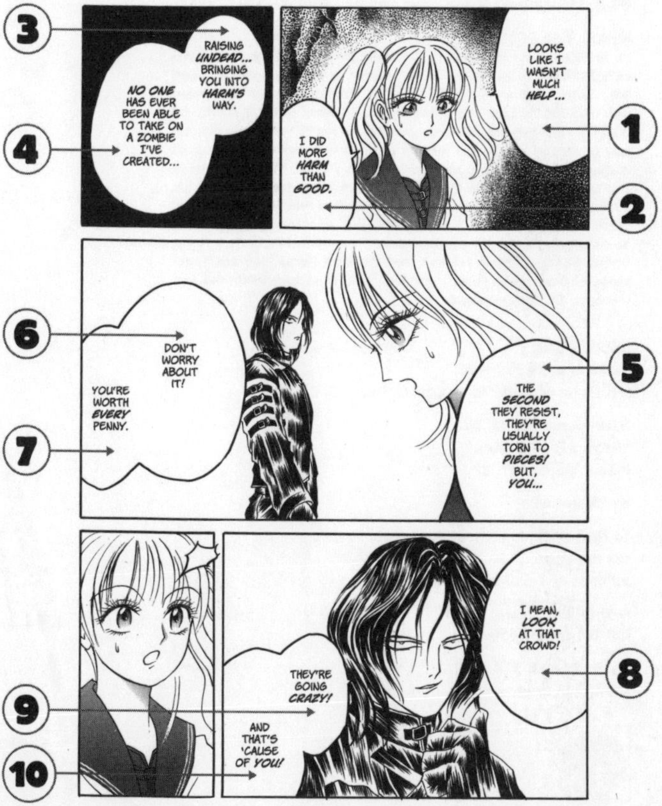
1
LOOKS LIKE I WASN'T MUCH HELP...
2
I DID MORE HARM THAN GOOD.
3
RAISING UNDEAD... BRINGING YOU INTO HARM'S WAY.
4
NO ONE HAS EVER BEEN ABLE TO TAKE ON A ZOMBIE I'VE CREATED...
5
THE SECOND THEY RESIST, THEY'RE USUALLY TORN TO PIECES! BUT, YOU...
6
DON'T WORRY ABOUT IT!
7
YOU'RE WORTH EVERY PENNY.
8
I MEAN, LOOK AT THAT CROWD!
9
THEY'RE GOING CRAZY!
10
AND THAT'S 'CAUSE OF YOU!